THE

HANDBOOK
OF
PROJECT
MANAGEMENT

THE

AMA

HANDBOOK
OF
PROJECT
MANAGEMENT

Paul C. Dinsmore, Editor

American Management Association

New York • Atlanta • Boston • Chicago • Kansas City • San Francisco • Washington, D.C.
Brussels • Toronto • Mexico City

This publication is designed to provide accurate and authoritative information in regard to the subject matter covered. It is sold with the understanding that the publisher is not engaged in rendering legal, accounting, or other professional service. If legal advice or other expert assistance is required, the services of a competent professional person should be sought.

Library of Congress Cataloging-in-Publication Data

The AMA handbook of project management / Paul C. Dinsmore, editor.
    p. cm.
  Includes bibliographical references and index.
  ISBN 0-8144-0106-6
  1. Industrial project management.   I. Dinsmore, Paul C.
II. Title: Handbook of project management.
HD69.P75A46   1993
658.4'04—dc20   93-6947
                                             CIP

Printing number

10 9 8 7 6 5 4 3 2

Advisory Editors

Supporting Editor

Contents

Contributors

Paul C. Dinsmore, Dinsmore Associates

John R. Adams, Western Carolina University
Russell D. Archibald, Integrated Project Systems
George C. Belev, General Electric Company
Manuel M. Benitez Codas, M. M. Benitez Codas
Jasjit S. Dhillon, Decision Management Associates
Ralph D. Ellis, Jr., University of Florida
Irving M. Fogel, Fogel & Associates, Inc.
David Gordon, University of Dallas
Robert J. Graham, R. J. Graham and Associates
Jerry Haar, University of Miami
Brian Hobbs, University of Quebec at Montreal
William N. Hosley, All-Tech Project Management Services, Inc.
Darrel G. Hubbard, Management Analysis Company, Inc.
Lewis R. Ireland, L. R. Ireland & Associates
Lee R. Lambert, Lee R. Lambert & Associates
Harvey A. Levine, Project Knowledge Group
J. Royce Lummus, Jr., General Dynamics Corporation
Jacques Marcovitch, University of São Paulo
M. Dean Martin, Western Carolina University
Antonio C. A. Maximiano, University of São Paulo
Pierre Ménard, University of Quebec at Montreal
Alan S. Mendelssohn, Budget Rent a Car Corporation
Peter W. G. Morris, Bovis Ltd.
Rainer A. Otto, Southern California Gas Company
Stephen D. Owens, Western Carolina University
Alfred I. Paley, NRI Associates
David L. Pells, Strategic Project Management International
Joseph S. Reams, Administrative Controls Management, Inc.
William H. Roetzheim, Booz-Allen and Hamilton, Inc.
Milton D. Rosenau, Jr., Rosenau Consulting Company
Larry A. Smith, Florida International University

Sri Sridharan, Alcatel Network Systems
Alan M. Stretton, University of Technology
Hans J. Thamhain, Bentley College
John Tuman, Jr., Management Technologies Group, Inc.
Thomas P. Watkins, Decision Management Associates
Francis M. Webster, Jr., Western Carolina University, retired
A. J. Werderitsch, Administrative Controls Management, Inc.
Richard E. Westney, Spectrum Consultants International, Inc.
Robert B. Youker, Management, Planning & Control Systems
Lois Zells, Lois Zells & Associates, Inc.

Acknowledgments

In completing this project I drew upon the knowledge, comprehension, patience, and diligence of many people. The cornerstones of the project have been the Supporting Editor, Frank Galopin, and the Advisory Editors—John R. Adams, Russell D. Archibald, Harvey A. Levine, and John Tuman, Jr.—to whom I am indebted for their guidance and counsel. I am also deeply thankful to the contributing authors who submitted the chapters that constitute the basic content of the *Handbook*. I also appreciate the highly professional comments of Myles Thompson, former AMACOM Acquisitions Editor, and Jacqueline Laks Gorman, who did the developmental and copy editing. Final thanks go to Maria de Lourdes Malta, who provided manuscript and office support for the project.

Preface

Paul C. Dinsmore
Dinsmore Associates

When the lunar module *Eagle* landed in the Sea of Tranquility at 13 hours, 19 minutes, 39.9 seconds Eastern Standard Time on July 20, 1969, an incredible space journey had just put the first men on the moon. President John Kennedy's commitment to the Apollo program had made the pioneering moon landing possible. The event was hailed as one of history's major milestones. But its importance went beyond that. One of the most fascinating and significant spin-offs of the U.S. space program was the development of flexible yet precise organizational structures, forms, and tools that allowed people to work together to reach challenging goals. Out of that grew the modern concept of project management.

Since the Apollo days, change has been taking place at an ever-increasing pace; as a consequence, project management, applicable both to individual endeavors or to a series of projects called programs, has been applied to new fields of activity. With the trend toward accelerated change, the scope of project management has expanded from construction projects and the space program to encompass areas such as organizational change, R&D projects, and high-tech product development.

Such change in the scope of project management led to the need for a new, comprehensive book in the field. *The AMA Handbook of Project Management* fills that need. The *Handbook* presents both overviews from noted experts and in-depth approaches from specialists for solving new and specific project problems. As such, the *Handbook* offers information that will help project management professionals:

- Establish project goals.
- Fix managerial philosophy and strategy.
- Carry out project planning on both high-level and operational plateaus.
- Design adequate organizational structures.
- Generate and maintain teamwork.
- Manage the project life cycle.
- Meet project objectives.
- Handle the transition to operational start-up.

The book provides a ready reference for everyone involved in project tasks, including upper management executives, project sponsors, project managers, functional managers, and team members. These people can be involved in any of the major program- and project-oriented industries, such as defense, construction, architecture, engineering, product development, systems development, public utilities, R&D, education, and community development.

Organization of the *Handbook*

The *Handbook* is organized in such a way that readers can use the volume as a reference and find their way to their particular areas of interest. The first part of the book, "Project Management Concepts and Methodologies," presents in sequential form the broad general concepts of project management. The second part of the book, "Project Management Applications," provides just that—discussions of specific areas in which project management is and can be used.

Part I: Project Management Concepts and Methodologies

Part I contains eight sections. They are as follows:

I. Overview

This section provides a helicopter view of project management. Webster's "What Project Management Is All About" sets the conceptual stage and defines the basics. In "An Overview of Project Management Principle for Executives," Dinsmore gives six lessons to ensure success in managing projects. And Stretton's "Developing a Project Management Body of Knowledge" discusses the universe of information encompassed in the project management discipline.

II. Managerial Strategies for Starting Up Successful Projects

In this section, Morris's "Strategies for Managing Major Projects" highlights the fundamental issues that determine the success of larger, complex projects. In Levine's "Project Initiation Techniques: A Strategic View," a framework for developing project strategies and getting things properly under way is presented. Finally, Archibald submits another strategic view, which also discusses project start-up workshops, and develops an integrated concept in his chapter, "Project Team Planning: A Strategy for Success."

III. Project Structures and Organizations

The organizational issues of project management, including the basic structural alternatives, are dealt with in a comprehensive chapter by Hobbs and Ménard, entitled "Organizational Choices for Project Management." A complementary essay by Dinsmore ("Flat, Flexible Structures: Organizational Answer to Changing Times") develops the idea that matrix structures are tending to spread to companywide levels and discusses the challenges one faces in using such structures.

IV. Planning the Details of Project Management

This section goes into developing project management plans and shows some of the alternative forms for doing so. Westney, in "Paradigms for Planning Productive Projects," shows examples of work breakdown structures, network diagramming, bar charting, resource histograms, and assignment modeling. Hubbard discusses in detail the idea of planning through "Work Structuring," as his chapter is titled. A planning approach for complex projects, such as major governmental undertakings, is outlined in Pells's "Project Management Plans: An Approach to Comprehensive Planning for Complex Projects."

V. Controlling Costs and Keeping on Schedule

Ellis, in his chapter "Project Cost Control Systems That Really Work," outlines a project costing system based on a construction industry format. Lambert summarizes the complex issues involved in applying earned value techniques to a set of criteria known to U.S. government contractors as C/SCSC, defined in the title of the chapter, "Cost/Schedule Control System Criteria (C/SCSC): An Integrated Project Management Approach Using Earned Value Techniques." Paley demonstrates in "Value Engineering and Project Management: Achieving Cost Optimization" that costs can be kept under control by applying ongoing value engineering techniques at various stages throughout the project.

VI. Teamwork and Team Building

Team concepts are developed in this section in two complementary chapters. Tuman shows the importance of team building in his "success modeling" approach and demonstrates the vital role of the stakeholder in his chapter, "Models for Achieving Project Success Through Team Building and Stakeholder Management." Dinsmore shows a classical team-building paradigm and highlights interpersonal abilities in "A Conceptual Team-Building Model: Achieving Teamwork Through Improved Communications and Interpersonal Skills."

VII. Power, Influence, and Leadership

Dinsmore, in "Power and Politics in Project Management: Upper-Echelon Versus Conventional Project Management," shows that power is wielded at various levels on projects and discusses strategies for handling the situations. Youker develops the concept of "Sources of Power and Influence" according to different models and relates them to some project management tools and techniques. Finally, Thamhain explores the leadership issue in additional detail in "Effective Leadership for Building Project Teams, Motivating People, and Creating Optimal Organizational Structures."

VIII. Quality in Project Management

Two views are taken on the topic of quality in project management. Mendelssohn, in "The Essence of Quality Management," proposes a process model to ensure final customer satisfaction. Ireland's study of three companies in his chapter "Quality in Project Management Services" sheds light on the challenge of performing project management services to the satisfaction of a highly particular client: the U.S. government.

Part II: Project Management Applications

The second part of the *Handbook,* on the applications of project management, contains six sections. They are as follows:

IX. Project Management and Change Management

Adams proposes that effecting change within an organization should be treated as a project in "Managing Change Through Projects." The chapter "Planning for Change" by Owens and Martin develops a methodology for dealing with environmental change, both external and internal to the project. Graham describes a process for changing an organization to a more project-oriented culture in "A Process of Organizational Change From Bureaucracy to Project Management Culture."

X. Engineering and Construction Concerns

In "Administrator-Engineer Interface: Requirement for Successful Contract Award," Belev explores the importance of closing the gap between engineering and procurement in the precontractual stages. Fogel demonstrates the need for engineers to manage more effectively during the predesign and design process in his chapter, called "Managing to Avoid Claims: A Design Engineering Perspective." Werderitsch and Reams comment further on the issue of claims, including delay and acceleration entitlement, in "Construction Claims: Entitlement and Damages."

XI. Information Systems and Software Projects

Roetzheim shows what is unique about developing a software project in a provocative chapter entitled "Managing Software Projects: Unique Problems and Requirements." This discussion is developed further in "Implementing Project Management in Large-Scale Information-Technology Projects" by Otto, Dhillon, and Watkins. Zells, in "Project Management for Software Engineering," explains the scientific method used to develop software projects and discusses the procedures and phases inherent to such undertakings.

XII. Research and Development Projects

How to do the right things and how to do things right on R&D projects are discussed by Hosley in "Managing High-Technology Research Projects for Maximum Effectiveness." High risk and uncertainty are what set R&D projects apart from other conventional projects; Lambert outlines how to adjust to that reality in "R&D Project Management: Adapting to Technological Risk and Uncertainty." Another side of the R&D picture is analyzed in a study performed by Marcovitch and Maximiano under the title "The Behavior of Knowledge Workers on R&D Projects."

XIII. Launching New Products and Build-to-Order Projects

"Faster New Product Development" by Rosenau explores various alternatives and proposes the phased approach as a solid procedure for launching new products. Gordon and Lummus propose the concept of the cross-functional team for integrated product development as the secret for success in their chapter "Innovative Program Management: The Key to Survival in a Lethally Competitive World." A specific case of product development is discussed by Sridharan in his chapter, "Product Development Challenges in the Telecommunications Industry."

XIV. International and Cross-Cultural Projects

Smith and Haar outline specific steps to assure success in the international arena in an overview entitled "Managing International Projects." Culture is proposed as the differentiating variable in international projects by Martin in "The Negotiation Differential for International Project Management." A case of integrating two cultures is presented in "Challenges in Managing International Projects" by Dinsmore and Codas.

A Contribution to the Field

The AMA Handbook of Project Management is designed to be a unique contribution to the burgeoning field of project management. It draws from experienced professionals affiliated with associations like the Project Management Institute and INTERNET (the European federation of project management associations). The book targets a broad audience, including not only the traditional project management faithfuls, but also professionals involved in organizational development, research, product development, and other associated fields.

Part I
Project Management Concepts and Methodologies

Section I
Overview

1

What Project Management Is All About

Francis M. Webster, Jr.
Western Carolina University, retired

What Are Projects?

Projects are ubiquitous: They are everywhere, and everybody does them. If they are so common, then why all the fuss? Very simply, better ways of managing projects have been and are being developed. Those organizations that take the lead in implementing these capabilities consistently perform their projects better and are more competitive in general.

Projects can also be looked upon as the change efforts of society. The pace of change, in whatever dimension, has been increasing at an ever-faster rate. Effectively and efficiently managing change efforts is the only way organizations can survive in this modern world.

Yet another way to describe projects is by example. Most such descriptions start with such things as the pyramids, the Great Wall of China, and other undertakings of ancient history. These were major construction projects, and indeed, construction is inherently a project-oriented industry. A modern construction project that rivals others is the English Channel Tunnel, a $12 billion dollar effort. There are other project-oriented industries, not the least of which is the pharmaceutical industry. The search for new drugs has led to a remarkably high level of health and life expectancy. The aerospace industry, also project-oriented, is noted by its accomplishments, not only in space but also for the technological developments that have changed the way we live and work.

But not all projects are of such great magnitude. Remodeling or redecorating the house is a project. A community fund-raising campaign is a project. A political campaign is a project. Developing a new product, developing the advertising program to promote that product, and training the sales and support staff to move and service the product effectively are all projects. Responding to an EPA complaint is a project, particularly if the complaint is substantial. Indeed, it is possible that most executives spend more of their time planning and monitoring changes in their organizations— i.e., projects—than they do in maintaining the status quo.

All of these descriptions focus on a few key notions. Projects involve change, the

5

creation of something new or different, and they have a beginning and an ending. Indeed, these are the characteristics of a project that are embodied in the definition of *project* as found in *The Project Management Body of Knowledge (PMBOK)* published by the Project Management Institute (PMI), a professional society servicing the needs of this career area. The definition in the *PMBOK* is as follows: "*Project:* Any undertaking with a defined starting point and defined objectives by which completion is identified. In practice, most projects depend on finite or limited resources by which the objectives are to be accomplished."[1] This definition, while useful to project managers, may not be sufficient for others to distinguish projects from other undertakings. Understanding some of the characteristics of projects and comparing projects to other types of undertakings may give a clearer perspective.

Some Characteristics of Projects

Projects are unique undertakings that result in a single unit of output. The installation of an entertainment center by a homeowner with the help of a few friends is a project. The objective is to complete the installation and enjoy the product of the effort. It is a unique undertaking because the homeowner is not likely to repeat this process frequently. It is not unusual, however, for multiple units to be involved in a project at one level of detail or another. A high-rise building typically involves multiple floors, each of which are nearly alike. Installing the windows in such a building certainly involves multiple units. Even though the building is managed as a project, these multiple elements may, in fact, be managed in another manner. There are more economical ways to produce multiple units of a product, such as the mass production techniques used on assembly lines.

Projects are composed of activities, usually nonrepetitive, operating on an interrelated set of items that inherently have technologically determined relationships. One activity must be completed before another can begin. Generally, these technological relationships are very difficult to violate, or to do so just does not make sense. For example, if getting dressed is considered a project, it just does not make sense to put your shoes on before your socks. Whether to put on both socks and then both shoes or to complete the left foot before the right foot is in most instances a question of preference. In modern project management, a network diagram is used to portray these technological sequences. Exhibits 1-1 and 1-2 illustrate the use of networks to describe alternative ways of putting on socks and shoes. In Exhibit 1-1, both socks are put on first, then both shoes. In Exhibit 1-2, the preference is for putting on the right sock and shoe before the left sock and shoe.

Exhibit 1-3 shows a parallel network and does not imply that both socks are put on at once. Rather, it provides flexibility to determine the actual sequence based on other criteria. It is important for planners to focus on the technological relationships to prevent implicitly scheduling a project before really understanding the alternatives

Exhibit 1-1. Network diagram with preference for putting both socks on first, then both shoes.

Exhibit 1-2. Network diagram with preference for putting right sock and shoe on first, then left sock and shoe.

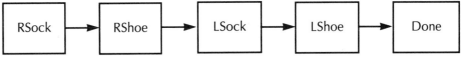

available. Exhibit 1-4 shows a network that would be nonsensical in most instances. Not only does it imply putting the sock on over the shoe but also putting both socks on the left foot.

Projects involve multiple resources, both human and nonhuman, which require close coordination. Generally there is a variety of resources, each with its own unique technologies, skills, and traits. This leads to an inherent characteristic of projects: conflict. There is conflict *between* resources as to concepts, theory, techniques, etc. There is conflict *for* resources as to quantity, timing, and specific assignments. Thus, a project manager must be skilled in managing such conflict.

The "project" is not synonymous with the "product of the project." The word *project* is often used ambiguously, sometimes referring to the project and sometimes referring to the product of the project. This is not a trivial distinction as both entities have characteristics unique to themselves. The names of some of these characteristics apply to both. For example, the life cycle cost of a product includes the cost of creating it (a project), the cost of operating it, the cost of major repairs or refurbishing (typically done as projects), and the cost of dismantling (often a project, if done at all). The project cost of creating the product is generally a relatively small proportion of the life cycle cost of the product. Exhibit 1-5 depicts the relationships that exist between the life cycles of projects and products of projects.

Consider a new product derived from basic research and then product research leading to design and then production. The first three phases of the product's life cycle—basic research, product research, and design—could each be one or more projects, each sharing the same objective: creation of a product. This product may require a facility for its production which, through the feasibility and acquisition

Exhibit 1-3. Parallel network diagram showing only technological relationships.

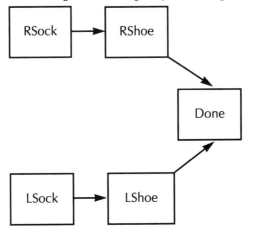

Exhibit 1-4. Nonsensical network diagram.

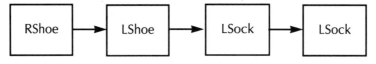

phases, is created by a project. That project in turn is composed of four phases that make up its life cycle: concept, development, implementation, and termination. Upon completion of the project, the operation of the facility is conducted in such a way as to prolong the life of the facility to the degree practicable. Integral to this process are a number of efforts to maintain and rehabilitate the facility, which are accomplished by projects. When the facility is no longer economically viable, it may be disposed of in some manner, often by a project.

When the product is designed and the facility completed, the product goes into production. The product goes through a marketing life cycle that is generally depicted as four phases: introduction, growth, maturity, and decline. Product introduction is a project and various aspects of the product growth phase are aided by performing

Exhibit 1-5. Comparison of project and product life cycles.

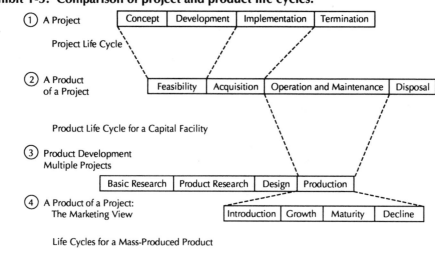

① A project to design and construct a building is presented.

② The building is the product of the project.

③ The purpose of the building is to house a process to produce a product in volume. Creating that process requires projects involving basic research, product research, and design of the product. Upon completion of these projects, the production of many units of that product begins.

④ This product is marketed and thus has its own life cycle characteristic of mass-produced items.

projects, such as the advertising campaign. Often, to extend the life of the product, various projects are undertaken to improve the product, develop alternative versions of the product, etc. To extend the useful life of the facility, other projects may be undertaken to improve or develop variations on the product.

Managerial emphasis is on timely accomplishment of the project as compared to the managerial emphasis in other modes of work. Most projects require the investment of considerable sums of money prior to enjoyment of the benefits of the resulting product. Interest on these funds is a major reason for emphasis on time. Being first in the market often determines long-term market position, thus creating time pressure. Finally, a need exists for the resulting product of the project, else the project would not have been authorized. Thus, time is of the essence. This time pressure, combined with coordination of multiple resources, explains why most project management systems have emphasized time management.

A Taxonomy of Work Efforts

It is helpful in understanding a concept to recognize and compare it to other similar concepts. This requires a taxonomy or classification of the modes in which work efforts are accomplished. There are five basic modes: craft, project, job shop, progressive line, and continuous flow. While most organizations perform some work in several of these modes, generally one mode is dominant in the core technology of the organization. All of these modes can be characterized as processes composed of one or more technologies/operations. Technologies in this sense does not imply just engineering or manufacturing but includes all sorts of office technologies, including the copier as well as the computer and the "technologies" involved in producing an advertising or political campaign, designing a training program or a curriculum, or producing a movie. The following are definitions and discussions of the four modes other than a project.

1. *Craft:* A process composed of a collection of one or more technologies/operations involving homogeneous human resources, generally a single person, producing a narrow range of products/services. This is best characterized by the single artist/craftsperson producing one unit of product at a time. Other examples are a single cook preparing a meal to order or a doctor examining a patient in the doctor's office.

2. *Project:* A temporary process composed of changing collections of technologies/operations involving the close coordination of heterogeneous resources to produce one or a few units of a unique product/service.

3. *Job shop:* A process composed of a loosely coordinated collection of heterogeneous technologies/operations to create a wide range of products/services where the technologies are located in groups by function and the time required at each workstation is varied. This is best characterized by the manufacturing plant in which equipment is located or grouped into departments by type or function, and the product/service is performed by moving the unit being worked upon from one department to another in a nonuniform manner. It is also the mode of operation of most kitchens and the one frequently used for physical examinations performed in hospitals.

4. *Progressive line:* A process composed of a tightly coordinated collection of heterogeneous technologies/operations to produce a large quantity of a limited range of products/services in which the technologies are located serially, the operator is directly involved in the work on the product, and the time allotted at each workstation is the same. The automotive assembly line is the stereotypical example, with the product moving from station to station in a cycle time of approximately sixty seconds. (Since this mode is used for both assembly and disassembly, the more general term *progressive line* is more appropriate than *assembly line*.) The progressive line is also the typical mode of serving for cafeterias and the mode in which physical examinations are given to large groups of people such as for the military. Note that manufacturing cells and *kanban* operations fit into this category. The progressive line mode can be used within a project. One example is a project to construct 740 houses in a development. The houses were in fact erected in the progressive line mode with multiple crews, each crew performing a very specific task on each house. On this line the *crews* moved from house to house with a cycle time of approximately one day.

5. *Continuous flow:* A process composed of a tightly coordinated collection of technologies/operations that are applied uniformly over time and to all the many units of a very narrow range of products/services, and in which the role of the operator is primarily to monitor and adjust the processes. Petroleum refineries are the most popular example of this mode. Other examples are electric generating stations, water as well as sewage treatment facilities, and automatic transfer lines such as those used in producing engine blocks and transmission housings.

Understanding the economics of these modes, as shown in Exhibit 1-6, reveals a fundamental driving force for attempting to move from the craft mode as far as

Exhibit 1-6. Economics of the five basic modes of work efforts.

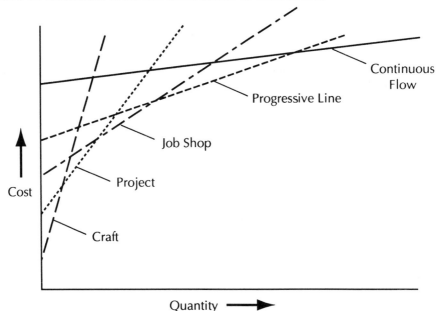

possible toward the continuous flow mode. For a given type of work, the craft mode generally requires the least capital investment or fixed costs but the highest variable cost per unit, while the continuous flow mode requires large capital investments or fixed costs and very low variable costs per unit. The other modes tend to be arrayed between these two extremes. Thus, regardless of the major mode for a given undertaking, there should always be a search for subsets of the work to be moved to the more economical mode. This was done, for example, for the 80,000 seats in the Pontiac Silverdome, which were installed in the progressive line mode. It is being done in the English Channel Tunnel project, where the digging, moving of tailings, and pumping of slurry to the tailings pit are all done in the continuous flow mode. (As a matter of fact, all modes can be observed on that project.) At a simpler level, programs for an athletic event such as a swim meet have been assembled in a progressive line mode while the overall effort to conduct the swim meet itself was a project.

A Further Abstraction

Given the definition that a project is a temporary process to produce one or a few units of a unique product/service, it is appropriate to examine the characteristics of the process. Consider the following: *The essential characteristics of the process by which a project is performed is the progressive elaboration of requirements/specifications.* A project is initiated by a person (perhaps a member of an organization) recognizing a problem or opportunity about which some action is to be taken. That person, alone or in concert, develops an initial concept of the action to be taken in the form of a product, be it a product for sale, a new facility, or an advertising campaign. Much work needs to be accomplished to take this meager concept to the reality of the product. This work, though often not conceived as such, is accomplished by instituting a project.

The general concept is expanded into a more detailed statement of requirements. These are examined for feasibility—market, technical, legal, organizational, political, etc.—resulting in further refinement of the specifications. These are then the basis for general design, the products of which become the basis for detail design. The detail designs are followed by production designs, tooling, production instructions, etc., each stage producing an elaboration on the specifications of the prior stage. Eventually, the product of the project takes shape, is tested, and is ready for operation. At this stage, give or take a few details, the project is completed. This characterization of projects permits the adaptation of modern quality management concepts into the management of projects.

The above is a rather lengthy discussion to clarify the nature of a project, but it is nevertheless an essential step in comprehending what project management is really all about.

Project Management

Project management as a unique career and profession is barely thirty years old. Its origins can be traced back to efforts such as U.S. Department of Defense major weapons systems development, NASA space missions, and major construction and maintenance efforts as well as comparable efforts in Europe. The magnitude and complexity of these efforts were the driving force in the search for tools that could aid management in the planning, decision making, and control of the multitude of activities involved in the project and especially those going on simultaneously.

A major misconception about project management is that it is no more than PERT (Program Evaluation and Review Technique), CPM (critical path method), or other methods of project scheduling using software. A more realistic view is that scheduling software is a small part of project management. Its importance is that it has permitted scheduling and cost management to be done much more efficiently and therefore in less time, in more detail, or both. Thus, a project can be planned and executed more precisely, leaving more time to perform the other aspects of project management.

An important way to view project management is that it is the management of change. This statement is more meaningful when contrasted with two other types of management: operations and technical. Operations management can be characterized as managing the steady state. Executives tend to be concerned about setting up a new operation (a project) to implement organizational strategy. As soon as the operation is established, the concern is more with maintaining the operation in a productive mode for as long as possible. Technical management tends to focus on the theory, technology, and practice in a technical field, concerning itself with questions of policy on strength of materials, safety factors in design, checking procedures, and the like. Project management, then, is the interface between general management, operations management, and technical management which integrates all aspects of the project and causes the project to happen.

Project Management Functions

PMI has developed a nominative model of the components of project management as represented in the "Function Impact Matrix Chart." It identifies three categories: the General Project Management Processes, Basic PM Functions, and Integrative PM Functions. The first category is subsumed under "General Framework," while the other two are composed of the eight "PM Functions" as discussed in Chapter 3. It may be useful to view project management as a fabric, consisting of woof, warp, and the diagonals. The General PM Process—the woof—ties these together into a whole. The Integrative PM Functions are the other threads that are added in, often at an angle, to give special texture to the fabric. In other words, they are the diagonals.[2]

The General PM Process: The Woof

Project Integration

If there is a single word that characterizes project management, it is *integration*. It is the responsibility of the project manager to integrate the efforts of the varied human resources; the variety of equipment, supplies, and materials; and the technologies to produce the product of the project in conformance with the requirements/ specifications, on schedule, and within budget.

The project environment is inherently dynamic. It is impractical, if not impossible, to predecide all aspects of the project, and inevitably things do not always go as planned. The project manager is the focal point for gathering the relevant information, making adjustments in plans, and communicating the new plans to all concerned. Project management is, by its very nature, a challenge to conceptualize, plan, implement, and close out the project within the triad of cost-schedule-performance.

Strategic Planning

The integration process is facilitated by having an overall strategy for the project: a strategic vision. Such a vision, if adequately communicated to the project team, can be the theme for subsequent integration and control actions. Strategic planning and the subsequent integration operate on at least three levels: technical, human, and schedule.

1. At the technical level, it involves combining the product components in a manner that best achieves the requirements. For example, in assembling a stereo system, the system performs up to the level of the most limiting component. This is true of any project.
2. At the human level, it is necessary to deal with concepts and work efforts. A well-defined strategic vision of how the project is to be carried out aids in achieving a common concept of the project for all team members. This is essential to ensure that all efforts are directed toward the same objectives in a consistent manner.
3. At the schedule level, the strategic vision aids in ensuring that all elements of the project are completed when required. And yet they should not be completed too early lest they have to be redone, become damaged, or get lost, not to mention the extra interest on the money expended to do the task if it is done too early. This vision is made explicit in this regard through the network plan for the project.

Control requirements and procedures need to be well designed and in place before substantial efforts on the project proceed so the records can be complete from the beginning. Valuable time and effort can be consumed in retracing the records after the fact, and control can be lost before the project really gets started. Furthermore, legal tests of prudency, common in the utility industry, are better dealt with when accurate and complete records of the project are available.

Resource Allocation

This is an essential process that both determines the cost of the project as defined and provides control over the project participants. Viewed simply, it is the budget. But even managing the budget per se neither brings the project in under budget nor on schedule. The project manager must ensure that the allocation of specific resources is adequate but not excessive and that the right resources are assigned to the right tasks. This is not a simple procedure because of the number of activities that can be in process simultaneously. Fortunately, modern project management software provides considerable assistance by identifying those activities which are most critical, the number of units of resource required by day for a given schedule, and the activities on which a critical resource is required. Nevertheless, having identified the critical decision areas, human judgment is still required to evaluate and make the final decisions.

The Basic PM Functions: The Warp

Scope Management

"The scope of a project can be either the work content or components of the project. It can be fully described by naming all activities performed, the end products which will result, and the resources consumed."[3] The scope statement is a vital document as it defines the project, not only what is included but what is not included. One manager of project managers commented that managing the scope of projects was his most important and troublesome assignment. On the one hand, he had to ensure that the client's needs had been met, but on the other hand, he had to ensure that any work content not in the originally contracted scope statement could be billed to the client.

Quality Management

The definition of quality is simply "conformance to requirements/specifications." If the requirements for the product of the project are consistent with the real, or perceived, needs of the client/customer, then the client/customer is likely to be satisfied with the product of the project. The product either conforms to these requirements or it does not. Quality should not be confused with excellence, luxury, prestige, "gold-plating," or other terms that describe the product of the project in qualifying degrees. These terms may be applied to the statement of requirements/specifications, but quality then refers to conformance to these requirements/specifications. There can be waste involved in producing a product or service that exceeds requirements just as surely as in producing a product that falls short of requirements. This definition of quality is the essential concept on which quality management operates.

The concept of a project as a process is essential for the application of process control to the management of projects, and more specifically, statistical process control applied to reduce variability. The concept of the progressive elaboration of specifications as the essential nature of the process fits with the quality concept that the customer is the next person/operation in the process. The "customer" is the next engineer, the tool builder, the ad layout person, and so on. If the product going to the customer has no defects, he or she can perform his or her task in the most efficient manner—and do the right thing right the first time.

It should be noted that this same concept of conformance can apply to the project itself as a measure of how well it was planned and executed relative to such things as environmental and safety expectations of society. *Quality Management for Projects and Programs*, a book by Lewis R. Ireland, published by the PMI, amplifies on these concepts.

Time Management

The management of time is crucial to the successful completion of a project. In some large projects that run for several years at costs in excess of $1 billion, the financing charges can approach $1 million per day. Even in many smaller projects, especially in a competitive market, it is essential to complete projects on time or lose the edge in the marketplace.

The function of time management has been divided into four processes: planning, estimating, scheduling, and control. Planning includes depicting what is intended to be done, how it will be done, and what will be used to do it. Estimating is the determination of the duration required to perform each activity. Scheduling determines the time period in which it is intended to perform the activity, recognizing both time and resource constraints. Control includes a recognition of what has happened and taking action to ensure that the project will be completed on time.

Cost Management

Cost management includes the processes that are required to maintain financial control of projects including economic evaluation, estimating, organizing, controlling, analyzing, reporting, forecasting, and taking necessary corrective action. Cost estimating is the process of assembling and predicting costs of a project over its life cycle. The cost budgeting process involves establishing budgets, standards, and a monitoring system by which the cost of the project can be measured and managed. Cost control entails gathering, accumulating, analyzing, monitoring, reporting, and managing the costs on an ongoing basis. Cost applications include special cost techniques, such as data banks to aid in estimating and product life cycle costing, and topics that affect cost management, such as computer applications and value analysis.

The Integrative PM Functions: The Diagonals

These functions of project management are pervasive throughout the project, providing the richness which gives the fabric its life and character. Projects can be performed with little attention to the details of these functions, but the probability of surprises, of conflicts among participants, and of misunderstandings are greatly increased when these functions are performed poorly. Ultimately, the probability of success of the project is greatly improved by knowledge and skilled use of these functions.

Risk Management

Risk management in the project context is the art and science of identifying, analyzing, and responding to the risk factors throughout the life of a project and in the best interests of its objectives. It may also include consideration of risks associated with the product after the project itself is completed. The term *risk management* tends to be misleading because management implies control of events. On the contrary, risk management must be seen as preparation for possible events in advance, rather than simply reacting to them as they happen. With time in hand, it is possible to identify alternative action plans and select that which is most consistent with project objectives. Risk management is the formal process whereby risk factors are systematically identified, assessed, and provided for. Such provisions constitute *response planning* and may include such defensive actions as mitigation by risk *avoidance*, *deflection* by insurance or contractual arrangement, and *contingency planning* such as the provision and prudent management of budgeted contingency allowances to cover uncertainties.

Human Resources Management

The project manager is responsible for developing the project team and building it into a cohesive group to complete the project. Two major types of tasks are recognized: administrative and behavioral. Administrative tasks include employee relations, compensation, and evaluation, as well as government regulations and evaluation. Much of the administrative activity of the project manager is directed by organizations and agencies outside the project. Understanding how these work can facilitate the process. The behavioral aspects deal with the project team members, their interaction as a team, and their contacts with individuals outside the project itself. Included in these are communicating, motivating, team building, and conflict management. The finite life and unique nature of projects places a premium on knowledge and skills in managing human resources.

Contract/Procurement Management

Inherent in the process of managing a project is the procurement of a wide variety of resources. In most instances, this requires the negotiation of a formal, written document, generally called a contract. Thus, procurement/contract management is essential knowledge. Different types of contracts are likely to elicit different types of behaviors by both the contractor and contractee. These need to be matched to the requirements of the project. The processes of initiating, evaluating, negotiating, and administering contracts are essential skills. In a global business environment it is also essential to understand varying social, political, legal, and financial implications in this process.

Communications Management

Successful project managers are constantly building consensus or confidence in decisions at critical junctures in a project by practicing active communications skills. The project manager must communicate to upper management, to the project team, and to other stakeholders. The communications process is not always easy because the project manager may find that barriers exist to communication, such as lack of clear communications channels and problems with technical language that must be used. The project manager has the responsibility of knowing what kind of messages to send, knowing to whom to send the messages, and translating the messages into a language that all can understand.

Conclusion

Projects fill an essential need of society. Indeed, projects are the major mode in which change is accomplished in a society. It is the mode in which corporate strategy is implemented.

Projects need be neither large, high-tech, nor complex. Their management is often complex because of the need to coordinate closely the heterogeneous resources in a manner to achieve the objectives of the project efficiently and effectively. This is further compounded by the fact that the mix of technologies/operations are constantly changing over the life of the project. And, this must be accomplished by doing the right thing right the first time, often each time with a completely new set of players.

It is clear that a project is a process. The essential concept of this process is that it is the progressive elaboration of requirements/specifications. From this it is easy to integrate the essential concepts of modern quality management, including conformance to requirements/specifications, do the right thing right the first time, the customer is the next person/operation in the process, and ultimately the reduction of variability through statistical process control.

Such a conceptualization and definition is critical to the future of project-oriented industries and organizations as they strive to match the performance of volume manufacturing organizations in achieving quality and reliability levels for which defects are measured in parts per million. It is critical to all organizations that hope to survive in a world where change is happening at an increasing pace, for projects are the means for responding to, if not proactively anticipating, the environment and opportunities of the future.

Acknowledgement

Appreciation is expressed to the Project Management Institute, P.O. Box 43, Drexel Hill, Penn. 19026, for permission to use extensively material contained in the *Project Management Body of Knowledge (PMBOK)*.

Notes

1. Project Management Institute, *Project Management Body of Knowledge* (Drexel Hill, Penn.: PMI, 1987).
2. Ibid.
3. Linn C. Stuckenbruk, *The Implementation of Project Management: The Professional's Handbook* (Reading, Mass.: Addison-Wesley/Project Management Institute, 1981).

2

An Overview of Project Management Principles for Executives: Six Lessons to Ensure Success

Paul C. Dinsmore
Dinsmore Associates

Project management, old in history and new as a management science (with most writings on the subject dating after 1960), is built around the cornerstone of accomplishing goals. The setting is generally complex and constrained by time, involving different groups and various technologies. The set of principles for gearing up, meeting goals, and winding down projects to completion in this complex environment is called project management.

Modern-day examples of projects include (1) physical construction, such as building bridges or industrial plants; (2) changes in organizational culture, like adopting participative management; and (3) undertakings with mixed objectives, such as putting in a new system that requires both physical adjustment (new layout and hardware installation) and changes in the way people perceive and perform their tasks. Exhibit 2-1 shows the type of project that executives may have to deal with, whether their primary function is managing projects or not.

In general management, just as in project management, goals also have to be met. The complexity of tasks, external environment, and time pressure make many activities appropriate for project management applications. Since project management is, by nature, aimed at managing change, executives in general management positions can gain from using a project approach. If, then, overall management can be divided into (1) managing the status quo (operational management), and (2) managing change (project management), and if change is happening at an increasing

This chapter was adapted from Paul C. Dinsmore, "Ideas, Guidelines and Techniques for Applying Project Management Solutions in the General Business Arena: Lessons for Executives." Reproduced by permission of Butterworth-Heineman Limited, Oxford, United Kingdom, from *The International Journal of Project Management*, Volume 8, February 1990, pp. 33–38.

Exhibit 2-1. Range of projects.

Physical (technical)	Mixed (systems and people)	Nonphysical (purely behavioral)
Building a bridge	New computer hardware and software system	Managerial training
Constructing an add-on to a factory	New materials-handling equipment	Quality awareness program
Establishing additional facilities	New corporate budgeting system	Organization change

Continuum including broad range of mixed-nature projects (involving systems and people), between the extremes of technical and purely behavioral projects.

pace, project management principles must inevitably become a bigger part of the overall management picture. Exhibit 2-2 shows the relationship between ongoing management and project management concepts.

Two common situations executives face are as follows:

1. *The executive as project manager in managing change and goal-oriented, time-constrained tasks in daily business activities.* Many executives face challenges that are not operational or repetitive. These challenges involve goal-oriented efforts with time

Exhibit 2-2. Typical components of ongoing management and project management.

Ongoing Management	Project Management
Business policies	Programming, scheduling
Marketing	Cost control
Human resources administration	Quality control
Finance and accounting	Scope management
Strategic planning	Contract management
Organizational behavior	Resources management
Standards and procedures	Interface management

Ongoing management principles — Overlap area — Project management principles

limits requiring coordination with other areas. Project management techniques—such as strategic project planning, work breakdown structures, problem solving, and feedback and evaluation methods—can help solve special general management tasks.

2. *The executive as project sponsor or other major stakeholder in relation to a conventional project.* Greater knowledge of project principles can help executives interact more effectively with project-oriented efforts within the company. Nonproject management executives may find themselves sponsoring a project or participating on a project management board for a conventional project related to their area. Or, other projects under way may overlap with the executive's area of responsibility.

Both situations are examined in this chapter. First, we look at the executive who manages a project within his or her area of responsibility, taking on the role, if not the title, of project manager. We then examine the executive who is sponsoring a project or is involved in a situation where there is overlap into the executive's territory.

The Executive as Project Manager

For starters, the executive acting as project manager needs to be aware of the basis of project management. Lesson 1 provides a set of project management commandments that summarizes the fundamentals for managing projects.

Lesson 1: Learning Project Management's Ten Commandments

These ten commandments summarize the recommended managerial posture for administering projects.

1. *Concentrate on interfacing.* Many projects involve interacting with other areas where the lines of interface are fuzzy. This calls for boundary spanning, involving both defining frontiers and making efforts at bridge building.

2. *Organize the project team.* If the project is going to involve a number of people, pick team members carefully, then motivate and integrate them. Test leadership abilities and delegate as much as possible.

3. *Plan strategically and technically.* Use a top-down planning approach, starting with overview thinking and then moving into details. Establish both what has to be done and how these planned tasks are to be accomplished. Break the project down into component parts using a work breakdown structure or other project logic.

4. *Remember Murphy's Law.* According to Murphy, "If anything can go wrong, it will." Strategies, plans, and systems should be tested to ensure fail-safe implementation. Don't leave the door open for Murphy to prove his theory.

5. *Identify project stakeholders.* Who are the interested parties who will influence important project decisions? Determine who has a stake in project outcome (clients, users, managers, financiers, suppliers of technology, higher management), and devise systems for involving and satisfying their needs.

6. *Be prepared to manage conflict.* In situations that involve people and change,

conflict is inevitable. In managing projects, effectively dealing with conflict may be instrumental in reaching proposed goals. Use conflict management techniques: negotiate when interests clash, promote collaboration when talents and capabilities are complementary, force the issue when important principles are at stake, and finally, set off conflict if necessary to meet project goals.

7. *Expect the unexpected.* Reducing the unexpected helps keep projects on track. In project environments, surprises can be warded off by participative planning, contingency allowances, judicious use of expert opinion, and statistical comparisons with similar prior projects.

8. *Listen to intuition.* Intuition is a subjective form of processing information. While it may not be entirely logical, it reflects the gut feeling formed by the experiences logged over the years. Intuition, therefore, should be one of the components used in making decisions on projects.

9. *Apply behavioral skills.* Projects are developed and carried out by people. Therefore, in the change-oriented project environment, behavioral influences may be substantial. Remember that resistance to change is a human characteristic. Work on integrating the project team, and try to foresee eventual people problems.

10. *Follow up and take corrective action.* The counterpart of planning is control. Set up a system for measuring progress, then evaluate that progress against initial plans and take corrective action.

Lesson 2: Planning Project Management

In actual practice, dozens of planning and control documents and instruments are needed to complete projects successfully. For complex projects, the types of documents may number in the hundreds. The minimum needed to structure most projects is summarized in the two strategic-type plans shown below: the project management plan, and the project plan.

Project Management Plan

This plan summarizes *how* the project is to be managed and should answer the following questions:

- ▸ What managerial philosophies, policies, and criteria should apply to the project?
- ▸ What are the primary goals and objectives of the project?
- ▸ What are the project milestones?
- ▸ What characteristics does the project have that require special managerial attention?
- ▸ How will upper management participate and support the project?
- ▸ What authority and responsibility will the project manager have?
- ▸ How will the project manager and project team interface with the client or end user, higher management, and other functional or support areas within the organization?
- ▸ How will the project team be organized?

- What systems and management tools will be used to plan, program, and control the project?

The project management plan is an up-front effort to harmonize the managerial philosophy to be used on the project. It should be used to involve the major influencing parties in reaching a managerial consensus as to how the project will be managed.

Project Plan

The project plan provides a macro view of *what* is to be done. This plan is aimed at summarizing the project itself, as opposed to the project management plan, which condenses the proposed managerial philosophy. Here are some of the cornerstones of the project plan.

- *Scope summary.* This summary reflects the essence of the project and defines project boundaries and interfaces. Objectives, goals, time, cost, and quality should all be dealt with in the scope summary.
- *List of documents to be issued.* To comprehend scope and time fully, a listing is needed of major documents such as drawings, specifications, requisitions, plans, and schedules.
- *Contracting plan.* When the project involves subcontracting vendors to supply equipment, materials, and/or services, a contracting plan is needed to define the work packages and how they will be handled.
- *Work plan.* In this section the physical work is described in terms of what is to be done and how it is to be done.
- *Master schedule.* This schedule demonstrates the time relationships between project activities, usually in bar chart form.
- *List of standards and procedures.* This outlines the managerial and technical rules of the game. These are determined by the standards that are chosen or especially prepared for the project.
- *Budget and cost control system.* This section describes budgeting and cost criteria and outlines cost codes and reporting periods.
- *Project breakdown structure and precedence diagramming.* Here the project is broken down into convenient work packages, and the sequential interrelationship is established between tasks and activities.
- *Equipment and materials lists.* These lists summarize the material components required to make the project a reality.
- *Detailed management plan.* Organizational structures, job descriptions, and administrative flow diagrams are the focus of this detailed version of the project management plan.
- *Communications.* In this section, all formal communications channels are established among client, contractors, managers, joint venture partners, etc.

Once the project plan and the project management plan have been outlined the project foundations have been set firmly in place. On top of this base, the remaining managerial actions can be taken with reasonable probability of success.

Lesson 3: Planning vs. the Process of Planning

The process of preparing the two plans mentioned above may be as important as the plans themselves. Involving those who are going to be responsible for project implementation in the planning effort pays dividends in terms of better decisions, higher motivation, and a "buy-in" to the plan that results from participative approaches.

The Japanese are masters at participative planning. They have demonstrated convincingly that integrated participative planning increases overall effectiveness and reduces implementation time. In spite of potential bogdowns at the beginning of the project, the slower start is offset by the natural synergy and capacity for foreseeing problems that grow out of the process. In other words, the process of planning can be as important as the plan itself. As Exhibit 2-3 shows, progress is made more quickly on projects utilizing participative planning rather than traditional planning.

This Japanese participative planning concept has spilled over to the Western world both in project applications and in traditional production-related efforts. A case in point is the simultaneous planning approach being used by U.S. auto makers for creating and launching new models. (General Motors uses the term "simultaneous engineering," Ford calls it the "team concept," and Chrysler applies "process-driven design.") The change came when U.S. auto makers discovered that their segmented approach to dealing with new models (planners plan, finance managers finance, engineers engineer, and sellers sell) led them to a concept-to-market time period of fifty-four months, which is long enough for consumers' tastes to change. Meanwhile, their Japanese counterparts could go from start to finish in as little as thirty-six months. Now the U.S. industry, by changing its approach to one involving simultaneous planning, aims to whittle down the cycle substantially and close the competitive gap.

Two significant changes are apparent when comparing the new Detroit planning format against traditional sequential approaches.

1. The new car model effort came to be seen as an integrated project requiring strong organizational interfacing.

Exhibit 2-3. Project progress with traditional planning vs. participative planning.

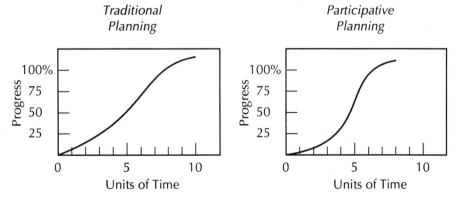

2. Planning became a participative effort, actively involving all stakeholders in the project.

Planning, then, is a major key to managing projects successfully. The plan itself, in terms of content and form, is a part of that success. Equal emphasis, however, needs to be given to the involvement of the stakeholders. The result is a better plan with greater probability for successful implementation.

Lesson 4: Managing the Project Cycle

Since projects evolve through a life cycle, management efforts require adaptation to each of the project's phases. Beginning a project calls for conceptual thinking. The development stage requires resource planning. The implementation phase calls for organization and productivity in carrying out the proposed work. Finally, termination involves wrapping up, reviewing, and turning over the completed project (facility, product, system, or service) to the user. Exhibit 2-4 shows the types of activities normally performed during each phase.

The most important concept for executives to remember in relationship to the life cycle is that each phase calls for a specific managerial approach. Successful project managers know how to shift gears from one stage to the next, starting off reflectively, moving into resource planning, then to the hands-on managing of actual implementation, and finally putting on pressure to bring the venture to a close.

Exhibit 2-4. Typical activities during phases of the project life cycle.

Phase 1 (Concept)	Phase 2 (Development)	Phase 3 (Implementation)	Phase 4 (Termination)
Conduct situation survey. Do alternative studies. Fix goals. Establish overall criteria. Outline strategies. Make preliminary costing and scheduling estimates.	Plan resource utilization: •People •Materials •Machines •Money Detail plans: •Scope •Time •Costs •Quality	Fully mobilize: •Organization •Communications Network Direct and monitor work. Pursue plans and adjust. Motivate and lead. Problem-solve.	Finish work. Turn over operations. Negotiate settlements. Evaluate and review. Finalize permanent record.

Resources (vertical axis) / Time (horizontal axis)

The Executive as Project Sponsor or Other Major Stakeholder

Project stakeholders are those that gain or lose as a result of perceived success in project implementation. Here are some hints for executives who find themselves in the role of project stakeholder.

Lesson 5: Dealing With the Stakeholder Role

The project manager and team are stakeholders since their competence, as seen by others, is tied to successful termination of the project. Others that stand to gain or lose are clients and end users, functional managers, technology suppliers, and joint-venture partners. Another major stakeholder is the project sponsor.

Ultimate responsibility for project success usually resides with the *project sponsor*, although the day-to-day burden is carried by the project manager. The sponsor is often the person or group to whom the project manager reports within the parent organization, although in some cases, a matrix or other corporate relationship may exist. The sponsor generally assigns the project manager to the task and relieves that manager if necessary. The project sponsor's function is to provide support, nurture high-level contacts, and monitor the project's overall performance. Here are some hints for executives who find themselves acting as project sponsors.

- Make sure to have a "contract" with the project manager. If both parties have worked together in the past and know one another's thinking patterns, fine. If not, spend time discussing the major issues. Use a review of the project manager's job description to see if both parties understand the job the same way.
- Get involved in the strategic project planning. Make sure that the project manager starts the project by involving the major stakeholders in the planning process. Give personal input and guidance during the initial planning stages.
- Provide support for the project manager at upper levels. For the project manager to work productively, he or she needs to be able to concentrate on daily management chores.
- Establish periodic formal review meetings with the project manager. In addition, keep channels open for informal communication.
- Since most competent project managers cannot simply be told what to do, think of yourself as the project manager's mentor: plant ideas, make suggestions, question points. Help the project manager see the big picture.

Clients or end users have a major stake in the final outcome of a project, but in many cases they are not responsible for the implementation phase. Yet they must live with the end result and operate it. Here are some ideas to help executives who are clients or end users.

- Try to influence the choice of the project manager. The manager will naturally be more acceptable to you if you have been involved in the matter. If the project manager has already been indicated, make it a point to establish as close a relationship as possible with that person.
- Since client/project team roles are often conflictive in nature, do your part to

reduce the tension. Recognize the difficulties, avoid being destructively critical, and be supportive whenever possible.

▸ Negotiate periodic formal contacts with the project team, and establish jointly acceptable procedures regarding approvals, design freeze criteria, preoperational activities, etc.

▸ Look ahead. Try to fix criteria and procedures that will reduce potential problem areas.

Other stakeholders, such as *functional managers,* also need to be aware of how they can best fit into the project picture. Here are some suggestions.

▸ Since one's capacity is a technical or support function, take advantage of the dynamics of the project organization to channel subjects that need action.

▸ Recognize the inherent conflict between functional groups (let's make sure we get it right) and project teams (let's get on with the job). Avoid interpreting conflictive situations as personal attacks.

▸ Insist on becoming involved in the planning stages that require using resources for which you are personally responsible. Give realistic time estimates.

▸ Participate in establishing procedures for project activities that involve personnel. Make suggestions and take initiative to ensure that policies are fixed before the action starts.

For other stakeholders, such as *joint-venture partners, suppliers of proprietary technology, development agencies,* and *financing institutions,* here are some general guidelines.

▸ Get it in writing. Personal rights and responsibilities must be clearly fixed in formal documents to enable a claim on one's stake in the project to be realized.

▸ Remember that having it in writing isn't enough. Those who negotiate projects are often not those who implement them. Therefore, get involved with the project team, at least at the strategic planning level, to ensure that your interests are being cared for.

▸ Don't overdo it. Recognize the limits of your claim on the project. Let other people do their jobs, even if they don't do things exactly the way you would prefer.

▸ Establish and follow through on a periodic review procedure that guarantees your right to monitor the project.

Lesson 6: Establishing a Project Management Council

One way for stakeholders to be represented adequately is through a project management council or steering committee. In the council meetings, the stakeholders are given a formal overview of project status, usually presented by the project manager, and then invited to participate in discussions regarding future trends. Project management council meetings are generally held quarterly, but depending on the size and time frame of the project, their frequency can be adjusted to meet project needs.

Initiative for forming the council is taken by the project manager and/or the project sponsor, who invites the members in an effort to involve and garner support from the project stakeholders. Here are examples of members of possible different project management councils.

- ► *Council No. 1.* Director of engineering, project manager, chief purchasing agent, outside consultant, head of production department, and chief of contracts and corporate investments.
- ► *Council No. 2.* Head of systems department, group leader, head of financial department, chief analyst, and third-party vendor of principal hardware and software.
- ► *Council No. 3.* Executive vice-president, head of project management, project manager, manager of finance, administrative manager, special assistant for operations, and joint-venture partner.

Conclusion

Executives face the challenge of adopting new management practices to meet the demands placed on business by the changing world. The new practices must include approaches that provide timely and cost-effective responses. The set of principles geared to reaching goals on schedule and within budget is labeled project management.

General management is moving more and more toward project management. Executives are expected to be managers of change, and managing change is what project management is all about. Modern-day executives, who are looked to as change managers, and who will also be exposed to conventional project work, can greatly increase their effectiveness by adding to their general management skills the dynamics of handling change through project management.

3

Developing a Project Management Body of Knowledge

Alan M. Stretton
University of Technology

Why a Project Management Body of Knowledge?

The most compelling argument for having a consolidated body of knowledge for project management is to help overcome the "reinventing the wheel" problem. A good body of knowledge should help practitioners do their job better, by both direct referencing and by use in more formal educational processes.

Koontz and O'Donnell express the need as follows: "In managing, as in any other field, unless practitioners are to learn by trial and error (and it has been said that managers' errors are their subordinates' trials), there is no other place they can turn for meaningful guidance than the accumulated knowledge underlying their practice. . . ."[1]

The Project Management Institute (PMI) took formal steps to accumulate and codify relevant knowledge by initiating the development of a *Project Management Body of Knowledge (PMBOK)* in 1981. The perceived need to do so arose from the PMI's long-term commitment to the professionalization of project management. As the PMI states, ". . . there are five attributes of a professional body. . . :

1. An identifiable and independent project management body of knowledge (PMBOK standards)
2. Supporting educational programs by an accredited institution (Accreditation)
3. A qualifying process (Certification)
4. Code of conduct (Ethics)
5. An institute representing members with a desire to serve (PMI)"[2]*

---

*Material from the *Project Management Body of Knowledge* is reprinted with permission of the Project Management Institute, P.O. Box 43, Drexel Hill, Penn. 19026, a worldwide organization of advancing the state-of-the art in project management.

The *Project Management Body of Knowledge* is central to the main thrust of PMI's professionalization program, which is aimed at a worldwide audience. This is tackling the "reinventing the wheel" problem on a grand scale! Some of the material in this chapter derives from the experiences of many members of the Project Management Institute, including the author, in the ongoing development of the PMI's *PMBOK*. (It should be emphasized that opinions and interpretations in this chapter are the author's alone and do not represent official policy or viewpoints of the Project Management Institute.)

What Are the Most Important Aspects of Project Management?

The many different perceptions as to what constitute the most important aspects of project management appear to derive from many causes, such as (1) normal differences between individual perceptions (even of the same event); (2) different actual experiences (even on similar projects); (3) differences in the projects themselves (in terms of such parameters as size, complexity, industry or technology, and type of project, e.g., R&D, construction, maintenance); and (4) the fact that any one individual can have had only limited hands-on experience across this increasingly diverse range.

There are also what could be called vested interest differences, as exampled by Kerzner: "Even in the academic community there exist differing views of project management: business colleges stress organizational responsibility and conflict management; engineering colleges (especially the civil engineering departments) stress scheduling and quantitative tools; and some engineering and business colleges provide interdisciplinary efforts in teaching cost control."[3]

Such wide-ranging differences in experiences and perceptions compound the difficulty of securing agreement on both the form and contents of a PMBOK, which is the primary topic of this chapter.

How Does a PMBOK Relate to Other Bodies of Knowledge?

An interesting way of illustrating intersections/overlaps between a PMBOK and other bodies of knowledge is given in PMI's 1987 *PMBOK*. There, it is stated that it is not uncommon for project management to be regarded as a subset of general management. This is typically the approach taken by schools of business, for example. However, Exhibit 3-1 shows these two as substantially independent bodies of knowledge, but with an overlapping area where a common body of knowledge is shared.[4] Many writers, including the author, have found this a very useful model when considering curricula for courses in project management. But there is also the possibility that general management, as we have understood it to date, may become subordinate to—or indeed be replaced by—project management (or "management by projects"). This is discussed in more detail toward the end of this chapter.

The intersection between the *PMBOK* and Technical or Industrial Bodies of Knowledge is an important one in actual practice, because all project management activity takes place within some industry, technology, or other specialist application area. The implications of this factor in project management education, and in the

Exhibit 3-1. Bodies of knowledge.

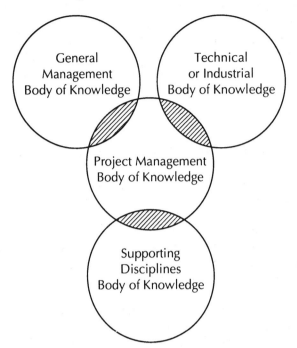

Source: This exhibit is reprinted from the *Project Management Body of Knowledge* (1987) with permission of the Project Management Institute, P.O. Box 43, Drexel Hill, Penn. 19026, a worldwide organization of advancing the state-of-the-art in project management.

development of project management bodies of knowledge, are also discussed in more detail in later sections of this chapter.

Finally, it might be argued that the topics in the Supporting Disciplines Body of Knowledge could be incorporated in the other two intersecting circles. However, the author has found this aspect of the model to be useful in developing project management curricula and would not push for such topics to be incorporated elsewhere.

It should be emphasized that the actual extents of the overlapping areas in Exhibit 3-1 are by no means clearly defined. It is difficult, for example, to make clear distinctions between project management techniques and the like that apply to all applications in all industries and technologies (i.e., which are truly "generic" to the *PMBOK*) and those that apply only in some application domains. This is one of the problems being addressed by the PMI in its ongoing development of the PMBOK, to which we now turn.

The Structure of PMI's PMBOK

The development of PMI's *PMBOK* is an ongoing process. In the words of an editor of the *Project Management Journal:* "It was never intended that the body of knowledge could remain static. Indeed, if we have a dynamic and growing profession, then we must also have a dynamic and growing body of knowledge."[5]

However, the development process is evolutionary, and the *PMBOK* will not change radically in the shorter term. One of the purposes of this chapter is to discuss some of the issues that are likely to influence the longer-term development of the *PMBOK*. We start by describing the basic structure of the *PMBOK*.

The *PMBOK* comprises nine basic sections: a Framework and eight Project Management (PM) Functions. These functions are:

Basic PM Functions

- ▸ Scope Management
- ▸ Quality Management
- ▸ Time Management
- ▸ Cost Management

Integrative PM Functions

- ▸ Risk Management
- ▸ Human Resources Management
- ▸ Contract/Procurement Management
- ▸ Communications Management

The PMBOK Framework

The Framework is a special area concerned with tying together all sections of the *PMBOK*. This has developed from simply a collection of the PM Functions, through two-dimensional matrix forms, toward a three-dimensional matrix format. The two-dimensional matrix form has the Basic PM Functions on one axis and the Integrative PM Functions on the other. The idea behind this matrix is expressed in the *PMBOK* as follows:

> *At each intersection in the body of the matrix is a "box" defined by the two dimensions of the matrix. Each "box" or block of knowledge consists of the relevant knowledge, skills, processes, activities, techniques, and tools consistent with the particular dimensions. Thus, individual blocks of knowledge can be clearly defined, and interrelationships or overlaps between them can be readily identified.*[6]

This idea has proved to be less productive than was originally expected. A suggested extension to this matrix, in the form of a third dimension consisting of the Project Life Cycle, appears to offer greater potential as an integrative framework for all components of the *PMBOK*. This is because all projects are progressed through a Project Life Cycle, which thus represents a major common baseline linking all projects for both practical and educational purposes. Exhibit 3-2 shows the three-dimensional *PMBOK* Framework model. As with the *PMBOK* itself, the Framework will continue to evolve. Its importance lies in the help it should give in tying together all components of a *PMBOK* into a coherent whole, particularly in view of the shortage of such integrative models.

Exhibit 3-2. Three-dimensional model of the *PMBOK* Framework.

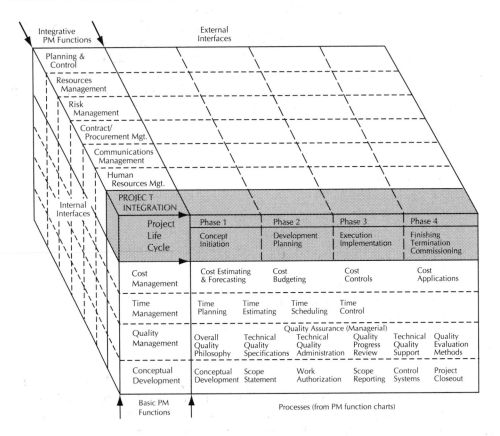

Source: Alan Stretton and John Thatcher, "Planned Developments of *PMBOK* and Associated Documents." Submitted for publication in *PM NETwork*.

The PM Functions

The treatment of each of the PM Functions in the *PMBOK* follows a thematic pattern. First, there is a discussion of the main features of the function. This is followed by a Function Chart, which is a detailed work breakdown structure into the function's component processes, activities, and relevant techniques. This is in turn followed by a function Impact Matrix Chart, which shows how each of the function's primary processes (from the Function Chart) impacts on each of the other PM Functions. Finally, there is a Glossary of Terms for each PM Function, covering each of the processes, activities, and techniques in the Function Chart.

Basic PM Functions

The Basic PM Functions are the management of scope, quality, time, and cost. (They are also varyingly described as "constraints," "restraints," or project "elements" in the *PMBOK* and elsewhere.) Scope, quality, time, and cost also represent the basic objectives that apply to all projects. The dual nature of these four Basic PM Functions was pointed out in the *PMBOK*'s predecessor, the "ESA Report": "The management of cost, time, scope, and quality are, in addition to being functions, also objectives to be attained within a project. . . . Cost, time, scope, and quality have a duality of character in that they are both functions and objectives."[7]

Although it is common usage to talk about "managing" scope, quality, time, and cost, it is worthwhile stopping for a moment to think about what these processes actually involve. Time management is a good example. In the literal sense, no one can actually manage time. Time management means the management of those project activities that are most relevant to the achievement of the project's time objectives. Similar comments apply to the other Basic PM Functions. What is involved in the management of scope, quality, time, and cost?

An examination of the Function Charts of each of these functions reveals some consistent patterns. (For the present purpose, we exclude the managerial component of quality management—i.e., the quality of human performance—and consider only the technical quality component.) The relevant primary processes are shown against each of the Basic Functions in Exhibit 3-2. Specifically, it can be seen that the primary processes of each of the four Basic PM Functions fit reasonably well into the typical project sequence for planning (including estimating and scheduling) and controlling (including reporting and progress reviews).

Now, it is common for books and articles on project management to focus primarily on planning and control activities, either as the core of project management in their own right, or as part of the four "classical" management functions of planning, organizing, leading (the human aspect), and controlling. However, *PMBOK* has chosen a different primary focus. It has separated out the primary project objectives of scope, quality, time, and cost and has separately nominated the corresponding managerial functions which are most directly concerned with their achievement. These heavily involve planning and controlling processes, which also apply to some of the other PM Functions, to which we now turn.

Integrative PM Functions

The Integrative PM Functions are the management of risk, human resources, contract/procurement, and communications. As the *PMBOK* states, these "integrative project management functions are quite independent of, and cut across, all these basic functions."[8]

There are three further functions that feature significantly in the *PMBOK*, namely the management of planning and control, management of project integration, and management of resources. These are included in Exhibit 3-2 but are not fully discussed as project management functions in their own right in the *PMBOK*.

On the basis of the above discussion on the Basic PM Functions, it is clear that planning and control are independent of the basic functions. Indeed, these processes not only apply to the basic functions but are clearly relevant to other integrative functions as well. However, all three of these additional functions have attributes that would be regarded as integrative in the normal usage of the word, and on that basis they would qualify for more detailed treatment in the *PMBOK*. This suggests the more general question, which frequently arises, as to just which functions should be included in a generic PMBOK.

One example of the types of questions to be resolved is instanced by the author's experience in managing R&D projects in which there were no contract/procurement activities whatever. Should this PM Function therefore be dropped from a generic PMBOK? More specifically, should we adopt a purist approach and exclude from a generic PMBOK any PM Function for which we find even one project where it is not applicable? Such an approach would appear to be basically counterproductive, as the usefulness of a PMBOK for both educators and practitioners could be substantially, or even dramatically, reduced.

Should we then adopt the opposite approach and include all potential candidates in a checklisting mode, so that those which do not apply for a particular application area can then be simply struck off? The problem with this approach is that such a list could be virtually never-ending, with attendant dangers of unbalancing and/or trivializing a PMBOK.

A third possibility, which is being adopted by PMI, is to include those PM Functions which are (agreed to be) common to most projects in most application domains. This approach could introduce some problems in deciding about specific inclusions and exclusions, because *most* is rather an elastic term. However, such potential problems would appear to be a small price to pay for increasing the usefulness of the *PMBOK*. Dealing with such problems of choice may also help ensure that the *PMBOK* remains dynamic and current.

The above discussion also suggests that there is a need for PMBOKs that are specific to particular industries, technologies, or other application areas, and we now turn to this topic.

Project Management in Different Application Areas

Industry/Technology-Specific Bodies of Knowledge

Most project managers operate within a particular industry and/or technology. The knowledge that is most relevant to them at any stage is that which is directly related to their current industry/technology. Indeed, it appears that much of the ongoing education in project management is done as a component of broader industry/technology-specific educational efforts. These include formal educational programs, such as engineering and other applied science degree programs, and continuing education programs, whether run by educational institutions, industry bodies, or individual organizations.

Thus, in many industries/technologies there is already a wealth of project management material, but this is often heavily intertwined with technical or other such materials particular to that area. One of the challenges for developers of industry/technology-specific PMBOKs is to isolate and extract the specific project management components.

Substantial bodies of knowledge have already been extracted in some areas, but there is also a good deal of material that is still "locked up" within individual organizations and therefore is not yet available to wider audiences. Academics often obtain some access to these materials and incorporate them in their writings. Other avenues for widening the availability of such materials need to be found.

An even greater challenge faces those working in industries and/or technologies that have only recently adopted the project approach to undertaking tasks. These groups will no doubt wish to develop their own domain-specific bodies of knowledge as soon as practicable, and they should be strongly supported in such efforts.

In the meantime, project managers in new application domains have only the more generic materials to fall back on to help develop their skills, and this is one very important reason why the generic PMBOK should continue to be developed.

Shared Domain–Specific Bodies of Knowledge

There is also a kind of "halfway house" approach that is currently being pursued by the PMI. It would appear that many different industries and technologies share many common project management activities. For example, such activities as engineering/ design, construction, and R&D are typically undertaken on a project basis in a wide variety of industries and technologies. There seem strong grounds for believing that each such set of project activities is carried out in a broadly similar way, irrespective of the particular industry or technology in which it is undertaken.

If it is so, then the codification of these shared domain–specific bodies of knowledge would offer considerable detailed help to a wide range of project managers in many industries and technologies. The PMI is actively pursuing the development of such bodies of knowledge, starting with the assembly of relevant case materials.

Toward Management by Projects

It is no accident that the project approach is becoming very widely used in diverse industries and technologies. Why is this so?

General management theory and practice evolved in eras when environments were relatively stable and certain, when technologies were relatively simple and changed slowly, and when "closed-system" assumptions about organizations were usual. This contrasts sharply with the general and business environments of the past two decades. The words "uncertain and turbulent" are habitually used now to describe the present and likely future environments in which managers must manage. Technologies are increasingly complex and change rapidly. The dynamic nature of business environments has forced "open-system" approaches to management.

The environments of projects have always had uncertain and turbulent characteristics, and project managers have learned how to achieve results in these circumstances. It would seem that a wider recognition of this may account (at least in part) for the accelerated adoption of the project approach over an increasingly diverse range of industries, technologies, and other domains.

Project management has the potential to expand much further. Indeed, it seems poised to move from being not only a distinct profession applying to distinctive tasks called projects, but also a valid (and often superior) form of general management in its own right. This movement from "project management" to "management by projects" represents an exciting prospect and challenge for both project managers and general managers.

Notes

1. H. Koontz and C. O'Donnell, *Essentials of Management* (New Delhi, India: Tata McGraw-Hill, 1978).
2. "Project Management Body of Knowledge: Special Summer Issue," *Project Management Journal* 17, No. 3 (1986), p. 15.
3. Harold Kerzner, *Project Management: A Systems Approach to Planning, Scheduling and Controlling* (New York: Van Nostrand Reinhold, 1979).
4. Project Management Institute, *Project Management Body of Knowledge* (Drexel Hill, Penn.: PMI, 1987), pp. 2–3.
5. "Project Management Body of Knowledge," p. 3.
6. Project Management Institute, pp. 2–5.
7. "Ethics, Standards, Accreditation: Special Report," *Project Management Quarterly* (August 1983), p. 20.
8. Project Management Institute, pp. 2–4.

Section II
Managerial Strategies for Starting Up Successful Projects

4

Strategies for Managing Major Projects

Peter W. G. Morris
Bovis Ltd.

The way one sets up a project largely determines how successful it will be. The crucial point about the model presented in this chapter is that *all* the items must be considered from the outset if the chances of success are to be optimized. The project must be seen as a whole, and it must further be managed as a whole as it is implemented. While this chapter is directed toward the management of large, broad, community-based projects, the same principles apply, on a lesser scale, to nonmajor projects.

The strategic model for managing projects discussed in this chapter is shown in Exhibit 4-1. Its logic is essentially as follows:

▸ The project is in great danger of encountering serious problems if its *objectives*, general *strategy*, and *technology* are inadequately considered or poorly developed, or if its *design* is not firmly managed in line with its strategic plans.

▸ The project's *definition* both affects and is affected by changes in *external factors* (such as politics, community views, and economic and geophysical conditions), the availability of *financing*, and the *project duration*; therefore, this interaction must be managed actively and well. (Many of these interactions operate, of course, through the forecasted performance of the product or products that the project delivers once completed.)

▸ The project's definition; its interaction with these external, financial, and other matters; and its implementation are much harder to manage and quite possibly damagingly prejudiced if the *attitudes* of the parties essential to its success are not positive and supportive.

▸ *Realization* of the project as it is defined, developed, built, and tested involves:

▸ Deciding the appropriate project-matrix-functional orientation and balancing the involvement of the owner, as operator, and the project implementation specialists

▸ Having contracts that reflect the owner's aims, which are motivational, and that appropriately reflect the risks involved and the ability of the parties to bear these risks

Exhibit 4-1. Strategic model for managing projects.

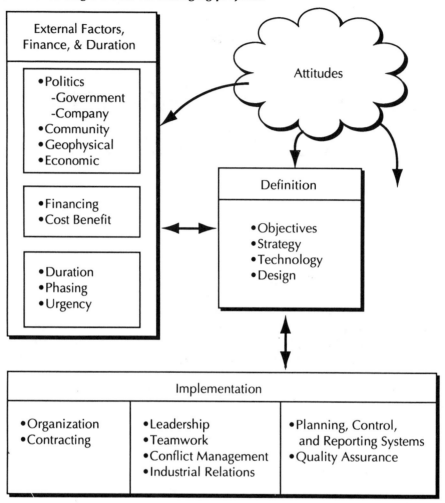

▸ Establishing checks and balances between the enthusiasm and drive of the project staff and the proper conservatism of its sponsors

▸ Developing team attitudes, with great emphasis put on active communication and productive conflict

▸ Having the right tools for project planning, control, and reporting

Let us examine these points.

Project Definition

The project should be defined comprehensively right from its earliest days in terms, for example, of its purpose, ownership, technology, cost, duration and phasing, financing, marketing and sales, organization, energy and raw materials supply, and transportation. If it is not defined properly "in the round" like this from the outset, key issues essential to its viability could be missed or given inadequate attention, resulting in a poor or even disastrous project later.

Objectives

The extent to which the project's objectives are not clear, are complex, do not mesh with longer-term strategies, are not communicated clearly, or are not agreed upon, compromises the chances of project success. The Apollo program, which placed the first man on the moon, was technically extremely difficult but its chances of success were helped immeasurably by the clarity of its objective.

It is interesting to compare the Apollo program with U.S. plans for a permanent, manned space station orbiting the earth. The space station objective is superficially clear—in President Ronald Reagan's words, "to develop a permanently manned space station and to do it within a decade." But the objective is in fact far from clear. What, for example, does *develop* really mean? Just design and construct? Surely not. And what is the station's real mission—and hence, what is the project's proper development strategy? Earth observation? A way station to planetary observation? Microgravity and other experimental purposes? Or a combination of these? The space station example illustrates that project, or program, objectives should match with viable long-term strategies, otherwise there will be confusion, uncertainty, changes, cost increases, and delays—as there indeed have been in the prolonged effort to establish a permanent manned space station.

Strategy

Strategies for the attainment of the project objectives should similarly be developed in as comprehensive a manner as possible, right from the outset. This means that at the prefeasibility and feasibility stages, for example, industrial relations, contracting, communications, organization, and systems issues should all be considered, even if not elaborated upon, as well as the technical, financial, schedule, and planning issues.

Some of the most valuable work on the need for comprehensive planning has come from the areas of R&D and new product development. Valuable work has also been done with regard to development aid projects. Hirshman's 1967 *Development Projects Observed*, for example, was one of the first writings explicitly to pull the "project success'" question into project management.[1] The 1980s insights of Cassens, Moris, and Paul encapsulate almost everything anyone of good sense would expect regarding what it takes to produce successful development projects.[2] The writings of Cooper, Manfield, and others on new product development similarly relate product implementation performance to environmental and market success.[3]

Technology and Design

The development of the design criteria and the technical elements of the project should be handled with the utmost care. The design standards selected affect both the difficulty of construction and the operating characteristics of the plant. Maintainability and reliability should be critical factors in determining the project's operating characteristics. Many studies have shown that technical problems have a huge impact on the likelihood of project overrun[4]: Thorough risk analysis is therefore essential. The rate of technological change in all relevant systems and subsystems should be examined; technology must be tested before being designed into production (as opposed to prototype) projects; design changes should be kept to an absolute minimum.

No design is ever complete; technology is always progressing. A central challenge in the effective management of projects is thus the conflict between meeting the schedule against the desire to get the technical base that fits better. The orderly progressing of the project's sequence of review stages—the level of detail becoming progressively tighter, with strict control of technical interfaces and of proposed changes (through configuration management)—is now a core element of modern project management.

Projects as widely different as weapons systems, process plants, and information systems now generally employ project development methodologies that emphasize careful, discrete upgradings of technology; thorough review of cost, schedule, and performance implications; and rigorous control of subsequent proposed changes. (Civil engineering and building, however, because of the split between design and construction still common in the United Kingdom, alone of today's major project-based industries, still tend not to have design management practices as a typically central part of the evolving total project management process.)

A major issue in project specification is how great a technological reach should be aimed for without incurring undue risks of cost overruns, schedule slippages, or inadequate technical performance. Up until about the 1980s this was perhaps the most difficult issue to get right on projects. During the 1980s, however, practice got better (though there have still been some spectacular disasters), partly because our basic technologies are not progressing into new domains at quite the rate they were before, but also partly because of the greater caution, care over risk assessment, use of prototypes, etc., which is now more common project practice. It is barely conceivable that we should embark on a brand new nuclear power reactor (AGR) or aerospace project (Concorde) today with the bravura that we did twenty to twenty-five years ago.

In setting up projects, then, care should be taken to appraise technological risk, prove new technologies, and validate the project design, before freezing the design and moving into implementation.

External Factors, Finance, and Duration

Many external factors affect a project's chances of success. Several may be identified but particularly important are the project's political context, its relationship with the local community, the general economic environment, and its location and the geophysical conditions in which it is set.

Political, Environmental, and Economic Factors

Project personnel have had notable difficulty in recent years recognizing and dealing with the project's impact on the physical and community environment and, in consequence, managing the political processes that regulate the conditions under which projects are executed. Most projects raise political issues of some sort and hence require political support: moral, regulatory, and sometimes even financial. National transportation projects, R&D programs, and many energy projects, for example, operate only under the dictate of the politician. The civil nuclear power business was heavily pushed politically. Third World development projects are especially prone to political influence. Even where the public sector is supposedly liberated to the private—as in build-own-operate projects—political guidance, guarantees, and encouragement are needed.

Do nonmajor projects also need to be conscious of the political dimension? Absolutely. Even small projects live under regulatory and economic conditions directly influenced by politicians; intraorganizationally, too, project managers must secure political support for their projects.

The important lesson therefore is that these political issues must be considered at the outset of the project. The people and procedures that are to work on the project must be attuned to the political issues and ready to manage them. To be successful, project managers must manage upward and outward, as well as downward and inward. The project manager should court the politicians, helping allies by providing them with the information they need to champion his or her program. Adversaries should be coopted, not ignored. (The environmental impact assessment process, which will be described shortly, is showing how substantive dialogue can help reduce potential opposition.)

Although environmentalism has been seriously prejudicing project implementation since the 1960s, most project personnel ignored it as a serious force at least until 1987–1988, when a number of world leaders, the World Bank, and others began to acknowledge its validity. Now, at last, most project staff members realize that they must find a way of involving the community positively in the development of their project. Ignoring the community and leaving everything to planning hearings is often to leave it too late. A "consents strategy" should be devised and implemented.[5] Dialogue must begin early in the project's development.

In a different sense, getting the support of the local community is particularly important in those projects where the community is, so to speak, the user—as, for example, in development projects and information technology. The local community may also be the potential consumer or purchaser for the project. Doing a market survey to see how viable the project economics are is thus an essential part of the project's management.

Changes in economic circumstances affect both the cost of the project's inputs and the economic viability of its outputs. The big difference today compared with twenty years ago is that then we assumed conditions would not vary too much in the future. Now, after the economic dislocation of the 1970s and 1980s, we are much more cautious. As with technology, then, so with economics: We should be more cautious in appraising and managing our projects today.

In the area of cost-benefit discounting and other appraisal techniques, practice has moved forward considerably over the last few years. Externalities and longer-term social factors are now recognized as important variables that can dramatically affect the attractiveness of a project. The basic project appraisal techniques of the 1960s have now been replaced with a broader set of economic and financial tools arrayed, in the community context with the use of environmental impact assessment procedures.

Initially resisted by many in the project community, the great value of environmental impact assessment (EIA) is that it (1) allows consultation and dialogue between developers, the community, regulators, and others; and (2) forces time to be spent at the front end in examining options and ensuring that the project appears viable. Through these twin benefits the likelihood of community opposition and of unforeseen external shocks arising is diminished. Further, in forcing project developers to spend time planning at the front end, the EIA process emphasizes precisely the project stage that traditionally has been rushed, despite the obvious dangers. We all know that time spent in the project's early stages is time well spent—and furthermore, that it is cost effective time well spent—yet all too frequently this stage is rushed.

Finance

During the 1980s there was a decisive shift from public sector funding to the private sector. There is a belief that projects built under private sector funding inevitably demonstrate better financial discipline. This is doubtless true where projects are built and financed by a well-managed private sector company. But private financing alone does not necessarily lead to better projects (as the record of Third World lending in the 1970s shows: weak project appraisals, loan pushing, cost and schedule overruns, white elephants, etc.). What is required is funding realism. The best way to get this is by getting all parties to accept some risk and to undertake a thorough risk assessment. Full risk analysis of the type done for limited recourse project financing, for example, invariably leads to better setup projects and should therefore be built into the project specification process. The use of this form of funding in methods such as build-own-operate projects has had the healthy consequence of making all parties concentrate on the continuing economic health of the project by tying their actions together more tightly to that goal.

The raising of the finance required for the English Channel Tunnel from the capital markets in 1986–1987 is a classic illustration of how all the elements shown in Exhibit 4-1 interact, in this case around the question of finance. To raise the necessary £6 billion required that certain technical work be done, planning approvals be obtained, contracts be signed, political uncertainties be removed, etc. Since the project was raising most of its funding externally, there was a significant amount of bootstrapping required: The tasks could be accomplished only if some money was already raised, and so on. Actions had to be taken by a certain time or the money would run out. Further, a key parameter of the project's viability was the likelihood of its slippage during construction. A slippage of three to six months meant not just increased financing charges but the lost revenue of a summer season of tourist traffic. The English Channel Tunnel thus demonstrates also the significance of managing a project's schedule and of how its timing interrelates with its other dimensions.

Duration

Determining the overall timing of the enterprise is crucial to calculating its risks and the dynamics of its implementation and management. How much time one has available for each of the basic stages of the project, together with the amount and difficulty of the work to be accomplished in those phases, heavily influences the nature of the task to be managed.

In specifying the project, therefore, the project manager spends considerable effort ensuring that the right proportions of time are spent within the overall duration. Milestone scheduling of the project at the earliest stage is crucial. It is particularly important that none of the development stages of the project be rushed or glossed over—a fault that has caused many project catastrophes in the past. A degree of urgency should be built into the project, but too much may create instability.

It is best to avoid specifying that implementation begin before technology development and testing is complete. This is the "concurrency" situation. Concurrency of course is sometimes employed quite deliberately, to get a project completed under exceptionally urgent conditions, but it often brings major problems in redesign and reworking. If faced with this, be under no illusion as to the risk. Analyze the risk rigorously, work breakdown element by work breakdown element, milestone phase by milestone phase.

The concurrency situation should be distinguished from a similar sounding but in fact quite different "fast build" practice. (This is sometimes also known as "fast track," but others equate fast track with concurrency. The terminology is imprecise and hence there is confusion—and danger—in this area.) Fast build is now being used to distinguish a different form of design and construction overlap: that where the concept, or scheme, design is completed but then the work packages are priced, scheduled, and built sequentially, within the overall design parameters, with strict change (configuration) control being exercised throughout. With this fast build situation, the design is secure and the risks are much less.

There are, in short, several lessons on how to deal with the challenge of managing urgent projects.

- ▸ Do not miss any of the stages of the project.
- ▸ Use known technology and/or design replication as far as possible; avoid unnecessary innovation.
- ▸ Test technology before committing to production (prototyping). Avoid concurrency unless prepared to take the risk of failing and of having to pay for the cost of rework.
- ▸ Avoid making technical or design changes once implementation has begun. Choose design parameters broad enough to permit development and detailing without subsequent change (fast build). Exert strict change control/configuration management.
- ▸ Order long lead items early.
- ▸ Prefabricate and/or build in as predictable an environment as possible and get the organizational factors set to support optimum productivity. Put in additional management effort to ensure the proper integration at the right time of the things that must be done to make the project a success: teamwork, schedule, conscious decision making, etc.

Each of these areas, then—external factors, finance, and duration—is both affected by and affects the viability of project definition. They must all be managed by the project executive. They must then be implemented through the project's life cycle.

Attitudes

Implementation can be achieved effectively only if the proper attitudes exist on the project. Unless there is a major commitment toward making the project a success, unless the motivation of everyone working on the project is high, and unless attitudes are supportive and positive, the chances of success are substantially diminished.

It is particularly important that there be commitment and support at the top; without it the project is severely jeopardized. But while commitment is important, it must be commitment to viable ends. Great leaders can become great dictators. It is important, then, if sane, sensible projects are to be initiated, that they be not insulated from criticism. Critique the project at its specification stage, therefore, and ensure that it continues to receive objective, frank reviews as it develops.

Implementation

I have suggested that project management has in the past been concerned primarily with the process of implementation. This is a pity since it implies that developing the definition of the project is somehow not something that is the concern of the project's manager. As the foregoing shows, this is absurd.

The key conceptual point is not only that the specification process must be actively managed, but that the specification process must consider all those factors that might prejudice its success—not just technical matters and economics, but also ecological, political, and community factors and implementation issues.

Organization

The two key organizational issues in projects are to decide the relevant project-matrix-functional orientation and the extent of owner involvement. Both of these must be considered from the earliest stages of project specification.

On the former, note that a full project orientation is expensive in resource terms and also that many projects start and finish with a functional orientation but "swing" to a matrix during implementation.[6] Note too that implementing a matrix takes time and that effort must be put into developing the appropriate organizational climate. Assistance from the area of organization behavior therefore should be considered when designing and building a matrix organization. (Indeed, this is also true for other forms of project organization.)

The crucial issues as regard the extent of owner involvement are the extent that the owner does not (1) have the resources, or (2) the skills, outlook, or experience, but (3) has legal or moral responsibility for assuring implementation of satisfactory standards. The first constraint is the most common. In building and civil engineering, for example, because of the nature of the demand, the owner rarely if ever has sufficient resources in-house to accomplish the project. Outside resources—principally designers, contractors, and suppliers—have to be contracted in. The owner, quite properly, focuses more on running the business.

Yet some degree of owner involvement is generally necessary. For if no project management expertise is maintained in-house, then active, directive decision making of the kind that projects generally require is not available. On the other hand, if operators who are not really in the implementation business get too heavily involved in it, then there is a danger that the owner's staff may tinker with and refine design and construction decisions at the expense of effective project implementation. The solution to this dilemma is not an easy one to determine. There is in fact no standard answer. What is right will be right for a given mix of project characteristics, organizations, and personalities.

The key point, ultimately, is for owner-operators to concentrate on predetermined milestone review points—the key markers in the project's development at which one wants the project to have satisfactorily reached a certain stage—and to schedule these properly and review the project comprehensively as it passes across each of them. Milestone scheduling by owners is in fact now much more accepted as appropriate rather than the more detailed scheduling of the past.

Contract Strategy

The degree of owner involvement is clearly related to the contractual strategy being developed. It is now generally recognized that the type of contract—essentially either cost reimbursable or incentive (including fixed price)—should relate to the degree of risk the contractor is expected and able to bear. If the project scope is not yet clear, it is probably better not to use an incentive or fixed price type contract: The contract can be converted to this form later. Contracts should be motivational: Top management support and positive attitudes should be encouraged.

The parties to a contract should put as much effort as possible as early as possible into identifying their joint objectives: It is better to spend longer working out how to make the contract a success than how to "do down" the other party. And while competitive bidding is healthy and therefore to be encouraged, adequate time and information must be provided in order to make the bid as effective as possible. Spend time, too, ensuring that the bases upon which the bid is to be evaluated are the best: Price alone is often inadequate.

People Issues

Projects generally demand extraordinary effort from those working on them, often for a comparatively modest financial reward with the ultimate prospect of working oneself out of a job! Frequently, significant institutional resistance must be overcome in order for the many factors here being listed to be got right—or anything like right. This therefore puts enormous demands on the personal qualities of all those working on the project, from senior management through the professional team(s) to the work force.

The different roles of project manager, leader, champion, and sponsor should be distinguished, as shown in Exhibit 4-2. Each is needed throughout the project, but the initial stages particularly require the latter three. Beware of unchecked champions and leaders, of the hype and overoptimism that too often surround projects in their

Exhibit 4-2. Leadership roles in projects.

Project Manager:	A manager is someone who gets others to do what he or she is not able to do alone. A project manager manages resources to achieve success, as defined principally by his or her "boss" or "client."
Leader:	A leader is someone who gets people to follow him or her.
Project Champion:	A champion promotes something. The project champion has an extremely important role early in the project, particularly in ensuring the project receives the attention and resources it needs in order to survive. Championship need not necessarily correlate with a successful project, and a project champion may or may not be knowledgeable on project management.
Project Sponsor:	A sponsor is the provider of resources. The sponsor must ensure the project makes operational sense once it is completed. He or she should be familiar with project management but the management of the project per se is not his or her remit. The sponsor is preeminently the guardian of the "business case."

early stages. The sponsor must be responsible for providing the objective check on the feasibility of the project.

We should recognize the importance of teamworking, of handling positively the conflicts that inevitably arise, and of good communications. Consideration should be given to formal start-up sessions at the beginning of a team's work (mixing planning with team building). The composition of the team should be looked at from a social angle as well as from the technical: People play social roles on teams and these must vary as the project evolves.

All projects involve conflict: Cost, schedule, and technical performance are in conflict. However, conflict can be used positively as a source of creativity. Conflict is managed in this way on the best projects. On some projects it is ignored or brushed over: at best, a creative tension is then lost; at worst, it becomes destructive.

Every effort should be made to plan for improved productivity and industrial relations. The last twenty years have seen considerable improvements in industrial relations, though much remains to be done. Productivity improvements still represent an area of major management attention. Total quality management (TQM), with its emphasis on determining real needs and of improving performance "continuously," has perhaps been one of the most potent concepts in this regard in recent years.[7]

Planning and Control

Plans should be prepared by those technically responsible for them and integrated by the planning and control group. Planning initially should be at a broad systems level with detail being provided only where essential and in general on a rolling wave basis. Similarly for cost: Estimates should be prepared by work breakdown element, detail being provided as appropriate. Cost should be related to finance and be assembled into forecast out-turn cost, related both to the forecast actual construction price and to the actual product sales price.

Implementation of systems and procedures should be planned carefully so that all those working on the project understand them properly. Start-up meetings should develop the systems procedures in outline and begin substantive planning while simultaneously building the project team. (A word of systems caution: It is vital that attention be given to managing the plant computer systems. There have been some spectacular cases recently of plant hardware being complete but the plant being unable to start up because the computer systems had not been managed as effectively as the rest of the project.)

Strategic Issues for Enterprises Working on Projects

For the management of projects, then, a strategic model can be said to exist. But what are the chances of anyone ever implementing it?* The key, probably, is in changing perceptions; and the keys to effecting that are, I believe, management and education.

The difficulty with project management is that it can encompass such a broad scope of services in different situations. The project manager for an equipment supply contractor on a power station, say, has a more narrowly defined task than the utility's overall project manager. The project manager for the specification, procurement, and installation of a major telecommunications system has a much broader scope than the project manager of a software development program. Yet all involve the elements of Exhibit 4-1 in some way.

The two strategic questions for enterprises working in project-related industries are to determine:

1. The level and scope of services that one's clients and customers need and are able to buy
2. Whether one has the organizational capability to supply this level and scope of services

There is little doubt that the most powerful set of ideas relevant to the first question—the level of services—is that of total quality. The TQM concept forces one to analyze what services one's clients want. (And there may be several different sets of clients in the production chain ranging from one's boss or bosses to, most obviously, the people who are using the services, whether as customers or as colleagues.) This approach to analyzing the effectiveness of one's services is directly relevant to determining not just the extent to which the factors identified in Exhibit 4-1 are needed but also the extent to which they need to be organized and delivered in an integrated fashion.

As long ago as 1959, the *Harvard Business Review* identified integration as the key

---

*The model presented in Exhibit 4-1 is of course a high-level one; it is bound to be since its essence is its comprehensiveness. Note, therefore, that as one gets into any particular subsystem, the level of detail increases. The two subsystems where models have more commonly been developed in detail are financing and implementation; that is, the areas traditionally discussed as project management.

project management function.[8] The question is, however, what needs to be integrated? By fundamentally addressing the client's real needs and the extent to which these are being satisfactorily met, a project manager may see, for example, that on this project the supply of finance, or the ability to provide better value for money, or to build faster, or to provide greater technical reliability, are issues that need better integration within the scope of project services to be provided.

As the level and scope of services become clearer, the second key strategic question arises: that of the organization's ability to deliver. Here, the principal difficulty is that our educational institutions are so far producing people with either a severely limited number of the vision or the ability to manage such a broad array of issues as those outlined in Exhibit 4-1. Few educational institutions have yet perceived that for projects to be managed successfully, so wide a range of factors may need integrating. Even fewer have any training across such a broad array, particularly in a project context. Yet there are signs that times are changing, and it is surely very much in the interests of all who work in project-related industries to support such change. Two items stand out as evidence of an increasing maturity in perceiving the breadth of professional formation in the management of projects.

First, the certification process being initiated now by the professional project management societies in the United States, the United Kingdom, and Australia are increasingly reflecting a broader "Body of Knowledge" than that of mere "on time, in budget, to technical specification"—the traditional scope of project management. Thus, the current Bodies of Knowledge put forth by the Project Management Institute in the United States and the Australian Institute of Project Management are built around:

- ▸ Cost management
- ▸ Time management
- ▸ Scope management
- ▸ Human resources management
- ▸ Communications management
- ▸ Quality management
- ▸ Contract/procurement management
- ▸ Risk management
- ▸ Resources management
- ▸ Planning and control[9]

The British project management society, the Association of Project Managers—whose certification program is becoming the basis for that of the European INTER-NET (the International Association of Project Management)—has an even broader scope.[10] This is shown in Exhibit 4-3. At last, then, the project management societies are beginning actively to broaden their members' perceptions of the fields in which professional project managers should have competence.

The second evidence of an increasing maturity of project management formation is the growing number of advanced project management educational programs, particularly at the postgraduate level. There are about ten in the United Kingdom; as many in Australia; several in Germany, Holland, Italy, Scandinavia, Spain, and France; and over thirty in the United States and Canada. Saudi Arabia, Singapore,

Exhibit 4-3. Association of Project Manager's Body of Knowledge

1. Project Management Techniques and Procedures

    1.1   Project
    1.2   Project Life Cycle
    1.3   Work Breakdown Structure
    1.4   Task Responsibility Matrix
    1.5   Planning and Scheduling
    1.6   Cost Estimating
    1.7   Resource Allocation and Management
    1.8   Cost Control
    1.9   Performance Measurement
    1.10 Risk Analysis
    1.11 Procurement

2. Organization and People Management

    2.1   Leadership
    2.2   Motivation
    2.3   Delegation
    2.4   Communications
    2.5   Conflict Management
    2.6   Negotiation
    2.7   Team Building
    2.8   Organization Design
    2.9   Contract Forms and Project Organization
    2.10 Owner/Sponsor Role vs. Project Manager Role
    2.11 Project Life Cycle
    2.12 Interface Management
    2.13 Industrial Relations
    2.14 Management Development
    2.15 Compensation and Evaluation
    2.16 Health and Safety

3. Technical

    3.1   Basic Knowledge of Technology
    3.2   Basic Knowledge of Industry
    3.3   Technology Management
    3.4   Systems Engineering
    3.5   Design Management
    3.6   Value Engineering
    3.7   R&D Management
    3.8   Quality

4. General Project Knowledge

    4.1   Project Appraisal
    4.2   Project Sponsor (i.e., "Client") Role

(continues)

Exhibit 4-3. (*continued*)

4.3   Project Success and Failure Criteria
4.4   Relevant "Industry" History
4.5   Project Environment

5. General Management

5.1   Information Technology/Management Information Systems
5.2   Human Resources Management
5.3   Finance and Accounting
5.4   Marketing and Sales
5.5   Law
5.6   Economics
5.7   Production Management
5.8   Business Strategy

6. General Management Competences

6.1   Operations
6.2   Finance
6.3   People
6.4   Information

7. Integrative Skills

7.1   Personality
7.2   Forms of Integration (Versus Different Sources of Differentiation)
7.3   Integration Knowledge Base
7.4   People Skills

and South Africa offer programs too, as do Venezuela and Brazil, and no doubt several other countries.

Postgraduate education is important because a considerable level of technical, organizational, and business integration is being required at senior levels on most of the more advanced projects and programs. Without a well-rounded educational background, as well as real frontline practical experience, there must be some doubt as to our ability to furnish managers capable of meeting the project management demands being made by today's projects.

Conclusion

The message of this chapter is, in short, that a model for the strategic management of major projects does exist. The framework sketched in Exhibit 4-1 indicates the main items that should be considered; the lessons outlined in the second half of this chapter furnish the meat that goes on that framework. All the items identified in

Exhibit 4-1 should be considered from the earliest stages of the project and should be kept in review as the project develops, receiving particular scrutiny at the major life cycle change points.

A fundamental task facing any senior manager on a major program or project is to work out how the various factors identified in Exhibit 4-1 should best be allocated and integrated on his or her project. For managers and educators, a major challenge facing the project management profession is to ensure that we have people with the intellectual breadth and the experience to tackle issues of the diversity and subtlety of those so often posed by today's projects. Every encouragement should be given to the professional societies and the schools and other organizations around the world to develop an appropriate, well-rounded professional formation for the management of projects.

Notes

1. A. O. Hirschman, *Development Projects Observed* (Washington, D.C.: Brookings Institution, 1967).

2. R. Cassens and Associates, *Does Aid Work?* (Oxford, England: Clarendon Press, 1986); J. Moris, *Managing Induced Rural Development* (Bloomington, Ind.: International Development Institute, 1981); S. Paul, *Managing Development Programs: The Lessons of Success* (Boulder, Colo.: Westview Press, 1982).

3. N. R. Baker, S. G. Green, and A. S. Bean, "Why R&D Projects Succeed or Fail," *Research Management* (November–December 1986), pp. 29–34; R. Balachandra and J. A. Raelin, "When to Kill That R&D Project," *Research Management* (July-August 1984), pp. 30–33; R. G. Cooper, "New Product Success in Industrial Firms," *Industrial Marketing Management* 11 (1982), pp. 215–223; A. Gerstenfeld, "A Study of Successful Projects, Unsuccessful Projects and Projects in Progress in West Germany," *IEEE Transactions on Engineering Management* (August 1976), pp. 116–123; E. Manfield and S. Wagner, "Organizational and Strategic Factors Associated With Probabilities of Success and Industrial R&D," *Journal of Business* 48, No. 2 (April 1975); R. Whipp and P. Clark, *Innovation and the Auto Industry* (London, England: Francis, 1986).

4. Ibid. See also F. P. Brooks, *The Mythical Man-Month* (Reading, Mass.: Addison-Wesley, 1982); T. E. Harvey, "Concurrency Today in Acquisition Management," *Defense Systems Management Review* 3, No. 1 (Winter 1980), pp. 14–18; O. P. Karhbanda and E. A. Stalworthy, *How to Learn From Project Disasters* (London, England: Gower, 1983); *Learning From Experience: A Report on the Arrangements for Managing Major Projects in the Procurement Executive* (London, England: Ministry of Defense, 1987); E. W. Merrow, *Understanding the Outcomes of Mega Projects: Quantitive Analysis of Very Large Civilian Projects* (Santa Monica, Calif.: Rand Corporation, March 1988).

5. B. Bowonder, "Project Siting and Environmental Impact Assessment in Developing Countries, *Project Appraisal* 2, No. 1 (March 1987), pp. 1–72; N. Lichfield, "Environmental Impact Assessment in Project Appraisal in Britain," *Project Appraisal* 3, No. 3 (September 1988), pp. 125–180; J. Stringer, *Planning and Inquiry Process*, MPA Technical Paper No. 6, Templeton College, Oxford, September 1988.

6. P. W. G. Morris, "Managing Project Interfaces—Key Points for Project Success,"

in D. I. Cleveland and W. R. King, eds., *Project Management Handbook* (New York: Van Nostrand Reinhold, 1988); C. E. Reis de Carvalho and P. W. G. Morris, "Project Matrix Organizations, or How to Do the Matrix Swing," 1979 *Proceedings of the Project Management Institute,* Los Angeles (Drexel Hill, Penn.: 1979).

7. W. E. Deming, *Out of Crisis* (Cambridge, Mass.: MIT Press 1989); M. Imai, *Kaizen* (New York: Kaizan Institute/Random House, 1986); J. M. Juran and F. M. Gryna, *Juran's Quality Control Handbook* (New York: McGraw-Hill, 1988).

8. P. O. Gaddis, "The Project Manager," *Harvard Business Review* (May-June 1959), pp. 89–97.

9. A. Stretton, "A Consolidation of the PMBOK Framework and Functional Components," *Project Management Journal* 20, No. 4 (December 1989), pp. 5–30.

10. "Project Managers and Their Teams: Selection, Education, Careers," *Proceedings of the 14th International Experts Seminar,* INTERNET, March 15–17, 1990, Zurich, Switzerland. See particularly the papers by R. Archibald and A. Harpham; E. Gabriel; and R. Pharro and P. W. G. Morris.

5

Project Initiation Techniques: A Strategic View

Harvey A. Levine
Project Knowledge Group

Perhaps the hardest part of the project planning process is getting started. Certainly, overcoming inertia usually contributes to the problem. And then, there's always the problem of getting some relief from your other duties. But the major cause of difficulty and procrastination is the lack of a framework for engaging in the process and developing the plan itself.

To start with, you want to address the crucial identification of project objectives, constraints, and stakeholders. Then you need to move on to organizing for the project and development of the project team. This team participates in the development of a strategy for achieving the project objectives and the clarification of the role of the various project stakeholders. The team then proceeds to the development of a framework for the work scope, timing, and budgeting aspects of the project. These include work breakdown structures (WBS), organizational breakdown structures (OBS), structures for cost accounting, and project milestone schedules.

It is not unusual to falter seriously at the project initiation stage. We don't quite know where and how to start. Some project managers put the process off until it's too late to develop a plan of their own choosing, getting stuck, instead, with a plan that is by now doomed to failure from the start. Other project managers attempt to produce a quick schedule, or a resource plan, or an expenditure plan (budget), or perhaps all three. What they soon find out is that they don't have all of the answers that they need and that their plans are full of holes. Indeed, that is the nature of the beast. In most cases, the project planning process starts off with a set of assumptions, and the project planning process is used to validate these assumptions. Rather than putting off the planning process until the missing pieces are found, the smart project manager uses the process to help generate the missing data.

Obviously, there is a lot of front-end work that must be executed prior to establishing the project schedule, resource plan, and budget. And, contrary to popular thought, a good deal of this effort does not involve the use of the computer. At this point, the project manager would do well to consider the following course of action:

- Examine the objectives for this project and the various constraints that impact upon these objectives.
- Identify the project stakeholders and how they, too, impinge upon those objectives.
- Develop a project strategy that supports the project objectives and stakeholders, while meeting the various constraints.
- Put together a project team and other required resources and evaluate what limits they impose on the execution of the project within time and budget constraints.
- Eventually, implement a planning and control procedure that can support the needs of the project while being able to be supported by the project team.

Defining Project Objectives

A project plan is a blueprint of how one intends to achieve the objectives of a project. In several aspects, it is not that different from a building drawing. To prepare such a drawing, the architect must focus on the purpose and use of the building, amass conceptual data, develop outlines, and conduct certain technical and cost inquiries. Once prepared and then approved by the owner, the drawing serves as the guide for the construction of the building. We can view a project plan in a similar light.

It naturally follows, therefore, that the very first item of order in this planning process is to make sure that the project objectives are perfectly clear and are defined in terms that can be used to develop the project plan. An inseparable part of this process is the identification of the constraints associated with the project.

The project objectives typically cover a number of elements, such as time objectives, budget objectives, technical objectives, and scope objectives. Let's consider, for instance, a banking group that has decided to develop a new computer-based transaction processing system. The objectives for such a project are as follows:

- *Technical objectives,* such as volume of transactions, turnaround time, ease-of-use, and error handling
- *Timing objectives,* such as initial implementation of the system, system cutover, and operator training
- *Budget objectives,* such as total system cost, operating cost (per transaction), and equipment costs
- *Scope guidelines,* such as type of transactions to be processed, equipment to be used, locations involved, communications, and training

All of these must be clearly identified before the project planning can commence in earnest.

Constraints would include:

- Time constraints
- Technology constraints
- Personnel constraints
- Cultural constraints
- Money constraints

These, too, must be clearly identified at the outset.

Developing the Project Strategy

Once the project manager has outlined the objectives and considered the constraints for the project, it's time to initiate the development of the project strategy. A project strategy is simply *how* the project objectives are going to be attained. If the term *strategy* hints at a more involved process than you might expect, that is intentional. It is not enough to choose a course of action to achieve project objectives. That course of action must be tested for its likelihood of success. The set of processes that have been developed within the discipline of strategic planning are equally applicable to the process of developing the strategy for a project.

Stakeholders

First, it is advisable for the project manager to identify all of the project stakeholders. Who are the people who will have an impact on project success, either positive or negative? Or, stated differently, who are the people who can make or break the project? For starters, don't forget the owners of the enterprise. They probably have the most to gain or lose from the project. The project manager and the owners have to evaluate whether the objectives of this project are consistent with the general mission of the enterprise. Will attainment of the project objectives enhance and be in harmony with the primary purpose of the business? Will implementation of the project represent an improved utilization of the business's financial, human, and physical resources? Will the successful completion of the project improve the position of the company in its overall business objectives?

There are two very important reasons for obtaining "yes" answers to these questions. The first is to check for a proper fit with the other business of the company. The lack of such a fit often places the company's resources in disarray, exacting a toll on both the new project and the other company business. The second is that, without this required fit, the project manager is unlikely to obtain the required support of his or her superiors. Without sponsorship in high places, a project eventually fails for lack of support in critical situations. This evaluation is the first of many instances where the project team is required to determine whether to continue the project, to make significant adjustments to objectives and strategy, or to abandon it.

Other stakeholders include the project sponsor, key project participants, company clients and prospective clients, regulatory agencies, suppliers and subcontractors, and users of the project product—essentially, anyone who can have an impact on the success of the project or who might be involved in the determination of the project success.

Opportunities, Threats, and Issues

In the traditional business strategic planning process, the next function is to attempt to identify significant opportunities, threats, and issues. This same process should be applied to a project. Any project involves risk. An early evaluation of potential threats helps the project team to prepare to deal with these and to minimize their impact. Any project involves opportunity. While the key opportunities are usually part of the original project purpose and justification, an evaluation of potential secondary opportunities may uncover additional benefits to the company and the project participants. An attempt to identify all issues that may impact on the project, to list them, and to discuss them with the project stakeholders should promote knowledge of and sensitivity to the issues and prevent them from having a severe negative impact on the project.

Involving the Project Team

The strategic planning process, as well as the project planning process, is not a one-person process. At this time, the project team must be identified and assembled. While it certainly is possible that the strategy that develops may impact upon the makeup of the project team, some of the key players should be involved in generating the data for the strategy development and analysis and in developing the project strategy. At a later point in the process, a strategy and project plan has to be adopted. It is most important that the project team understand the strategy and support it. The more that people participate in the development of a plan, the more likely they are to support it. This "buy-in" of the strategy is a key to success of the project.

Addressing Specific Concerns

Of all of the phases of the project initiation process, it is the act of dealing with strategies, stakeholders, and the organization that has the greatest impact on project success. Ideally, many of these issues were addressed while the project was first being considered or proposed. Once the project has been officially authorized or awarded, it may be too late to do much about some of these issues. Unfortunately, projects often come into being without full consideration of these issues. Regardless of the level of attention given to this area in the preproject stages, the sage project manager repeats the process at the initiation of the project. The following is an expansion on some of the strategic and organizational concerns that should be addressed.

Strategy and Organizational Culture

Most projects exist within the larger sphere of an existing, ongoing business. They are accomplished by people who generally are part of this business and its organization and culture. Yet many organizations treat projects as though they take place in a different, separate environment from that of the organization. When this happens, project managers and their senior managers tend either to ignore or to change independently key practices that are crucial to maintaining the organization's essential structure, culture, and business strategy.

Clearly, there are important differences between managing a project and the day-to-day operations of a business. But when the project unfolds independently or outside of an organization's mainstream operations and culture, it can often have an adverse impact on the integrity of the business. In many industries, project objectives are virtually synonymous with an organization's business goals. In such instances, the success of key projects may have a major impact on the ability of the business to continue to be competitive—even to survive.

Therefore, organizations that apply traditional strategic planning practices to a project must focus on integrating the project into the organization and its culture. This requires analyses of several project constituencies—the project sponsor, other project stakeholders, the organization in which the project unfolds, and the project team—as well as of the strategic planning process itself.

Stakeholder Analysis

How do we align the project objectives with the goals and expectations of the stakeholders so as to minimize the potential for conflicts that could adversely affect the project's success? One way to do this is to expand our view of project success.

The traditional view of project success is the accomplishment of all of the schedule, budget, and technical objectives as planned. Couldn't we also define project success as accomplishing the goals of everyone who has a stake in the project? If so, then the stakeholder analysis must ask:

- Who are the project stakeholders?
- What do they want?
- How can they impact success?
- How can they be satisfied?

Carrying this thesis further, we might say that project success is determined by:

- The power and influence of the project stakeholders
- The difficulty and risk involved in the stakeholders' goals
- The talent and resources available to accomplish these goals
- The perceptions of the stakeholders of what was actually accomplished[1]

Organizing for Project Management

If you are in the business of doing projects, then your company has probably modified its organizational structure to help it to respond to the demands of the project environment. Your company, like most, has probably migrated from a primarily functional or line type of organizational structure to the currently ubiquitous matrix format. Conceptually, the matrix approach implies that the responsibility for achieving project objectives is shared equally by the functional and project managers. All too often, the company makes these organizational changes in a vacuum, giving little attention to the corporate culture, and with insensitivity to the corporate resources. As a result, these changes fall far short of achieving the objectives and, in fact, become an actual impediment to effective project implementation and success.

The matrix management structure is available as a practical solution to bringing a project's capability into an ongoing business. It is difficult to dispute the premise that a matrix organizational approach is probably best for most situations. We must be careful, however, to avoid two problems that are common to the establishment of the matrix structure.

The first problem is that the new organization often addresses and changes areas of responsibility, but fails to change the methods of measurement and reward. If people are asked to perform to new standards, but are measured and rewarded by the old structure, the behavior and performance changes that are supposed to occur from the reorganization will not happen. Human nature dictates that most of us perform so as to support the measurement and reward practices. If project and line supervisors are asked to perform on a shared basis, but continue to be measured and rewarded on the basis of individual performance to old and different standards, how can we expect to achieve our objectives?

The second problem in moving to a matrix mode is that the role of the functional or line manager is often diminished in the new organization. Or, at least, the line managers perceive their role to be diminished in relation to that of the project manager. Yet the real importance and contribution of the line manager can never be underestimated or undervalued. The resources and the standards essential to the successful completion of most projects are controlled by these key contributors, and their importance to this success must be clearly identified, acknowledged, and rewarded.

In short, a diagram of an organization, matrix or otherwise, should not be mistaken for the organization itself. An organization is a living, working organism. The organization chart is similar to a bar chart. It doesn't get the work done—it only shows how the organization might work. Lots of things can break down between the diagramming of an organization and its successful implementation.

Bringing a successful project management capability into an organization requires significant change, but it does not require a total dismantling of existing cultures. Like any other change, it should retain what works, fix what's broken, and recognize that the very people involved in these changes must buy into the new practices if these practices are to succeed.

Role of the Project Team

If we acknowledge the importance of both project and line management, then there is little need to define a set of rules and responsibilities for the project team. Each member of the team must respect what the other members bring to the project. Each member must also remember that he or she is supposed to contribute to the attainment of the project objectives, as well as his or her individual, functional measurement.

A frequent cause of project problems is the lack of project team participation in making decisions. The following case history exemplifies this.

THE PROJECT

The design and installation of a new factory steam supply.

THE INCIDENT

The field superintendent calls the project manager to report a problem with the boiler installation. There is an unexpected interference of the water inlet piping with some adjacent crane rails. The superintendent recommends a quick field fix by moving a 90 degree bend that is currently six feet out from the inlet nozzle to two feet out, to avoid the interference. The project manager, wishing to respond quickly, approves the change without involving other disciplines.

Some time later, when the system is put into operation, the operating engineer reports seemingly erroneous water flow readings. The problem is reported to the design engineer, who eventually finds out about the piping change. It seems that no one bothered to discuss the piping change with the design engineer. If anyone had, he or she would have been told that the six-foot run of pipe at the inlet was required for the flow instrumentation to function properly. *Now,* the project manager wants Engineering/Design to fix the problem.

The message here should be clear. Project team members should neither overstep their bounds nor ignore the responsible contributions of the others. When there is a problem or a decision to be made, the project manager and the others involved would be wise to seek the widest participation possible in the solution. This approach not only increases the potential for the best solution, but gets the other team members to buy into that solution.

Developing Subproject Strategies

The concept of strategic planning can be applied at several levels of the project. Up to now, we have been looking at project-level strategies. Eventually, we will move from our top-level objectives to the next level (the deliverable end items), and then on to the work package detail and to the individual activities themselves. At the intermediate levels, the project team members must develop a strategy and plan. They start with a set of givens or assumptions. Then, for each of the key areas, they look at the objectives, the current situation, the favored plan, constraints, and alternatives.

Let's look at how this approach might be implemented. In a hypothetical situation, the Clinton County Community College (CCCC) is engaged in a project to upgrade its athletic facilities. The overall objective is to increase the school's prestige and revenue by elevating its sports program to a higher competition division. This requires an expansion of the CCCC stadium and the supporting infrastructure. One of the key project areas (deliverable end items) is the athletic field parking lot. The project team develops a planning worksheet as shown in Exhibit 5-1.

This is just one illustration of the kind of orderly, strategy-oriented thinking that should be employed in developing a project plan. In many instances, this subproject strategic planning is part of the preproject estimating function. On the other hand, there may be times that the project team would not have this level of detail available at the initial planning stages. You have to work with what you have and make assumptions for the rest. Eventually, all of the data have to be confirmed. And at all times, this planning should be tested for consistency with the overall project objectives, the overall business objectives, and the criteria for project success.

Creating a Project Framework

We have repeatedly noted that a key factor to getting a project off the ground is the development of a structured approach toward identifying the work scope and timing

Exhibit 5-1. Planning worksheet for athletic field parking lot project.

Design Objectives:

1. Provide parking for 3,000 vehicles.
2. 1,000 of that capacity to be paved.
3. 1,000 to be gravel base (for later paving).
4. Remainder to be overflow on grass field.

Budget Objectives:

1. Costs to be charged to capital improvement budget—not to exceed $250,000 for all infrastructure items.

Timing Objectives:

1. Complete repaving before annual homecoming football game. Do not interfere with any other scheduled games.

Current Facilities:

1. Paved parking for 1,000 cars. Needs repaving.
2. Adjacent level field for 1,000 cars. Dirt base.
3. Additional adjacent field (undeveloped) available for 1,000 cars.

Favored Plan:

1. Repave existing 1,000-car lot
   Area = 270,000 sq. ft.
   Cost = $0.40 per sq. ft. = $108,000

2. Improve old overflow area with gravel base.
   Area = 270,000 sq. ft.
   Costs
   Gravel: 3,400 tons of #1 crushed gravel @ $6/ton = $20,400
   Trucking @ $30/25 ton load = $4,080
   Spread and compact = $13,500
   Total cost = $37,980

3. Clear and grade new overflow area.
   Area = 270,000 sq. ft.
   Cost = $6,000

4. Paint stripes in paved area.
   Quantity = 20,000 linear ft.
   Cost = $5,000

Constraints:

1. Planning Board approval.
2. Funding approval.
3. Timing interface with football games and other events at the stadium.

Strategic Considerations and Alternatives:

1. If repaving/curing of paved lot cannot be completed prior to the homecoming weekend, consider completing gravel placement in old overflow lot plus grading of new overflow lot and using these for homecoming parking.
2. If insufficient funding is available for all infrastructure items, hold off on repaving old lot.

for the work. It is easy to be overwhelmed by just the mass of the project. Furthermore, most project estimates and proposals are not prepared in a format that lends itself to easy conversion to a project plan. Although a definition of the project work scope may be present in the precontract documents, it almost always requires a major restructuring in order to turn these data into a pragmatic project plan. Another aspect of this project initiation phase is bringing the preproject plan up to date. The preproject documentation defines the project "as proposed." In the development of the latest project plan, these data have to reflect the definition of the project "as sold." These are often not the same.

A major component of the front-end work required to plan and initiate a project effectively is the development of a framework for the project model. This framework, or structuring, of the project is important to the development of a complete and organized project plan. It is also essential to permit the sorting, selecting, grouping, and summarization of the project data which, in turn, are essential to support recognized management-by-exception techniques and reporting to the various stakeholders.

If we define the process of project planning and control as the integration of the project work scope, timing, resource usage, and cost, then we need to develop a structured base for each of these, as follows:

- *Work Scope:* A top-down hierarchical model, called a *work breakdown structure (WBS)*. And, perhaps, an alternate hierarchical model, by responsibility or performer, called an *organizational breakdown structure (OBS)*.
- *Timing:* A *project milestone schedule.*
- *Resources and Cost:* A set of *resource codes and cost accounts,* used to facilitate selection, sorting, summarization, and interrogation of resource and cost data.

Work Scope: The Work Breakdown Structure

The first step in creating a project framework is usually to define the WBS, as this is the framework for the project work scope. If you cannot define the work scope, then you cannot define the schedule, resources, or budget for the project. The WBS first helps with this work scope definition and then becomes the framework for the identification of the details of the project. The WBS is an organization chart for the project work. If you were to draw a typical project WBS, it would look just like a typical business organization chart. At the top would be a single box, for the project. Under that would be the main divisions of the project. A popular term for this level is project deliverables. The WBS can also be depicted in an outline form.

The approach works for any type of project. For instance, if your project is a prototype bomber for the Air Force, the WBS, at the deliverables level, might look like Exhibit 5-2. If your project is the development of a new product, like a new cereal, the WBS might start off as shown in Exhibit 5-3.

The deliverables section gives us our first level of project definition and a framework for further structuring. Each of these items can usually be traced back to a basic project objective. Each of these items can usually be assigned to a specific responsible individual, for accountability. The development of the WBS continues in increasing levels of detail. Returning to the Air Force bomber project, we can expand the first item of the WBS as shown in Exhibit 5-4.

Exhibit 5-2. WBS for Air Force prototype bomber project.

Air Force Prototype Bomber Project

Aircraft Structure

Propulsion Systems

Aircraft Control Systems

Armaments Systems

Thus far, we have illustrated the WBS in an outline format. Exhibit 5-5 shows more of the Air Force prototype bomber WBS in the alternate organization chart format.

Eventually, each of the lower items can be subdivided even further, into work packages and individual activities. A hierarchical numbering system can be used to imbed the WBS into the activity identification code. There is rarely an ideal work breakdown structure for a given project. The important thing to keep in mind is to develop a framework that truly is indicative of how the project itself is structured and how the participants are likely to follow its execution.

Note that with this numbering system, your project management software system should permit you to use these codes to select specific portions of the project, to group activities within a common code, to sort activities by that code, and to summarize certain activity data at higher levels. A few products have recently introduced an outlining function that allows you to develop your project activity details in an outline form. Most of the other programs provide user code fields for this purpose. The outliner format offers greater simplicity but is usually limited to a single WBS type framework. User code fields—which may range from two to twenty

Exhibit 5-3. WBS for new product development project.

Almonds & Molasses Cereal Project

Product Formulation

Lab Testing

Pre-production

Test Marketing

Package Design

Advertising Program

Sales & Distribution Program

Certification/Regulation

Production Engineering

Production Facilities

Exhibit 5-4. Expansion of WBS for Air Force prototype bomber project.

---

1 Air Force Prototype Bomber Project

1.1 Aircraft Structure

    1.1.1 Fuselage
        1.1.1.1 Cowling
        1.1.1.2 Cockpit
        1.1.1.3 Body

    1.1.2 Wings
        1.1.2.1 Fixed Portion
        1.1.2.2 Trim Portions

    1.1.3 Tail
        1.1.3.1 Fixed Portion
        1.1.3.2 Trim Portions

    1.1.4 Landing Gear
        1.1.4.1 Main Landing Gear
        1.1.4.2 Nose Landing Gear

---

code fields, depending on the product—offer greater flexibility and the ability to have more than one WBS.

Why would anyone want more than one WBS? The answer is to support the information needs of all of the stakeholders. The deliverables-oriented WBS may be a handy way for the project manager to group the work. But the functional or line manager may want to look at it from a responsibility-oriented point of view. To facilitate this, we often develop a second framework, called the organizational breakdown structure. Using the OBS, we can assign codes by responsible manager or department. Additional activity coding schemes can be used to assign physical locations, project phases, priority codes, budget divisions, etc. Each of these codes can be used to sort and select activities and for grouping and summarization.

The WBS and other structures, established in a coding scheme or an outliner, allow for the efficient and effective display and reporting of vast amounts of project data to the various interested parties. Also, once established, the WBS can be used as a checklist for additional project work that may be similar to an earlier project.

Timing: The Project Milestone Schedule

The development of the WBS and other structures does not necessarily occur all at once. During the project initiation process, the WBS is initiated and developed down to some intermediate level. At that time, it is also advisable to develop a timing framework for the project.

Exhibit 5-5. WBS in organization chart format for Air Force prototype bomber project.

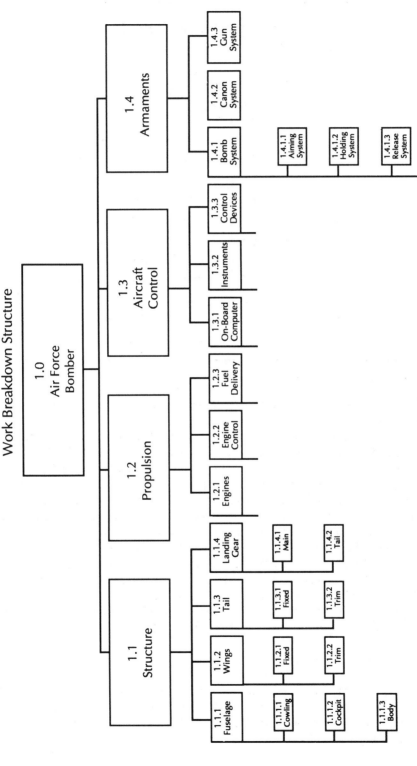

Work Breakdown Structure

Source: Harvey A. Levine, *Project Management Using Microcomputers* (Berkeley, Calif.: Osborne McGraw-Hill, 1986).

The WBS is a framework for the definition of the project work scope. Another framework is the project milestone schedule. The PMS is a framework for the timing of the project and provides a structure for the project detailed schedule. Again, we face the question of where to start. And again, we note that the development of the schedule is an iterative process. We may initiate that process when the top levels of the WBS are developed, and continue to increase the level of detail as we define the project in greater detail. Continuing the schedule development, we then integrate the schedule data with expected resource constraints. Finally, we attempt to optimize the schedule by balancing timing, resources, and other constraints, until we accept the schedule as part of a baseline plan.

The PMS, as the framework and first part of this scheduling process, is a vehicle for recording the time constraints, time objectives, and other givens pertaining to the schedule. Therefore, the process for developing the PMS is as follows:

▸ *Start with the key dates that you already know.* These may be a given project start date, a target or contractual project end date, and interim milestone dates.
▸ *Note any special time-based constraints.* This could be a plant shutdown, a critical design review, a company board meeting, a trade show commitment, and any contract commitment dates.
▸ *Add any internal interim milestone dates and preliminary high-level time frames.* These include target starts and completions for various phases, resource-based timing objectives, arbitrary time dividing elements, weather-dictated factors, and known or typical time cycles for major components or effort-driven work.

The project milestone schedule provides guidance by defining the time windows into which the task scheduling attempts to fit. Exhibit 5-6 shows such a schedule for the almonds and molasses cereal project described earlier. Exhibit 5-7 is an example of a PMS for a turnkey power plant project.

Resources and Cost Frameworks

Up to this point, we have been talking about work scope and timing structures for activities. In a project management database, each activity may have one or more resource or cost elements associated with it. There are people associated with the project who are more interested in an aggregation of resource and cost information than in the activity view. This collection of information is achieved by assigning resource codes to each resource (or each task) and defining a cost account structure for the system. If possible, you may set up a resource hierarchy so that resources can be put into groups. Unfortunately, many of the commercial project management software programs do not support this feature. Most programs, however, do not support some kind of cost account numbering system.

If you intend to use any performance measurement procedures, you need to establish a structured basis for subdividing the project into collective elements that are meaningful to those people who are interested in the project performance results. Most programs provide at least one data field that can be used to define a code of accounts for the system.

Effective cost management through the utilization of project management software systems is an elusive objective. The integration of work measurement (schedule

Exhibit 5-6. Project milestone schedule for new product development project.

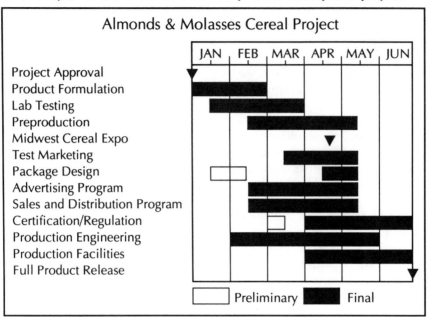

progress) and cost measurement, the main ingredients required for project perform-ance measurement and control, is built into most project management software products. Yet that potential is not often achieved by the system users. There are three significant causes of this failure.

1. Difficulty in synchronizing the timing for the progress measurements and the cost measurements
2. Linking of the project management systems to the accounting systems
3. The tendency to set up different measurement categories for the progress and the cost

The latter two items can be addressed when we develop the activity and cost structures for our project. It is imperative that you identify and recognize the way that cost data is collected for your project. If the project database is set up to one structure and the cost data is being collected to a different structure, the integration of the two is obstructed. Useful project performance measurement requires the integration of the progress and cost data, which mandates the establishment of a common set of pigeonholes into which to funnel the experience data.

Effective Project Initiation: A Key Factor in Project Success

Getting started may be the hardest part of the project planning process. But the diligence applied at the initiation stage almost certainly pays large dividends at the conclusion of the project. This is where we build the foundation for the project.

Exhibit 5-7. Project milestone schedule for turnkey power plant project.

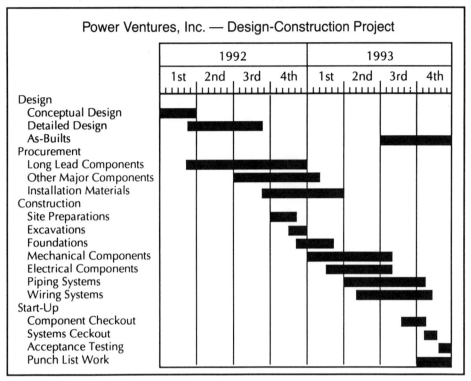

▸ We look at organization and culture and establish plans to work within the existing environment and the overall business strategy.
▸ We identify the project stakeholders and look at how they measure success.
▸ We develop a project strategy that is fully consistent with the business and stakeholders and addresses the opportunities, risks, and issues associated with the project.

These front-end activities are essential to the initiation of a project, regardless of the automated project management tools employed, if any. We then move on to building the frameworks for the project plan.

▸ We develop a set of structures (the WBS, OBS, PMS, code of accounts, etc.) so that there is a framework for the project database.
▸ We use these structures as an aid in identifying the project work scope and in developing the baseline schedule and budget.
▸ Assuming that some kind of project management software is being used, we then use these same structures to sort the data, to select sections of the data, to group the data, and to roll up activity, resource, and cost data to various summary levels.

No project is ever easy to manage, and no project management software system is a panacea. But we can be pretty certain that the application of automated project management tools will fail to deliver its potential without a decent framework. Without a proper foundation of strategic thinking and organized structures, the project will crumble to the ground.

Note

1. John Tuman, Jr., "Success Modeling: A Technique for Building a Winning Project Team," 1986 *Proceedings of the Project Management Institute* (Drexel Hill, Penn.: PMI).

6

Project Team Planning: A Strategy for Success

Russell D. Archibald
Integrated Project Systems

Recognition of the need for project team planning has grown out of the increased awareness of: (1) the weaknesses in the more traditional project planning approaches, (2) the difficulties in getting functional managers and team members to be committed to a plan that has been created by others, and (3) the need to accelerate the project planning and team-building processes at the very beginning of the project. The concept of project team planning applies equally to the inception of the conceptual phase and to the starting up of any subsequent phase of a project. It can also be used effectively when any major change in scope is required or when a major, unforeseen problem is encountered.

The Project Team Planning Process

Project Start-Up Workshops

Although the importance of getting a project off to a good, well-planned start has long been recognized, it has only been within the last ten years that the concept of systematic, well-planned project start-up workshops has been widely accepted and used. The INTERNET Committee on Project Start-Up—which was established in 1982 under the leadership of Dr. Morten Fangel—has been instrumental in promulgating and documenting this concept. (The committee's *Handbook of Project Start-Up* provides detailed information on the concept and methods and many examples of experience in its application in various industries and geographic areas of the world.)

The fundamental essence of the concept of these systematic project start-up workshops is *project team planning*. The start-up workshop, when properly conducted, provides the setting and well-planned process that enables the project team to work together effectively to produce integrated plans and schedules in a very short time

Parts of this chapter were adapted from Russell D. Archibald, *Managing High-Technology Programs and Projects, Second Edition* (John Wiley & Sons, 1992), Chapter 11. © Copyright 1992 by R. Archibald.

period. (The phrase *project start-up* may be misleading since the concept applies not only to the very first "start-up"—say, at the beginning of the conceptual phase of a project—but also to those at the beginning of each subsequent phase: definition, planning, or proposal; execution or implementation; and project closeout. Thus, the term *project phase transition workshop* may be more appropriate than *project start-up workshop*.)

Elements of the Team Planning Process

The basic elements of an effective team planning process are:

- Adequate preparation
- Identification of the key project team members
- Interactive exchange of information
- Physical setting conducive to the process
- Capture of the "team memory"
- Use of a planning process facilitator

Each of these is discussed in the following sections.

Adequate Preparation

Prior to bringing together a project team for a team planning session, it is vital to prepare adequately for the meeting. This includes:

- Defining the specific objectives of the team session and the results to be achieved
- Establishing a well-planned agenda
- Preparing sufficient project planning information in preliminary form (e.g., project objectives, scope definition, top levels of the PBS/WBS, team member list, and established target schedules, if any)
- Setting the session date sufficiently in advance to ensure that all team members can attend
- Announcing the session through appropriate authoritative channels to ensure higher management interest and support and to ensure that all team members show up
- Defining and understanding the planning process to be used and the roles and responsibilities of the project manager and the planning process facilitator
- Arranging for a suitable meeting facility and related logistical support

Identification of the Key Project Team Members

It seems obvious that in order to have a project team planning session, it is necessary to identify the team members. However, this is often not a simple task. Who are the *key* project team members? Which functions must be included, and what level of manager or specialist from each function should be identified and invited to the team planning session? How many people can participate effectively in such a session?

A few basic rules can be helpful in answering these questions.

▸ Each of the important functional specialties contributing to the project must be represented. This may include people from within and outside of the organization (contractors, consultants, major vendors, etc.).
▸ The "functional project leader"—the person holding responsibility and accountability for the project within each functional area—must be present.
▸ If a functional project leader cannot make commitments of resources for his/her function, then that person's manager (who *can* make such commitments) should also be invited to participate in the team planning session.
▸ If there are more than twenty key team members, special efforts are needed to assure appropriate interaction (such as breaking into smaller working team sessions).
▸ The project manager obviously plays a vital role in the team planning sessions. If available and assigned, project planning, scheduling, and estimating specialists should also participate in—but not dominate—the sessions.

Interactive Exchange of Information

Central to the project team planning concept is the need for intensive interaction among the team members during the planning process. The session preparation, the information provided, the physical setting, and the methods of conducting the planning sessions must be designed to promote, not inhibit, this interaction. If the project manager goes too far in preparing planning information prior to the meeting, and he or she presents this information as a fait accompli to the team in a one-way presentation, there will be little or no interaction, and the objectives of the team planning session will not be met.

Robert Gillis has pioneered the development of such sessions over several decades in his work in Canada. Exhibit 6-1, drawn from Gillis's paper on "Strategies for Successful Project Implementation," illustrates several important factors in achieving the interactive exchange of information that is needed for effective project team planning. As indicated in the exhibit, the interaction process is based on the following steps:

1. *Immediate recording of keyword abstract of what is said (recall trigger).* Here the group facilitator writes key words in bold letters on display cards.
2. *Immediate display of group memory.* Then, each card is affixed to a wall so all participants can see them.
3. *Exploration of what it means (through interactive discussion).* The facilitator ensures that there is adequate discussion to guarantee group focus.
4. *Fitting the keyword card in the right information structure.* The cards are then arranged in groups and subsets so that the commonalities and differences become evident.
5. *Continuing the process until the objectives of the session have been reached.* The process is repeated as many times as necessary until consensus or decision is reached.

Physical Setting Conducive to the Process

As shown in Exhibit 6-1, Gillis uses the term *planning theater* for the room in which the interactive team planning sessions are held. This is an important factor in

Exhibit 6-1. Overview of interactive team planning process.

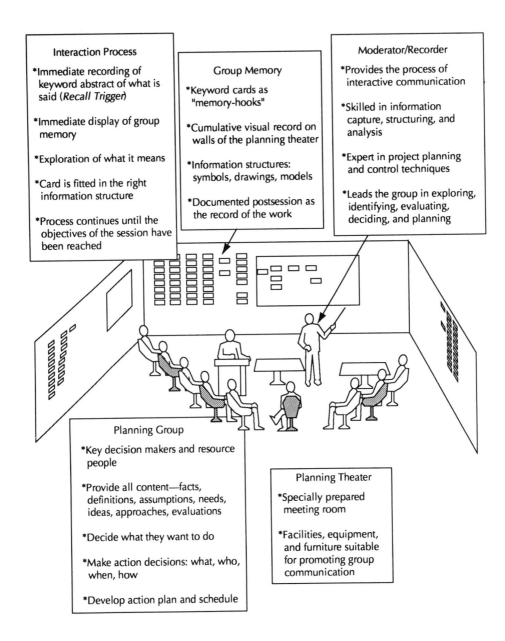

Source: R. Gillis, "Strategies for Successful Project Implementation," in M. Fangel, ed., *INTERNET Handbook of Project Start-Up* (Hilleroed, Denmark: INTERNET Committee on Project Start-Up, 1989).

achieving the interaction desired. The theater does not have to have an elaborate design, but it must provide a setting conducive to the process, with:

- Plenty of wall space with good lighting for display of the team memory and planning results
- Open access to the walls by the team members (elimination of tables and other impediments to individual movement to fill in keyword cards and place them on the walls)
- Sufficient space to enhance individual comfort, movement to view other walls, and open communication

Capture of the "Team Memory"

The team memory (also called "group memory") is based on:

- Using the keyword cards as "memory hooks" to recall specific ideas
- Creating a visual record on the walls of the planning theater or meeting room
- Proper information structures that are appropriate to the planning work being done: models, matrices, drawings, symbols, and charts

The team memory resulting from capturing and structuring the information exchanged and produced during the planning sessions provides an agreed, understood, postsession record of the plans created by the team.

Use of a Planning Process Facilitator

The facilitator (called the moderator/recorder in Exhibit 6-1) is a crucial player in the project team planning process. This person:

- Provides the process of interactive communication
- Is skilled in information capture, structuring, and analysis
- Is expert in the application of project planning and control methods and techniques and other aspects of project management
- Leads the team during the planning sessions in exploring, identifying, evaluating, deciding, and planning
- Maintains the process discipline to adhere to the established agenda for the planning session

The Project Manager's Role in Team Planning

It is widely recognized that the key characteristic of the project manager's role is that of integration. In project team planning, the integrative role of the project manager becomes quite obvious. The project manager must assist the project team members in developing an acceptable plan and schedule that achieve the objectives of the project and reflect the plans and available resources of the various team members. The project manager usually holds the lead responsibility for preparing for the team planning sessions, as discussed earlier.

During the planning sessions, the project manager must be alert to real or potential conflicts in plans and bring these to the surface for resolution. He or she must concentrate on identification of the key project interface events, or those points of transition of responsibility from one team member to another, since one of the key tasks of the project manager is to manage these interfaces properly. A second key role in the project team planning process, that of the process facilitator, can also be taken by the project manager, but experience shows that it is much more effective for another person to carry out the facilitator role.

Setting the Stage for Detailed Planning

The plans, schedules, and other planning documents created during a team planning session should be limited to integrated plans at the overall project level. Of course, these require definition of the project down to the major functional task level, so that responsibilities can be assigned to, agreed upon, and understood by the team members. The team-produced project master schedule shows the agreed target dates for key milestones, reflecting the team's judgment on the overall allocation of time to accomplish the intermediate and final objectives.

Team planning sessions are not intended to produce detailed, functional plans, schedules, and budgets. To attempt to do so would be an extravagant waste of valuable time. Rather, these team sessions are intended to set the stage for truly effective detailed planning, scheduling, and budgeting. Based on the results of the top-down planning performed by the project team, under the integrating influence of the project manager and guided by the planning process facilitator, the stage is set very effectively for the detailed planning needed to validate the team's efforts and prove whether their judgments are correct.

At this point, the project manager—often with the assistance of planning, scheduling, and estimating specialists—can proceed with the more detailed, integrated planning that is necessary to ensure effective monitoring and control of the project. The top-level project plans produced by the team can be entered into the computer software to be used on the project. The more detailed functional plans and schedules can also be entered in the planning and control system, to the extent that this is warranted and practical. At this stage, the planning, scheduling, and estimating specialists may well work one-on-one with the various functional contributors to develop the detailed plans within the framework developed by the project team.

An Example of Team Planning in Action

An example of team planning in action took place in the telecommunications industry. The projects involved designing, manufacturing, installing, and testing complex voice/data communications/information systems by AT&T under contract to companies and agencies purchasing the new systems. AT&T had sound project management practices in place, but the company needed to accelerate and improve its project planning, scheduling, and team-building efforts for these major projects. The team planning start-up workshops typically were conducted in two or three sessions of one full day apiece, usually one week apart (to allow time for cleanup of each day's results and preparation for the next planning session). The first two days usually included fifteen to twenty internal AT&T team members and managers (although on one very large project the team comprised forty people). The third day included the AT&T team members plus the client project team members.

The Planning Deliverables Produced

The specific planning deliverables produced during these team planning sessions were:

- A list of key concerns and major open issues
- A list of all project team members, including the client team members, with office and home telephone numbers and electronic mail addresses. Also included were the names of immediate bosses and their office and home telephone numbers, for use in solving unresolved problems or conflicts
- Project scope and objectives
- Agreed upon definition of the project in the form of a project breakdown structure (PBS), usually down to four or five levels
- Agreed upon task/responsibility matrix, based on the PBS, with codes showing for each task: (1) who does the work, (2) who must be consulted, (3) who must be notified or receive a copy of the results, and (4) who must approve the results
- A list of the key project interface events, indicating who would be the originator and who the receiver
- The project master schedule, based on the PBS, with team commitments thereto
- Agreed upon project monitoring and control procedures
- Action assignments from the planning sessions
- The *Project Handbook,* a three-ring binder with dividers for retention of the above documents, for use by each project team member throughout the life of the project. As the plans were revised and updated, the latest documents were placed in these handbooks

Conduct of the Planning Sessions

For each AT&T project, the assigned project manager planned and prepared for each team planning session, following the guidelines described earlier in this chapter. An experienced facilitator assisted the project manager in this preparation and in conducting the sessions. For each planning deliverable, the facilitator gave a brief presentation of the project planning concept, and then the project team immediately applied that concept to the project. In developing the project breakdown structure and the task/responsibility matrix, small teams of four or five people worked together on the specific portions of the project for which those team members held responsibility. The small teams reported their results to the full project team to ensure complete agreement and understanding.

Results Achieved

The results of these team planning sessions were and continue to be excellent. The projects have been completed on schedule and without crash efforts near the end date, saving money and increasing quality. Improvements have been noted in getting the projects started more quickly and smoothly, in increased cooperation with the client, in better communications, and in better teamwork. The functional team members have reported that this approach requires less of their time for planning than the more traditional methods used previously. Team planning through start-up workshops has been incorporated into the AT&T corporate project management process and is used on all major projects within this business segment of AT&T.

Hidden Agenda Items

Several hidden agenda items have been reported as benefits of the team planning approach:

- Introducing uniform project management methods
- Hands-on training of project team members in project planning
- Tapping the team wisdom
- Creating a shared vision of the project and its objectives
- Demonstrating the power of open team communications
- Exchanging experience and developing skills
- Creating a team and getting commitment

Benefits and Limitations of Project Team Planning

There are a number of basic benefits of project team planning.

- The plans produced are based on how the work will actually be accomplished.
- The persons responsible for performing the work have a greater sense of commitment to the plans and to the project.
- Only one set of plans exist: those that the project team has created and is following.
- The time required for planning by the key project team members is minimized.
- The project plans reflect a top-down approach using the total wisdom of the project team, which then sets the stage for more effective, detailed, bottom-up validation of the plans.

Other benefits, including the hidden agenda items, are discussed above.

There are also limitations to the process. The decision to use project team planning should be based on the characteristics of the project in question. It would not be appropriate to insist on this type of project team planning if it is an effort that is very well known to the organization and very repetitive of many previous projects, with project team members who are all experienced in this type of project, and planners who can produce plans and schedules that are valid and acceptable to all concerned.

The primary limitation in project team planning is probably the time required of the project team members to devote to the team planning sessions. Although planning should be given a high priority in any organization, frequently it is viewed as unproductive and even wasteful, hence it is difficult to convince the project team members that they should devote even a few days to developing the project plans. Top management understanding and support is required to overcome these ingrained attitudes and habits. A successful project team planning session can also do a lot to demonstrate the power and usefulness of this approach.

Section III
Project Structures and Organizations

7

Organizational Choices for Project Management

Brian Hobbs
University of Quebec at Montreal

Pierre Ménard
University of Quebec at Montreal

How should a particular project be organized? There is no clear and simple answer to this question. The project management literature on organization structures presents the problem as one of a choice among three alternatives:

1. The functional structure
2. The project or fully projectized structure
3. The matrix structure

This approach has the advantage of providing a clear conceptual framework for the analysis of organizational structures. However, it is of limited usefulness to the manager who must decide how to organize a specific new project without restructuring the whole organization.

Projects are often undertaken by organizations whose main activities go much beyond these projects. These organizations already have a structure for managing their activities, whether it be a functional, product, matrix, or hybrid structure, and they are not considering restructuring to accommodate a new project. The problem that the manager faces, then, is not which structure to choose for the organization but rather:

- How should the project be positioned with respect to the existing organization, and what relationships should be established between the project and the existing organization?
- How much autonomy and authority should be given to the project manager? What should his or her status be?
- What management practices and systems should be used to manage this project? To what extent should they be different from those in use in the existing organization?

This chapter attempts to answer these questions by drawing on the project management literature and on the authors' experience with several organizations that manage projects.

Organizing Projects as Distinct Entities

Our approach is based on two fundamental ideas or postulates. Postulate 1 is that *in order to maximize the chances of project success, it is generally better to organize the project as an entity distinct from the rest of the organization and thus minimize the interdependencies between the project and the rest of the organization.* Most project managers wish to be as free as possible from the constraints of the existing organization. They constantly demand more authority and autonomy.

Several factors help explain why autonomous projects tend to be more successful. First, they and their results are more visible and thus attract more management attention. Second, autonomous projects suffer less from conflicts over priorities than activities managed within the existing structure; this facilitates both schedule and cost control. Third, maintaining relationships between the project and the organization means the project manager has more interfaces to manage, more effort to put into coordination, and more authorizations to obtain. In addition, the manager is more exposed to organizational pathologies such as conflicts and power struggles. This requires additional management effort by the project manager and increases project risk.

If our first postulate is true, why are all projects not organized as autonomous units? Two factors can help answer this question. The first is that the creation of an autonomous organization is not always the most economical solution for the organization. The assignment of resources to the project on a full-time basis is not always justified by project requirements. If this is the case and the project is cost sensitive or if the resources it needs are scarce and critical to the ongoing operations of the existing organization, the creation of a distinct and autonomous unit may cause serious difficulties.

The second factor is a much more frequent phenomenon than the first and thus a more relevant explanation of why projects are often not organized as autonomous units. We present this as our second major postulate.

Integrating the Project Into the Existing Structure

Postulate 2 is that *when an organization undertakes a new project, strong pressures exist to integrate the project into the existing structure and management systems and practices.* These pressures can come from several sources, not the least of which is resistance from department managers within the existing structure. The decision to create an autonomous unit to manage a project is, at the same time, a decision not to give the project to existing departments and their managers, some of whom may feel that they are capable of managing the project and that the project falls within their department's jurisdiction. Thus, such a decision may be perceived as a loss of prestige, jurisdiction, and resources for them and can even be seen as a sign of lack of confidence in their ability to manage on the part of upper management. They may also feel penalized if in addition to losing the project they also lose some of their best resources to the project team. In addition, the creation of an autonomous unit normally reduces the level of influence the functional department managers would otherwise have on technical decisions. If this is their perception of the stakes involved in the choice of an organizational arrangement for a project, then one should expect that they would exert considerable pressure to have the project integrated into the existing structure.

Personnel may also resist being transferred to the project on a temporary basis. This resistance would be expected if the assignment is perceived as risky, particularly in terms of reintegration.

The setting up of special arrangements for a project requires adaptation and extra effort on the part of support functions such as accounting and personnel. In addition to resisting extra effort, these functions are likely to resist the creation of special arrangements because special arrangements are counter to their organizational mission to develop and promote standardized methods and procedures.

From the overall organizational and the upper management points of view, creating distinct units for projects has the advantage of making these projects more visible and more amenable to direct management action. However, projects that are organized as distinct units require more effort and attention on the part of upper management, both in setting the projects up and in monitoring them throughout their life cycles. The existing organization usually provides for orderly monitoring, reporting, and controlling of activities. Distinct and autonomous projects break up this order. If a larger number of distinct projects are under way at any one time, upper management may become overloaded with the extra effort and attention they require. Upper management may thus resist giving special status to a project because of the extra effort and attention it would then require.

Projects have a horizon that barely goes beyond their own existence, but the organization has a horizon that is both broader and longer than that of a single project. The project manager of an autonomous project would be expected to optimize the performance of his or her project. But optimal project performance may not mean optimal organizational performance. Many things that organizations do are justifiable from a global point of view but not from the more limited point of view of a single project—for example, the development of human resources; the standardization of methods, designs, components, etc.; and the integration of procurement activities into an overall procurement strategy and policy. Project autonomy can be seen as a threat to these integrative activities, and those responsible for them can be expected to resist.

If the organization that is to be put in place to manage a particular project involves management practices and behavior patterns that are different from those of the existing organization, then resistance to change can come from more cultural sources. These are more subtle and more difficult to overcome. They involve changing human attitudes and behavior. They can come as much from contacts with the existing organization as from within the project team, especially if the team is recruited from the existing organization.

All of these factors help explain why there are pressures to integrate the project into the existing structure and management systems and practices and where these pressures come from. But beyond this, there is the very context within which a decision on project organization and structure is usually made. Those pulling for project autonomy are usually the project manager and possibly a core team. The project manager usually has relatively low status within the organization. On the other side, those pulling for project integration into the existing organization are many, and among them are higher-status managers. The dice are therefore loaded toward integration unless a member of upper management acts as project sponsor and actively promotes project autonomy.

This discussion of the pressures toward project integration into the existing organization describes the context within which top management must decide on the appropriate organizational arrangements for a specific project. Should management resist these pressures and establish arrangements that are specific to the project? If so, to what extent should the project be distinct and autonomous from the existing organization? The answer to these questions depends on the specific context. Many factors intervene, but these can be grouped into three categories as shown in Exhibit 7-1.

1. The structural type of the existing organization
2. The factors related to the organization: the organizational contextual factors
3. The factors related to the specific project: the project factors

The choice of an appropriate organizational arrangement for the project depends on these groups of factors and the relationships among them. We will now describe in more detail each category of factors and how they are related to the choice of a project organization.

Exhibit 7-1. Decision model for organizational choice.

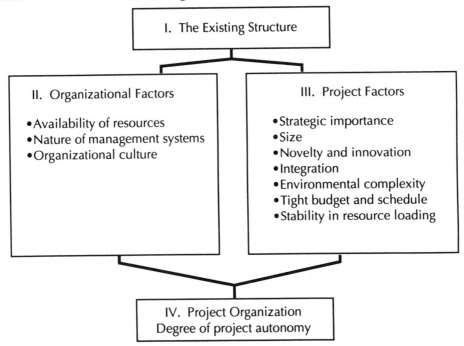

The Existing Structure

An organization is a complex system. The most effective and efficient way to analyze such a system is to compare it to one of a limited number of organizational types. In our analysis of the factors a manager should consider when deciding how to organize a particular project, we will first discuss organizational type, as this is the most important factor and the one that allows the broadest and most integrative approach. We will follow this discussion with an analysis of several organizational contextual factors.

We propose the following typology of organizational structures:

- ▸ The functional structure
- ▸ The fully projectized structure
- ▸ The project-functional matrix structure
- ▸ The organic structure

The Functional Structure

The functional structure is a widespread organizational form. As can be seen in Exhibit 7-2, its principal components are functions or areas of technical and administrative specialization. The main objectives in organizing units according to their specialty are:

Exhibit 7-2. The functional structure.

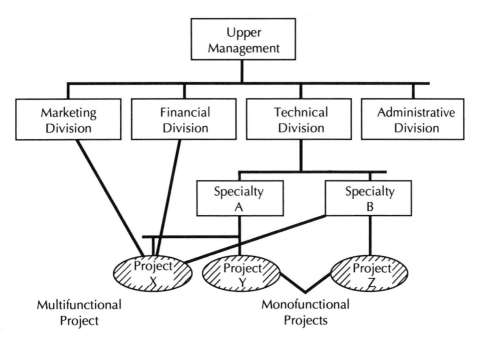

Multifunctional Project

Monofunctional Projects

- To facilitate supervision by grouping similar activities in the same unit
- To group similar activities and resources so as to benefit from economies of scale
- To facilitate the development and maintenance of technical competency in the areas that are essential to the organization's survival

It is generally recognized that the development and maintenance of technical competency in a specialized field is facilitated when specialists are grouped together in the same department under the same boss. The specialized department and its manager can then pursue clear and easily reconcilable objectives: the long-term development of technical competency and the short-term production of products offering the best quality/price ratio possible. This arrangement also fosters the development of competency because of the synergy created when specialists work in the same physical setting and stimulate each other.

The functional structure generally has a pyramidlike shape and is built on a vertical and hierarchical conception of authority. A series of management principles is often associated with this pyramidlike structure. These principles aim to ensure simplicity, order, and harmony inside the organization. Note particularly the following:

- Each employee must have only one superior (the principle of unity of command).
- Each person's responsibilities must be clearly defined and distinct from those of all others.
- The individual must be held accountable. This requires a clear chain of command and clearly defined and distinct areas of responsibility.
- Information must mainly be circulated vertically so that the hierarchy can assume its full responsibility.
- Lateral relations, when necessary, must be controlled by a set of rules and procedures as complete and precise as possible.

Certain practices have been added to these principles and have been internalized to such an extent that they are perceived as the only modus operandi possible. These include:

- Only an expert from a given field can supervise experts from the same field.
- Technical expertise + seniority = progression in the hierarchy.

These characteristics facilitate the control of quality, costs, and individual performance. In addition, the almost complete control that this structure provides to superiors facilitates long-term planning and flexibility and economy in the use of resources, which can be distributed according to management's priorities and transferred from one activity to the next as the need arises.

A career in a functionally structured organization tends to follow a path up the hierarchy within the functional department. Rotation between specialized areas is very difficult and infrequent. This lack of rotation and of diversified experience combined with the homogeneity of technical training tend to foster the creation of a vision of problems that is limited to the dimensions that are relevant to the function, thus fostering the development of a professional-specialist culture within each of the functional departments. The development of a professional-specialist culture has several consequences for project management:

- Priority given to technical elegance at the expense of cost and schedule
- Conflicts with other specialist groups when working on multifunctional projects
- Tendency to neglect relations with the external environment and particularly with the client and other stakeholders

Despite its many advantages, this type of structure also has many inconveniences. This is particularly the case for the manager of a major project involving more than one type of specialized resources. Exhibit 7-3 presents a partial list of the characteristics of functional structures.

When a project is integrated into a functionally structured organization, the responsibility is usually assigned to the functional unit that will make the greatest technical contribution to the project. The head of the functional unit has a multitude of responsibilities; he or she must manage the regular activities of the unit, ensure its long-term development, and, in addition, assume responsibility for one or many projects. In the normal context of limited resources, the functional head may well be unable to reconcile the requirements of pursuing normal activities with the requirements of the projects. It would therefore be natural for the functional head to accord priority to the unit objectives with negative consequences for the project schedule.

Obviously, the functional head can solve the dilemma by delegating responsibility for the projects to project managers chosen from among the specialists in his or her unit. However, this can put the specialist in a delicate position with respect to the heads of the other functional units because of his or her lower status, particularly if he or she must refer to the functional head for important decisions. Furthermore, the project manager within the functional unit often pursues an objective that is compatible with the functional unit's mission. In the case of technical departments, this tends to be high technical quality. In a situation where a technical specialist becomes a project manager and must seek a compromise among divergent requirements relative to quality, time, and cost objectives, it is probable that he or she will favor quality at the expense of time, cost, or both.

There are other difficulties when the responsibility for a multidisciplinary project is assigned to one of the specialties. Given the competitive climate that exists inside organizations, it is quite possible that the functional head will have difficulty obtaining the necessary cooperation from his or her colleagues in the other functions involved; they probably have other organizations that they consider to be of higher priority. In addition, the functional head may be tempted not to call upon all of the resources whose contribution could be beneficial to the pursuit of project objectives. The smaller the portion of the primary function or specialty, the greater the risks. The following rule of thumb is a good guideline: Do not assign the management of a project to a functional manager when his or her specialty represents less than 75–80 percent of the total project.

Projects can be executed well within purely functional structures when each project can be executed almost exclusively by one primary function or when the projects can be broken down into subprojects that require little integration and thus

Exhibit 7-3. Characteristics of the functional structure.

Advantages	*Inconveniences*
Technical competency	
▸ Development and maintenance of technical competency in specialized fields ▸ Synergy among specialists	▸ Filtered perception; lack of an overall view ▸ Difficulty in integrating several specialties: possible conflicts among specialists ▸ Difficulty in creating motivation for the project ▸ Lack of openness to the environment ▸ Risk of neglecting the aspects not related to the specialty
Objectives	
▸ Concentration on the objectives of the function ▸ Pursuing long-term development objectives ▸ Easy reconciliation of internal objectives	▸ Conflict of priorities with other functional activities ▸ Difficulty in making effective compromises between the variables quality-time-cost ▸ Nobody is exclusively responsible for project objectives ▸ Subordination of the managerial to the technical
Permanence and stability	
▸ Horizontal relations are clear ▸ Clear definitions of roles and responsibilities ▸ Efficiency improved by standardization ▸ Stability in interpersonal relations ▸ Well-defined career paths ▸ The possibility for organizational learning	▸ Difficulty in adapting; resistance to change ▸ Difficulties in the internal circulation of information ▸ Slow decision making
Control	
▸ Easier control of quality and performance ▸ Flexibility and economy in the use of labor	▸ The time variable is less well controlled ▸ Limited liaisons with the outside ▸ Lack of visibility for the client ▸ Limited development of management capabilities among the personnel

can be assigned to different functional departments. Furthermore, functional organizations tend to perform better on projects in which the development of technical content is the primary consideration. It would therefore be appropriate to integrate small development projects under reimbursable-cost type contracts into a functional structure by assigning them to the appropriate department.

Multidisciplinary projects that require the integration of system components, the management of external interfaces, and the negotiation of trade-offs among time, cost, and quality requirements should, however, not be assigned to one department of a functional organization. We turn now to a description of the project organization that in many ways is the exact opposite of the functional organization.

The Fully Projectized Structure

When an organization is given responsibility for the execution of a major project, it often places the project in a temporary structure more or less independent from the rest of the organization. This is referred to as a project organization or fully projectized structure. Specifically, the organization is seeking to:

- ▸ Concentrate the responsibility for the conduct of the project in the hands of one person whose only preoccupation is the success of the project and the attainment of project objectives
- ▸ Facilitate the integration of different technical specialists required by the project as well as other relevant dimensions, such as political, cultural, economic, and environmental
- ▸ Ensure that decisions affecting either the content or the managing of the project are the result of an optimum compromise among the different objectives of the project; in other words, avoid the undue and systematic predominance of one objective, particularly the technical objective

Many variations on the project structure exist, but they all have in common a project manager with more or less full authority over his or her resources. Obviously, this type of structure is chosen for special temporary organizations designed to execute one or several specific projects. In practice, all the necessary resources are not always placed under the exclusive supervision of the project manager. Certain support functions such as accounting, legal services, and information services often remain integrated into the parent organization's management systems.

The advantages and inconveniences of the project organization are relatively obvious. As the project manager has no functional responsibility, conflicts in objectives and priorities are minimized. However, conflicts may arise in establishing priorities between projects or between the projects and the parent organization concerning the sharing of resources. The project team is less likely to have a strong bias for a particular specialization. This facilitates taking an overall view of the project. There is no undue bias for technical quality, which permits an effective compromise among the quality-time-cost variables. The project manager has clear authority over his or her resources. This reduces ambiguity and permits better coordination, as well as promoting effective collaboration among the resources. This authority also makes the project manager the hub of all formal communications related to the project. He or she thus becomes a credible spokesperson for the project in relation with the client and other outside stakeholders.

The project organization avoids the inconveniences associated with the functional structure. However, it does not offer the same advantages. The disadvantages of the distinct and autonomous project were discussed earlier either as limiting conditions for the use of this structural arrangement or as sources of resistance to its implementation. The advantages and inconveniences of this structural arrangement are summarized in Exhibit 7-4.

The fully projectized structure is thus an appropriate organizational choice for major projects that require systems integration; trade-offs among cost, schedule, and quality; and clear communications channels with outside stakeholders. An organization that wishes to execute one such project but feels that its existing structure would not be appropriate may create a temporary independent project organization just for this project. In this way, the organization can effectively execute the project while minimizing the descriptive effect it might have on the going organization. This is what organizations do, for example, when they create task forces for special projects. We turn now to a discussion of the matrix structure.

The Project-Functional Matrix Structure

The matrix structure is an organizational form that seeks to combine the advantages of the functional structure and the project organization while avoiding their inconveniences. As the typical organization chart (as shown in Exhibit 7-5) illustrates, the matrix structure is characterized by the simultaneous presence of both project and functional components. These components are administratively independent, but interdependent in the execution of projects. This arrangement permits functional

Exhibit 7-4. Characteristics of the fully projectized structure.

Advantages	Inconveniences
▸ Clear identification of overall project responsibility	▸ Duplication of effort and resources
▸ Good systems integration	▸ Limited development and accumulation of know-how
▸ More direct contact among different disciplines	▸ Employment instability
▸ Clear communications channels with client and other outside stakeholders	
▸ Clear priorities	
▸ Effective trade-offs among cost, schedule, and quality	▸ May tend to sacrifice technical quality for the more visible variables of schedule and cost
▸ Client-oriented	
▸ Results-oriented	

Exhibit 7-5. The matrix structure.

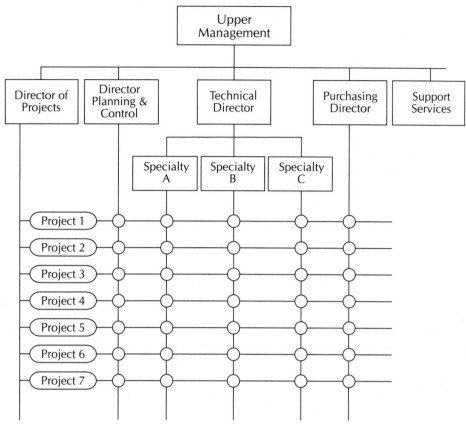

components to maintain an independent existence and to pursue, where appropriate, their regular activities while providing specialized resources necessary for the execution of projects. In general, the specialists remain permanently under the authority of their functional head, but their services are lent to the projects on a temporary basis in accord with project needs. The functional components thus become centralized reservoirs of specialized resources.

The autonomous existence of the project components permits the organization to benefit from most of the advantages of a project organization. The project components are comprised of project managers directing temporary multidisciplinary teams whose composition may frequently vary as the project progresses through the different phases of its life cycle.

The matrix structure places the project and functional sides of the organization in a situation of high interdependence. The two must collaborate if the structure is to work well. Despite the high level of interdependency and the need for close cooperation, the matrix structure performs better if the responsibilities of each party are made as clear and as distinct as is reasonably possible. Generally, the responsibilities are distributed between the two dimensions as follows:

1. The project dimension is:
   - ▸ Responsible for results
     - ▸ Attaining project objectives
     - ▸ Producing the desired deliverables to meet schedules
     - ▸ Respecting budgetary constraints
     - ▸ Minimizing costs
   - ▸ Responsible for liaison with the client and other external stakeholders
2. The functional dimension is:
   - ▸ Responsible for the technical quality of projects and maintaining technical excellence
   - ▸ Responsible for the efficient use of specialized resources
   - ▸ Responsible for the management of specialized resources
     - ▸ Hiring and initiation
     - ▸ Training, development, and acculturation
     - ▸ Evaluation
   - ▸ Responsible for developing the organizational memory

The project manager is generally responsible for overall project planning; identifying project objectives, deliverables, and the principal elements of the work breakdown structure; determining the key elements of the schedule; and establishing a preliminary budget for the work packages. The functional representatives assume responsibility for identifying the required resources, defining the content of the work packages, and monitoring work progress and quality.

Our objective in describing the matrix structure is not to provide a detailed analysis of this complex structural arrangement but rather to describe the structural context within which an answer must be found to the question as to how to organize a specific project. The project-functional matrix is a structure that is designed to manage projects. Most projects would therefore normally be managed through the existing structure. However, projects that because of their specific characteristics could be managed effectively in a functional structure could also be assigned directly to the appropriate functional department in the matrix structure. An example might be a small in-house development project that calls upon the resources of only one department. Likewise, a project whose characteristics would justify the creation of a distinct and autonomous structure could be set up in this way alongside the existing matrix structure. An example of this might be a major project that required the full-time and stable use of considerable resources over an extended period of time or that drew heavily on outside resources. But this would be an exceptional situation.

For projects that are managed through the matrix structure, the question then becomes twofold. First, what should be the reporting relationships between the project manager and the resources working on the project? Exhibit 7-6 provides guidelines for such relationships as they vary with the importance of contributions made by the different human resources. Second, what level of authority should be invested in the project manager, particularly in his or her relations with the functional managers? Here again, the characteristics of the specific project determine the appropriate sharing of power between the project and functional managers. We refer you to the discussion of project-related factors later in this chapter. We turn now to a discussion of organic structures.

Exhibit 7-6. Reporting relationships in the matrix structure.

Contribution to the Project		*Reporting Relationship to Project Manager*
Limited or occasional contribution	⟶	Direct relations with the project manager
Significant contribution	⟶	Full members of the project team
Major contribution throughout the duration of the project	⟶	Detached from their administrative units and assigned exclusively to the project manager

The Organic Structures

Small R&D or other highly professional organizations often have organic structures. These are organizations that have few formal structural arrangements. In these organizations, teams form around problems or projects. Recruitment onto project teams is rather informal, as are reporting relationships. In these organizations projects often are initiated lower down in the organization. A project manager or team leader recruits the resources he or she needs to form a team from among the organization's resources in a rather informal manner.

The question as to whether or not to integrate a new project into this structure depends on the characteristics of the specific project. The organic structure works well for small, very creative projects. These can therefore be integrated into the existing organization by finding a project manager who will champion the project and see that the necessary resources come together to form a project team. However, a project that because of its characteristics could be managed as a separate and distinct unit could be set up as such, parallel to the workings of the existing organization. An example in this case might be a larger project with more precise requirements or one over which management wishes to maintain tighter control.

Organizational Contextual Factors

Each of the four organizational types we have discussed is often associated with a particular organizational context. There are, of course, many ways in which organizations of the same structural type can vary from one to the next. We have chosen to discuss three groups of variables that are particularly relevant to the decision as to whether or not a particular project should be integrated into an existing organization or set up as a separate unit. These are:

1. The availability of resources
2. The nature of the organization's management systems
3. The organization's culture

The Availability of Resources

The ready availability of resources facilitates the establishing of an autonomous project unit. Inversely, a severe constraint on the availability of a critical resource may necessitate the sharing of resources with the parent organization. This will reduce project autonomy and partially integrate the project and the organization.

If a particular category of resources is very rare both within the organization and in the outside market, it may not be practical or possible to assign these resources exclusively to the project team, since this would create a shortage within the parent organization and thus jeopardize the pursuit of its other activities. Both physical resources, such as special equipment and human resources, may be in short supply. It may not be practical to recruit or purchase new resources because of lack of availability in the outside market or because the duration for which they would be needed would not justify either purchasing new equipment or hiring and training new personnel. Then again, a tight project schedule might preclude either of these options.

In any case, the project will likely have to share resources with the parent organization. This sharing of resources will effectively integrate the project partially into the parent organization. More coordination effort will be needed to adjust to both project and other organizational demands and the project manager will need to devote more time and effort to managing the interface with the departments with which the project must share resources. This is the unavoidable consequence of constraints on resource availability and the resulting need to share some resources.

The Inadequacy of the Organization's Management Systems

The less the organization's existing information systems and administrative policies and procedures are able to adequately serve project needs, the more the project needs to have specific and dedicated systems and procedures. Specific and dedicated systems and procedures are almost impossible to establish and maintain, except when the project is set up as an autonomous unit. The setting-up of separate systems and procedures has the effect of making the project unit even more autonomous from the parent organization.

Projects tend to have very specific needs in terms of planning, control, procurement, delegation of decision-making authority, reporting, and other administrative activities. Existing administrative procedures and information systems may be more or less adequate in meeting these needs. In the case of a project-driven organization, unless a new project has needs that are radically different from those of other projects, existing management systems may well be adequate for managing the new project. However, organizations whose main activities are not organized on a project basis have management systems, and particularly information systems, that may or may not be adequate for supporting the project.

Several years ago, few information systems in nonproject-driven organizations could support project-oriented planning and control, and even in some project-driven organizations, the management information systems were less than adequate. Typically, the categories that the rest of the organization used for budgeting and controlling were inappropriate for project planning and control, and the systems were not flexible nor powerful enough to be able to adapt to project requirements. Report-formatting has also been a problem, as some systems *do* contain the necessary information, but are not designed to produce a concise project report; the information is often buried in a mountain of printouts and reports, and thus remains virtually unaccessible to project personnel. Projects often operate within a time frame that is different from that of the rest of the organization. The imperatives of the project schedule and the interdependencies that exist among different activities within the project often require that information be timely so that decisions can be made quickly.

Administrative policies and procedures that may be appropriate for the rest of the organization are often poorly adapted to project requirements. Procurement policy and procedures; personnel policies and procedures in such areas as personnel selection, salaries and benefits, personnel evaluation, and the hiring of temporary personnel; sub-contracting policy and contract management procedures in general, and the system of standards and authorizations for obtaining certain resources such as additional space and equipment and travel expenses are all examples of areas where following established policies and procedures may impede project performance. The reason is either the project time frame is different from that of the rest of the organization or the decision criteria implicit in these policies and procedures are inappropriate within the context of the project.

Many project managers take pleasure in telling stories of how a particular policy or procedure was shown to be petty and ridiculous in the context of their project. They are also highly critical of information systems that do not meet their expectations. The solutions they propose to solve these problems are the setting-up of an autonomous information system for the project and the freeing of the project from many of the policies and procedures that constrain the management of the project. These solutions inevitably involve some duplication of work being done elsewhere in the parent organization. Typically, the project will acquire additional equipment and personnel and develop administrative procedures and methods for treating information. Many administrative functions are thus effectively accomplished by the project office. Summary data is provided to the parent organization in order to meet the information requirements of the organization's reporting system, project managers are often willing to support the cost and effort required to establish and operate separate and dedicated systems in order to get access to timely and accurate information and to have more freedom and flexibility in the use of the project's resources.

This is inevitably opposed by the functional departments within the parent organization that are responsible for information-processing and administrative functions. The role of these departments is to rationalize, standardize, and control. Allowing a project to establish autonomous, dedicated systems and procedures undermines their ability to fulfill their mission and weakens their position within the organization. The system that adequately meets project needs may not adequately meet the organization's legitimate requirements and concerns. It also creates some duplication of effort and requires that administrative functions adapt to the specific system the project might set up. If many projects set up separate and different systems, the organization's whole management system may become overloaded or chaotic.

In many organizations, a conflict exists between project managers and administrative functional departments. The relationships between the two are often characterized by very infrequent communication and a lack of understanding. Some project managers react by setting up unofficial parallel systems on which they rely for accurate and timely information, while neglecting the information requirements of the organization's systems. This, in turn, makes the conflict worse, while confirming in their minds that the other side is either incompetent or is acting in bad faith.

The decision as to whether separate systems and procedures should be set up should be based on an analysis of the needs of both the project and the organization—and of the capacity of the organization's existing systems to serve both. An approach we have used has been to first plan the project and specify its critical information and decision-making requirements, then to present these to the relevant functional departments. The objective is to obtain either a commitment on the part of the functional departments to adequately respond to project requirements or their approval for, and possibly support in, the setting-up of project-specific systems. In our experience, the presenting of project requirements to functional support groups before project execution can greatly reduce previous levels of mutual misunderstanding. This often results in better support for the project from existing systems and can help avoid the extra cost and inconvenience of setting up separate dedicated systems.

The Organization's Culture

The more the organization's culture differs from the project management culture, the more the project should be isolated from the organization by setting it up as a separate unit.

Project management is more than the use of planning and control techniques and a way of organizing. It is also a system of attitudes and behavior patterns that can be referred to as a project-management culture. The decision as to whether a particular project should be integrated into the existing organization should be based, partly, on a comparison between the culture that would support project success and the existing culture in the organization and on an analysis of the likely impact the existing organization's culture might have on the project.

A detailed and structured analysis of organizational culture would be beyond the scope of this chapter. However, Exhibit 7-7 presents several of the attitudes and behavior patterns that are either supportive of or detrimental to project success.

Not all projects are dependent on the creation of a project-management culture and not all organizations are unsupportive of this type of culture. But this is certainly not uncommon in functional organizations. The decision to isolate the project from the rest of the organization in order to reduce cultural contamination should thus be based on an analysis of the specific project and the impact that contact with the organization might have.

The Project Factors

The way a project is organized should be adapted to the specific characteristics of the project. There are seven factors that should influence the decision on project organization: (1) the project's strategic importance; (2) the project's size; (3) the project's novelty and the need for innovation; (4) the need for integration; (5) the environmental complexity; (6) the need to meet severe budget and time constraints; and (7) the stability of resource loading.

Exhibit 7-7. Attitudes and behavior patterns supportive of or detrimental to project success.

Supportive	Detrimental
▸ Open communications and free circulation of information	▸ Guarded communications and restricted information flows
▸ Frequent lateral communications	▸ Communications following the chain of command
▸ Willingness and ability to make decisions	▸ Conformity to multistep multiperson approval process
▸ Flexibility; organic	▸ Rigidity; bureaucraticness
▸ Collaboration	▸ Power struggles; conflicts
▸ Proactive; willingness to take initiatives, risks	▸ Reactiveness; waiting for assignments, approvals
▸ Confrontation of ideas	▸ Avoidance and submission: "The boss is right"
▸ Assuming responsibility for results	▸ Avoiding responsibility
▸ Prime loyalty to project	▸ Prime loyalty to function
▸ Behavior regulated by project needs (e.g., work on evenings, weekends)	▸ Behavior regulated by rules (e.g., the 9-to-5 syndrome)

The Project's Strategic Importance

The greater a project's strategic importance for the organization, the more it should be isolated from the existing structure and set up as a separate unit.

There are two arguments that support this position. First, as shown before, integrating the project into the existing organization increases organizational risks, particularly with respect to slow and fragmented decision processes and internal conflict. If the success of the project is of crucial importance to the organization, its chances of success would be increased if it was not subjected to these risks.

Second, a project that is detached from the existing structure is much more visible and subject to management scrutiny. Inversely, a project that is integrated into the existing structure may become more difficult to monitor as its activities are fragmented and partially integrated with other activities of the organization. Projects of high strategic importance should receive much more upper management attention, and their being managed separately from the rest of the organization facilitates top management monitoring and control.

The Project's Size

The greater a project's size, the more it is appropriate to set up a separate organization to manage it.

The larger a project is, the more economically justifiable it is to create a separate structure and to assign resources to it on a full-time basis. In addition, managing a very large project within the existing organization would require major adjustments.

By setting up a separate structure, the impact on the existing organization can be minimized, thus allowing the organization to pursue its other activities while managing this large project.

The Project's Novelty and the Need for Innovation

The more a project's content differs from the regular activities of the organization and the more the project requires new and innovative solutions, the more the project should be isolated from the rest of the organization by being set up as a separate unit.

Project novelty often takes the form of technological uncertainty or unfamiliarity, but many aspects of the project may differ from normal activities or ways of operating. The more a project differs from other organizational activities, the less the organization's present skills are relevant for solving the problems that are specific to the project. But, more importantly, if the project requires new and innovative solutions, it is important to protect the project's creative and entrepreneurial efforts from being unduly hampered as they might be if the project was given to organizational units with vested interests in certain technological options or if project resources are shared part-time with other activities. The best way to protect the project from these influences is to set it up as an autonomous unit.

The Need for Integration

The more a project requires integration, the more it should be separated from the existing organization and set up as a separate unit.

The amount of integration a project requires is a function of several factors.

▸ *The number of components.* The more components there are to a project, the more effort that needs to be spent on integration. The term *components* refers to physical parts or systems, to different functional contributions (e.g., marketing, finance, production), as well as to different vested interests of stakeholders (e.g., environmental impact, economic development, technology transfer).

▸ *The degree to which the project's components are different from each other.* These differences may be differences in functional specialization—for example, marketing, production, and financial components of a commercial project—or the differences may originate from the different technologies used in producing the different components or subsystems of a physical product. The differences may even stem from the national origins of those contributing to the project. Whatever the basis on which project components differ, these differences make integration more difficult and thus increase the level of integrative effort required on the part of the project manager.

▸ *The level of interdependence among project components.* If the project components can be produced separately and independently from each other, then the project manager can establish the specifications for each component and have them produced without personally needing to invest heavily to integrate them into a final product.

Independent project teams are very powerful integrating mechanisms, whereas ongoing organizations are very poor at obtaining the cooperation between departments that is necessary in order to ensure that their various contributions will be well integrated to produce a coherent end product. Therefore, if a project requires considerable integrative effort, then it should be set up as a separate and independent unit. Organizationally and physically separating the project's resources from the existing organization greatly reduces the required level of integrative effort.

If, however, the project can be executed almost entirely by one existing organizational unit and little coordination is required to integrate the contributions of others, then the project can be assigned to the appropriate unit. Likewise, if the project can be broken down into independent subprojects, each of which can be executed by one existing organizational unit with little coordination with other units, then the level of integrative effort required is low and the project can be managed as several independent subprojects within existing units. A project manager or project coordinator might still be necessary to ensure a minimal level of coordination.

The Environmental Complexity

The more complex the project's external environment and the more a project's success is dependent on this environment, the more the responsibility for management of external interfaces should be assigned to a project manager in an autonomous unit.

The argument concerning relations with the external environment is quite similar to that regarding project internal coordination or integration, as discussed in the previous point. In fact, here it is again a question of integration, but in this case, the integration between the project and its external environment.

Several factors contribute to environmental complexity and the project's dependency on its external environment.

- *The number of external interfaces that must be managed.* As this number increases, it becomes more difficult to manage the external environment coherently.
- *Uncertainty.* If the external environment is predictable, then it is much less complex an interface to manage.
- *Dependency.* If the project is dependent on the external environment for resources, authorizations, permits, or the clarification of project content, then managing external interfaces is more critical and more complex.
- *Hostility.* If segments of the external environment are hostile to the project, then the management of external interfaces with these segments, with the media, or with other groups that might be influenced by hostile actions becomes very critical and very complex.

Relations with the external environment are generally managed better if the project manager in an autonomous unit is given overall responsibility for managing external interfaces, than if the responsibility is diluted and shared with several stakeholders in the parent organization. Centralizing overall responsibility in the hands of the project manager ensures more coherent relations with the environment, while setting up an autonomous unit reduces interference from the hierarchy in the existing structure.

The Need to Meet Severe Budget and Time Constraints

The greater the need to meet severe budget and/or time constraints, the more the project should be separated from the existing organization and set up as an autonomous unit.

Projects with very tight budgets and/or schedules have a better chance of meeting these constraints if they are set up as autonomous units for several reasons.

▸ *Visibility of results.* Increased visibility facilitates the monitoring of results both by the project team and by upper management.
▸ *Better control of resources.* Focusing decision authority with the autonomous project manager and project team allows much better control of resources than if this authority is diluted and shared with several managers in the parent organization. Better control of resources leads to more flexibility and adaptability in their use.
▸ *Clear objectives and priorities.* The autonomous project has only its own objectives to pursue. When it is autonomous it can pursue these with a minimum of conflict of priorities with the organization's other objectives.
▸ *Isolation from interference.* The autonomous project organization is less vulnerable to interference from the hierarchy of the existing organization.
▸ *Quicker and better.* The autonomous project manager and project team have better and quicker access to project information and with appropriate decision-making autonomy can react more quickly to changing situations than the parent organization can. This results in faster and better decisions that are particularly critical in attempting to meet tight schedules and/or budgets.

The Stability of Resource Loading

The more constant the resource levels required by a project, the more economical and practical it is to dedicate resources to the project and thus create an autonomous project unit.

If resource loading varies considerably throughout the project life cycle, then setting the project up as an autonomous unit may result in inefficient use of resources and in considerable effort being spent on managing their mobilization and demobilization. More constant resource requirements would reduce these problems and make the setting up of an autonomous project organization more feasible.

The Choice of a Project Organization

As suggested at the beginning of this chapter, the problem of deciding on the most appropriate organization for a given project often takes the following form:

▸ Should we integrate the project in the existing structure (whatever it is) or create a more or less autonomous unit?
▸ If the second option appears more appropriate, what should be the degree of autonomy granted to that unit?

Therefore, a decision on project organization is largely a decision as to the project's degree of autonomy from the existing organization. This can vary from zero autonomy (total integration) to total autonomy (the fully projectized structure).

We suggest that a rational decision-making process regarding the choice of a project organization includes the following steps:

Exhibit 7-8. Decision table for the choice of project organization.

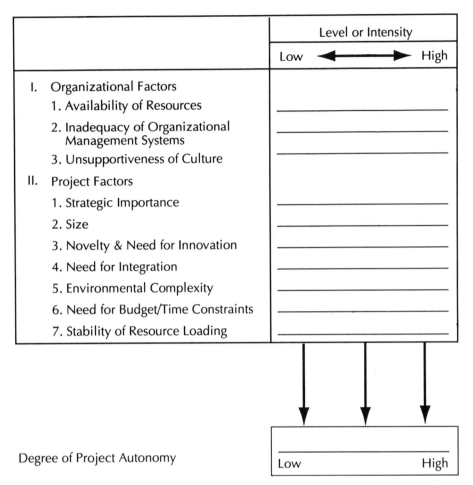

1. Using the decision table presented in Exhibit 7-8 to evaluate the organizational contextual factors and the project factors.
2. Taking all these factors into consideration, making a subjective judgment as to the desired level of project autonomy.
3. Keeping in mind the desired level of autonomy and the factors that have influenced this judgment the most, making a decision as to whether a separate unit should be set up to manage the new project or not. This decision must be based on an evaluation of the existing structure. If the existing structure is:
    ▸ A projectized structure, the question is usually irrelevant as the organization regularly establishes new units for its new projects. Only in cases where the factors on the decision table are evaluated as very low should a new unit not be established.
    ▸ A matrix structure, projects requiring a moderate level of autonomy are normally integrated into the matrix because a project in a matrix structure

has a moderate level of autonomy. Projects that score very high on the factors in the decision table would require very high levels of autonomy and should be set up as separate units. These would normally be exceptional cases. Similarly, a project that scores very low on the factors in the decision table might be assigned directly to the relevant functional department. Here again, this would be an exceptional case.

▸ A functional structure, projects that require moderate to high levels of autonomy should have separate units set up to manage them.

By following this three-step decision process, the organization can logically analyze a very complex situation and arrive at practical answers to the questions, "Should a separate structure be set up to manage the new project?" and "How much autonomy should be given to the new project?"

The level of project autonomy can be influenced by a large number of organizational parameters. Management must make a series of decisions regarding these parameters in such a way that the net effect produces the desired level of project autonomy. Exhibit 7-9 summarizes the most important parameters, which include:

▸ *Project manager selection.* If top management comes to the conclusion that a given project requires a substantial amount of autonomy, perhaps the most critical decision is the choice of the right project manager. That person must be able and willing to function in an autonomous mode and assume full responsibility for project decisions and full accountability for project performance. The selection criteria would

Exhibit 7-9. Organizational parameters regarding degree of project autonomy.

▸ Project manager selection
  − Ability and willingness to manage the project in an autonomous mode

▸ Project manager's role & status
  − Percentage of time assigned to the project
  − Reporting level in the organization and access to top management
  − Degree of responsibility for managing external and internal interfaces

▸ Project manager's control over resources
  − Proportion of human resources fully dedicated to the project
  − Control over selection and management of resources
  − Control over budget allocations and expenditures

▸ Project manager's control over project content
  − Authority on technical choices
  − Control over content of mandates assigned inside and outside the parent organization
  − Control over changes in project content

▸ Project manager's degree of operational autonomy
  − Project-specific management & control systems, procedures, etc.
  − Project resources located together
  − Physical separation from parent organization

then include experience, training, personality, and attitudes congruent with a project management culture.

▸ *Project manager's role and status.* If a project manager is assigned full-time to a project, he or she has greater autonomy than if his or her time and attention must be shared with other priorities. In addition, if the project manager is to operate with a high degree of autonomy, he or she should report directly to the highest possible level in the hierarchy or have direct access to upper management.

Finally, the greater the autonomy required by the project, the more pervasive and complete should be the project manager's authority and responsibility for the management of external interfaces (client and other stakeholders, suppliers, regulators, media, etc.) and for the coordination of various contributing departments within the parent organization. Any dilution of that authority would most probably result in added coordination requirements and organizational risk.

▸ *Project manager's control over resources.* The degree of project manager autonomy is largely determined by the degree of authority over resources. Although there are many possible indicators of that degree of authority, we believe that the following are generally the most useful.

- The proportion of human resources fully dedicated to the project under direct supervision of the project manager
- The project manager's degree of control over the resource selection process (internal and external) and over their management (job description, remuneration, evaluation)
- The project manager's control over the budget allocation process and the level of his or her discretionary power over procurement and authorization of expenditures

▸ *Project manager's control over project content.* The greater the project manager's control over the technical content of the project, the greater the autonomy of the project organization. This degree of control over project content can be determined by the following three indicators.

1. The degree of project manager control over technical decisions, and particularly over trade-offs
2. The degree of project manager control of the content of mandates assigned to various units of parent organization and of contracts allocated to other organizations
3. The degree of project manager control over changes in project content

▸ *Project manager's degree of operational autonomy.* This last organizational parameter deals mostly with the degree of project proximity to the parent organization in day-to-day operations. The project is more autonomous if:

- The project uses (or is allowed to use) its own management systems and procedures rather than the standard systems and procedures of the parent organization (project planning and control system, procurement procedures, etc.)
- Resources that make significant contributions to the project are physically located together to maximize project identification and minimize coordination efforts
- The project is physically separated from the parent organization

Implementing an appropriate level of autonomy for a project requires management to make a decision on each of these parameters.

The complete decision process requires that management assess the existing organizational structure, the organizational contextual factors, and the factors specific to the project. It must then make decisions as to whether or not a separate unit is to be set up to manage the project. And if this is done, it must decide on the appropriate level of autonomy for the project. In implementing the desired level of project autonomy, management must make a series of operational and policy decisions, each of which impacts on the level of autonomy that the project experiences. This decision process is illustrated in Exhibit 7-10.

The Decision Model in Action

To illustrate the application of this decision model, we refer to the case of a major utility where we recently used the model in choosing the appropriate organizational format for a very important project. The parent organization in question has a functional structure with a culture that is quite unsupportive of project management needs. Likewise, its management systems cannot adequately serve project needs in terms of planning, control, and general administration. The project is constrained by a severe shortage of the very specialized human resources required for the project as they are needed badly to keep the ongoing operations rolling effectively. The project has the following characteristics.

▸ *High strategic importance.* Technical failure could mean a major public catastrophe.

▸ *Medium to large project.* Total project cost will be around $200 million, and project duration is estimated at six years.

▸ *High need for innovation.* The project consists of replacing the present control system of a very large and complex power distribution network. The desired technology is not readily available on the market. Although several members of the project team participated in the design and implementation of the current system back in the early 1970s, the conceptual design of the new system is extremely complex and is based upon the very latest state of the art in both software and hardware and has yet to be implemented anywhere in the world.

▸ *High need for integration.* The project requires contributions from several technical departments, and these contributions are highly interdependent.

▸ *Medium to high environmental complexity.* The two main environmental factors relevant to this project are the number of external interfaces and the high level of dependency on suppliers. The project impacts on a very large number of various types of users who have to be involved in the design and implementation process. Because of the large number of stakeholders and the visibility the press has given to the shortcomings of the present system, the project is politically very sensitive. The project is in a situation of high dependency in its relations with its suppliers because it relies heavily on highly specialized consulting services and software/hardware producers and because the number of potential suppliers is extremely small. In

Exhibit 7-10. Decision process on degree of project autonomy.

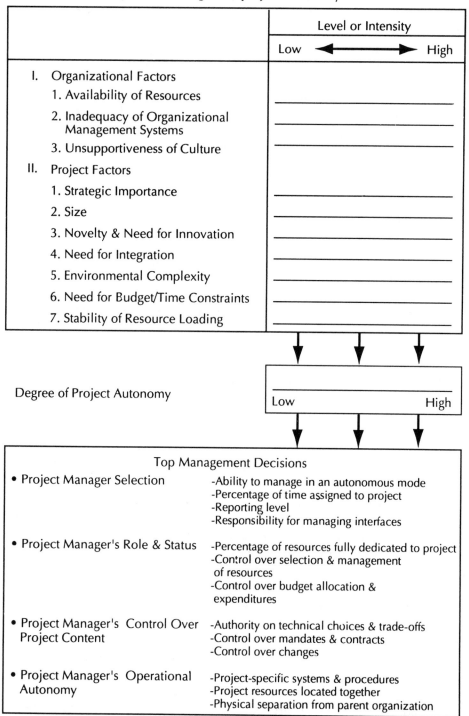

addition, environmental uncertainty is high because the whole industry is currently in a state of turmoil (incapacity to successfully terminate contracts, bankruptcies, mergers, etc.).

▸ *Medium budget and time constraints.* Although there is no magic deadline for the new system to be operational, time is an important factor as the risk of severe problems with the current system will increase significantly after the target completion date. The budget constraints are not critical for the time being, but as we are in a period of economic recession, cost issues get closer attention from top management.

▸ *Medium stability of resource loading.* The level of internal resources assigned to the project varies from phase to phase but the most critical resources (core project team) will be with the project for the entire six-year period.

As we can see below, the pattern of values for the various organizational and project factors leads to a nonequivocal solution: The parent organization needed to set up a project organization with a large degree of autonomy. But they have to solve the problem of the very limited number of specialized human resources. In setting up the project organization, management used the decision process shown in Exhibit 7-11 and took the following steps:

▸ They selected a project manager with a great deal of knowledge and experience; indeed, he was a key member of the project team for the design and implementation of the current system and was eager to take on this highly challenging assignment.

▸ The project manager was assigned full-time to the job and, although he is still reporting to the same functional boss, he was given the green light to communicate directly with top management when required. He was also given full responsibility for managing both internal and external interfaces.

▸ He was assigned a full project team under his direct supervision including several key technical contributors. He could get virtually any human resources he asked for and was given more authority than usual over budget allocations and expenditures subject to his boss's approval.

▸ He was not given full authority on technical choices as the new control system needs to be integrated with many other systems under the responsibility of various functional departments. On the other hand, he can exert considerable influence in all technical decisions. Furthermore, he has more or less full authority on negotiating the technical contents of mandates and contracts within his project.

▸ He set up a project-specific planning and control system but was not authorized to bypass the parent organization approval and administrative procedures. He was allowed to rent space in another building to accommodate the full project team as well as consultants working on the project.

▸ During the very early stages of the project, rare and specialized human resources were shared between the project team and the functional departments in the parent organization. This situation was judged as unsatisfactory for both the project and the functional departments. Therefore, for the next phases, the project was allowed to recruit its own resources from both the parent organization and the outside market. The functional departments also hired and trained new personnel to

Exhibit 7-11. Example of decision process on degree of project autonomy.

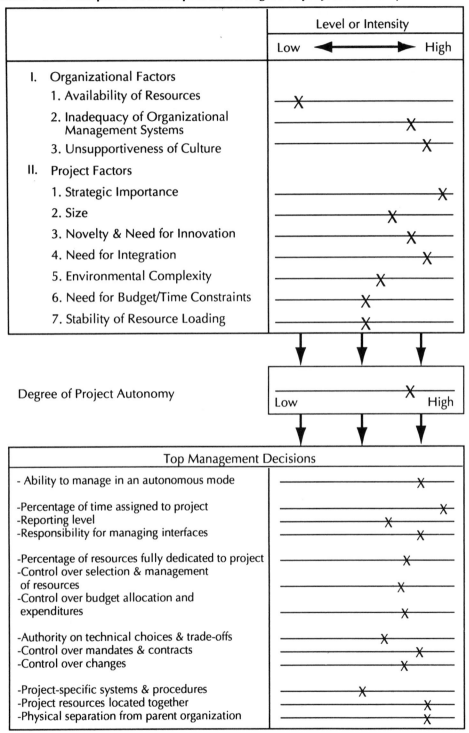

replace those who joined the project team. The hiring of full-time resources was justified by the project duration of six years and by the relatively constant level of effort required by the project.

Thus, the project organization is not completely autonomous from the parent organization, but nevertheless, it represents, for this organization, a major departure from the usual way of organizing and managing projects.

8

Flat, Flexible Structures: The Organizational Answer to Changing Times

Paul C. Dinsmore
Dinsmore Associates

Company organization structures that are purely functional or purely projectized are becoming relatively rare. Because of the pressure set off by constant external change, more commonly found are organizations with characteristics similar to the classic matrix formation used in managing projects. While these organizations may carry strong functional or project overtones, the interconnecting web of relationships and responsibilities characteristic of matrix philosophy is always present. This evolution has come about as companies have scrambled to survive and subsequently positioned themselves to gain competitive advantage.

This chapter discusses the evolution of matrix structures traditionally used for managing projects toward the FFS (flat, flexible structure), which is proposed as a companywide solution to deal with rapidly evolving change.

The change toward flatter, more flexible structures on a companywide basis is normally made through drastic organizational measures. These changes may be made all at once or over a period of time. Here are some common top management actions that contribute to creating these "leaner and meaner" organizations.

- Reducing middle management numbers at dramatic rates (downsizing to as much as one-third the previous number of managers)
- Cutting back the number of management levels by as much as 50 percent
- Giving importance to position titles and organization ranking
- Taking strong measures on a companywide basis to trim costs
- Injecting breakthrough technologies in information and communications into the organization
- Expecting professionals to perform more creative and dynamic roles

These actions represent pieces that compose the FFS organizational puzzle. Each contributes toward creating a more agile structure and more responsive organization. Yet making the change to the FFS is not an easy one.

What Is a Flat, Flexible Structure, Anyway?

Flat, flexible structures are organizations designed to deal with dynamic and complex situations through the delegation of responsibility to results-oriented participants who are charged with achieving high levels of quality and customer satisfaction. These structures are generally applied on a companywide basis. Matrix structures, on the other hand, although having similar characteristics, are generally applied in more restricted project settings.

The matrix structure and the FFS have things in common and things that set them apart. The commonalities far outshine the differences, yet there are enough differences to identify the organizations as distinct. Exhibit 8-1 compares the characteristics of the two structures.

Difficulties in Developing an FFS

Flat, flexible structures are an evolutionary thing and the trend is gaining ground, whether companies are in a traditional project-driven setting or simply in a customer-oriented organization trying to keep up with the times. This change means that the company faces dramatic organizational challenges. Here are some of the difficulties involved in developing an FFS on a companywide basis.

▸ Making the organizational change to the FFS means breaking old patterns, taking risks, creating new visions, and establishing commitment for organization members.

Exhibit 8-1. Matrix structure vs. flat, flexible structure.

Characteristics	Matrix Structure	Flat, Flexible Structure (FFS)
Optimizing resources	X	X
"Fuzzy" boundaries of responsibility	X	X
Adaptable to new situations	X	X
Companywide structure		X
Dual-focus project settings	X	
Conflict-prone	X	X
Consensus-based decision process	X	X
Requires training in managerial behavior	X	X
May be used in downsizing organizations		X
Synonymous with "lean and mean" organizations		X
Multiple-project ambiguous settings	X	X

▸ Although top management and direct, production-related employees favor "lean and mean" organizations, middle managers tend to resist the change.

▸ An FFS may not be applicable in all situations; a setting of change, ambiguity, and multiple projects is a prerequisite.

▸ Tools used in an FFS call for multiproject planning, scheduling, and tracking capabilities that can adjust to constantly shifting scenarios. Such capabilities must exist in the company.

▸ Moves to the FFS are not always crowned with glory. Failure results when structures are improperly designed or training is inadequate.

Facilitators in Developing an FFS

To make an FFS work, it takes more than isolated management moves. The change must be made within a framework of organizational philosophy. A list of facilitating policies, characteristics, and actions follows.

▸ In an effective FFS, the customer is brought as close as possible to the organization so that the final user's expectations are met.

▸ Artificial intelligence may offer a means for reaching a new quantum level in flexible, agile organizations.

▸ To maintain overall performance standards, the successful FFS needs to operate under some form of total quality management program.

▸ Beginning stages in the life of a complex project are particularly critical; therefore, free-flowing structures need to be put in place early on?

▸ Empowerment (the acceptance and prudent yet energetic use of delegated power) is needed for an FFS to be successful.

▸ An FFS requires coupling work breakdown structures for the various projects into overall corporate strategies.

▸ A corporate policy establishing clear criteria on risk management takes on particular importance in an FFS.

Changing to More Flexible Organization Forms

Changing to a flexible organization mode is a project in itself that calls for management through various stages, whether it be to the matrix in a traditional project setting or to the FFS on a widescale corporate setting. Here is a summary of the stages that need to be managed.

1. *Initial awareness.* In the "kickoff" stage, the participant learns of the new organizational concept and becomes aware of the ideas. Once this stage has been achieved, future references to the proposal are processed more rapidly.

2. *Cognitive understanding.* Here the person involved not only recognizes the new organizational concept but is able to discuss and explain the basic ideas.

3. *In-depth understanding.* In this stage, the understanding is internalized, and the participant is capable of analyzing situations and proposing solutions.

4. *Conceptual acceptance.* At this point the psychological barrier to acceptance is

broken. The participant not only understands that the new organizational concept is valid and good but also fully believes in it.

5. *Individual behavior change.* The participant now demonstrates visible signs of operating in a new organizational mode and begins demonstrating changed behavior.

6. *Organizational behavior change.* Here the group involved, influenced by individual behavior, starts to act in ways different from the past, consistent with the new philosophies absorbed by the individuals.

The change to a flat, flexible structure calls for a "management-over-time" approach. The process must respect the phenomenon of resistance to change and the time factor involved for people to absorb and internalize new concepts. Each of these phases calls for specific action to nurture along the change process.

Practical tools and activities are required for ensuring that the proposed organization change passes through all the necessary phases and achieves behavior change on an organizational level. These tools and activities are the change initiators that make the proposed mutation come about. Exhibit 8-2 shows some of the specific tools and activities used at specific stages to facilitate the change process toward more flexible forms.

Exhibit 8-2. Tools and activities that facilitate the change process toward more flexible structures.

	Phases of Organizational Change					
	1 Initial Awareness	2 Cognitive Understanding	3 In-Depth Understanding	4 Conceptual Acceptance	5 Individual Behavior Change	6 Organizational Behavior Change
An organizational behavior change plan	X					
Setting examples	X	X	X	X	X	X
One-on-one coaching			X	X		
Lectures and expert presentations	X	X				
Roundtable discussions		X	X			
Meetings	X	X	X	X	X	X
Promotional campaigns	X	X				
Structured seminars		X	X	X		
Planning workshops	X	X				
External facilitators/experts	X			X		
Programmed reading	X	X	X			
Activities that elicit involvement	X	X	X	X	X	X
Videos/Cumputer-based training	X	X				

It takes persistence and the right combination of change-making facilitators to achieve the goals of organizational change. Each organizational setting calls for a tailormade approach.

Conclusion

The FFS approach expands the free-flow of the traditional matrix concept to a corporate level in search of establishing a rapid response to the expanding customer-driven market. The intent in establishing the FFS is much the same as that of the matrix organization: to create a more responsive and resource-efficient organization. Although the FFS and matrix organizations are not implemented on the same scale or for the same purpose, the culture that results from implementing each is basically identical.

Both the FFS and matrix are effective to the extent that they are handled as behavioral change model. When that concept is grasped, the move to less structured, more agile organizational models becomes a simpler task, involving adjusting employees' behavioral patterns to the requirements of "leaner and meaner" organizations. Once the organizational behavior has been adjusted, the "structure" itself loses some of its relevance. The organization begins to follow the newly defined behavior, not because it has been so "designed" structurally, but because organizational change toward a more flexible form has taken place. This trend toward flat, flexible structures calls for expansion of the traditional matrix concept to application on a companywide level and the use of all the necessary organization change tools for the company to make the transition to a more dynamic organization.

Bibliography

Graham, Robert J. *Project Management as if People Mattered.* Bala Cynwyd, Penn.: Primavera Press, 1989.

INTERNET. *Management by Projects.* 10th INTERNET World Congress Proceedings, Vol. 1, Vienna, Manz Verteg., 1990.

Section IV
Planning the Details of Project Management

9

Paradigms for Planning Productive Projects

Richard E. Westney
Spectrum Consultants International, Inc.

Projects are the method by which organizations change, improve, introduce new products, and ensure competitiveness. If a company fails to perform project work well, its eventual demise is virtually ensured. Project planning is therefore a manager's job. A manager must make certain that the organization and systems are in place to ensure project success, that problems have been identified and corrective actions taken. Yet many managers who should and could plan their projects do not do so. Instead they delegate that responsibility to others.

Managers who delegate too much planning responsibility are unilaterally disarming themselves of one of the most powerful weapons in the project manager's arsenal. Are they irresponsible? Or are they just unaware of the numerous new paradigms for planning that are provided by personal computer programs?

What are these new paradigms for planning? This chapter describes the numerous ways that today's managers can take advantage of personal computer software to gain the power of computerized planning in a way that is appropriate for a manager's use.

Planning: Key to Project Management

It's no secret that success in project management is often the result of thorough and thoughtful planning. Most current studies, such as the research conducted by the Construction Industry Institute, emphasize the payoff in project performance from early, effective planning. The planning process provides the basis for strategic and tactical decision making, as well as the most effective tools available for communication of job responsibilities, timely problem identification, and control of progress and productivity.

So, effective managers are also effective project managers, and effective project managers understand and use today's management-oriented planning methods. But planning—predicting future actions and problems—is inherently difficult, some managers would even say unnatural. Everyone much prefers to deal with the certainty of the here-and-now to the uncertainty of tomorrow. In response to this problem, planning methods have evolved such that a manager can now choose from a variety of ways of visualizing the future and translating that vision into specific planning data. These methods make use of today's interactive personal computer interface to give a manager easy and effective ways to plan. They are the diverse paradigms that are discussed in this chapter.

What Is a Planning Paradigm?

A *paradigm* may be defined as a pattern or model by which we think about things or perform tasks. A *planning paradigm*, then, is a pattern or method for defining a project in terms of tasks, durations, resources, and costs. Software, by its very nature, encourages a formal, standardized method for doing something and is therefore a frequent example of a paradigmatic approach to a management or technical problem.

While a paradigm for planning may imply rigidity and lack of flexibility (often the kiss of death for a management method), with planning paradigms this need not be the case. Not only does planning software provide different paradigms for planning, it often provide them within the same program. This means that each person dealing with the plan can use the paradigm that suits him or her best; while the integrity of the data is maintained at all times.

Planning From Diverse Perspectives

A manager's interest in planning a project may focus on one or more of the following variables:

- ▸ *Time.* The schedule of activities that comprise the project
- ▸ *Resources.* The people, equipment, and materials required to perform the work
- ▸ *Assignments.* When and how each resource is to be assigned

The planning paradigms provided by personal computers today are defined accordingly. The view a manager chooses often depends on his or her role in the organization as well as his or her priorities. They include:

- ▸ Task planning
- ▸ Resource planning
- ▸ Assignment scheduling

Each of these three planning paradigms is described below.

Task Planning

The manager who focuses on task planning is most interested in defining what work is to be done and when it is to be done. Personal computer software today provides the following paradigms for task planning:

- Outlining
- Work breakdown structure
- Interactive network drawing
- Bar charting

These task planning paradigms all attempt to provide an easy way to think as a planner: to define a project in terms of a sequence of required tasks.

Planning by Outlining

Outlining is perhaps the easiest and most intuitive method available for planning. It closely follows the way most managers think: Define a problem in broad terms and then refine different aspects as appropriate. Perhaps the greatest advantage of the outlining paradigm is that it helps a person get started in defining the plan: Once started, the rest seems easy.

To illustrate the outlining method, let us imagine a project to develop a management system. The planning of such a project might begin with an outline like this:

Phase I: Define Requirements
Phase II: Define System Specification
Phase III: Develop and Test Programs
Phase IV: Document, Test, and Train Users

In this example, each heading represents a phase of the project. Headings could also be used to group information by area, group, or system. At this point, headings are input with only a title; no other data need be added.

Now each heading is defined in more detail by adding subtasks beneath each heading as follows:

Phase I: Define Requirements
- Interview users
- Review existing practices
- Define problem areas
- Define hardware and software constraints

Phase II: Define System Specification
- Define input and output
- Define required processing
- Evaluate hardware and programming options
- Prepare report and review with users

Phase III: Develop and Test Programs
- Program user interface
- Program database
- Program output drivers
- Test modules
- Test full system
- Beta test with users
- Incorporate user comments

Phase IV: Document, Test, and Train Users
- ▸ Prepare user guide
- ▸ Install systems
- ▸ Conduct training classes

As these subtasks are defined, the software "rolls up" the data to summarize it in the heading. As a result, the duration, work-hours, and costs of the heading are the sum of the total for all its subtasks.

The outline can be expanded into additional sublevels of detail as the project progresses and more information becomes available or as various tasks need to be defined in more detail.

An important feature of outlining is that it allows the plan to be represented at different levels of detail. For example, a management-level presentation would show only the main headings, a presentation for discussion of Phase I would show only the details of Phase I, and a detailed planning meeting would use a display in which all headings and tasks are shown.

In addition, outlining programs allow headings and tasks to be input in any order that they occur to the planner and then be moved up and down or in and out on the outline. The input data for each task may include the duration, resource requirements, costs, and descriptive notes.

The next step in outlining is to define the constraints (i.e., dependencies) between tasks and headings. This is also usually done on the outline format by highlighting the predecessor and successor tasks. Note that the ability to define constraints between headings (e.g., all the subtasks for Phase I must be complete before Phase II can begin) often results in a simpler plan with fewer constraints.

Once the outline is complete, the planning process proceeds in the manner of traditional critical path method analysis. Most software presents a network diagram and bar chart derived from the outline data.

Planning With a Work Breakdown Structure

Unlike the other planning paradigms, the work breakdown structure (WBS) concentrates on the physical systems and components of the project and uses these as an aid in defining the tasks to be performed. The WBS method requires the planner to view the project in terms of its physical components and to break these down into ever-increasing detail until each component is of manageable size. The tasks necessary to create that component are then defined, and these tasks become the basis of the plan.

To illustrate the use of a WBS, imagine that you are the manager of a major program to create a new fighter aircraft. This is a project of such size and complexity that it might be impractical to simply start planning task-by-task. Therefore, we might begin with a WBS that simply defines the project in terms of its major systems as follows:

Project: FX100 Fighter Plane
        Major Systems:
                Propulsion
                Airframe

Avionics
Weapons

These systems are still too large for planning, so we might take each major system and break it into components.

Project: FX100 Fighter Plane
    Major System: Airframe
        Components:
            Fuselage
            Wings
            Empennage
            Landing Gear

The analysis might continue in this way until enough detail has been reached to facilitate the planning of tasks. For example:

Project: FX100 Fighter Plane
    Major System: Airframe
        Components:
            Wings
        Tasks:
            Define Area, Sweep, Aspect Ratio
            Select Airfoil
            Test in Wind-Tunnel
            Fabricate Prototype
            Stress-Test Prototype
            Prepare Shop Drawings
            Manufacture Wings

Exhibit 9-1 shows an example of how a portion of this WBS might look.

Many users of the WBS also find this paradigm to be useful in defining a coding system whose hierarchical structure is similar to that of the WBS itself. For example, the activity "Select Airfoil" could have a code that identifies it as:

Task number 2
in the Component "Wings"
which is part of the System "Airframe"
which belongs to the Project FX100 Fighter Plane

These WBS codes are very useful in the database operations found in planning software. The codes can be used in conjunction with a "filter" command (i.e., a selection criterion) to select, for presentation and analysis, only those data that are of interest. For example, the WBS code for the FX100 project could be used to extract just the task data that involves work on designing the wings.

Planning With Interactive Network Drawing

The traditional critical path method (CPM) of planning seeks to define a plan in terms of a network diagram—i.e., a diagram showing each task and the constraints

Exhibit 9-1. Work breakdown structure.

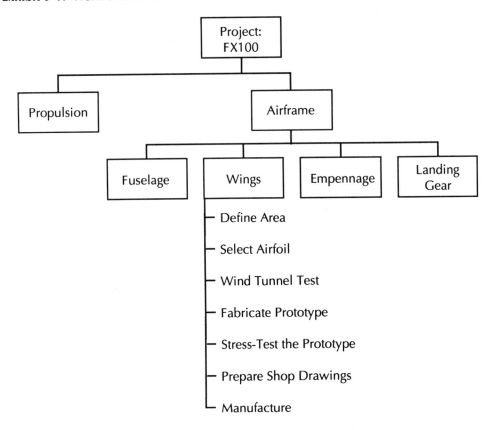

between them. Network diagrams may be drawn in "arrow" or "precedence" formats. For those managers or planners who are accustomed to thinking in this way, many planning programs offer the capability to use a mouse to place tasks on the diagram and actually to draw the constraints between them. This type of planning paradigm is enhanced considerably by the use of a graphical user interface that makes the process of drawing easy and intuitive. For an example of a network plan drawn with a mouse, see Exhibit 9-2.

A good rule for effective planning with networks is to keep them simple. When the total number of activities exceeds fifty, the value of the network as a tool for communication diminishes greatly. Networks can be kept simple, even for very large projects, through the use of subprojects—a capability found in most planning software.

Planning With a Bar Chart

Everyone who has been concerned in any way with projects and schedules is used to seeing the bar chart (also known as Gantt chart) representation of a schedule.

Exhibit 9-2. Network diagram in precedence format.

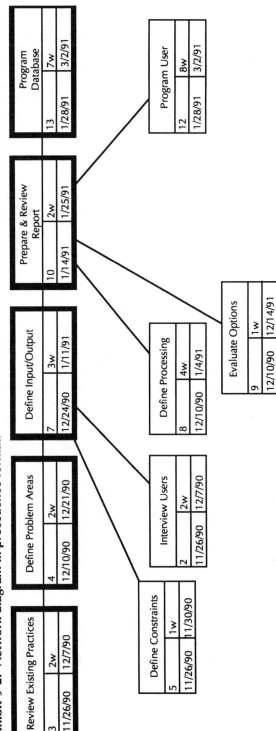

Prepared using Microsoft Project software from Microsoft Corporation, Redmond, Washington.

This is such a familiar format that many planning programs provide it as a paradigm for planning, even though a bar chart does not usually show the essence of a plan: the dependencies between tasks.

In the bar chart paradigm, the planner defines tasks and their dependencies and sees the result instantly represented in the form of a bar chart schedule. A network diagram, showing the dependencies, is usually available as an alternative view.

Bar chart planning is also aided considerably by the use of the graphical user interface that allows the length, position, and appearance of the bars to be varied easily. Bar charting is also frequently displayed together with outlining. (See Exhibit 9-3.)

Resource Planning

Plans and schedules are useless unless the resources are made available to do the work—when and where required. Managers therefore rely on resource planning to define:

- ▸ Realistic project schedules—consistent with the organization's ability to provide resources
- ▸ Work schedules for different resources
- ▸ Organizational plans—hiring or restructuring

Resource planning information is most commonly represented by a resource histogram. (See Exhibit 9-4.) The resource histogram can be thought of as a schedule of resource requirements, just as a bar chart is a schedule of tasks. Any change in the task schedule results in immediate change to the resource histogram, and vice versa. Therefore, it is also useful to view the project as a combination bar chart–histogram. Some programs allow manipulation of the bar chart so that one can see the effect on the histogram.

When working with resource histograms and bar chart schedules, the technique of resource leveling is useful. This allows the manager to input the limits of availability of a resource and have the program calculate a schedule that is achievable without exceeding those limits. Today's programs not only carry out the leveling calculation, they also show the delay (if any) on each task caused by the lack of resources. Since the result of resource leveling is not optimized—that is, there may be extensive periods of unused capacity—the manager usually interacts with the program to experiment with different scenarios until an acceptable solution is found.

Assignment Scheduling

When a manager considers the tasks that must be performed, the resources that are to perform the tasks, and the schedule for doing the tasks, he or she is actually thinking in terms of assignment scheduling. We can define assignment scheduling as defining:

which specific *resource*
will perform which specific *task*
using which *skill*

Exhibit 9-3. Bar chart schedule.

ID	Name	Duration	Quarter (Nov Dec)	1st Quarter (Jan Feb Mar)	2nd Quarter (Apr May Jun)	3rd Quarter (Jul Aug Sep)	4th Quarter (Oct Nov Dec)	1s (Jan)
1	Phase I: Define Requirements	25.38ed						
2	Interview Users	2w						
3	Review Existing PRA	2w						
4	Define Problem Area	2w						
5	Define Constraints	1w						
6	Phase II: Define Specifications	46.38ed						
7	Define Input/Output	3w						
8	Define Processing	4w						
9	Evaluated Options	1w						
10	Prepare & Review Report	2w						
11	Phase III: Develop & Test	200.38ed						
12	Program User Interest	8w						
13	Program Database	7w						
14	Program Output Drive	4w						
15	Test Modules	5w						
16	Test Full System	4w						
17	Beta Test	6w						
18	Incorporate User Comments	3w						
19	Phase IV: Document, Train	39.38ed						
20	Prepare User Guide	4w						
21	Install System	3w						
22	Conduct Training	2w						

Project:
Date: 12/2/90

Critical	Milestone
Noncritical	Summary
Progress	Total Slack

Prepared using Microsoft Project software from Microsoft Corporation, Redmond, Washington.

Exhibit 9-4. Resource histogram.

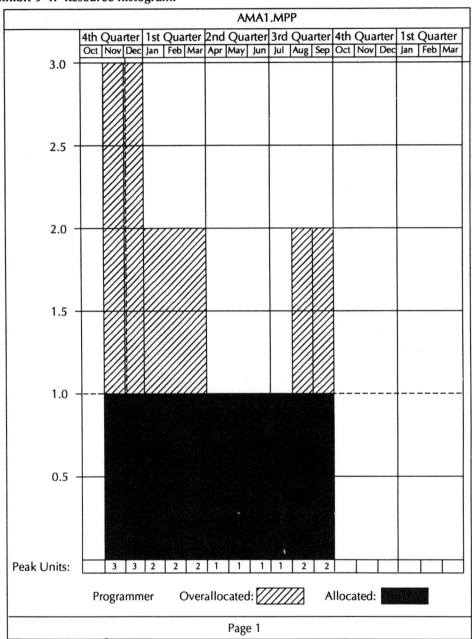

Prepared using Microsoft Project software from Microsoft Corporation, Redmond, Washington.

at what level of *effort*
between which *dates*

Although methods using the CPM can address this problem through resource leveling as described above, they cannot determine an optimum way to make specific assignments. Nor can they reflect real world complexities such as the ability of a resource to have more than one skill with different levels of productivity in each skill.

A new methodology has therefore been developed for addressing this problem. Called assignment modeling, it uses artificial intelligence (AI) techniques to model the way a resource manager makes assignments. By so doing, it provides an ability to define an optimum assignment schedule, something that is not possible otherwise.

Assignment modeling, as seen in Exhibit 9-5, provides a complement to traditional critical path methods of project planning. The CPM assumes that dependent tasks are being planned and that the planner/manager has responsibility for a broad number of diverse tasks. In a matrix organization, however, these tasks must often be managed by a functional or resource manager—and neither the functional manager nor the people actually doing the work are under the direct control of the project manager. The functional or resource manager often finds that project management programs are not particularly helpful, since the resource manager's view of his or her workload is apt to be one of many parallel, independent tasks.

This classic problem of matrix organizations is alleviated by assignment modeling, which is primarily a tool for the functional or resource manager. As such, it helps the resource manager to be better able to use resources efficiently and therefore satisfy project requirements.

The AI aspect of assignment modeling works through a process of ranking. Tasks are defined in terms of the efforts required by each skill and are given deadlines and priorities. Resources are defined in terms of their availability (which may be limited

(text continues on page 130)

Exhibit 9-5. Assignment modeling.

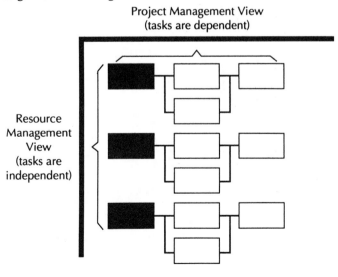

Exhibit 9-6. Resource summary bar chart.

Erudite Corporation
Resource Summary Bar Chart – Daily
Report No.: 1-1 for all resources

Date: 26 June 1990
Time: 10:05
Page: 1

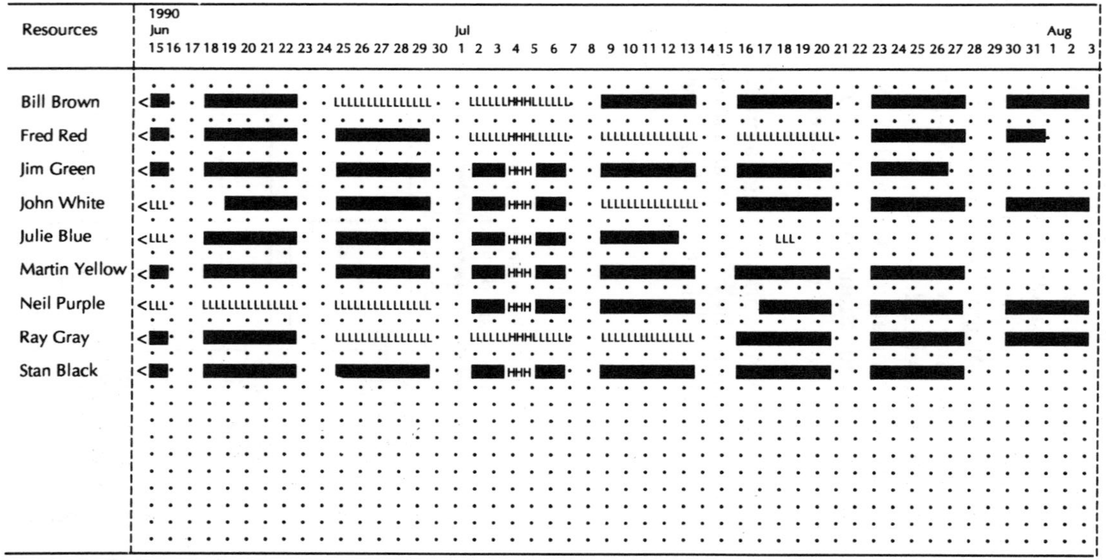

Legend:
■ = Resource assigned
L = Leave   H = National holiday
< Bar displayed starts before beginning of chart
> Bar displayed finishes after end of chart
  as of date (06/07/90)
1 character (*, X etc) represents 0.33 days

Sagacity

Erudite Corporation

Prepared using Sagacity software from Erudite Corporation, Burlingame, California.

Exhibit 9-7. Task summary bar chart.

Erudite Corporation
Task Summary Bar Chart – Design Group
Report no.: 1-2 for all tasks

Tasks	1990 Jun	Jul	Aug	Sep	Oct	Nov	Dec	1991 Jan	Feb	Mar	Apr	May	Jun	Jul	Aug
Dg Brake Recall															
Supervising															
Dg Study Steer															
Tg Test Brake															
Tg Design Brake															
Dg Design Steer															
Dg Test Steering															
Tg Suspen Recall															
Tg Optim. Brake															
Tg Optim. Study															
Tg Study Brake 08															

Legend: ■ Task assigned
< Bar displayed starts before beginning of chart
> Bar displayed finishes after end of chart
as of date (06/07/90)
1 character (■, L, H) represents 3 days

Sagacity   Erudite Corporation

Prepared using Sagacity software from Erudite Corporation, Burlingame, California.

by vacations, transfers, etc.), their billing rate, their skills, and their capability at each skill. The inference engine then proceeds to rank the skill requirements of each task in order of importance. Resources that may provide the skill to the most important task are then identified and ranked in order of desirability. Reassignment may be necessary so that skilled, efficient resources are always put on the most important tasks. The calculation proceeds in this way until all resources are assigned and all task requirements met.

Since AI cannot take the place of human judgment—and this is especially true in the complex arena of matching resources to tasks—the assignment modeling method provides two ways for the resource manager to insert his or her own judgment. The first way in which the manager can affect the AI calculation is in the definition of preferences that allow the AI rules to be tailored to different situations. For example, one manager might make assignments so that the most projects are completed in the least time, whereas another might want to accomplish the most work for the least cost. The second way in which the manager affects the solution is through direct interaction. This could include specifying the resources to work on a task, locking in one or more resources once the task begins, defining overtime or weekend work, and changing scheduled vacations and leaves.

The result of the assignment modeling calculation is an assignment schedule that can be displayed graphically as seen in Exhibits 9-6 and 9-7. Thus, assignment planning provides a new paradigm for planning from an assignment perspective.

10

Work Structuring

Darrel G. Hubbard
Management Analysis Company, Inc.

Managers, like craftspeople, require tools to perform their work. Craftspeople use physical tools and skill; managers use administrative processes and techniques. In management, as in a craft, improper or inept use of a tool creates lost time and wasted resources, while masterful use of a tool maximizes resource application and the efficient use of time. Many of the business management techniques that allow us to cope in a changing environment and that simultaneously support the need for control by management are based on one premise: Break "it" down (whatever "it" may be) into manageable pieces. Founded on the concept of cascading analysis, this management technique takes and dissects the entire "it" into successively lower levels of detail until management control is possible and, in most processes, until the level of breakdown can be quantified. This analytical concept is used in many project management areas, including:

- Business management: Management by objectives
- Administrative management: Plan, policy, and procedure hierarchy development
- Project control: Work breakdown structuring
- Software management: Structured systems design

A project is goal- or objective-oriented and is defined by the technical or operational objectives to be achieved. It is a specific task that is unique, complex, time-limited, and resource-limited and is composed of many smaller interrelated tasks. The key to organizing and interrelating these tasks is structuring the work. One of the most useful management skills, therefore, is the ability to organize the many tasks required in any process or project, and one of the first project management tools to be used in project planning is work structuring. In project management tools to be used in project planning is work structuring. In project management this involves taking an entire job—the project—and breaking the work effort down into small, manageable segments such as work packages, tasks, and activities.

Work structure planning in a project environment can best be described as the function of (1) selecting the project objectives; (2) establishing a predetermined course of action; and (3) creating the structures of policies, plans, procedures, and work tasks necessary to achieve the objectives within a forecasted environment. The degree of detail required for this depends upon the complexity of the project and the level of management visibility chosen to ensure adequate project control.

Work structure planning is a decision-making process because it involves choosing among alternatives. Work structuring serves to organize the project by defining all the processes and tasks that must be performed in the conception, design, development, fabrication, construction, and testing of the project, hardware, software, facilities, or services. The work structure is prepared at the earliest possible point in the project life cycle. At the same time, formal change control procedures are established to ensure the project's currency and accuracy. This process eliminates the need for personnel to be able immediately to comprehend and structure complex problems involving interacting factors while they are in the process of performing work.

The work structure must fulfill all the work definition and control needs, while at the same time accommodating the numerous business and organizational factors of a competitive environment. To be successful at this process, project managers must understand why work structures are prepared; what benefits work structures provide; what effect business influences have; how and by whom work structures are developed; and how work structures can be used by project and functional managers for effective work scope planning, performance measurement, and change control.

Why Are Work Structures Prepared?

For a project to be manageable and controllable, planning documentation is necessary to describe the intent of the project and to identify the actions necessary to accomplish the project objectives. This documentation includes not only plans and procedures, but also the work structures.

The first step in planning any project is defining the work to be accomplished and the pieces of the project that must be managed. No realistic overall project plan is possible without first developing a work structure that is detailed enough to provide meaningful identification of all project tasks. This work structure is more than an element of the project plan: It is the framework upon which the project is built. Therefore, the work structure is usable from the start to the finish of the project for planning, tracking, and reconciliation. The other elements of the project plan are produced based on this work structure.

The work structure is a product- and goal-oriented work task structure, as opposed to the traditional functional organization, production code of accounts, or similar breakdowns for scope and cost, which use completely separate work task planning and scheduling on an activity or other basis. In structuring the work, a project is progressively subdivided into smaller increments of work until a manageable task for planning and control purposes is reached. The reason for this subdivision of effort is simple: Projects are subdivided for purposes of control. Project control therefore becomes synonymous with the integration of tasks, where the project manager must act as the integrator using the work structure as the common framework.

Project management requires effective and precise communication of information throughout all phases of the project and with all involved personnel. Better information at all levels results in a more effective management effort; this in turn leads to a more successful project. This distribution of information requires that all project work be defined and broken down into performable pieces for which the scope is known, the cost can be determined, and the schedule can be established.

The successful accommodation of both project and corporate objectives requires a structured plan with statements of work that define the entire work effort and assign the work responsibility for each task to a specific performing organizational element. Work definition and structuring is the single most important process in project plan development. Because the work is broken down into smaller elements, there is a greater probability that every major and minor activity will be accounted for. Whenever work is structured, understood, easily identifiable, and within the capabilities of the staff, a high degree of confidence exists that the objective can be reached.

Benefits of Work Definition and Structuring

As a management tool, the work structure provides several benefits. First, it allows total project work to be structured as a summation of subdivided elements. This is accomplished by:

- Uniquely identifying and hierarchically relating the tasks, services, hardware and software products, and facilities needed to accomplish project objectives
- Describing detailed tasks required for engineering, licensing, research, development, construction, installation, demonstration, operation, or production of the facility, unit, plant, major items, or product
- Defining the relationship between the elements

The work structure establishes responsibility for all work. This is done by:

- Assigning responsibility for accomplishing work structure elements to specific performing organizations and individuals
- Identifying responsible organizations for each work structure element and thereby preventing gaps in responsibility assignments

Planning, budgeting, and scheduling is facilitated by:

- Providing a method for clear definition of the project scope early in the project life cycle
- Linking objectives and work to resources in a logical manner and providing a basis for allocation of resources
- Interrelating scope, cost, schedule, and productivity on a work structuring basis, thereby enabling scope, cost, and schedule to be integrated
- Helping to identify work requiring special attention, such as replanning or additional breakdown

Performance measurements are obtained by:

- Making the structure the basis for meaningful schedule and cost status reporting, monitoring, and coordination, thereby ensuring that all work to be done can be compared to a well-defined baseline

▸ Using the structure for the orderly summarization of work performance to selected levels of consolidation

Communication and information reporting are facilitated by:

▸ Helping all participants to understand the project clearly during the initial project stages by means of the work structure development process
▸ Using the work structure as the basis upon which all communication between information systems is established, and allowing for written correspondence with reference to a single applicable work structure element
▸ Using the work structure whenever project information is collected or issued to ensure that all information collected, reported, and forecasted has a common meaning, regardless of the source of the information
▸ Establishing an effective basis on which to establish communications systems, policies, and procedures

Thus, a properly selected, designed, and developed work structure, with its codes and statements of work, supplies the common basis for all scope, cost, schedule, and productivity information and forms the foundation for quality project management for any project. The work structure provides the common communications link, the common language, and the device whereby diverse users can freely communicate from the beginning of the project to its completion.

Successful Work Structures

Why do some work structures provide the expected benefit while others do not? What factors have contributed to the success of many work structures? A review of the literature and lessons learned from various projects provide the answer. The most common factors leading to success can be divided into business management factors and project management factors.

Business Management Factors

The business management factors leading to success are as follows:

▸ Project objectives are clear or well defined by senior management.
▸ Practical assessments of realistic requirements and constraints are prepared.
▸ Personnel with training, practice, or experience in work structuring are involved.
▸ Task descriptions are required, thereby providing the structure elements with work scope definition.
▸ Structure is prepared before work begins.
▸ Work product end-item orientation of the work structure is not confused by introducing company functions, organizations, or financial accounts.
▸ Work structure development is not constrained or driven by the finance system.

Project Management Factors

The project management factors leading to success are as follows:

- ▸ Project objectives are clarified and refined.
- ▸ Development is by a project team composed of those who manage and perform the work and not by a single project individual or an administrative staff.
- ▸ Adequate time is allowed for development, and task-coding is well conceived.
- ▸ Developers are concerned with the structure, ensure that it has all the work elements, and provide the necessary and sufficient levels of task breakdown required for control.
- ▸ Work structure change control is adequate and prohibits mixing old and new scope in the same element.

To emulate these success factors and to create a work structure useful for management, the work structure must be planned and developed in a managed, structured, and systematic approach.

Work Structure Design and Development

Building a work structure is an art rather than a science and is based upon experience, techniques, and needs. As previously stated, work structuring uses the work breakdown technique for subdividing a total project into its component elements. The project is broken down level by level into subprojects and finally into tasks, where a task is a single, identifiable job with clearly defined start and finish times and a unique task description called a statement of work.

The work structuring process produces a multilevel task-oriented structure that defines, organizes, and graphically displays the work required to achieve the commitments and end objectives of the project. Each level becomes progressively more specific about the work to be accomplished. As shown in Exhibit 10-1, the basic requirement for the configuration of the structure is that it must be in pyramid format; in other words, the lower-level elements must relate to and logically sum up to one, and only one, next higher element. A project's products may be hardware (e.g., facilities, steam generators), services (e.g., plant operation, test and evaluation, project management), data (e.g., technical reports, engineering data, management data), or other quantified objectives. Work definition and structuring serve as the unifying theme between these products and the project objectives. It reflects ordering of the detailed products and the work to be accomplished, relates these elements to each other and to the project's prime objective, and provides the conceptual framework for planning and controlling the project work.

Work structures are hardware- or product-oriented, but not always end product–oriented. For example, the breakdown includes products that are undoubtedly end products, such as equipment and facilities. The work structure includes level-of-effort tasks that result in the end products. It also includes "products" such as licensing, quality assurance, project administration, and research. For a successful work structure, the design and development must consider a number of factors, which are discussed in the rest of this chapter.

Exhibit 10-1. Work breakdown structure pyramid.

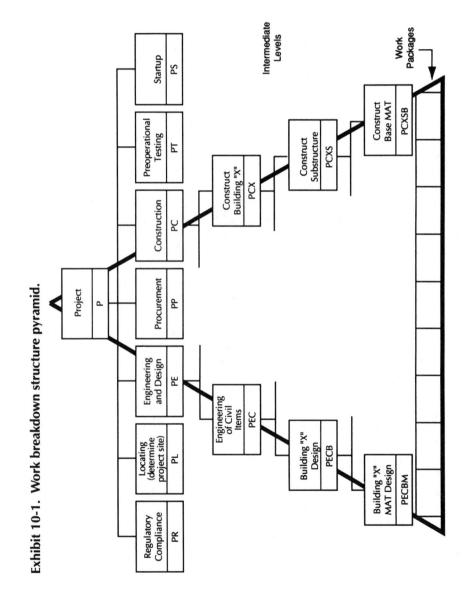

Business Influences

Business influences affect the development of a project work structure more than they affect any other area of project planning and control. Business factors that influence selecting and creating a work structure include various needs for assigning performance, performance measurement, desired level of client/owner visibility versus performer's needs, required degree of control, and required amount of cost identification. Other business factors that influence the framework of the work structure include project phases and project type or a mixture of project types. As various factors are added, the complexity of the methodologies required to develop a work structure increase. These items are reviewed and analyzed, and their influence on the configuration and content of the work structure is established.

Project Objectives

The primary prerequisite to the preparation of any work structure is the clear understanding and statement of project objectives. Work structuring can be used to reach such diverse objectives as lowering costs, eliminating jurisdictional work disputes, or lowering scrap factors. Therefore, the first step in designing a work structure is to identify, determine, and define the project objective and overall project scope. Once established, the overall project objective provides insight and guidelines for identifying the project subobjectives. The work structure is then subdivided into subobjectives with progressively finer divisions of effort. These subobjectives interact to support the overall project objective in the same manner that subsystems support a total system capability. By defining subobjectives, greater understanding of the work and clarity of action are added for those individuals who perform the work. This process of identifying and defining subobjectives assists in structuring the contributing elements during work structure preparation.

Development Responsibilities

The preparation of the work structure plan is the responsibility of the project manager in accord with senior management directives. The project manager is responsible for developing the complete task structure and element definition for all project-related work. To prepare the project work structure, the project manager first develops the project summary work structure, based on the project objectives and the appropriate summary work structure elements. Participating organizations supporting the project develop, coordinate, and submit individual work structures for their work. Finally, the project manager integrates the performers' work structures with the project summary work structure to obtain the total project work structure. During the process of breaking down the project, the project manager, the staff, and all involved managers and contractors are forced to think through all aspects of the project.

Top-Down Approach

Work structures are traditionally developed using a top-down approach to ensure that the total project is planned and that all derivative plans and associated work contribute directly to the desired end objectives. The work structure is developed using a top-down approach, because projects are developed and tasks are defined in the same way.

This is particularly true when projects have recently been authorized. When projects have been in existence for a period of time or when certain tasks are prespecified, there may be a requirement to develop portions of the work structure from the bottom-up. To achieve the best results for large projects, however, work structures should be developed from the top-down.

The top level of the structure is defined as the total project scope. This level is then subdivided into finer sublevels. As the levels become lower, the scope, complexity, and cost of each subproject become smaller, until a level is reached where the elements represent manageable units for visibility, planning, and control and where tasks can be accomplished. At the lowest levels of the work structure, individual work packages are identified (as shown in Exhibit 10-2). The work package is the lowest-level element of an integrated cost and schedule work structure. A fully developed work package is a single, definable, monitorable, and controllable segment of work. It is the point at which cost and schedule are integrated, and responsible and performing organizations can be assigned.

At any level of the work structure, a monitoring element may be identified. This is an element of the structure chosen to monitor and control a specific portion of the work at or above the work package level (as shown in Exhibit 10-2). Each monitoring element is a management control point at or below which actual costs and schedule status can be accumulated. This level is often referred to as the cost account level, and it represents the work assigned to one responsible organizational element.

The outcome of top-down structuring is information flow and summing patterns designed to be compatible with anticipated project management requirements.

Rolling Wave Work Structure Planning

The development of the work structure must take into account the fact that the creation of work definition, cost, and schedule information is evolutionary: Tasks further out in time mature or become more detailed and precise as the project progresses. All project work must eventually be planned and controlled through fully developed and detailed packages of work. The work package size should be small enough to permit realistic estimates, but not so small as to result in excess control costs. However, such detailed planning cannot usually be produced at the beginning of the project.

The rolling wave work planning concept acknowledges that a person or organization has a sufficient depth of information to plan in detail today's work (the near term), but lacks that depth of information about tomorrow (the future). Therefore, those future tasks are planned and scheduled at a more summary level starting with planning packages. A planning package is a logical aggregation of work within a higher-level work structure element. As the project progresses and information matures, more detailed scope, schedule, and cost estimates are developed, and the summary tasks are broken down into multiple lower-level tasks and finally into work packages.

Content

The overall design of the work structure is the key to an effective working project control system. Therefore, the work structure must be carefully studied from an

Exhibit 10-2. Hierarchical relationship of project information using work structure.

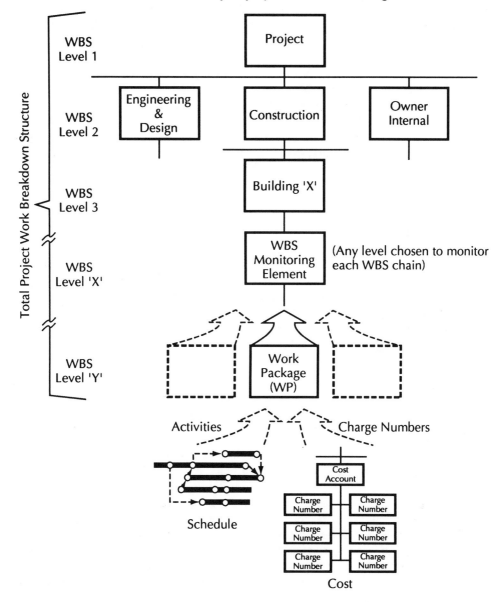

information input and output point of view. The structure must be based on the most likely way the project will be worked, managed, and controlled. Critical products or services to be subcontracted should be identified and treated as individual elements. An element or series of elements applicable to support tasks (such as test equipment, spare and repair parts, transportation, and training) should also be included.

Each work structure element must be a meaningful grouping of related tasks and a unique, single, definable, goal-oriented segment of project work. Each element must be able to be summed without allocation with other related work structure elements, in a logical manner, to the work structure element above it, thereby providing defined scope, schedule, and cost parameters for all elements of the work structure. Each summary-level element must be meaningful from the viewpoint of project control, such as how the work will be controlled, performed, and/or contracted.

Structure and account codes must be applied to the work structure element to ensure that relationships are meaningful and summarization is possible.

In developing the project work structure as a communications tool, the work structure must be defined with regard to all the base elements that are required to make it a working entity: project objectives, structure, coding, and reporting. Before integrating these elements, each must be analyzed separately, and then the relationships of the elements to each other must be studied. The design of the structure, the codes, and the reports should contain as much input as possible from the performing and responsible groups that will be using them.

Types of Structure

The approach to the design of the work structure and its development depends upon the management and contracting philosophy adopted. Five primary work structures can be considered for use on most projects: The work structure can be oriented toward (1) products, or end items, (2) contracts, (3) systems, (4) phases, or (5) facilities. The work structure may also be a combination of these structures. The structure is usually displayed in a tree formation representing the hierarchical components of the project.

Level of Detail

The number of subdivisions in the work structure varies according to the complexity of the work. The work is progressively and logically subdivided into manageable tasks down to the levels where work will be monitored and controlled (a monitoring element) and/or performed and statused (a work package). The work is subdivided to a level at which tasks are assignable, identifiable, and manageable by the organizational units performing the work. For example, the work structure for a hardware end-item system would be subdivided further than that for a training process.

The reasons for the different levels of detail are often quite subtle. Engineering and manufacturing planning and control and, thus, configuration management require a level of subdivision that identifies all of the configuration items. However, the level required for assignment and control by the performing organization is usually higher than the level required for detailed planning of configuration items. Regardless, the work structure must be identical for configuration management and project control purposes and must be detailed until that level in the structure is reached. The level of detail should be clearly defined so that no duplication of effort occurs within or between performing organizations.

Integration

The project control process is built on the concepts of integrating data related to scope, performing organization, schedule, and cost and of producing performance measurements by assimilating and evaluating all information on a common basis. Therefore, each work structure element must interface with the organization responsible for accomplishing that element. Flexibility must be provided to establish these interfaces at meaningful and appropriate levels. Otherwise, existing management systems and management by those assigned responsibility may be impaired. Whatever type of planning and control technique is used, all the important interfaces and interface events must be identified. To integrate project data properly, five major interfaces to the work structure are established in developing the work structure design:

1. Work structure/organization relationship
2. Work structure/schedule relationship
3. Work structure/cost relationship
4. Work structure/technical relationship
5. Work structure, cost, and schedule interrelationships

Statement of Work

A major part of defining and structuring the work for a project is the preparation of a statement of work (SOW), which provides the detailed descriptions of work contained in each element of the work structure. The reason for producing SOWs is to provide a careful documentation of each work structure element with regard to scope, schedule, cost, resource requirements, and technical requirements so that all users have a common understanding of the content and meaning of each work structure element.

The descriptions must indicate what materials, equipment, facilities, people, and other resources are necessary. The description of work must be clear and concise and capable of standing alone as a "miniature project." Work must neither be duplicated between work structure elements nor should any project work be omitted. Where confusion might be possible, the SOW for each element explicitly states the work that is *not* included as well as the work that is included; where other similar work is included, the SOW should reference the work statement. The work descriptions from the summary SOWs for the upper work structure levels, together with those from the more definite monitoring element SOWs and the detailed SOWs for the work packages, provide a basis for checking the work structure.

Iteration, Revision, and Maintenance

The work structure development process is iterative as the project evolves and contracts are awarded. Work structure revisions also result from work expansion or contraction with project/contract scope changes and the movement of a project through various phases (e.g., research, design, development, fabrication, construction, testing, demonstration, and operation). The approved project work structure is maintained and revised to incorporate changes throughout the life of the project to ensure that the project work efforts are traceable. When changes in the project concept, objectives, approach, work scope, or resource levels occur after the initial work structure has been defined, a formal change process is used to update the structure.

Conclusion

The work structuring methodology for integrated scope/schedule/cost planning and control is a proven methodology used to manage successful projects. The project work structure is the heart of the project planning effort. It is more than just an element of the project plan; it is the basic project structure providing the framework for developing and maintaining cost/schedule planning, budgeting, and data collection, as well as performance evaluation. It provides streamlined information flow, improvement in communication, reduction in redundancy, and improved visibility. The work structure is the device by which the users—such as the owner, contractors, and the government—can communicate among themselves and with the people performing the actual work.

The work structuring methodologies work equally well with any of the standard organizations used for projects: functional, pure project, or matrix. The methods and techniques are flexible and may be applied to varying degrees, depending on the size, needs, and characteristics of the specific project and the desires of the project manager. If properly applied, the work structuring techniques and methods give project managers and functional managers a powerful tool to provide and communicate all needed project information.

Management-directed project work structuring offers creative technical approaches to project and business management challenges. It allows management integration of many processes, work phases, and organizations, and it also ensures integration of scope, schedule, and cost. Management-based work structuring offers a means for complying with both project objectives and multicompany objectives and can accommodate ever-changing work priorities. Project managers who employ work structuring as a key management tool increase efficiency on their projects and gain a more competitive contract edge.

11

Project Management Plans: An Approach to Comprehensive Planning for Complex Projects

David L. Pells
Strategic Project Management International

Preparation of a project management plan (PMP) is a simple, straightforward approach designed to promote and ensure comprehensive project planning. The PMP is a combination of two plans that are often prepared separately: the traditional management plan, which describes operational management systems and approaches, and the project plan, which includes the work breakdown structure (WBS), logic, schedules, and cost estimates. PMPs are intended to be more comprehensive than either management plans or project plans. They reflect an awareness that the people, the system, and the detailed planning are all critical to project success.

This chapter provides an introduction to PMPs. It outlines PMP contents, including traditional issues such as work breakdown structures, critical path networks, Gantt charts, and earned value. It introduces new ideas such as planning for organizational development, health and safety planning, and risk planning. Most importantly, it provides a framework for comprehensive project planning.

The project management plan typically contains seventeen items. They are:

1. Introduction/Overview
2. Mission and objectives
3. Work scope
4. Planning basis
5. Work breakdown structure
6. Organization development plan
7. Resource plan
8. Procurement and logistics plan
9. Logic and schedules
10. Cost estimates, budgets, and financial management

11. Risk analysis and contingency plan
12. Quality and productivity plan
13. Environmental, safety, and health protection plan
14. Security plan
15. Project planning, control, and administration plan
16. Documentation and configuration management plan
17. Appendix

This chapter discusses these items, with descriptive information as well as suggestions as to how to address the topics during the planning process and what to include in the project management plan.

Introduction/Overview

The PMP introduction/overview includes an introduction both to the specific project and to the PMP document itself. Some background information may be included to set the stage or to provide perspective on the information that follows, such as how the project was initiated, who the customer or sponsor is, how the project is funded, or other critical factors that are important to those who read the PMP. Introductions are always short, allowing the reader to move into the remainder of the PMP quickly but with initial perspective. Additional external or historical information can be referenced or included in the Appendix.

External factors important to the initiation or health of the project should be discussed. External factors may include general or specific economic trends, constraints, or opportunities; political or governmental conditions; population demographics; or internal organizational factors.

Mission and Objectives

The purpose or mission of the project is stated in one or two paragraphs, followed by a set of concrete objectives. The mission statement is all-encompassing, establishing why the project exists. Mission statements can be general or specific. They also reference the customer if the project is being performed under contract or for a third party.

Project objectives are outlined as specific goals to be accomplished and to which status can be applied. For instance, objectives for a small construction project might include a good location; modern energy-efficient economic design; a fully furnished facility; a complete set of project documents; compliance with all laws, codes, and requirements; standard profit margin; and completion date.

Planning becomes straightforward when objectives are defined for key areas. Objectives can be established for every aspect of the project, including scope of work, organization, management, systems, environment, safety, and overall completion of the project (i.e., final cost and schedule dates). Established objectives in the following areas facilitate detailed planning, systems development, and work performance:

▸ Technical objectives
▸ Schedule objectives

- Cost objectives
- Organizational/personnel–related objectives
- Quality objectives
- Environmental safety and health objectives
- Contracting/procurement objectives
- Management system objectives

Well-defined objectives enhance the reliability of subsequent planning. Once objectives are stated in concise terms, they allow for the development of the project scope of work and the work breakdown structure.

Work Scope

The work scope section of the PMP is the heart of the plan. It demonstrates how well the project is understood. This section includes narrative descriptions of all elements of the project's scope of work. It clearly identifies the products or services to be provided to the customer. The statement of work contains enough information to allow development of the work breakdown structure, schedules, and cost estimates, as well as assignment of responsibilities.

The work scope section can address the project phases and include special plans associated with those phases, such as the R&D plan, engineering/design plans, construction plan, manufacturing plan, facility start-up plan, or transition plan. The work scope section may also describe the systems management activities, including systems engineering and integration, to ensure project life cycle perspective. In other words, it shows that the activities necessary to ensure that the design and final products meet customer requirements are all planned and managed properly and can be integrated and operated as intended, and that start up, transition, operation, and completion activities are also planned and managed properly.

To simplify preparation, the work scope can be prepared in outline form, which can then be used to develop the WBS. Often the WBS and work scope are prepared in parallel, with the resultant narrative description of the work called a WBS dictionary.

Planning Basis

The planning basis section provides for the documentation of key approaches, assumptions, requirements, and other factors considered during preparation of the PMP. The following topics are addressed in this section:

- Project deliverables/end products
- Requirements
- Constraints
- Approaches/strategies
- Key assumptions
- Specifically excluded scope

Project Deliverables/End Products

A list of all products, documents, and services to be delivered to the customer over the life of the project is required. When the project is being performed under a contract with the U.S. government, this list may be prepared during contract negotiations and attached to the contract itself. Every project manager, however, should have a complete list of project end products, in order to ensure delivery of those items on schedule.

Requirements

Requirements are specifications or instructions that must be followed during project performance. They may include technical requirements, facilities requirements, data requirements, management requirements, or special instructions. Technical requirements may include codes, standards, laws, engineering or design specifications, models, or examples for mandatory or recommended compliance on the project. When there are mandatory requirements, such as laws, these must be identified and listed, or project performers run the risk of noncompliance and legal prosecution.

Facilities requirements include an initial assessment of types, amount, and quality of facilities needed for the project, along with related utilities, furniture, and equipment. This provides initial bases for estimating quantities and costs associated with those resources. Overlooking facilities issues during project planning leads to schedule slippages, cost overruns, unhappy project participants, and untold headaches for the project managers. For small projects, facility requirements may not be a big issue; for larger projects, they can be critical.

Functional and operational requirements (F&DRs) spell out what the system, facility, or product being produced is intended to do. F&DRs provide the basis for the engineering, design, and planning of the system, facility, or product. Where F&DRs exist, listing or identifying them greatly simplifies and facilitates the design process. Mandatory data requirements, management directives, or special instructions are also identified and documented during the planning process. Special instructions may include directions from the customer or upper management or may be spelled out in contract documents.

Constraints

Constraints may include known technical limitations, financial ceilings, or schedule "drop dead" dates. Technical constraints may be related to state-of-the-art capabilities, interface requirements with other systems, or user-related issues (e.g., software that must run on certain types of personal computers). Financial and schedule constraints can be introduced by the customer, lead time associated with procured hardware, or funding/budgetary limits.

Approaches/Strategies

The approach or strategies to be utilized can have a major impact on subsequent planning. For instance, if all project work is to be performed within the parent (host) organization, with minimum subcontract support, that approach impacts planning of resources and organizational issues. If work is to be "fast-tracked" by overlapping design and construction activities, or by performing more work in parallel, then that approach can be described. Communication of strategies to project participants can be done effectively by devoting several paragraphs to that topic in this section of the PMP.

Key Assumptions

Every project is planned under some degree of uncertainty. Therefore, assumptions are required to estimate work scope, schedule durations, resource requirements, and cost estimates. Assumptions are also required when defining the management strategies, systems, and procedures to be utilized.

Major assumptions are to be documented since they can have a significant impact on planning and estimating. This is true on all projects, regardless of size. Large projects, which involve numerous participants and major complexities, generally depend on more key assumptions during project planning than smaller projects. The major reason for documenting key assumptions is to provide the project manager with a basis for revising plans when the assumptions are changed (i.e., when a customer changes his or her mind).

Specifically Excluded Scope

This subject is included for communications purposes, but it may also be needed to limit the scope of work. It is intended to highlight specific and relatively obvious issues, such as documentation, training, or follow-on support, which customers often assume but which cost money and have not been included in the project plan. Clarification of these scoping questions saves headaches later, in some cases even avoiding litigation.

Work Breakdown Structure

The WBS is a product-oriented hierarchy of the scope of work and is embodied in a numbering structure that provides a system for organizing the scope in a logical manner. The WBS is prepared in conjunction with the scope of work, and it should be developed to the level of detail where responsibility for work performance is assigned. Responsibility for each element of a WBS is then established.

The most popular portrayal of a project WBS is in graphic form, similar to an organization chart. This WBS chart displays project elements and tasks in levels and boxes, representing smaller parts of the project. The WBS is a mandatory requirement for the PMP.

The WBS facilitates the following:

- Understanding of the work
- Planning of all work
- Identifying end products and deliverables
- Defining work in successively greater detail
- Relating end items to objectives

- Assigning responsibility for all work
- Estimating costs and schedules
- Planning and allocating resources
- Integration of scope, schedule, and cost
- Monitoring cost, schedule, and technical performance
- Summarizing information for management and reporting
- Providing traceability to lower levels of detail
- Controlling changes

The WBS provides a common framework for planning and controlling the work to be performed. It provides a common, ordered framework for summarizing information and for quantitative and narrative reporting to customers and management.

Organization Development Plan

This section of the PMP addresses the following organization-related issues:

- Organization structure
- Responsibilities
- Authorities
- Interfaces
- Personnel development

For every project, how the people involved are organized, assigned responsibilities, and directed needs to be defined and communicated to the participants. In addition, interfaces among participants both inside and outside the project team require planning. Equally important, training and team-building plans need to be established to promote quality and productivity on project work.

Organization Structure

While not all participants may be involved during early project planning, key positions and participating organizations are identifiable fairly early. A preliminary organization structure in graphic form can be prepared and included in the PMP. Where possible, names, titles, and phone numbers are included on the chart, to promote understanding and communication. Organization charts are dated but not finalized until resource allocation plans are prepared, based on detailed work planning and cost estimates.

Responsibilities

Specific responsibilities of individual project participants are defined as clearly as possible, to promote communication and teamwork and to avoid confusion. For large projects, responsibilities of positions or participating organizations are defined and included.

Authorities

Much has been written about the "authority versus responsibility" issues in project management, especially in matrix organizations. Project managers or other project participants are "responsible" for project accomplishment without "authority" over the resources being employed. For all projects, it is helpful to recognize these issues and document procedures for resolving conflicts as necessary. For larger projects, authority levels are formally established for key positions in the project organization and documented in the PMP. Where multiple companies or organizations are integrated into a project organization, contract relationships are referenced or defined, as appropriate. Procedures for resolving problems related to work direction may also need to be established. This section of the PMP provides an opportunity to document and communicate plans and procedures that reduce conflict in these areas.

Interfaces

On projects involving technical activity, it is common for personnel from the customer's organization to talk directly with technical staff in the project organization. However, when multiple project participants are interfacing with outside entities— either customer representatives, the general public, the press, or others—it is easy for conflicting information to be transmitted. These interfaces can generally be identified and controlled, normally via procedures or established protocols.

On large, complex projects, it is fundamental to identify interfaces among project participants. Clearly defining interfaces highlights where communication is needed and which areas may cause potential communications problems. Interface planning reduces these problems.

Personnel Development

Skills and techniques related to teamwork and effective communication can be critical to a project's success, allowing problems to be solved, schedules accomplished, and objectives met. Many of those skills and techniques, however, may be new or difficult for new project participants. This is an issue common to all large projects.

This section of the PMP outlines the types of training and team-building activities planned for the project. Simply establishing a plan in this area can be enormously important, as it points out that the project leaders are aware of the issue and plan to improve communication, teamwork, and productivity on the project. In addition, other types of training are necessary on projects, especially if the project utilizes technologies, equipment, systems, or approaches that participants are not familiar with.

Resource Plan

The resources needed to accomplish the project—including personnel, supplies, materials, facilities, utilities, and information/expertise—are identified in this section of the PMP. The availability of those resources also needs to be determined, that is, when the resources are needed and whether they are available when required. For example, the expertise needed for the project may not be available within the organization and may need to be found outside, via hiring, contract, or partnership. Materials required may be available only "on the other side of the world," requiring additional planning, time, and expense to secure.

The primary resource planning issues are:

- Identification and qualification of the resources required
- Availability of those resources
- Quantification, or amount, of the resources required
- Timing, or "allocation," of the resources needed

Identification and availability of resources are addressed in this section of the PMP. Quantities and timing of those resources are established during the cost-estimating process and finalized after schedules have been defined. Pricing of resources is how cost estimates are established and becomes the basis for project budgets. However, preliminary estimates of resources required and projected dates needed are included in the PMP, then finalized when cost estimates and schedules are established. Because of inflation, cost of capital, and other factors, accurate pricing of resources cannot occur until resources have been scheduled, so this process is also fundamental to the cost-estimating process. Resource allocation is also normally included in the cost estimate section of the PMP, in the form of a time-phased cost estimate.

Procurement and Logistics Plan

Advance planning of the contracting and procurement activities is particularly critical on large projects. In addition, logistics issues related to major equipment, supplies, or materials need to be planned in advance to ensure manufacturing, transportation, and storage by cost-efficient, safe, and timely means. This section of the PMP includes the following:

- Subcontracting plans
- Procurement plans
- Logistics plans

Subcontracting Plans

Subcontracting activity has a direct effect on project costs, schedules, and overall success, so it normally receives attention early in the planning process. It may be directly related to the original structure of the project organization if, for instance, joint ventures, consortia, or other partnering arrangements are established to perform a project. A primary contracting organization may have overall project management and planning responsibilities, but one or more other subcontractors will perform portions of the project. In those cases, the subcontracting arrangements are planned early, or project work can be delayed.

An early planning activity is identifying major subcontracts needed to accomplish project work. This occurs during the resource planning process. The selection, negotiation, and award of major subcontracts is a rigorous, difficult, and time-consuming process, involving complex legal arrangements and extensive documentation and approvals.

This section of the PMP also includes identification of subcontracting laws, regulations, and requirements to be complied with; identification and description of the major subcontracts anticipated for the project; timing of those subcontracts; potential problems or issues associated with the contracts; and approaches and expertise to be employed during the contracting process.

Procurement Plans

The procurement of equipment, materials, and supplies requires planning to reduce the risk of impacting project schedules and to ensure efficient and cost-effective acquisition. On large projects or projects involving R&D or manufacturing of new systems, key equipment or parts may themselves need to be developed and specially manufactured. In those cases, vendors may also go through the R&D, design, engineering, and manufacturing processes just to deliver the equipment to the project. In cases involving long lead time items, procurement planning occurs long before the items are needed on the project, in order to initiate the design and procurement processes for those items. Failing to do so means the equipment or parts will not be available when needed, causing the project schedule to slip and costs to rise.

Logistics Plans

For construction projects of all kinds and sizes, logistics planning is critical. The timing, transportation, delivery, storage, and usage of project materials, supplies, parts, or equipment must be planned, coordinated, and managed for the project to be successful. Unavailability or damage during shipment, storage, or handling causes major problems at the job site. These same issues apply to any projects involving large quantities of procured materials or equipment.

This section of the PMP includes plans related to the physical aspects of procurement: when items will be delivered by vendors; transportation and handling during shipment; warehousing, storage, kiting, and handling at the job site, including inspection, testing, and acceptance procedures; and distribution to project participants as needed for completion of project tasks. Systems and expertise needed to track, manage, and report status on procured items are identified, along with the schedule and approach for establishing those systems and functions. Responsibilities and procedures are identified and defined.

Logic and Schedules

All project work must be scheduled. Schedules include milestone lists, summary schedules, and detailed schedules. This section of the PMP includes those schedules and the logic and network plans necessary to develop them.

Networks and Logic

Network planning is applied to projects during early planning processes, so that activity relationships are identified, understood, and factored into the schedule. In their simplest form, network plans are simple flow diagrams displaying the order in which activities are to be performed, which activities cannot be started or completed before other activities are started or completed, and what activities must be completed before the overall project is complete. Logical network plans are important for project planning, but they are complex, detailed, and cumbersome for displaying schedule information. While networks are necessary, they may be referenced in the PMP or attached later. The PMP, however, should describe the logic applied and establish networks as the basis for the schedules.

Summary Schedules

The summary schedule corresponds to the upper levels of the WBS and identifies key milestones. Additional levels of schedules are developed as required and are compatible with each other, the management summary schedule, and the WBS. Schedules provide information for measuring physical accomplishment of work, as well as identifying potential delays.

Schedules normally include lists of tasks and activities, dates when those tasks are to be performed, durations of those tasks, and other information related to the timing of project activities. That information is displayed in many ways. The most popular tends to be the bar chart, produced by project scheduling software programs.

Milestone schedules are simple lists of top-level events (i.e., the completion of the key tasks or activities) with planned dates. These same lists are used for reporting schedule progress by adding a column for completion date information.

Milestone schedules, networks, bar charts, and activity listings are included in the PMP as desired. Detailed schedules may be provided in the Appendix and referenced in the body of the PMP. They are maintained current over the life of the project to reflect current working plans. Schedules also normally identify critical activities so they can receive special attention.

Cost Estimates, Budgets, and Financial Management

Every PMP includes a cost estimate, a budget, or both. The cost estimate is normally in table format and includes a summary of costs for each major task or element of the project. Financial management includes systems and procedures for establishing budgets, for reporting financial information, for controlling costs, and for managing cash flow.

Cost Estimates

The most straightforward method of estimating costs is to use the WBS and schedule. Each element of the WBS or each activity in the schedule or network can have a cost associated with it. Therefore, the approach is to go down the list of activities or WBS elements and estimate the cost for each one. Costs are estimated by identifying the resources needed for each activity, in what quantities, and at what price. The pricing of the resources depends on the timing, so normally a cost estimate is not finalized until the project activities have been scheduled.

Budgets

Budgets are cost estimates that have been approved by management and formally established for cost control. Actual costs are compared to budgets as the project is completed, to identify variances and potential problems and to provide information on what the costs will be. The budgeting process includes extensive reviews and revisions of the cost estimates, to arrive at the final budget figures.

Financial Management

The requirements, systems, procedures, and responsibilities for project financial planning, management, and control are addressed in this section. Financial control includes cash flow management as well as conventional cost control (standard cost accounting cost performance reporting, and cost productivity assessment).

Cash flow management involves traditional income and expenditure reporting and analysis. On most projects, funding and funds management are critical, representing the timing at which resources can be scheduled and work accomplished. Cash flow planning and reporting procedures and responsibilities are established in the PMP, ensuring that funds are available as needed on the project. Many projects are financed by multiple customers, government agencies, or organizations, making it necessary to keep track of which money is spent for which project activities.

Risk Analysis and Contingency Plan

Projects need to be assessed to identify areas containing high degrees of risk—for instance, those activities associated with new research, technical developments, or other tasks that have never been done before. Risk may also be associated with the external environment, such as economic conditions, political uncertainties, weather, geography, public opinion, or labor-related factors. This section of the PMP provides an opportunity to consider project risks and to develop contingency plans to offset those risks. Topics suggested for this section are:

- ▸ Risk identification
- ▸ Risk analysis
- ▸ Risk minimization plans
- ▸ Contingency plans and reserves

Risk Identification

The WBS is used to identify risks associated with specific elements of the project. Each WBS element is assessed for risk, based on the following:

- ▸ Status of technology being utilized
- ▸ Status of planning
- ▸ Status of the design (project stage)

Risk is higher when new or unproven technologies are required. Greater uncertainty is also expected when all aspects of a task or project element are not yet planned in detail. Finally, risk is generally higher during the early stages of a project or task than when nearing completion.

Risk Analysis

Risk analysis includes a detailed discussion of the risk, including both internal and external factors. An impact table is prepared with factors assigned based on technology status, planning status, and design/project status. Finally, the potential cost and schedule impact is assessed. The impact table includes a worst-case cost estimate for each of the project elements included.

Risk Minimization Plans

Once the risks to the project have been identified and assessed, strategies are needed to minimize those risks. Such strategies may include technology development, modeling, demonstrations, peer reviews, replanning, changes in project logic, reorganization of project participants, or even contractual changes. The idea is to adapt a proactive, planning-based approach to risk assessment and to minimize project risks through specific actions.

Contingency Plans and Reserves

Changes in technical performance or schedules imply a new look at cost estimates and a reevaluation of contingency reserves. Risk analysis therefore can be performed in conjunction with cost estimating when estimates of contingency reserves are calculated. Regardless of the timing, effort, or risks, cost estimates may be inaccurate for various reasons, such as engineering errors or oversights, schedule changes, cost or rate changes, external factors, construction or implementation problems, or estimating errors. The amount of reserves depends on a number of factors, including funds available, overall riskiness of the project, and the management approach.

Quality and Productivity Plan

Project management planning itself is an effective productivity improvement process. Productivity improvement can also be an established project objective. This section of the PMP is where that planning is addressed and includes:

- Total quality management planning
- Quality management systems planning
- Quality assurance/quality control
- Technical performance measurement
- Productivity improvement

Total Quality Management Planning

Total quality management (TQM) requires the commitment and involvement of top management and all employees. TQM in a project environment requires clear policy statements, attention by senior company management, the commitment of the project manager, and the involvement of all project participants. Training programs and major improvements in procedures, systems, and approaches may be involved. The steps to be taken for implementing TQM on a project are described in this section of the PMP.

Quality Management Systems Planning

While quality may be defined in terms of technical performance of end products, value to the customer is now regarded as a key measure. Technical quality and customer satisfaction are increased by establishing systems and procedures for ensuring high performance. That means well-defined project requirements or specifications, systems for comparing progress to specifications, and effective feedback mechanisms. This part of the PMP contains or refers to quality management systems or procedures to be utilized on the project.

Quality Assurance/Quality Control

Quality assurance (QA) is a process of establishing performance standards, measuring and evaluating performance to those standards, reporting performance, and taking action when performance deviates from standards. Quality control (QC) includes those aspects of QA related to monitoring, inspecting, testing, or gathering performance information, as well as actions needed to ensure that standards are met. QA and QC both require discipline and systematic approaches to defining and measuring technical performance. For large projects, formal systems and procedures are necessary, and these can be described or listed in this section of the PMP.

Technical Performance Measurement

Technical performance measurement is the evaluation of performance against standards, criteria, or requirements established for a project. A procedure is established to evaluate each element of the WBS for technical performance status and for taking corrective action. Evaluation can be by a design committee, chief engineer, QA organization, or group of technical experts. The plan for technical performance management is included or referenced in the PMP.

Productivity Improvement

Productivity improvement, or reductions in the time and costs to accomplish project objectives, also calls for planning and monitoring. Plans, schedules, and cost estimates can be evaluated for process improvements and efficiencies and performance improvements. Cost-saving methodologies, such as value engineering, can be applied to designs and technical plans. Cost estimates can be subjected to "sensitivity analysis," which identifies areas of the project where the most probable savings can occur. Company procedures, systems, or processes can be reassessed for improvements regarding paperwork, staffing, or time. New products, methodologies, or technologies might increase productivity. Employees also may be encouraged to identify productivity improvements, cost savings, or time-saving processes. This section of the PMP identifies which of those strategies are used on the project and outlines when and how they will be used.

Environmental, Safety, and Health (ES&H) Protection Plan

This section of the PMP identifies all the environmental compliance laws, regulations, and requirements that must be satisfied on the project. The plans for complying with those requirements are also described. The PMP describes the steps to be taken by the project team to protect the environment, the public, and project participants and includes:

- ▸ Safety and health protection plan
- ▸ ES&H management/information systems
- ▸ Emergency preparedness plan

Safety and Health Protection Plan

The PMP contains the project safety plan. Each element of the WBS is assessed for safety issues, including potential hazards, opportunities for accidents, and government regulatory requirements. The systems, procedures, and steps to be employed to ensure a safe workplace are also described.

ES&H Management/Information Systems

The systems and procedures to be used for managing and reporting information related to environmental, safety, and health (ES&H) activities on the project are identified and described. Responsibilities and interfaces with outside organizations, often key to compliance with ES&H regulations, are also documented. A matrix chart is used for projects where multiple regulations, systems, and organizations are involved.

Emergency Preparedness Plan

Emergency preparedness involves addressing such issues as fires, tornadoes, floods, power outages, sabotage, terrorism, and the loss of key personnel. Preliminary planning identifies the people who will take charge in each type of emergency. Public services such as fire stations, ambulances, hospitals, police, and evacuation means are identified. A fully developed PMP contains or references plans and procedures for all types of emergencies.

Security Plan

Every project involves security issues that need to be dealt with in the PMP. The major topics are:

- ▸ Physical security
- ▸ Property protection
- ▸ Information security

Physical Security

Limiting physical access may require gates and fences, guards, electronic access systems or surveillance devices, badges, or contracted security services. Plans for providing physical security—including requirements, responsibilities, tasks and activities, timetables, and procedures—are described or referenced in the PMP.

Property Protection

Property protection against loss, theft, or damage is needed whenever a project involves acquisition or use of materials or equipment, including hardware, software, vehicles, tools, or other devices. The more important those materials or equipment are to the success of the project, the more important are property protection plans, systems, and procedures. Property protection may also require detailed property management information systems, procurement tracking systems, training, and experienced personnel.

Information Security

For some projects, information security may be the most important security issue facing the project manager. As a project proceeds, key information is generated, including technical information (i.e., design specifications, vendor data, engineering data), cost and schedule information, contract-related information, correspondence, plans, and progress information. This section of the PMP contains the plans for ensuring against loss or damage of key project information. An information security manager for the project may be needed to control access to information; to coordinate passwords, codes, and file names; to ensure backup systems and databases; and to ensure proper usage of procedures and protocols. These issues can all be included in the security plan.

Project Planning, Control, and Administration Plan

This section is intended to describe the management approaches and systems to be used for managing the project. The section should be clear and straightforward, referencing additional systems or documents as required.

Project Planning

The PMP represents the major plan for the project, yet it may be one of many plans prepared—especially if the project is large, complex, and involves many different organizations.

Management Plans

If more than one management plan is prepared for the project, they are identified and described here. On large projects a hierarchy of management plans is common, with each participating organization preparing a management plan for its portion of the project. A table should be prepared identifying all the plans to be prepared and their relationship to one other.

Detailed Work Package Plans

Work packages are the lowest level of project work assigned to individuals who then plan and manage detailed project activity. Project activity at the lowest levels of the WBS is planned in work packages, which describe in detail the work scope, schedules, and costs associated with the work. Work package plans are summarized and consolidated to support the information contained in the PMP. The work package planning process to be used, the assignment of responsibilities, the formats to be used, and the planning procedure can be described in this section of the PMP.

On large U.S. government–funded projects, detailed work packages and cost accounts are required. When this is the case, a description of the procedures are included or referenced here.

Schedules and Budgets

Summary information tends to be included in management plans, with detailed scope, schedule, and cost information contained in detailed work package plans. Schedule and budgets are fully described in other sections of the PMP.

Project Control

Project control involves procedures, processes, and methods used to determine project status, assess performance, report progress, and implement changes. In addition, on large projects there may also be the need for a formal work authorization process, which documents task agreements prior to the start of work. These issues are addressed in this section of the PMP.

Work Authorization

Work authorizations are documents that describe work to be performed, have cost estimates (or budgets) and scheduled performance dates identified, and are negotiated and agreed to by a "requesting" organization and a "performing" organization. Work authorizations are common in large companies doing business with the U.S. government. The work authorization forms and procedures to be used on a project are described in this section of the PMP.

Cost and Schedule Performance Measurement

The methods and procedures to be used to assess schedule status and how much work has been accomplished over the life of the project are described in this section of the PMP. For instance, the process and responsibilities for assessing the completion status of each activity in the project schedule are outlined here, as well as any methods to be used for measuring quantities of work completed.

Systems and procedures for cost collection, accounting, and reporting are outlined in this section. Where projects are being performed within a company, organization, or larger project where cost accounting systems and procedures are already established, those systems and procedures are referenced. For one-of-a-kind projects, however, systems and procedures may need to be developed.

Change Control

The procedures, systems, and responsibilities for administering and controlling changes to a project's work scope, schedule, and budgets (or cost estimates) is described in this section of the PMP. Formal change control systems are required to ensure that plans, baselines, design, and documentation are not revised without appropriate reviews and approvals.

Project Administration

This section of the PMP describes the reports, meetings, and record-keeping processes associated with project management and administration.

Reporting

Different types of management reports are identified and described here. Formats, procedures, and responsibilities are outlined and defined for major reports. A list of reports to be prepared, with distribution and responsibilities identified, can be included in this section or in the Appendix. Reports for both internal and external distribution should be included.

Meetings

Major management meetings to be conducted are identified, including review meetings with customers or management, status meetings, change control meetings, and special meetings to transmit key information.

Administrative Document Control

The system, procedures, and responsibilities for administrative records management on the project are described along with the outline of the filing system. This may be addressed in the document control section of the PMP, or it can be included here with reference to the overall project systems.

Subcontract Management/Control

This section contains an overview of procedures and responsibilities associated with administering key contracts on the project. Performance measurement and reporting by contractors is described, contract requirements identified, and subcontract management activities identified, including site visits, meetings, and technical reviews.

Documentation and Configuration Management Plan

Documents include plans, administrative documents and records, technical data, engineering and construction documents, procedures and systems-related documents, reports, and correspondence. This section of the PMP identifies the documents to be prepared on a project and establishes the administrative approach, systems, and procedures to be used to manage that documentation.

Document Control

Documentation management includes the following:

- ▸ List of key documents
- ▸ Responsibilities
- ▸ Document storage and access
- ▸ Document control systems and procedures

List of Key Documents

For each major element of the WBS, a list of documents or type of paperwork for each participating functional organization is developed. That list includes documents related to management and administration; technical specifications and requirements; R&D, design, and engineering; manufacturing; construction; start-up; and operation or production. The list also includes contracts, compliance documents, and documents prepared by entities external to the project.

Responsibilities

Responsibilities for dealing with the documents are identified as follows:

- ▸ Initial preparation of the documents
- ▸ Reviews and approvals
- ▸ Changes to the document
- ▸ Distribution list
- ▸ Storage

A document responsibility matrix is a simple, straightforward method for communicating the plan for document control. The responsibility matrix lists the documents, then identifies responsibilities for document preparation, revisions, approvals, distribution, and storage.

Document Storage and Access

Document storage is a huge issue for large projects. Document storage may include entire storage facilities, filing rooms, filing cabinets, computers, computer diskettes, compact disk systems, tapes, and microfiche. Document storage issues include:

- ▸ Document identification (numbers or codes)
- ▸ Document type (hard copy, disk, files, etc.)
- ▸ Physical location
- ▸ Document and data security

- ▸ Access to documents and information
- ▸ Document control procedures

A document numbering system is developed to store, administer, and access project documents. It can be based on the WBS, the project organizational structure, the date, or any other logical order. The numbering system is then used to organize and store project documents and to find the documents over the life of the project.

Document Control Systems and Procedures

The system, methods, and equipment needed for document storage depend on the type of documents, data, or information to be managed. Those may include hard copies (i.e., of reports received), on-line files, compact disks, or tapes. The physical location of document storage facilities depends on facility requirements (i.e., air conditioning, size, layout), facilities available, frequency of anticipated access, volume of project documentation, or many other considerations.

Data and document security calls for specific procedures. When sensitive or classified information is involved, access may need to be controlled via format security plans. Security against fire, damage, or theft is also addressed and described in the PMP, as are backup files for automated data storage systems.

Access requirements and plans are also described, including a list of those who will need access, what kind of access (i.e., on line, complete, extracts, etc.) frequency, and how that access will be monitored. This may mean simply allowing project participants to walk into a document storage room, find the document, review or extract information, and return the document to storage. In other instances elaborate on-line document storage and retrieval systems may be used, requiring instruction or assistance in the process.

The procedures for project document control are identified and described in the PMP. Where existing systems and procedures will be used, they are referenced. Procedures to be developed, procured, or implemented for document control are specified, outlined, described, or identified. In some cases only a brief description may be included, to be completed or fully described later. It is important, however, to address the need for document control systems and procedures in the PMP.

Configuration Management

Configuration management can be defined as the process of identifying and documenting the functional and physical characteristics of products, facilities, or systems; of controlling changes to those items and associated documents; and of reporting status of the items or changes to those who need to know. The objective is to keep project technical documentation consistent with the project systems, products, hardware, or facilities involved. Where a comprehensive document control system has been implemented, configuration management can be an expansion of the processes for the technical documents and systems.

Configuration management plans include the following:

- ▸ Configuration management requirements
- ▸ Configuration identification

▸ Configuration control
▸ Configuration status reporting

Configuration Management Requirements

On projects for government agencies, configuration management requirements may include compliance with detailed laws, regulations, or contract clauses. This is especially true in such industries as nuclear power, military/weapons systems and procurement, space-related contracting, transportation, and other areas potentially involving environmental, health, or safety issues concerning the general public.

Configuration Identification

The technical systems, components, facilities, and products that comprise the project and associated technical documents are identified in the PMP. These are the elements that define the "technical baseline" drawn from the WBS. Technical baseline documents consist of the documents associated with research, design, engineering, fabrication, installation, construction, start up, and operation of each of the technical systems/components of the technical baseline. This section of the PMP consists of a list of the technical baseline systems/components and associated documents that will be subjected to configuration control.

Configuration Control

Configuration control involves the procedures for administering and controlling changes to the technical baseline and associated documents. Configuration control parallels the more general document control process but places more emphasis on controlling changes to the design and technical configuration of the system themselves. Control of technical documentation ensures that those documents accurately reflect the latest status of the technical baseline.

The configuration control section identifies how changes to the technical baseline are made and fixes the associated responsibilities and procedures for keeping technical documents current. Procedures and responsibilities are identified in a matrix format along with necessary narrative explanations.

Configuration Status Reporting

A method is established for communicating configuration changes and status information to those who need that information. In general, a procedure with distribution lists for specific documents or system will suffice, provided that responsibilities are assigned for distribution of technical information and documentation.

Appendix

The PMP Appendix includes the following types of information:

▸ Referenced technical data (e.g., technical specifications, test requirements)
▸ Support exhibits (e.g., detailed WBS)

- ▸ Detailed schedules
- ▸ Detailed cost estimate support data
- ▸ Work package documentation procedures
- ▸ Example reports
- ▸ Change control charter
- ▸ Current working plans

The Appendix provides a place to put supporting information, allowing the body of the PMP to be kept concise and at more summary levels. In some cases, where a section of the PMP is prepared as a separate document (for instance, when required by law), it can be included in the Appendix and referenced in the PMP.

Bibliography

Bellows, Jerry L., and Stephen L. Osborn. "Development of the Project Management Plan." 1980 *Engineering Foundation Conference,* August 10–15, 1980 (Henniker, N.H.: AACE, 1981).

Cleland, David I., and Harold Kerzner. *A Project Management Dictionary of Terms.* New York: Van Nostrand Reinhold, 1985.

Cleland, David I., and William R. King, eds. *Project Management Handbook.* 2nd ed. New York: Van Nostrand Reinhold, 1988.

Cori, Kent. "Project Work Plan Development." 1980 *Proceedings of the Project Management Institute.* Drexel Hill, Penn.: PMI, 1989.

Dinsmore, Paul C. "Planning Project Management: Sizing up The Barriers." 1984 *Proceedings of the Project Management Institute.* Drexel Hill, Penn.: PMI.

DOE Order 4700.1. *Project Management System.* Washington, D.C.: U.S. Department of Energy, March 6, 1987.

Humphreys, Kenneth K., ed. *Project and Cost Engineers Handbook.* 2nd ed. New York: American Association of Cost Engineers/Marcel Dekker, 1984.

Kerridge, Authur E., and Charles H. Vervalin, eds. *Engineering and Construction Project Management.* Houston: Gulf Publishing, 1986.

Kerzner, Harold. *Project Management: A Systems Approach to Planning, Scheduling and Controlling.* 3rd ed. New York: Van Nostrand Reinhold, 1989.

Kerzner, Harold, and Hans J. Thamhain. *Project Management for Small and Medium Size Businesses.* New York: Van Nostrand Reinhold, 1984.

Lock, Dennis, ed. *Project Management Handbook.* London, England: Gower, 1987.

Pells, David L. "Project Management Standards at the Idaho National Engineering Laboratory." *Proceedings of the Northwest Regional Symposium,* jointly sponsored by the American Association of Cost Engineers and the Project Management Institute, April 22, 1988, Vancouver, Canada. Drexel Hill, Penn.: PMI.

Pells, David L., "Project Management Upgrade at the Idaho National Engineering Laboratory." 1989 *Proceedings of the Project Management Institute/INTERNET Joint Symposium.* Drexel Hill, Penn.: PMI.

Section V
Controlling Costs and Keeping on Schedule

12

Project Cost Control Systems That Really Work

Ralph D. Ellis, Jr.
University of Florida

In the design and implementation of a project cost control system, the individual characteristics of the organization performing the project and of the project itself must be considered. However, the following criteria should be considered regardless of the specific situation:

- *Validity.* The information reported must accurately reflect actual versus estimated costs.
- *Timeliness.* The cost data must be reported soon enough so that managerial action can be taken if a problem arises.
- *Cost-effectiveness.* Collection and reporting of cost data must be done in a way that does not hinder project progress.[1]

Cost control systems can work if they are set up with these criteria in mind. This chapter covers how to design and implement an effective project cost control system. The examples given are drawn from the construction industry, yet these same principles are applicable to other types of projects.

Developing a Project Cost Control System

Establishing a Project Cost Control Baseline

The project cost control baseline is developed from the project cost estimate.[2] Initially, during the conceptual phase, the cost estimate exists only as a preliminary or order of magnitude estimate;[3] as the engineering design progresses, more precise estimates of cost can be developed. A detailed cost estimate, based upon work quantities determined from completed project drawings and specifications, provides the most precise estimate of cost. It is this detailed cost estimate that forms the basis of the project cost control baseline.

However, the detailed cost estimate often cannot be directly used as a control

budget. Usually some transformation is required. For example, for bidding or negotiating purposes, the estimate may originally have been organized in a form convenient for the project owner. The project contractor may find it advantageous to
reorganize the estimate into a form that matches his or her cost control preferences.
Also, the level of detail provided by the estimate may not be appropriate for the
control budget.

Several factors should be considered when deciding upon the appropriate level
of detail for the cost control budget.

- How many individual cost elements can the office and field personnel be
  expected to break actual project costs into for reporting purposes?
- How many individual cost elements can the project management team effectively review and monitor?
- How can Pareto's Law be taken into account—that 80 percent of the total
  project cost is probably represented by only 20 percent of the cost items?

The answers to these questions and the selection of an appropriate level of detail
depends upon the characteristics of the project and upon the management resources
allocated to manage the project. If, for instance, a cost engineer is assigned to assist
the project manager in supervising the collection and reporting of cost control
information, greater detail may be practical. Generally, it is desirable to maintain
more detail on cost items that represent a more significant portion of the project cost.

Consider a project in which structural concrete represents a large percentage of
the total project cost. In this case the structural concrete costs should be broken down
into a number of cost subaccounts categorized by work operation, such as formwork,
reinforcing, and concrete placement. Further subclassification by structural component, such as foundation, slabs, columns, and beams, may also be appropriate. On
the other hand, if only a relatively small percentage of the total project cost involves
masonry, then all of the masonry cost items in the estimate might be transferred to
the project cost control budget as a single summary. Exhibit 12-1 provides an
illustration of how the project cost estimate information might be transferred to the
cost control budget.

Establishing a standard organizational listing and coding of all cost items is a
prerequisite to the preparation of both the detailed cost estimate and the cost control
budget. The standard organization listing consists of a comprehensive list of all
conceivable cost items. In the construction industry, such a list might be prepared
using the Masterformat published by the Construction Specifications Institute (CSI).[4]
The CSI Masterformat provides an extensive classification and coding of cost items
relevant to the construction industry and is widely used by manufacturers, architects,
contractors, and other professionals.

The standard cost code system should be tailored to the organization's needs.
Some cost items found in the CSI standard can be deleted if not within the scope of
work performed. Other cost categories can be expanded to provide additional detail
in critical areas.

The level of detail resulting from the cost coding system can be adjusted by
means of a system of account hierarchy. The highest category is represented as a
major account. Each major account is subdivided into subaccounts and subsubac-
counts. Cost data can be summarized and collected at any level within the account

Exhibit 12-1. Transfer of project cost estimate information to the cost control budget.

Detailed Cost Estimate

Cost Code Number	Item	Material	Labor	Total
03	Concrete			
03100	Concrete Formwork	71920	125602	197522
03200	Concrete Reinforcement	208105	83100	291205
03310	Cast in Place Concrete	391400	42700	434100
03350	Concrete Finish	0	18900	18900
04	Masonry			
04210	Brick Masonry	4200	3510	7710
04220	Concrete Unit Masonry	2810	3640	6450
04420	Cut Stone	400	720	1120

Cost Control Budget

Cost Code Number	Item	Material	Labor	Total
03100	Concrete Formwork	71920	125602	197522
03200	Concrete Reinforcement	208105	83100	291205
03310	Cast in Place Concrete	391400	42700	434100
03350	Concrete Finish	0	18900	18900
04000	Masonry	7410	7870	15280

hierarchy. The CSI contains sixteen major cost accounts. Exhibit 12-2 provides an example of how the account hierarchy system can be used.

Just as the standard cost code is tailored to the general operation of the organization, the project cost control budget is tailored to satisfy the cost control needs of the specific project. Cost control account categories and levels of detail are matched to the particular characteristics of the project. Then the cost figures are transferred from the cost estimate to the appropriate account in the cost control budget.

A well-designed and accurately prepared cost control budget is an essential requirement for a successful project cost control system. The cost control budget becomes a cost baseline used as a benchmark for monitoring actual cost and progress during the entire project. The cost control budget is also an important ingredient for practically all of the project management activities.

Collecting Actual Cost Data

The collection of project cost data falls within the scope of activities normally conducted by the organization's accounting system.[5] Project costs are collected, classified, and recorded as a routine accounting function. Individual project costs, when collected at the organizational level and compared with overall income, are a basic component in determining profitability of the enterprise.

Although job cost accounting is a fundamental part of most accounting systems, the job cost accounting format used frequently does not satisfy the requirements of project cost control. Classification and level of detail used in the accounting system may not match with the cost control budget developed for the project. For example, we may wish to examine the labor and material costs associated with a certain category of work tasks such as formwork for cast-in-place concrete. However, the job cost accounting system may provide only a summary of all concrete costs.

Obviously, the greatest efficiency is obtained when the accounting system can directly provide the information required by the cost control system. A great deal of progress has been made in this area, particularly with the use of computerized cost accounting systems. Increased flexibility in the assignment of cost account codes and the production of specialized reports have significantly improved recent computerized accounting packages.

However, as a practical matter, some of the detailed cost breakdown data required by the cost control system may have to be generated separately from the general accounting system. This involves reviewing source documents such as supplier's invoices, purchase orders, and labor time sheets at the project level. The cost data required for cost control purposes can be extracted and recorded in the cost control records.

Exhibit 12-2. Example of cost code hierarchy.

Level 1	03000	Concrete
Level 2	03300	Cast in Place Concrete
Level 3	03365	Post-Tensioned Concrete

Regardless of how the actual cost data are collected, they must be organized in accord with the project cost control budget. Comparisons of actual to budget costs can be made only when both categories of costs are classified, summarized, and presented in identical formats. We do not want to compare apples with oranges.

Determining Earned Value

Earned value is the portion of the budgeted cost that has been earned as a result of the work performed to date. Cost values originally assigned to the various items in the cost control budget represent total costs. However, as work on the project progresses, we must periodically compare actual costs with budget costs. In order to make this comparison, the amount of earned value of the total budget must be determined.

Several methods are available for measuring project progress. Each method has different features and provides a somewhat different measure of progress. Sound managerial judgment must be applied no matter which method is used. Progress estimates require honest and realistic assessment of the work accomplished versus the work remaining.

Some of the more common methods of determining earned value are as follows:

▸ *Units completed.* This method involves measuring the number of work units that have been accomplished and comparing the number of completed units with the total number of units in the project.[6] No subtasks are considered, and partially completed units are generally not credited. For example, suppose that 420 linear feet (LF) of 4-inch diameter steel pipe has been installed. If the total project requires 2,100 LF of pipe, then the percentage of completion is 20 percent (420 LF divided by 2,100 LF).

▸ *Incremental milestones.* When the work task involves a sequential series of subtasks, the percentage of completion may be estimated by assigning a proportionate percentage to each of the subtasks.[7] For example, the installation of a major item of equipment might be broken down as follows:

Construct foundation pad	10 percent
Set equipment on foundation	60 percent
Connect mechanical piping	75 percent
Connect electrical	90 percent
Performance testing and start up	100 percent

Percentage of completion is estimated by determining which of the milestones have been reached. The accuracy of this procedure depends upon a fair allocation of percentage to the subtask in relation to costs.

▸ *Cost to complete.* When properly applied, this method can provide the most accurate representation of project cost status.[8] The cost to complete the remaining work for a given task is first estimated. This detailed cost estimate utilizes both the original cost estimate and any historical cost data acquired so far on the project. The idea is to develop the best possible estimate of the cost required to complete the task. The percentage of completion is calculated as follows:

$$\text{Percentage of Completion} = \frac{\text{Actual Cost to Date}}{\text{Estimated Total Cost}}$$

$$\text{Percentage of Completion} = \frac{\text{Actual Cost to Date}}{\text{Actual Cost} + \text{Estimated Cost}}$$
$$\text{to Date} \qquad \text{to Complete}$$

For example, if the actual cost to date for structural steel erection is $18,500 and the estimated cost to complete the task is $6,500, the percentage of completion is calculated as follows:

$$\text{Percentage of Completion} = \frac{18,500}{18,500 + 6,500}$$

$$\text{Percentage of Completion} = 74 \text{ percent}$$

With each of the methods used to estimate the percentage of completion, earned value is calculated as the percentage of completion times the original budget cost for the task.

Reporting and Evaluating Cost Control Information

Cost control status reports can be custom-tailored to suit the preferences of individual managers and to accommodate specific project differences. However, in general, cost status reports should provide an item-by-item comparison of actual cost to earned value.[9] Estimated cost to complete and projected total cost can also be shown. Variations from the cost budget can be presented as a percentage or as an actual value, and categorical breakdowns of the cost status can also be shown. It is often useful to separate material, labor, equipment, and subcontract costs.

Exhibit 12-3 is an example of a monthly cost control status report. The figures listed as "Total Budget Amount" represent the originally estimated costs for each of the cost account categories. Actual costs to date are compared with earned values, and variances are listed. Estimated costs to complete are also given. The projected total cost has been calculated by adding the actual cost to the estimated cost to complete. This report could have been expanded to provide a separate listing of material, labor, equipment, and subcontract costs. The amount of detail can be structured to meet the requirements of the project manager.

Managers will be particularly interested in the variance between actual cost and earned value, and the resulting total cost projection.

Accuracy and timeliness are equally important in reporting cost control status. If the information is to be of any value to the project manager, it must be provided soon enough to allow for corrective action. Monthly cost control reports should be provided as soon as possible after the end of the month. The time lag between the cutoff of the cost period and production of the report should be as small as possible.

Material suppliers and subcontractors are normally paid monthly; therefore, a monthly cost report seems appropriate for summarizing these costs. However, labor costs are typically paid on a shorter interval, such as weekly. Labor costs are also likely to be more variable and consequently are normally the subject of greater

Exhibit 12-3. Monthly cost control status report.

Project: New River Office Complex

Item	Cost Code Number	Total Budget Amount	Percentage Complete	Earned Value	Actual Cost	Percentage Variance	Variance Cost	Estimated Cost to Complete	Projected Total Cost
General Requirements	1000	$ 48,523	55.2%	$ 26,785	$ 22,478	16.1%	$ 4,307	$ 40,721	$ 63,199
Site Work	2000	478,925	98.1	469,825	458,799	2.3	11,026	467,685	926,484
Concrete	3000	798,147	74.6	595,418	762,396	−28.0	(166,978)	1,021,979	1,784,375
Masonry	4000	589,991	26.2	154,578	156,887	−1.5	(2,309)	598,805	755,692
Metals	5000	387,240	58.0	224,599	206,251	8.2	18,348	355,605	561,856
Carpentry	6000	142,364	12.0	17,084	16,841	1.4	243	140,342	157,183
Moisture Protection	7000	98,755	0.0						
Doors and Windows	8000	124,721	0.0						
Finishes	9000	211,766	0.0						
Specialties	10000	45,889	0.0						
Equipment	11000	267,451	0.0						
Furnishings	12000	89,010	0.0						
Special Construction	13000	15,600	0.0						
Conveying Systems	14000	82,710	0.0						
Mechanical	15000	1,752,335	12.5	219,042	219,042	0.0	0	1,752,336	1,971,378
Electrical	16000	987,143	18.9	186,570	186,570	0.0	0	987,143	1,173,713
Total Project		$6,120,570	33.2%	$1,893,901	$2,029,264	−7.1%	($135,363)	$5,364,616	$7,393,880

management attention. It may be appropriate to generate weekly status reports of labor costs.

Graphical representations of the cost-schedule data are often useful in providing a quick visualization of cost control status. One of the most common is a cost-schedule graph in which actual and budget costs are plotted against performance time. Exhibit 12-4 is an example of a cost-schedule graph. This example provides a graphical representation of the data included in the cost control status report given in Exhibit 12-3. In this example, the project is approximately one week behind schedule in time, and total actual costs have exceeded the cost budget by 7.1 percent.

Taking Corrective Action

One of the primary functions of the cost control system is to identify problem areas to the manager early enough so that corrective action can be taken. Although we would not expect actual costs and earned values to be identical, a significant variance indicates a problem. Determining the source of the problem requires an investigation by the project manager. There are many possible causes such as an estimating

Exhibit 12-4. Cost-schedule graph.

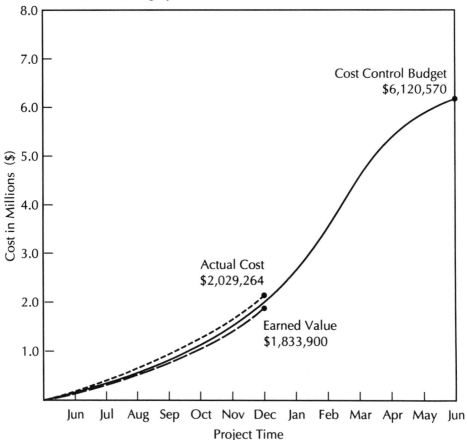

mistake, a change in material prices, a change in labor wage rates, or a change in work productivity. The cost control system cannot identify the cause of the problem, but tells the manager where to look for the cause. Additionally, the cost control system furnishes feedback to the manager, showing the effect of any corrective action.

Achieving Project Success by Controlling Costs

Project success depends to a great extent upon management's ability to control cost. Although there may be other important project goals, cost remains a universal measure of success. Projects with substantial cost overruns are rarely considered successful.

Maintaining cost control requires a well-designed and implemented project cost control system. A sound project cost control system performs four basic functions:

1. Establishing baseline cost
2. Collecting actual cost data
3. Reporting and evaluating (including earned value)
4. Taking corrective action

The level of cost detail and the format of the report documents should be matched to the requirements of the specific project and the management team. Exhibit 12-5 provides an illustration of the elements involved in a project cost control system and their interrelationship.

Exhibit 12-5. Elements of a cost control system.

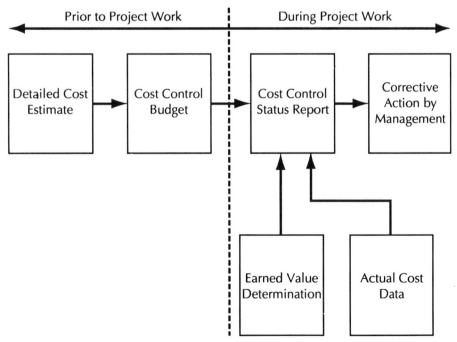

Establishing an adequate project cost control system requires an investment. Project managers must take the time before starting project work to develop the structure of the cost control system. They must decide upon cost classification and the appropriate level of cost detail to be monitored. They need to work out actual cost collection procedures. How will the cost control system interface with the organization's accounting system? Reporting frequencies, procedures, and formats must be determined. Administration of the cost control system also requires the allocation of staff time. However, if management is willing to commit the necessary systems, it is possible to have a project cost control system that really works. Operating without effective cost control is gambling in the dark.

Notes

1. D. Bain, *The Productivity Prescription* (New York: McGraw-Hill, 1982), p. 62.
2. Construction Industry Institute, *Project Control for Construction* (Austin, Texas: CII, 1989), p. 6.
3. R. L. Peurifoy and G. D. Oberlender, *Estimating Construction Costs* (New York: McGraw-Hill, 1989), p. 422.
4. Construction Specifications Institute, *Masterformat* (Washington, D.C.: CSI, 1989).
5. K. Collier, *Fundamentals of Construction Estimating and Cost Accounting With Computer Applications* (Englewood Cliffs, N.J.: Prentice-Hall, 1987), p. 44.
6. Construction Industry Institute, p. 14.
7. Ibid.
8. Fails Management Institute, *Financial Management for Constructors* (New York: McGraw-Hill, 1981), p. 4.
9. S. E. Powers and B. H. Brown, *Walker's Practical Accounting and Cost Keeping for Contractors* (Chicago: Frank R. Walker, 1982), p. 116.

13

Cost/Schedule Control System Criteria (C/SCSC): An Integrated Project Management Approach Using Earned Value Techniques

Lee R. Lambert
Lee R. Lambert & Associates

The purpose of this chapter is to introduce the concept of cost/schedule control system criteria (C/SCSC), often referred to as earned value. The use of C/SCSC is obligatory on many U.S. government contracts, yet the criteria is generally applicable to other contracts as well. The material that follows shows some of the key characteristics that make the C/SCSC approach one of the most powerful and productive concepts used in managing complex projects in private, commercial, or government environments.

In the world of C/SCSC, the role of the cost account manager (CAM) is pivotal in the process. The project manager and all of the other traditional project management contributors are active participants and have significant responsibilities that can't be underestimated. However, because of the critical role of the CAM, the material is targeted at helping him or her plan and manage the assigned tasks.

The C/SCSC process is essentially the same at all levels of the project or organization. Individual components of the C/SCSC address work authorization through reporting. Descriptions of cost accounts, authorized work packages, and

This chapter was adapted from Lee R. Lambert, *Cost/Schedule Control System Criteria (C/SCSC): An Integrated Project Management Approach Using Earned Value Techniques—A Lighthearted Overview and Quick Reference Guide*. © 1990 Lee R. Lambert & Associates.

planned work packages have been emphasized because of their significance in the C/SCSC approach in general and, specifically, because of the ability of the cost account manager to be successful at the difficult job of balancing the many project management requirements and tasks.

Process Overview: Introduction to the Concept

History

The first C/SCSC concept was introduced in the 1960s, when Department of Defense Instruction 7000.2–Performance Measurement of Selected Acquisitions exploded on the management scene. The criteria included in the instruction constitute standards of acceptability for defense contractor management control systems. The original thirty-five criteria were grouped into five general categories—organization, planning and budgeting, accounting, analysis, and revisions—and were viewed by many, government and contractor personnel alike, as a very positive step toward helping to solve management problems while achieving some much needed consistency in the general methods used throughout the Department of Defense and, eventually, the Department of Energy and other project worlds.

In the early 1990s, more than 200 contractors, including most of the highly respected organizations in the world, were working within the boundaries of the criteria, having received validation or certification by the U.S. government. These organizations represented hundreds of government and private projects and programs. Hundreds of other contractors have been using the principles of C/SCSC without any requirements to do so. They have clearly found the concepts and techniques useful on all work, not just that for the U.S. government.

It should be noted that not everyone agrees that C/SCSC is the best project management approach. However, investigation reveals these same critics are subtly adapting various components of the C/SCSC concept on their projects and finding them extremely valuable and productive tools. After all, it is hard to argue with the sound business management concepts upon which C/SCSC is based.

In this chapter, numerous abbreviations and terms are employed in a description of C/SCSC. A list of these abbreviations and terms is found in Exhibit 13-1.

Understanding the Critical Data Elements of C/SCSC

There are three critical elements involved in C/SCSC. The budgeted cost of work scheduled (BCWS), the actual cost of work performed (ACWP), and the budgeted cost of work performed (BCWP).

Budgeted Cost of Work Scheduled

The BCWS is the amount of resources, usually stated in dollars, that are expected to be consumed to accomplish a specific piece of work. The BCWS is more commonly known as the spend plan or cost estimate and has long been employed in the world of management. In C/SCSC applications, the emphasis is placed on achieving the closest possible correlation between the scope of work to be completed (work content) and the amount of resources actually required.

Exhibit 13-1. C/SCSC abbreviations and terms.

ACWP	—Actual cost of work performed
AWP	—Authorized work package*
BAC	—Budget at completion
BCWP	—Budgeted cost of work performed = EV
BCWS	—Budgeted cost of work scheduled
CA	—Cost account
CAA	—Cost account authorization*
CAM	—Cost account manager
CAP	—Cost account package*
CBB	—Contract budget base
CD	—Contract directive*
CFSR	—Contract funds status report
CPR	—Cost performance report
C/SCSC	—Cost/schedule control system criteria
C/SSR	—Cost/schedule status report
CWBS	—Contract work breakdown structure
EAC	—Estimate at completion
EV	—Earned value = BCWP
FM	—Functional manager*
FTC	—Forecast to complete
LOE	—Level of effort
LRE	—Latest revised estimate
MPMS	—Master phasing milestone schedule
MR	—Management reserve
PCR	—Package change record
PM	—Project manager
PMB	—Performance measurement baseline
PWP	—Planned work package*
RAM	—Responsibility assignment matrix
SOW	—Statement of work
UB	—Undistributed budget
VAR	—Variance analysis report
WBS	—Work breakdown structure
WBSM	—WBS manager*
WPM	—Work package manager

*These abbreviations are not common in C/SCSC. Organizations may use their own terminology.

Actual Cost of Work Performed

The ACWP is the amount of resources, usually stated in dollars, that were expended in accomplishing a specific piece of work. The ACWP is more commonly known as the actual incurred cost or actuals, and it has also been employed in the world of management since its beginning. In C/SCSC applications, the emphasis is placed on expending and recording resource expenditures with a direct correlation to the scope of work that has been planned to be completed at the same point in time.

Budgeted Cost of Work Performed

The BCWP is a measure of the amount of work accomplished, stated in terms of a percent of the budget assigned to that specific scope of work. The work accomplishment status, as determined by those responsible for completion of the work, is converted to dollar form and becomes the focal point of all status and analysis activities that follow. The BCWP is the only new data element required when utilizing C/SCSC management techniques. The BCWP, when compared with the BCWS and ACWP, provides the foundation for comprehensive management evaluations, projections, and (if necessary) corrective actions.

What's in It for the User?

In-the-trenches experience has resulted in two separate observations on utilizing C/SCSC. There is good news and there is bad news. Let's take the good news first. The C/SCSC approach:

- ▸ Provides information that enables managers and contributors to take a more active role in defining and justifying a "piece of the project pie"
- ▸ Alerts you to potential problems in time to be proactive instead of reactive
- ▸ Allows you to demonstrate clearly your timely accomplishments
- ▸ Provides the basis for significant improvement in internal and external communications
- ▸ Provides a powerful marketing tool for future projects and programs that require high management content
- ▸ Provides the basis for consistent, effective management system–based training and education
- ▸ Provides a more definitive indication of the cost and schedule impact of project problems
- ▸ Allows tremendous flexibility in its application

On the downside, C/SCSC also most likely:

- ▸ Results in the customer asking for more detail
- ▸ Results in greater time spent on paperwork by someone in the organization, although this is becoming less and less of an issue with today's computer capabilities
- ▸ Requires more structure and discipline than usual
- ▸ Costs money and organizational resources to develop and implement

Experience clearly shows the net result to be significantly in favor of utilizing the C/SCSC approach. Exhibit 13-2 shows the benefits in graphic form. Without earned value, the example shows an "under budget" situation. Using earned value, the real status of the project is revealed, showing a project behind schedule and over budget. But even with C/SCSC, the management user must remember at all times that using C/SCSC will not:

- ▸ Solve technical problems
- ▸ Solve funding problems, although it might help

Exhibit 13-2. Benefits of using C/SCSC.

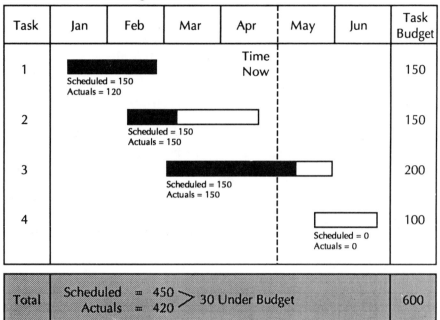

Project Control Without Earned Value

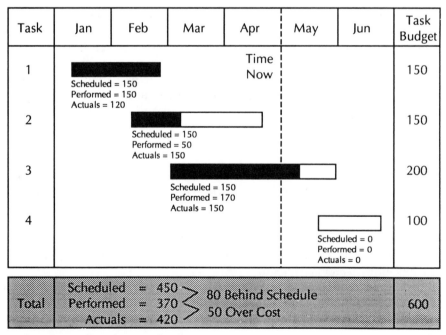

Project Control With Earned Value

  ‣ Make decisions for you, although it will help
  ‣ In any way "manage" your program, project, or task

C/SCSC will, however, provide sound, timely information—the most useful commodity for today's managers faced with making extremely difficult decisions.

The System: C/SCSC Process Description

C/SCSC can be successful only if the user recognizes the need for a hierarchical relationship between all the units of work to be performed on a project. This hierarchical relationship is established via the work breakdown structure (WBS). Work is done at the lowest levels of the WBS; therefore, these critical elements have particular significance when it comes to achieving the most beneficial results from using C/SCSC.

The C/SCSC process involves numerous specific tasks and efforts, which are described in detail below.

Cost Account

The cost account (CA) is the focus for defining, planning, monitoring, and controlling because it represents the work associated with a single WBS element, and it is usually the responsibility of a single organizational unit. C/SCSC converges at the cost account level, which includes budgets, schedules, work assignments, cost collection, progress assessment, problem identification, and corrective actions.

Day-to-day management is accomplished at the CA level. Most management actions taken at higher levels are on an "exception" basis in reaction to significant problems identified in the CA.

The level selected for establishment of a CA must be carefully considered to ensure that work is properly defined in manageable units (work packages) with responsibilities clearly delineated.

Authorized Work Package

An authorized work package (AWP) is a detailed task that is identified by the cost account manager for accomplishing work within a CA. An AWP has these characteristics:

  ‣ It represents units of work at the levels where the work is performed.
  ‣ It is clearly distinct from all other work packages and is usually performed by a single organizational element.
  ‣ It has scheduled start and completion dates (with interim milestones, if applicable), which represent physical accomplishment.
  ‣ It has a budget or assigned value expressed in terms of dollars and/or labor hours.
  ‣ Its duration is relatively short unless the AWP is subdivided by discrete value milestones that permit objective measurement of work performed.
  ‣ Its schedule is integrated with all other schedules.

Planning Work Package

If an entire cost account cannot be subdivided into detailed AWPs, far-term effort is identified in larger planned work packages (PWPs) for budgeting and scheduling purposes. The budget for a PWP is identified specifically according to the work for which it is intended. The budget is also time-phased and has controls, which prevent its use in performance of other work. Eventually, all work in PWPs is planned to the appropriate level of detail for authorized work packages.

Work Authorization

All project work, regardless of origin, should be described and authorized through the work authorization process, an integral part of C/SCSC. The C/SCSC relates not only to work authorization, but also to planning, scheduling, budgeting, and other elements of project control, which reflect the flow of work through the functional organizations.

Although the cost account manager is most concerned with the work authorization process at the authorized work package and cost account levels, the total process is presented to provide the CAM with a sense of his or her role in the total system. The authorization flow is traced from customer authorization through contractual change authorization through the following five steps:

1. Authorization for contracted work consists of two parts: the basic contract, and the contractual scope changes.

2. Work authorization for contracted work is provided as follows: The organization general manager, in coordination with the finance director, provides authorization to the project manager to start work via a contract directive (CD). This directive approves total project scope of work and funding

3. WBS planning target authorization is as follows:
- The WBS manager prepares the WBS planning target authorization.
- The project manager approves the WBS target goal for expansion to the functional cost account.
- The WBS target is later replaced by the WBS-package budget rollup of CAs.

4. The procedure for cost account planning target authorization is as follows:
- The cost account manager prepares target the cost account goal for expansion to work packages.
- The CA target is later replaced by CA-package budget rollup of all planned work packages.

5. Change control is processed as follows:
- The CAM submits or signs a marked-up work package sheet to the C/SCSC information department. Markups show any internal replanning or customer contractual baseline change that:
  - Alters work by addition/deletion, causing CA budget adjustments
  - Causes adjustment of work or budget between CAs
- The processing department completes a package change record (PCR) for audit trail of baseline revisions (baseline maintenance).
- The project manager or delegated WBS manager approves the add/delete

transactions to the management reserve contingency account controlled by management if the budget adjustment is outside the single cost account. (*Note:* Parties to the original budget agreements must approve revisions.)

▶ The CA budget cannot be changed by such actions as cost overruns or underruns; changes that affect program schedules or milestones because of work acceleration or work slippage; or retroactive adjustments.

Planning and Scheduling

This description of planning and scheduling from the project level down gives the CAM an overall view of his or her function. Eight factors are involved.

1. Planning and scheduling must be performed in a formal, complete, and consistent way. The customer-provided project master schedule and related subordinate schedules through the cost account/work package levels provide a logical sequence from summary to detailed work activities. The C/SCSC logic works as the tool to make work package schedules compatible with contract milestones, since the networks are derived from the work package database.

2. Network logic must be established for all interfaces within the framework of the contract work breakdown structure (CWBS).

3. The responsibility assignment matrix (RAM) is an output of WBS planning. It extends to specific levels in support of internal and customer reports. The RAM merges the WBS with the organization structure to display the intersection of the WBS with the cost account–responsible organizations.

4. When work plans are detailed, the lower-level tasks are interfaced and scheduled. These tasks are usually identified as either:

▶ *Discrete effort:* Effort that can be scheduled in relation to clearly definable start and completion dates, and which contains objective milestones against which performance can be measured

▶ *Level of effort (LOE):* Support effort that is not easily measured in terms of discrete accomplishment; it is characterized by a uniform rate of activity over a specific period of time.

Where possible, tasks should be categorized in terms of discrete effort. LOE should be minimized.

5. The general characteristics of schedules are as follows:

▶ Schedules should be coordinated (with other performing organizations) by the C/SCSC manager.

▶ Commitment to lower-level schedules provides the basis for the schedule baselines.

▶ All work package schedules are directly identifiable as to CA packages and WBS elements.

▶ After a baseline has been established, schedule dates must remain under strict revision control, changing only with the appropriate C/SCSC manager's approval.

6. Two categories of project schedules are used.

▶ Project level schedules are master phasing/milestone schedules, program schedules, or WBS intermediate schedules.

▸ Detailed schedules are either cost account schedules or work package schedules.

  ▸ Cost account schedules: (1) have milestones applicable to responsible organizations; (2) are developed by the organizations to extend interfaces to lower task items; (3) are at the level at which status is normally determined and reported monthly to the project level, for updating of higher-level schedule status and performance measurement; (4) have planned and authorized packages that correlate with the CA, WBS, and scope of work (SOW) and with reports to the customer; and (5) document the scheduled baseline for the project.

  ▸ Work package schedules: (1) provide milestones and activities required to identify specific measurable tasks; (2) supply the framework for establishing and time-phasing detailed budgets, various status reports, and summaries of cost and schedule performance; (3) are the level at which work package status is normally discussed and provide input for performance measurement; (4) are the responsibility of a single performing organization; (5) provide a schedule baseline against which each measurable work package must be identified; and (6) require formal authorization for changes after work has started and normally provide three months' detail visibility.

7. Regarding schedule change control, the cost account managers can commit their organization to a revised schedule only after formal approval by at least the WBS manager.

8. Work package schedule statusing involves the following:

▸ Objective indicators or milestones are used to identify measurable intermediate events.

▸ Milestone schedule status and BCWP calculations are normally performed monthly.

Budgeting

In accord with the scope of work negotiated by the organization with the customer, the budgets for elements of work are allocated to the cost account manager through the C/SCSC process. These budgets are tied to the work package plans, which have been approved in the baseline. The following top-down outline, with five factors, gives the CAM an overview of the C/SCSC budgeting process.

1. Project-to-function budgeting involves budget allocations and budget adjustments.

  ▸ Budget allocations involve the following:

    ▸ The project manager releases the WBS targets to the WBS managers, who negotiate cost account targets with the cost account managers. The CAMs then provide work package time-phased planning.

    ▸ When all project effort is time-phased, the C/SCSC information department produces output reports for the project manager's review. When the performance measurement baseline (PMB) is established, the project manager signs WBS package printouts, which are summarized from the cost accounts.

- ▸ The WBS manager signs the cost account package printouts, which are summed from work package planning. The time-phased work package budgets are the basis for calculating the BCWP each month.
- ▸ Regarding budget adjustments, the performance measurement baseline can be changed with the project manager's approval when either of the following occurs:
  - ▸ Changes in SOW (additions or deletions) cause adjustments to budgets.
  - ▸ Formal rebaselining results in a revised total allocation of budget.
2. PMB budgets may not be replanned for changes in schedule (neither acceleration nor slips) or cost overruns or underruns.
3. Management Reserves (MRs) are budgets set aside to cover unforeseen requirements. The package change record is used to authorize add/delete transactions to these budgets.
4. Undistributed Budgets (UBs) are budgets set aside to cover identified, but not yet detailed or assigned SOW. As these scopes of work are incorporated into the detail planning, a PCR is used to authorize and add to the performance measurement baseline.
5. Regarding detailed planning, the planned work package is a portion of the budget (the BCWP) within a CA that is identified to the CA but is not yet defined into detailed AWPs.

Cost Accumulation

Cost accumulation provides the CAM with a working knowledge of the accounting methods used in C/SCSC. There are six things involved in cost accumulation accounting (for actual costs).

1. Timekeeping/cost collection for labor costs uses a labor distribution/accumulation system. The system shows monthly expenditure data based on labor charges against internal work packages.
2. Three factors are involved in nonlabor costs.
   - ▸ Material cost collection accounting shows monthly expenditure data based on purchase order/subcontract expenditure.
   - ▸ The cost collection system for subcontract/integrated contractor costs uses reports received from the external source for monthly expenditures.
   - ▸ Regarding the funds control system (commitments):
     - ▸ The funds control system records the total value of purchase orders/ subcontracts issued, but not totally funded.
     - ▸ The cumulative dollar value of outstanding orders is reduced as procurements are funded.
3. Regarding the accounting charge number system:
   - ▸ The accounting system typically uses two address numbers for charges to work packages: (1) the work package number, which consists of WBS–department–CA–work package; and (2) the combined account number, which consists of a single character ledger, three-digit major account, and five-digit subaccount number.
   - ▸ Work package charge numbers are authorized by the work package manager's release of an AWP.

4. Regarding account charge number composition, an example of an internal charge number is 181–008–1–01. External charge numbers are alphabetized work package numbers. An example is 186–005–2–AB.
5. Regarding direct costs:
   ▸ All internal labor is charged to AWP charge numbers.
   ▸ Other direct costs are typically identified as: (1) Purchase services and other; (2) travel and subsistence; (3) computer, and (4) other allocated costs.
6. Indirect costs are elements defined by the organization.
   ▸ Indirect costs are charged to allocation pools and distributed to internal work packages. They may also be charged as actuals to work packages.
   ▸ Controllable labor overhead functions may be budgeted to separate work packages for monthly analysis of applied costs.

Note that actual cost categories and accounting system address numbers vary by organization. Extra care must be taken to integrate C/SCSC requirements with other critical management information processes within the specific organization.

Performance Measurement

Performance measurement for the cost account manager consists of evaluating work package status, with BCWP calculated at the work package level. Comparison of planned value (BCWS) versus earned value (BCWP) is made to obtain schedule variance. Comparison of BCWP to actual cost (ACWP) is made to obtain cost variance. Performance measurement provides a basis for management decisions by the organization and the customer. Six factors must be considered in performance measurement.

1. Performance measurement provides:
   ▸ Work progress status
   ▸ Relationship of planned cost and schedule to actual accomplishment
   ▸ Valid, timely, auditable data
   ▸ The base for estimate at completion, or latest revised estimates
   ▸ Summaries developed by the lowest practical WBS and organizational level
2. Regarding cost and schedule performance measurement:
   ▸ The elements required to measure project progress and status are: (1) work package schedule/work accomplished status; (2) the BCWS or planned expenditure; (3) the BCWP or earned value; and (4) the ACWP or recorded cost.
   ▸ The sum of AWP and PWP budget values (BCWS) should equal the cost account budget value.
   ▸ Development of budgets provides these capabilities: (1) the capability to plan and control cost; (2) the capability to identify incurred costs for actual accomplishments and work in progress; and (3) the cost account/work package BCWP measurement levels.
3. Performance measurement recognizes the importance of project budgets.
   ▸ Measurable work and related event status form the basis for determining progress status for BCWP calculations.

▸ BCWP measurements at summary WBS levels result from accumulating BCWP upward through the cost account from work package levels.

   ▸ Within each cost account, the inclusion of LOE is kept to a minimum to prevent distortion of the total BCWP.

   ▸ There are three calculation methods used for measuring work package performance: (1) Short work packages are less than three months long. Their earned value (BCWP) equals BCWS up to an 80 percent limit of the budget at completion until the work package is completed. (2) Long work packages exceed three months and use objective indicator milestones. The earned value (BCWP) equals BCWS up to the month-end prior to the first incompleted objective indicator. (3) Level of effort: Budget (BCWP) is earned through passage of time.

   ▸ The measurement method to be used is identified by the type of work package. Note that BCWP must always be earned the same way the BCWS was planned. (See Exhibit 13-3 for alternate methods of establishing BCWS and calculating BCWP.)

4. To develop and prepare a forecast to complete (FTC), the cost account manager must consider and analyze:
   ▸ Cumulative actuals/commitments
   ▸ The remaining CA budget
   ▸ Labor sheets and grade/levels
   ▸ Schedule status
   ▸ Previous quarterly FTC
   ▸ BCWP to date
   ▸ Cost improvements
   ▸ Historical data
   ▸ Future actions
   ▸ Approved changes

5. The CAM reports the FTC to the C/SCSC information processing department each quarter.

6. The information processing department makes the computer entry and summarization of the information to the reporting level appropriate for the project manager's review.

Variance Analysis

If performance measurement gives results in schedule or cost variances in excess of preestablished thresholds, analyses must be made to determine the cause. The CAM is mainly concerned with variances that exceed thresholds established for the project. Analyses of these variances provide opportunities to identify and resolve problems. Three factors are involved in variance analysis.

1. Preparation
   ▸ The cost-oriented variance analyses include a review of cumulative and at-completion cost data. In-house performance reports exhibit cost and schedule dollar differences from the cost account plan.
   ▸ The calendar-schedule analyses include a review of any (scheduling subsys-

Exhibit 13-3. Alternate methods of establishing BCWS and calculating BCWP.

0/100	Take all credit for performing work when the work package is complete.
50/50	Take credit for performing one-half of the work at the start of the work package; take credit for performing the remaining one-half when the work package is complete.
Discrete Value Milestones	Divide work into separate, measurable activities and take credit for performing each activity during the time period it is completed.
Equivalent Units	If there are numerous similar items to complete, assume each is worth an equivalent portion of the total work package value; take credit for performance according to the number of items completed during the period.
Percentage Complete	Associate estimated percentages of work package to be completed with specific time periods; take credit for performance if physical inspection indicates percentages have been achieved.
Modified Milestone-Percentage Complete	Combines the discrete value milestone and percent complete techniques by allowing some "subjective estimate" of work accomplishment and credit for the associated earned value during reporting periods where no discrete milestone is scheduled to be completed. The subjective earning of value for nonmilestone work is usually limited to one reporting period or up to 80 percent of the value of the next scheduled discrete milestone. No additional value can be earned until the scheduled discrete milestone is completed.
Level of Effort	Based on a planned amount of support effort, assign value per period; take credit for performance based on passage of time.
Apportioned Effort	Milestones are developed as a percentage of a controlling discrete work package; take credit for performance upon completion of a related discrete milestone.

tem) milestones that cause more than one month criticality to the contract milestones.

▸ Variances are identified to the CA level during this stage of the review.
  ▸ Both cost variance and schedule variance are developed for the current period and cumulative as well as at-completion status.
  ▸ Determination is made whether a variance is cost-oriented, schedule-oriented, or both.
  ▸ Variance analysis reports are developed on significant CA variances.
2. Presentation
  ▸ Variance analyses should be prepared when one or more of the following exceed the thresholds established by the project manager: (1) schedule variance (BCWP to BCWS); (2) cost variance (BCWP to ACWP); or (3) at-completion variance (budget at completion to latest revised estimate, or LRE).

3. Operation
   ▸ Internal analysis reports document variances that exceed thresholds: schedule problem analysis reports for "time-based" linear schedule, or cost account variance analysis reports for dollar variances.
   ▸ Explanations are submitted to the customer when contractual thresholds are exceeded.
   ▸ Emphasis should be placed upon corrective action for resolution of variant conditions.
     ▸ Corrective action should be assigned to specific individuals (cost account managers) and tracked for effectiveness and completion.
     ▸ Internal project variance analyses and corrective action should be formally reviewed in monthly management meetings.
     ▸ Informal reviews of cost and schedule variance analysis data may occur daily, weekly, or monthly, depending on the nature and severity of the variance.

Exhibit 13-4 presents some sample comparisons of BCWS, BCWP, and ACWP.

The Appendix of this chapter contains additional graphic examples that show how the relationships between BCWS, BCWP, and ACWP are interpreted and applied to tracking project progress.

Reporting

There are two basic report categories: customer and in-house. Customer performance reports are contractually established with fixed content and timing. In-house reports support internal projects with the data that relate to lower organizational and WBS levels. The CAM is mainly concerned with these lower-level reports.

1. Customer reporting
   ▸ A customer requires summary-level reporting, typically on a monthly basis.
   ▸ The customer examines the detailed data for areas that may indicate a significant variance.

Exhibit 13-4. Comparisons of BCWS, BCWP, and ACWP.

BCWS	BCWP	ACWP	Condition
$100	$100	$100	On Schedule—On Cost
$200	$200	$100	On Schedule—Underrun
$100	$100	$200	On Schedule—Overrun
$100	$200	$200	Ahead of Schedule—On Cost
$100	$200	$100	Ahead of Schedule—Underrun
$100	$200	$300	Ahead of Schedule—Overrun
$200	$100	$100	Behind Schedule—On Cost
$300	$200	$100	Behind Schedule—Underrun
$200	$100	$300	Behind Schedule—Overrun

- ▸ The cost performance report (CPR) is the vehicle used to accumulate and report cost and schedule performance data.
2. In-house reporting
   - ▸ Internal management practices emphasize assignment of responsibility for internal reports to an individual CAM.
   - ▸ Reporting formats reflect past and current performance and the forecast level of future performance.
   - ▸ Performance review meetings are held: (1) monthly for cost and schedule; and (2) as needed for review of problem areas.
   - ▸ The CAM emphasizes cumulative to-date and to-go cost, schedule, and equivalent manpower on the CA work packages.
      - ▸ It is primarily at the work package level that review of performance (BCWP), actuals (ACWP), and budget (BCWS) is coupled with objective judgment to determine the FTC.
      - ▸ The CAM is responsible for the accuracy and completeness of the estimates.

Internal Audit/Verification and Review

The cost account manager is the most significant contributor to the successful operation of a C/SCSC process and to successful completion of any subsequent internal audits or customer reviews. Day-to-day management of the project takes place at the cost account level. If each CA is not managed competently, project performance suffers regardless of the sophistication of the higher-level management system. The organization and the customer should place special emphasis on CAM performance during operational demonstration reviews.

A Final Warning

The C/SCSC approach to project management may be the most comprehensive and effective method of developing plans and providing decision-making information ever conceived. But to achieve maximum potential benefit, the extensive use of a computer becomes inevitable. Software especially developed to support C/SCSC applications is currently available for nearly every computer hardware configuration: micro, mini, and mainframe.

When considering which computer hardware/software combination will best satisfy your needs, carefully evaluate your specific project application, i.e., size of projects, frequency of reporting, ease of modification, potential for expansion, and graphic output requirements. This computer hardware/software decision could be the difference between success and failure in a C/SCSC application, so don't rush it! Make your selection only after a thorough investigation and evaluation. Don't let anyone sell you something you don't need or want.

References

Lee R. Lambert, *Consideration of a Cost/Schedule Control System by Research & Development/Demonstration Personnel or What's In It for Me?* Battelle Memorial Institute, October 1981.

Lee R. Lambert, "Cost/Schedule Control System Criteria (C/SCSC)—A Lighthearted Introduction for the Technical Non-Believer." *American Association of Cost Engineers Symposium Proceedings* (July 1988).

Lee R. Lambert, "Program Control From the Bottom Up—Exploring the Working Side." *Project Management Journal* (March 1985). Also presented at 1983 *Joint Project Management Institute/INTERNET Symposium*, Boston.

Lee R. Lambert, "Project Management Education Becomes Knowledge—The Migration of Academic Theory to Applied Reality." *Project Management Journal* (August 1984).

Lee R. Lambert, "Understanding the Value of Earned Value or Where Have All Your Dollars Gone?" *American Association of Cost Engineers Symposium Proceedings* (June 1989).

U.S. Government Documents on C/SCSC

U.S. Department of Defense, Instruction 7000.2, "Performance Measurement of Selected Acquisitions," Washington, D.C.

U.S. Department of Energy, Order 2250.1, "Cost and Schedule Control System Criteria (C/SCSC) for Contract Performance Measurement," Washington, D.C.

Appendix

DATA UTILIZATION FORMULAS
FOR ANALYSIS

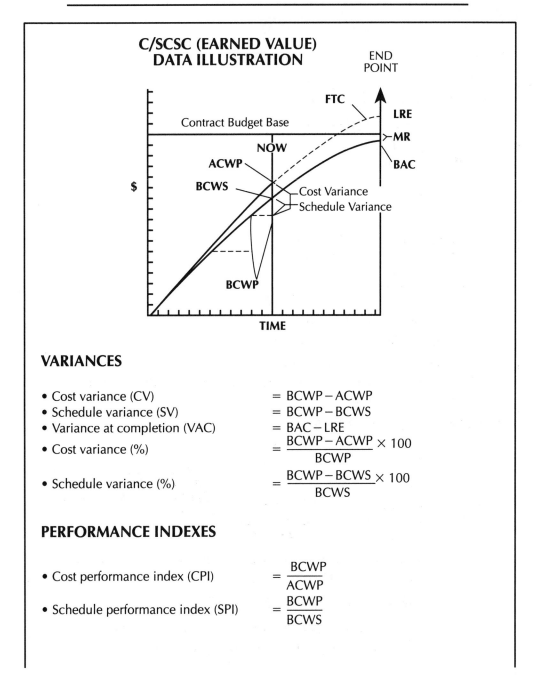

VARIANCES

- Cost variance (CV) $= BCWP - ACWP$
- Schedule variance (SV) $= BCWP - BCWS$
- Variance at completion (VAC) $= BAC - LRE$
- Cost variance (%) $= \dfrac{BCWP - ACWP}{BCWP} \times 100$

- Schedule variance (%) $= \dfrac{BCWP - BCWS}{BCWS} \times 100$

PERFORMANCE INDEXES

- Cost performance index (CPI) $= \dfrac{BCWP}{ACWP}$

- Schedule performance index (SPI) $= \dfrac{BCWP}{BCWS}$

(continues)

"TO COMPLETE" PERFORMANCE INDEX (TCPI)

At EAC, or at LRE

- $\dfrac{\text{Work remaining}}{\text{Money remaining}} = \dfrac{\text{BAC} - \text{BCWP}}{\text{EAC or LRE} - \text{ACWP}}$

At BAC

- $\dfrac{\text{Work remaining}}{\text{Budget remaining}} = \dfrac{\text{BAC} - \text{BCWP}}{\text{BAC} - \text{ACWP}}$

% SCHEDULED/COMPLETE/SPENT

- % scheduled $= \dfrac{\text{BCWS}}{\text{BAC}} \times 100$

- % spent $= \dfrac{\text{ACWP}}{\text{BAC}} \times 100$

ESTIMATED AT COMPLETION
(CONSIDERS COST VARIANCES ONLY)

- EAC or LRE $= \dfrac{\text{BAC}}{\text{CPI}}$

ESTIMATED AT COMPLETION
WITH PERFORMANCE FACTORING (PF)*

- EAC or LRE $=$ ACWP $+$ PF (BAC $-$ BCWP)

* The performance factor (PF) is a prediction of what it will cost for each $1 of planned work remaining.

SCHEDULE CONVERSIONS

- Months ahead or behind $= \dfrac{\text{SV}}{\text{Average monthly BCWS**}}$

NOTE: *This conversion may be misleading. Distortion occurs if network schedule/critical path activities aren't properly considered.*

- Projected at completion months ahead or behind $= \dfrac{(\text{BAC/SPI}) - \text{BAC}}{\text{Average monthly BCWS**}}$

**The average BCWS may be calculated using the total contract months to date or a selected number of recent months.

MATERIAL PRICE AND USAGE VARIANCES

- Usage variance $=$ (planned quantity $-$ actual quantity) $\times$ planned price
- Price variance $=$ (planned price $-$ actual price) $\times$ actual quantity

SAMPLE
COST/SCHEDULE VARIANCE THRESHOLDS

Project variances for current month, cumulative-to-date, and at-completion: Project variances at selected reportable WBS levels shall be explained in narrative whenever the percentage (%) AND the associated dollar variance (V) EXCEED these tolerances:

Type of Variance	Variance Thresholds for Each Reportable WBS Level
Current Month	$\% = \pm\ 10\%$ $V = \pm\ \$25,000$
Cumulative or Fiscal Year-To-Date	$\% = \pm\ 10\%$ $V = \pm\ \$25,000$
At-Completion	$\% = \pm\ 10\%$ $V = \pm\ \$25,000$

Where V (cost) = BCWP (−) ACWP

or V (schedule) = BCWP (−) BCWS

And the Cost Percentage = V (cost) ÷ BCWS = $\dfrac{\text{BCWP (−) BCWS}}{\text{BCWP}} \times 100$

or the Schedule Percentage = V (schedule) ÷ BCWS =
$\dfrac{\text{BCWP (−) BCWS}}{\text{BCWS}} \times 100$

At Completion Percentage = V (at-completion) ÷ BAC = $\dfrac{\text{BAC (−) LRE}}{\text{BAC}} \times 100$

Also, regardless of the combined (percentage and dollar value) tolerances: (1) any dollar variance greater than $100K in the current month, cumulative or at-completion, or (2) any milestone slippage that causes more than one-month criticality to the contractor's project plan, or (3) any performance indicator milestone forcast that is more than one month later than scheduled, **shall be explained.**

Variance of the above magnitudes require analysis of cause, impact, and potential corrective actions during preparation of a Problem Analysis Report.

Note: Variance thresholds should be throughly evaluated and established for each project. Type and size of project determine thresholds.

SAMPLE LOGIC AND
CONSISTENCY CHECKS

LOGIC CHECK	EXPLANATION
CURRENT BCWP/BCWS RATIO INDICATES POOR PLANNING	The amount of work performed during the reporting period was less than half the amount of work scheduled.
CURRENT BCWP/ACWP RATIO INDICATES POOR EARNING METHOD	The actual cost of the work performed during the reporting period was less than half the budgeted cost for such work.
CUMULATIVE BCWS WITH NO CUMULATIVE BCWP	No work has been performed to-date, in a category for which work was scheduled in this or an earlier reporting period.
BCWP INCREASE WITHOUT ACWP INCREASE	Cost has increased without work being performed.
ACWP CHARGED TO UNOPENED TASK	Task has not started; therefore, no cost should be charged.
BAC OR BCWS INCONSISTENCY—DATA SHOULD BE CORRECTED	Cumulative time-phased budget assigned to task cannot be greater than total budgeted value.
LREAC OR ACWP INCONSISTENCY— DATA SHOULD BE CORRECTED	Money spent to date cannot exceed the total amount to be spent for a task.
LREAC POSSIBLE INCONSISTENCY—LREAC DOES NOT REFLECT CUMULATIVE COST OVERRUN	Indicated contractor's LREAC is unrealistic when compared to performance date.

14

Value Engineering and Project Management: Achieving Cost Optimization

Alfred I. Paley
NRI Associates

Value analysis/value engineering (VA/VE) provides project managers with a powerful tool for maintaining quality standards while eliminating unnecessary costs and giving visibility for cost reduction efforts in the event of cost growth. In essence, it provides a "how to" answer to the question, "What can be done to reduce costs, yet maintain technical performance?"

Management of costs is one of the three major tasks of project management, and in fact it is the bottom line in the measurement of project success. In addition to completing the project with technical excellence, and on time, the project must be completed within budget to be fully successful. Project management requires that the following activities and actions take place: the project must be planned; the resources must be obtained and organized; progress must be monitored; and control must be exercised so that program goals and objectives are met. The plan must allow for the establishment of the organization and development of the structure to communicate and manage staffing and material and provide the visibility to understand what is happening in each phase of the project. Monitoring the status of the plan is necessary so that control can be effected. However, in the event that monitoring has indicated a problem, monitoring alone does not suggest solutions.

Cost growth is one of the most difficult items to correct in a project management task. Tools for cost management are often not sufficiently detailed, and cost management is left to the simple statement that a "good cost control system" should be used. Most modern cost control systems are based on the work breakdown structure (WBS), which is used as a basis for developing the budget. Feedback of charges against the WBS is designed to detail the project status with regard to "actuals." The actuals are a record of what has taken place, the historical and precisely accurate accounting of charges to the project. The actuals are compared with the previously established budgets, and in that way, deviations are detected so that corrections can be made. This methodology also provides the measurement tool for design-to-cost programs. However, it is one thing to detect cost growth, and another to know what to do after the growth has occurred. Correction of cost overruns on individual WBS items often leads to reducing the quality of the overall project in an attempt to achieve cost goals. In addition, problems may be encountered because of the fact that budgeting skills are not easily learned. Many project management systems provide the ability to learn from past experience by capturing actuals from previous projects for comparison purposes. The cost history from previous projects is then used to develop estimates for the present project, with consideration for complexity, learning curves, personnel changes, and experience factors.

The difficulty encountered in managing costs is apparent from the number of projects that experience cost overruns. As a project management adage states: "No project has ever been done within cost, and yours will not be the first!" The methodology of value analysis/value engineering is most useful in the cost control aspect of project management, since it addresses itself to maintaining quality while eliminating unnecessary costs, which are present in all designs, products, processes, and procedures. VA/VE used up-front in the concept stage avoids unnecessary costs from the beginning. The application of function-oriented VA/VE methodology provides insight into relationships of functions so that cost drivers, customer needs, and identification of unnecessary costs are provided and intelligent management decision making can occur. Function-oriented VA/VE is used in the product planning, design, and support phases.

Historical Beginnings

Value analysis began in the United States after World War II as a result of experiences by members of the War Production Board on their major project management task: winning the war. After the successful conclusion of the war, the members of the War Production Board returned to their previous positions in industry. During debriefing, members who returned to the General Electric Company reported the following observation: Quite often, in order to maintain the flow of materials and parts needed in the war effort, substitutions had to be made for items in short supply or delayed; more often than not, the substitutions worked just as well, but cost less. The reasons were not understood by the observers or the investigators.

At General Electric, a study was undertaken to understand the phenomenon and perhaps to be able to obtain the benefits of reduced costs on purpose, instead of by accident. The study resulted in the realization that what had been required in the instance of the specification of the part or material was the "function" of the part or material, and not necessarily the specific part or material ordered. The study found that if in a design or other requirement, function was determined initially, and a search was made for alternative ways to accomplish the function, then less expensive items could be selected to accomplish the function. Lawrence D. Miles, a GE engineer assigned to the purchasing department for the study, published the results in *Techniques of Value Engineering Analysis* (McGraw-Hill, 1956). In the book, he also developed the concept of orders of functions (basic and supporting secondary) and of how to identify unnecessary functions. From this original effort, the discipline of VA/VE developed and has proved to be a significant methodology for eliminating unnecessary costs in existing products, processes, and procedures and during design and planning phases of all forms of efforts, while maintaining the specified function.

The function-oriented discipline of VA/VE was coupled with structured problem solving to develop the methodology that is now called by various names, including analysis, value engineering, value management, value control, and value assurance. For most individuals in the field, the terms are synonymous. In this chapter, the acronym VA/VE is used.

The VA/VE Methodology

The VA/VE process embodies the function analysis discipline within a structured problem-solving methodology. Function analysis is the core of VA/VE and is the basic discipline that provides the power that makes the methodology work.

Function is defined as that which makes the product, process, or procedure (the item under study, or IUS) work. Sometimes the definition is extended to include the concept that the product, process, or procedure must both work and sell. The question "what does it do?" is asked of the IUS. For example, if a toaster were under analysis, the answer to the question would be, "It burns bread." *Burn bread* is a function. However, there are many other functions included in the toaster, such as heat the element, generate heat, conduct electricity, lower bread (to heating element), pop up bread (when toasted), control degree (of burn of the bread), contain parts, provide pleasant decor, and provide protection (of the table surface). Identification of all the function is necessary for the analysis to be effective.

The functions are defined, as much as possible, using two words: a verb and a noun. The verb is an active word, such as *provide, contain, emit,* or *generate.* The noun is a measurable word, such as *light, heat, parts, liquid,* or *solid.* The noun must be measurable. (How much liquid? How much heat? What weight of parts?) The two-word approach forces a concise definition of the functions and focuses the thinking of the team of analysts who are performing the VA/VE study on a specific point.

The functions identified for the IUS are then analyzed to identify the relationships of the functions. A *basic function* is identified. The rules of function analysis are that everything has one and only one basic function. The test for proper identification of the basic function is that if it were not needed, then all the other functions could be eliminated. In our example of the toaster, if it did not burn bread, all the other functions would be irrelevant.

A relationship between functions is obtained through use of a function analysis system technique (FAST) diagram. A form of FAST diagram is shown in Exhibit 14-1. Noted on it are the rules for developing the diagram. The diagram provides graphic two-dimensional presentation of the functions and identifies the basic function, secondary and supporting functions, higher-order functions, and various other variations. It also assists in defining a critical path of functions starting from the initiating element through the supporting functions and basic function, to the higher-order function. The order of the functions follows a logic arrangement in which functions going in the left direction answer *why* (why is the function to the right performed?), and the functions going in the right direction answer *how* (how is the function to the left performed?). The FAST diagram also identifies unnecessary

Exhibit 14-1. FAST diagram.

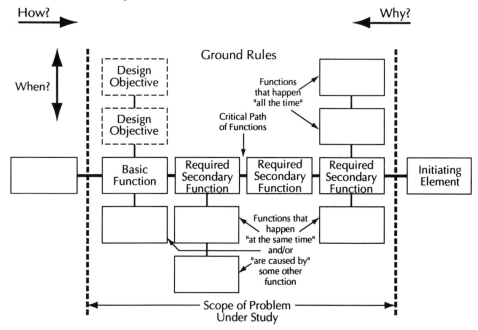

functions that may exist in the IUS. These functions are identified by examination of the how-why logic and reveal themselves in the analysis.

After the FAST diagram is generated, the next step is to assign costs to each function to establish a cost-function relationship. This step is important, as it reveals the problem and where it really exists. The costs associated with the IUS must be divided and allocated to the functions. Since the basic function is the most important, the majority of costs would be assumed to be allocated there. What is invariably seen is that a disproportionate division of costs exists, with little regard given to the importance in the critical path of functions. The FAST diagram may show that the major cost factors are not even on the critical path of functions. The problem then becomes one of finding less costly ways to accomplish the secondary functions without sacrificing performance or quality.

The FAST diagram does not provide the solution, but it defines the problems and shows the cost imbalances so that analysts can search for alternative solutions, which can reduce the costs of secondary functions or eliminate unnecessary functions and the costs associated with them.

Structured problem solving requires the use of a procedure that defines the order to be followed in the search for the solution to the problem. One such problem-solving procedure is diagrammed in Exhibit 14-2. The first step is the examination of the unsatisfactory situations. From the examination, the problems are defined (Step 2). Once the problems are defined, the use of creative thinking processes, such as brainstorming, are employed in Step 3 to develop a choice of possible solutions. The fourth step is the evaluation to select the best solution for the defined problems. And finally, in Step 5, action to implement the selected solution is presented to the decision makers. The most difficult and most important step in the procedure is the

Exhibit 14-2. Five steps in problem solving.

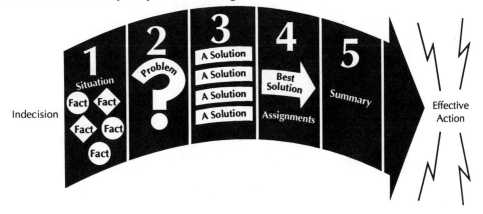

problem definition, since if the problem is not properly identified and defined, successful solutions will not be found, and the real problem will never be solved. Solutions for symptoms or unsatisfactory situations are generally not solutions to problems. A key element in problem solving is to complete each step in the outlined procedure before the next step is begun.

An example of the solution to a symptom is illustrated in the case of a wet floor that becomes slippery and causes people to fall with risk of injury. The apparent solution is to dry the floor. This works in the short term, but it is inadequate if the problem stems from rainwater passing through a hole in the roof. The problem is the hole in the roof, which is not remedied by the obvious solution to a wet floor: drying the floor.

The VA/VE Workshop

The VA/VE process generally includes a VA/VE workshop. The workshop employs a multidisciplinary team to analyze a product, process, or procedure to answer the following five questions:

1. What is it?
2. What does it do?
3. What does it cost?
4. What else can do the job?
5. What does that cost?

The objective of these questions and the answers to them is to provide visibility into function and cost and to establish the cost-function relationship for the multidisciplinary team. This visibility results in creative discontent of the team members, both individually and as a group. The creative discontent is used to develop alternative solutions in the search for increased value (see Exhibit 14-3). The purpose of the procedure is to obtain maximum value, which is achieved when the lowest cost is realized to perform the required functions.

Exhibit 14-3. Use of creative discontent.

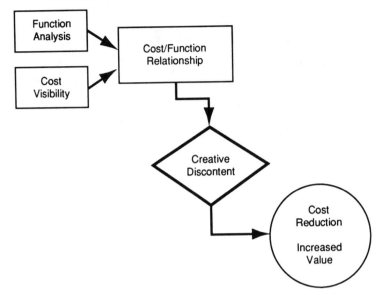

The VA/VE workshop follows a prescribed job plan that provides a disciplined procedure to achieve the answers to the five questions. The phases of the job plan are:

Phase 1: Information Phase. This involves several procedures.
- ▸ Define the scope of the task or problem to be analyzed. This answers, "What is it?"
- ▸ Define function or functions by developing the FAST diagram. This answers, "What does it do?"
- ▸ Provide cost visibility and develop cost-function relationships using the FAST diagram. This answers, "What does it cost?"
- ▸ Reexamine scope. At this point, based on the cost-function relationships and the identification of cost drivers and basic and secondary functions, the team may through creative discontent want to reconsider the scope of the analysis to study a particular function in more depth.

Phase 2: Speculative Phase. In this phase, creative brainstorming takes place in search of alternative ways to achieve, alter, or eliminate unnecessary functions. This answers, "What else can do the job?"

Phase 3: Evaluation Phase. The new ideas are considered and sorted, and costs are determined for comparison and selection of the best alternatives. This answers, "What does that cost?"

Phase 4: Planning Phase. Here, the team determines the approach for implementing the new ideas.

Phase 5: Execution Phase. Follow the plan of Phase 4.

Phase 6: Report Phase. The team documents and presents the results of the workshop to the decision makers showing the concept, detailed solutions, and cost benefits.

Exhibit 14-4. Outline of VA/VE workshop.

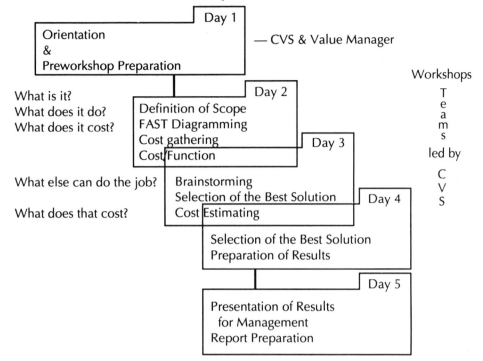

Teams, CVS, & Value Manager

A VA/VE workshop generally requires forty hours to conduct. During that period, a trained leader (a certified value specialist—CVS—certified by the Society of American Value Engineers, is recommended) leads teams of five or six individuals working on related pieces of the system being studied. Training of the teams in the techniques of value analysis is done concurrently as part of the workshop.

Fundamental to achieving the results of improved value (reduced cost for the same quality requirements) are:

▸ Following the job plan rigorously
▸ Training the teams in the VA/VE techniques
▸ Generating team enthusiasm and motivation for creativity enhancement

Exhibit 14-4 outlines the job plan and its timing during a five-day VA/VE workshop.

Application of Value Analysis/Value Engineering

VA/VE has become a standard in construction, manufacturing, government contracting, military procurement, and other areas of business and industry. Many construction contracts call for a VE workshop at the 35 percent point in design. The U.S.

government includes value engineering clauses in military procurement contracts in which savings are shared with contractors submitting approved value engineering change proposals, and it requires other government agencies to utilize the value engineering clauses in their procurements. The use of VA/VE in project management provides an effective tool for the control of costs, while maintaining performance and quality standards.

Section VI

Teamwork and Team Building

15

Models for Achieving Project Success Through Team Building and Stakeholder Management

John Tuman, Jr.
Management Technologies Group, Inc.

This chapter presents innovative techniques for building successful project teams. Specifically, the chapter defines project success; identifies who determines project success; describes techniques for measuring project success; and explains how to develop a model for creating a winning team. The goal of the chapter is to help project managers build teams with a success culture—that is, teams that have success ingrained in their values, beliefs, processes, procedures, and management style.

What Is Project Success?

A project is a success if all the work goes as planned. This assumes the project has developed a good plan and there are no surprises. In a successful project, objectives are well defined, work is accomplished as scheduled, and resources are used efficiently. Furthermore, the client is pleased with the final results. Most important, the whole job is done without mishap, controversy, or lawsuit. In addition, management acknowledges a fine job and rewards everyone handsomely.

Projects seldom work out this way. One reason is that project objectives have different meanings for different people. Work tasks run into roadblocks, get delayed, and consume resources. Critics attack the project, unexpected problems develop, and people get discouraged and quit. Project success means handling all the unexpected problems and getting the job done to project stakeholders' satisfaction. Project teams increasingly address a complex mix of issues, problems, and aspirations. These include not only the goals and ambitions of project participants but also of outside parties. To be successful, project teams must understand who determines success, what their motivations are, and what the costs involved are.

Who Determines Project Success?

In every undertaking there are parties with a vested interest in the activities and results of the project. The motivations of the project sponsors and those who do the work are obvious. Individuals affected by the project are concerned. Still others are motivated by political, social, environmental, and economic interests. These parties are called *stakeholders:* individuals with some kind of stake, claim, share, or interest in the activities and results of the project.

The role of the stakeholders and the influence they have is not always understood by project managers. This can be a serious problem for several reasons. First, the project manager has to build a project team that has the skill to address all stakeholder requirements and concerns. Second, the team must develop strategies for dealing with different levels of stakeholder power. Finally, resources must be obtained to deal with stakeholder issues that are beyond normal project demands. Project managers must study the different stakeholders to understand how they can influence project success.

Project stakeholders can be categorized into four main groups, as shown in Exhibit 15-1. These include: (1) project champions, (2) project participants, (3) community participants, and (4) parasitic participants. The potential role and influence of each group is discussed in the sections that follow.

Project Champions

Project champions are those who have some reason to bring a project into being. These stakeholders include the developers, investors, and entrepreneurs motivated by profit. The group also includes the visionaries who are trying to create something for the future or for the benefit of others. Also included is the client or customer with a specific need. Project champions can also include politicians, community leaders, and others who want to satisfy the needs of their constituents. The role of the project champion is significant; in most cases the project cannot exist without them. Furthermore, the judgments, evaluations, and perceptions of these stakeholders probably have the greatest effect in confirming project success. The project champions must be fully satisfied, or the project is not a success. Obviously, the composition of the project champions as well as their needs and perceptions can vary widely. In some cases, the individual goals and objectives of those within this group are in conflict with each other.

Project Participants

This group of stakeholders includes organizations and individuals who are responsible for planning and executing the project. Typically, this includes the project manager and project team, engineers, constructors, vendors, suppliers, craftspeople, and regulatory agencies at the local, state, and national levels. The involvement of the project participants is again fairly obvious. Success from their viewpoint means accomplishing the project goals and receiving appropriate recognition.

Exhibit 15-1. Four groups of project stakeholders.

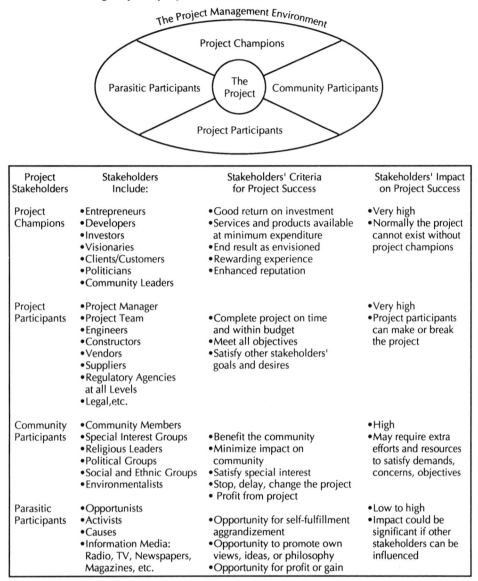

Project Stakeholders	Stakeholders Include:	Stakeholders' Criteria for Project Success	Stakeholders' Impact on Project Success
Project Champions	•Entrepreneurs •Developers •Investors •Visionaries •Clients/Customers •Politicians •Community Leaders	•Good return on investment •Services and products available at minimum expenditure •End result as envisioned •Rewarding experience •Enhanced reputation	•Very high •Normally the project cannot exist without project champions
Project Participants	•Project Manager •Project Team •Engineers •Constructors •Vendors •Suppliers •Regulatory Agencies at all Levels •Legal,etc.	•Complete project on time and within budget •Meet all objectives •Satisfy other stakeholders' goals and desires	•Very high •Project participants can make or break the project
Community Participants	•Community Members •Special Interest Groups •Religious Leaders •Political Groups •Social and Ethnic Groups •Environmentalists	•Benefit the community •Minimize impact on community •Satisfy special interest •Stop, delay, change the project • Profit from project	•High •May require extra efforts and resources to satisfy demands, concerns, objectives
Parasitic Participants	•Opportunists •Activists •Causes •Information Media: Radio, TV, Newspapers, Magazines, etc.	•Opportunity for self-fulfillment aggrandizement •Opportunity to promote own views, ideas, or philosophy •Opportunity for profit or gain	•Low to high •Impact could be significant if other stakeholders can be influenced

Community Participants

These stakeholders include groups or individuals who are directly affected by the project. Community participants create the environment that surrounds the project. The group can materialize because of environmental, social, political, economic, health, or safety concerns. These stakeholders can be a few households concerned about increased traffic from a new facility or a religious group opposed to a new technology. They can have a profound impact on a project. For example, antinuclear groups have stopped the construction of nuclear power plants, environmentalists have halted highway construction programs, and religious groups have challenged genetic research projects.

Parasitic Participants

This group of stakeholders presents an interesting and important challenge to project managers. Parasitic participants consist of organizations and individuals who do not have a direct stake in the project. In this group we find the opportunists, the activists, and others who are looking for a focal point for their energies, internal drives, and desires to promote their personal philosophies and views. By definition, this group is distinct and different from those whose members have legitimate concerns about the impact of a project on their community or way of life. The distinction is that the primary motivation of the parasitic participant is one of self-aggrandizement. The project provides the parasitic participants with an opportunity for activity, visibility, and self-fulfillment and a platform to promote their philosophy or ideas.

This group also covers the information media: radio, TV, newspapers, magazines, etc. The information media use the interest, attention, concerns, or controversy that can surround a project as a vehicle to sell their products. If projects can be made to appear controversial, sensational, dangerous, exciting, or risky, they become more newsworthy. Usually, the information media have no direct stake in the project, yet their influence on the project can be devastating.

Success Modeling

Can we model success? Experience and common sense teach us that some project teams function better than others. Most of the time we do not see what the team actually does; however, we do see and judge the final results. To learn from others, we need to look at the specific actions that make them different, better, or unique. Ideally, we want to capture this experience in a way that helps to guide our thinking and spark our creativity.

Success modeling provides a tool and a methodology that disciplines project managers to define consciously and deliberately the criteria for success of the project. In addition, success modeling provides a framework for team building, strategy development, and actual planning and control of project success.

Models can be used to represent a project (see Exhibit 15-2). Furthermore, we can simulate the project environment to test the soundness of the project models. Thus, it is possible to test different assumptions about project plans and organizational approaches before actually starting the project. The goal of modeling and simulation is to determine if the project team, plans, procedures, and systems are correct before committing resources to the project.

We can use modeling techniques to build a team for a specific undertaking within a specific environment. Furthermore, these techniques can help to create a cultural framework for team success. Creating a success model involves a number of specific steps that are discussed in the following sections.

Establish Project Success Goals

Defining the project success goals sets the baseline for measuring project success. The success goals must include the stakeholders' needs and desires as well as the

Exhibit 15-2. Project management model.

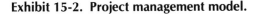

Elements of the Project Management Model	
People	The designated project participants. Identify the key decision makers and contributors to the planning, organizing, and controlling of the project activities and resources.
Situations	The specific problems defined within the context of the conditions, wants, and limitations thathe actual project ios expected to experience.
Issues and Requirements	The specific concerns, problems, and requirements that the project will face. This includes cost, schedule, and technical issues of the project as well as organization, staffing, communications, legal, political, cultural and social issues.
Environmental Conditions	The outside influences that impact the project. They may include physical conditions (i.e., geographic, climate, etc.), political, legal, social/cultural, economic, infrastructural, etc.
Project Simulation	Special exercises and problems in which the project participants interact to deal with specific issues and requirements for given situations and conditions.
Simulation Results	Data on how the project participants interacted with each other; their reactions to problem situations and environmental conditions and the actual decisions and solutions formulated to address specific problems.
Analysis and Action Plans	An evaluation of the simulation results against the issues and requirements of the project, to determine if the project team can effectively carry out their responsibilities. The specific actions relative to people, procedures, plans, systems, and resources to be taken.

cost, schedule, and technical objectives of the project. We can get information about the stakeholders by talking to them and opening lines of communication—i.e., advertising, surveys, public meetings, information hot lines, etc. Also, the relationships among stakeholder goals must be established. Are there conflicting goals? Are any of the goals mutually supportive? Do these goals have a positive or negative impact on the project?

A stakeholder study is called for in the conceptual phase. For a straightforward project, the stakeholders' goals may be simple and easy to understand. They may even be compatible with the project team's goals. However, for a complex or controversial project, there is usually a bewildering array of stakeholders' concerns and interests. The project team must sort out the different concerns and interests and determine which stakeholders have the leverage to hinder project success.

Exhibit 15-3 presents a technique for identifying and ranking project stakeholders. This technique produces numerical values to establish the power of the stakeholders and the degree of difficulty of their goal. In evaluating project stakeholders' success goals, we look at the characteristics of the goals (difficulty, conflict with other goals, etc.) and the power that each stakeholder has (to impact project resources, success, and so on). Then, a simple 1 to 5 scale is used to rate each factor. Each rating is multiplied by that factor's weight to obtain the weighted scale. The scales and weights used should reflect management's requirements. For example, a finer scale would be used for a project that has many factors to consider.

The final weighted scores are then used to develop a stakeholder success grid, as shown in Exhibit 15-4. The success grid shows the relationship between the difficulty of the stakeholders' goals and their power to influence project success. The informa-

Exhibit 15-3. Technique for identifying and ranking success goals of stakeholders.

Project Stakeholders	Power Factors and Weights			Success Goal Factors and Weights			
	Impact Resources (0.35)	Impact Success (0.65)	Weighted Score (x-Axis)	Difficulty 0.5	Risk/ Unknowns 0.35	Conflict 0.15	Weighted Score (y-Axis)
Project Champions							
• Developers	3	4	2.60	5	4	2	4.20
• Client/Customers	2	4	3.30	3	4	2	3.20
• Politicians	1	5	3.60	3	1	3	2.30
• Community Leaders	4	5	4.65	5	1	4	3.45
• Visionaries	1	3	2.30	2	1	2	1.65
Project Participants							
• Project Management	5	2	3.05	3	3	3	3.00
• Vendors	1	2	1.65	3	4	1	3.05
• Regulators	1	2	1.65	4	5	5	4.50
• Constructors	4	1	2.05	2	2	1	1.85
Community Participants							
• Special Interest Groups	2	2	2.00	5	1	5	3.60
• Environmentalists	3	2	2.35	4	1	5	3.10
Parasitic Participants							
• Media	4	5	4.65	4	5	1	3.90
• Activists	4	3	3.35	5	5	5	5.00

tion from the success grid is ranked by quadrant. In the example shown in Exhibit 15-4, stakeholders not directly involved in the project—activist groups, the media, and community leaders—have a major impact on project success.

From these analyses, the project team members can develop plans and processes to focus their energy and resources where they will do the most good.

Identify the Success Process

Management processes are required to accomplish project work effectively and efficiently. Project work involves planning, organizing, and directing resources and people to address stakeholder issues and project cost, schedule, and technical objectives. Often, stakeholders focus on the qualitative aspects of the project. Their concerns include health, safety, reliability, quality, and environmental issues. Nevertheless, the team must implement a process to manage all the project's requirements and activities in a systematic manner. For simplicity, we can break down the project's responsibilities into two types of activities: hard and soft.

Hard activities relate to the business of planning and controlling work scope, task, resources, practices, and standards. Hard activities also encompass the basic management functions of communicating, information processing, and decision making. Soft activities relate to behavioral modifications and opinion shaping. These

Exhibit 15-4. Stakeholder success grid.

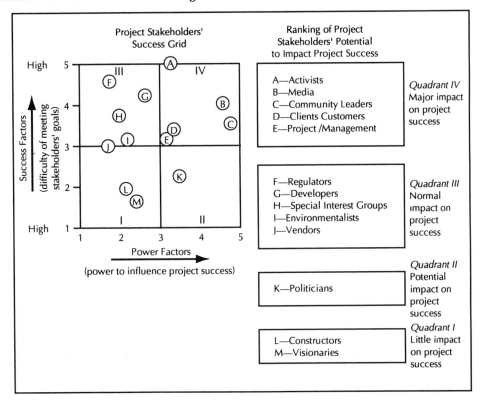

include training, team building, community relations, advertising, and promotion. Later in this chapter we will discuss ways of dealing with soft project activities.

Map the Success Characteristics

Successful project teams develop a culture and a management style that fits the project environment. These teams understand the political, legal, social, and economic situation as well as the infrastructure and physical conditions. Project teams must analyze their project environment as a military leader evaluates the terrain before a battle. The team must thoroughly evaluate the demands of its project environment and ask the question, "What must we do and how must we act to be successful under these conditions or in these situations?"

Project success mapping, as shown in Exhibit 15-5, first looks at the five components that are vital to project success: (1) the resources available; (2) the difficulty of the project itself; (3) the demands and perceptions of the stakeholders; (4) the conditions and problems presented by the project environment; and (5) the level of management and sponsor commitment. The second step is to determine the project team's ability to (1) control, (2) influence, and (3) react/respond to all of the requirements and problems presented by the five main components for project success.

The project team controls, influences, or reacts/responds to needs and situations by engaging in both hard and soft activities. In hard activities, the team controls, influences, or reacts/responds to project requirements by managing resources, applying practices or standards, or doing more or less work (scope of work). The team can also control, influence, or react/respond to project requirements through soft activities. That is, the team can seek to shape opinions and attitudes and modify behaviors through training, team building, advertising, promotion, and community relations.

Project success mapping thus provides a simple way for the project team to identify the activities, demands, and conditions that they must manage. From this analysis the team can determine the kinds of people they want on the team.

Develop a Project Success Scenario

Project teams must decide at the outset how they will deal with stakeholders, handle problems, and respond to emergencies or unexpected events. Team members can describe in brief vignettes how to operate in different situations to ensure success. Project success scenarios help the team members establish the values, standards, norms, and management style that are best for their project environment.

Define the Project Team's Modus Operandi

Success scenarios provide a way for project teams to develop ideas about their culture and philosophy of operation. However, the team must formalize its thinking and define a specific management style and way of doing business. The team should develop a modus operandi that describes its philosophy, values, vision, and mission. This document is broader in scope than the typical project management manual. The modus operandi is the charter that guides the development of the project team and its policies, procedures, and systems throughout the life of the project.

Exhibit 15-5. Project success mapping.

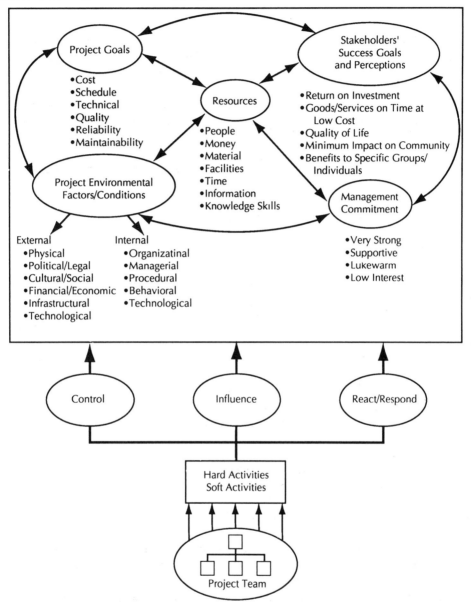

In summary, the success model is designed to reduce the real-life cost of on-the-job learning. By forcing the team to examine the project environment and the stakeholders' demands, we hope to avoid many project pitfalls. However, a success model is a dynamic instrument, and it should be refined as the project evolves. Thus, the project team can build a knowledge base of ideas, plans, decisions, and results and continually improve the model for future undertakings.

Building the Winning Team

The team-building program described in this chapter is based on the writer's experience as a project manager and consultant. After years of project and consulting work, I have concluded that team building must mirror the actual project work environment. Effective team building is accomplished only when team members interact to solve real project problems.

To build an effective team, project leaders should decide who is on the team, the scope of their responsibilities, and the policies, procedures, and systems they will use to get the job done. The team-building program that can make this happen is given in Exhibit 15-6. As the exhibit shows, team building is not a once-and-done exercise, but a process that continues throughout the life of the project. A discussion of the major steps in building a winning team follows.

Step 1: Conceptualize the Winning Team

Formal team building must start early in the project. Team leaders should meet to discuss the project and conceptualize the winning team. Studies and analysis from the success model help define the attributes of the winning team. The goal is to design a team that is well suited to the demands of the project environment. These demands are defined by: (1) the stakeholders' success criteria, (2) project environmental factors, (3) potential risks and unknowns, (4) resource constraints, (5) management support and commitment, and (6) the difficulty of the project itself. Information about each of these areas can be developed using the project success mapping technique referred to in Exhibit 15-5.

The output of Step 1 is a specification that defines the structure and character of the project team. Initially, this specification is used to identify potential team members. Later, the specification helps guide the actual formation and development of the team.

Project participants must be informed of the team development process and their role in this process. Prospective team members must understand that they are the ones who establish the team, conduct the team building, and manage the project.

Step 2: Follow the Phases of Team Building

Successful team building is an integrated process that continues throughout the life of the project. The intensity of the team building is high during the early stages; however, it must persist through all phases of the project. Every success or failure is an opportunity to strengthen the team. The team-building phases include: (1) project simulation, (2) project conditioning, and (3) team maturing.

Phase I: Project Simulation

We can use modeling and simulation techniques to organize, train, and build a team for a specific environment. These techniques involve uniquely structured workshops (see Exhibit 15-7). In these workshops, project participants can address vague, nonquantitative problems and situations in a real-time interactive, natural-language mode of operation. Participants are brought together in a predefined setting

Exhibit 15-6. Team-building program.

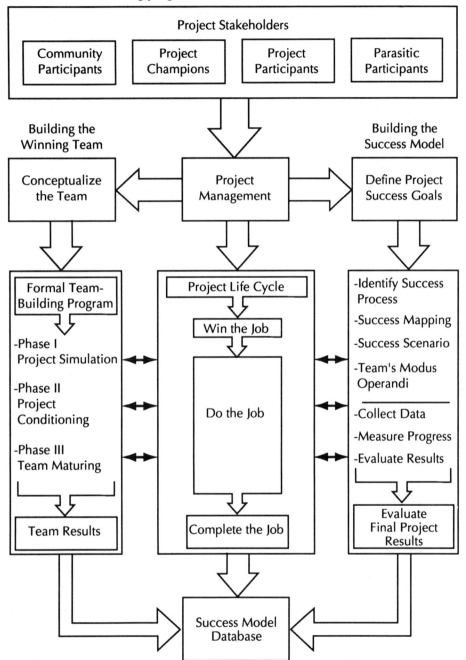

Exhibit 15-7. Project management simulation workshops.

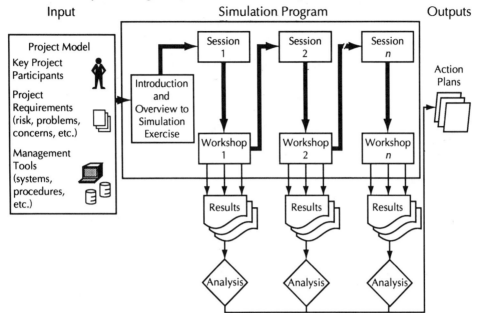

to work on problems directly related to their project. Thus, the team formulates solutions in advance of real problems. The objective of project simulation is for the team members to learn to work together and develop their management style. Project participants learn to function as a team before the start of the project, which helps reduce problems and inefficiencies common to new organizations.

Phase II: Project Conditioning

The first major problem, failure, or success the team encounters is a good time to strengthen the team by establishing appropriate response policies. These response policies define the team's behaviors, actions, and attitudes for dealing with problems or unexpected events. Regardless of the nature of the problem, the degree of seriousness, or who made a mistake, team members are conditioned to respond proactively to the situation.

Project conditioning is a formalized event-response, problem-solving methodology. When problems are uncovered or unexpected conditions develop (both good and bad), the team will respond according to a predefined constructive methodology. Proactive responses involve classical problem-solving techniques, problem-decomposition methodologies, brainstorming sessions, and seminars. Conditioning prepares the project team to accept problems and unexpected events as a normal part of the work. The goal is to develop a team culture that considers the vagaries of the project environment as an opportunity for learning and improvement. Project conditioning disciplines the team to be confident in volatile, high-stress situations. It also eliminates fault finding and blame fixing. Team members must feel secure about the decisions they make and the actions they take. They develop a high level of confidence when they know that, by design, the whole team is there to help. Thus, the success psyche is designed into the project organization at the outset and continually reinforced throughout the life of the project.

At a minimum, the team needs to participate in some type of self-appraisal workshop after each key milestone. Situations within the project determine the timing of the team's self-appraisals. However, the activity should not be deferred because of a heavy work load or problems. To the contrary, this is probably the most opportune time for the team members to step back and take an objective look at how they are doing.

Phase III: Team Maturing

The process of maturing the project team involves work assignments as well as formal and informal training. The goal of team maturing is to evolve a team that becomes better, smarter, and more effective and produces something of value for the stakeholders.

Team maturing involves the realization that projects are life-limited: Project team members are working themselves out of a job. Teams that establish plans for professional growth, development, and advancement can minimize this unsettling aspect of the project environment. These plans can include formal courses of study, self-study programs, seminars, workshops, tours of other projects, and related activities. The goal is to expand the skills and knowledge of team members concurrent with project work. Teams should also devise job-rotating assignments for their members to help ensure that members remain vital and enthusiastic about the project.

Other actions that help the team remain vibrant are recreational activities, motivational programs, incentive programs, rewards, and special recognition programs. However, the real impetus to perform well comes from a team that creates a culture that strives to be the best of the best.

The team-building effort described provides inputs for a success model database that documents the team's goals, plans, decisions, actions, and final results. The model database provides the foundation and the frame of reference for measuring project success.

Measuring Project Success

Success has different meanings and different degrees of importance for various stakeholders. For the project team, success means having to satisfy everyone else whenever possible. The project team tries to strike a balance between conflicting stakeholder goals, project goals, and the resources available. Some stakeholder goals are easy to define and measure; others are more subjective. Yet all goals must be identified, measured, and evaluated to ensure that they are accomplished as planned. The process for ensuring project success is as follows:

- ▸ Define the success objectives for the project stakeholders in quantitative and/or qualitative terms.
- ▸ Determine how to measure accomplishment of the stakeholders' goals.

▸ Collect data, then measure and evaluate the results.
▸ Take corrective action as needed.

We can quantify, measure, and evaluate progress on certain project goals easily. For example, personhours, dollars, material, and products are simple to define and measure. On the other hand, qualitative goals involving reliability, serviceability, safety, quality, and social values are more difficult to define and measure. Yet in highly competitive environments, these goals can spell the difference between success and failure. A formal method is needed to define and measure both the quantitative and qualitative project goals. These goals define the criteria for success and establish the bases for spending project resources.

Establish the Success Criteria

The Success Analysis Matrix shown in Exhibit 15-8 presents a technique for evaluating stakeholders' goals and devising project strategy. The matrix: (1) identifies the project stakeholders, (2) defines their goals, (3) establishes the levels of importance of the goals (by their impact on project success), (4) estimates the team's ability to achieve the goals, and (5) quantifies the cost of achieving these goals.

The Success Analysis Matrix makes a pragmatic evaluation of the stakeholders and the costs required to fulfill their goals. A careful analysis of the nature and cost of the stakeholders' goals may reveal some interesting facts. In some situations, no amount of effort, time, or money can satisfy a particular stakeholder's criteria for success. However, if the stakeholder's power is limited, it may not matter. On the other hand, it is possible that only some small effort may satisfy a particularly powerful stakeholder. Foresight, planning, and a willingness to understand the stakeholder's needs and concerns can make the difference. The Success Analysis Matrix provides insight into stakeholder demands.

Establish a Measurement Scheme

Many of the elements identified in the Success Analysis Matrix are easy to quantify and measure. Thus, expenditures and progress can be evaluated against the plan. However, qualitative or subjective success goals present more of a problem. Subjective goals are described as good, bad, high, low, effective, ineffective, valuable, and desirable. Fortunately, everyday language is sufficient to define most qualitative goals. The more difficult problem is to measure the progress made in accomplishing these goals. One approach is to have the stakeholders actually provide goal definitions and progress measurements.

Collect Data and Evaluate Results

To control a project, the team must collect data on how work is progressing. Data collection and analysis is straightforward for conventional cost, schedule, and technical objectives. However, for subjective goals the problem requires a different approach. Data are collected on these items by: (1) having a third party query the stakeholder, (2) establishing stakeholder feedback procedures, (3) using survey and sampling techniques, and (4) observing stakeholders' reactions to project conditions

Exhibit 15-8. Success Analysis Matrix.

Left margin notes:

Establish the Success Criteria

1. Define stakeholders' goals and impacts on success

2. Evaluate the other factors that may impact project success

3. Determine the project team's ability to fulfill goals and address other factors

4. Determine cost of fulfilling goals and meeting other requirements

5. Identify the high-risk areas; focus on areas that will substantially impact project success

6. Devise strategy for addressing all requirements

		Impact on Success	Ability to Accomplish	Cost to Accomplish	Success Strategy
I. STAKEHOLDER	**SUCCESS GOALS**				
Project Champions					
-Developers	High rate of return	5	3	5	Complete project on schedule and under budget
-Customers	Minimum price for product	5	3	5	Use advanced process techniques
-Community Leaders	Minimum impact on community	4	3	3	Opinion-shaping program
Project Participants					
-Project Management	Meet all objectives	5	3	5	Early team building
-Vendors	Deliver on time	4	2	2	Use resident expeditors
-Regulators	Fulfill all regulations	4	5	2	Early filings
Community Participants					
-Special Interest Groups	Stop project	3	2	3	Heavy public relations program
-Environmentalists	Minimum impact on environment	4	4	4	Implement environmental program
Parasitic Participants					
-Media	Obtain high level of interest	5	1	3	Appoint special team to work with media
-Activists	Obtain exposure	5	1	3	Appoint special team to manage
II. PROJECT ENVIRONMENT	**CONDITIONS AND REQUIREMENTS**				
External Factors					
-Physical	Severe climate	3	4	3	Condition team to work in this climate
-Political/Legal	Unstable political climate	5	1	5	Implement early warning system
-Financial	Poor	4	4	3	Obtain backup financing
-Infrastructural	Not well developed	4	3	2	Develop external support systems
Internal Factors					
-Organizational	Needs development	3	4	3	Hire outside consultants for assistance
-Management	Needs training	3	5	2	Implement training programs
-Procedural	Adequate	2	5	2	Use existing procedures
-Behavioral	Not known	4	2	3	Implement testing programs
-Technological	State of the art	5	2	5	Develop contingency plans
III. RESOURCES	**AVAILABILITY**				
-Funding	Adequate	5	1	1	Implement tight budget program
-Manpower	Limited	4	2	5	Selective recruiting program
-Facilities	Poor	4	4	5	Use mobile facilities
-Equipment	Limited	3	4	5	Purchase additional equipment
IV. PROJECT GOALS	**REQUIREMENT AND DEGREE OF DIFFICULTY**				
-Technological	Advanced state of the art	5	3	5	Obtain best specialist available
-Cost	Restrictive	5	3	5	Strict budget program
-Schedule	Realistic	3	3	3	Use computer-based PERT program
-Reliability	Very high: difficult	5	2	5	Detailed test program
-Maintainability	Very high: difficult	5		5	Design into initial concepts
V. MANAGEMENT COMMITMENT AND INTEREST	**PRESENT SITUATION**				
	Committed to project	2	2	1	Maintain close contact and high visibility
	Other priorities dominate attention	2	3	1	Look for opportunities to get management attention

Success and Cost Rating Scale

5 - Very demanding: high risk, difficult to accomplish
4 - Significant; risky but manageable; can be accomplished
3 - Average: typical project risk, within capabilities of most teams
2 - Low: routine situations
1 - Not significant: little or no risk

Accomplish Rating Scale

1 - Probably can't be done
2 - Very difficult to accomplish
3 - Difficult but realistic
4 - Typical project effort required
5 - Well within project's ability to accomplish

and activities. Each technique has advantages and disadvantages, and it is up to the project team to determine which technique is suitable.

Bibliography

Ballou, Paul O., Jr. "Decision-Making Environment of a Program Office." *Program Manager* (September-October 1985).

Cohen, Judith L., and John R. Adams. "Learning From Project Managers: Lessons in Managing Uncertainty." 1984 *Proceedings of the Project Management Institute,* Philadelphia. Drexel Hill, Penn.: PMI.

Davidson, Jeffrey P. "Teaming Up to Solve Problems." *Today's Office* (December 1984).

Fitzgerald, J. W. H. "Because Wisdom Cannot Be Told." *Program Manager* (September-October 1985).

Gadeken, Owen C. "Why Engineers and Scientists Often Fail as Managers." *Program Manager* (January-February 1986).

Grove, Andrew S. "How to Make Confrontation Work for You." *Fortune* (July 1984).

Hadedorn, Homer J., and Arthur D. Little. "Profiling Corporate Culture." *Today's Office* (October 1984).

Marutollo, Frank. "Taking Issue With Theory 'Y'." *Program Manager* (July-August 1984).

Mitchell, Eddie. "Creating High-Performing Programs by Modeling, Assessing, and Implementing Excellence." *Program Manager* (March-April 1986).

Muntz, Peter, and Robert Chasnoff. "The Cultural Awareness Hierarchy: A Model for Promoting Understanding." *Training and Development Journal* (October 1983).

Owens, Stephen D. "Project Management and Behavioral Research Revisited." 1982 *Proceedings of the Project Management Institute,* Toronto, Canada. Drexel Hill, Penn.: PMI.

Owens, Stephen D. "Leadership Theory and the Project Environment: Which Approach Is Applicable?" 1983 *Proceedings of the Project Management Institute,* Houston. Drexel Hill, Penn.: PMI.

Shearon, Ella Mae. "Conflict Management and Team Building for Productive Projects." 1983 *Proceedings of the Project Management Institute,* Houston. Drexel Hill, Penn.: PMI.

Shell, Richard L., Ray H. Souder, and Nicholas Damachi. "Using Behavioral and Influence Factors to Motivate the Technical Work." *IE* (August 1983).

Sink, Scott D. "State-of-the-Art Approaches to the Problem of Unlocking Employee Potential." *IE* (August 1983).

Tuman, John, Jr. "Improving Productivity in the Project Management Environment Using Advanced Technology and the Behavioral Sciences." 1983 *Proceedings of the Project Management Institute,* Houston. Drexel Hill, Penn.: PMI.

Tuman, John, Jr. "Project Management Modeling and Simulation for Planning, Organizing and Team Building." 1984 *Proceedings of the Project Management Institute,* Philadelphia. Drexel Hill, Penn.: PMI.

Tuman, John, Jr. "Modeling and Simulation Techniques for Project Planning, Organizing, Training and Team Building." 1985 *Proceedings of the Eighth World Congress on Project Management*, Rotterdam, Netherlands.

Whitney, Diana K., and Linda S. Ackerman. "The Fusion Team: A Model of Organic and Shared Leadership." *Journal of the Bay Area OD Network* 3, No. 2 (December 1983).

Wilemon, David L. "Learning in High Technology Project Teams." 1983 *Proceedings of the Project Management Institute*, Houston. Drexel Hill, Penn.: PMI.

Wilemon, David L., and Hans J. Thamhain. "Team Building in Project Management." 1979 *Proceedings of the Project Management Institute*, Atlanta. Drexel Hill, Penn.: PMI.

Wilemon, David L., and Hans J. Thamhain. "A Model for Developing High Performance Project Teams." 1983 *Proceedings of the Project Management Institute*, Houston. Drexel Hill, Penn.: PMI.

16

A Conceptual
Team-Building Model:
Achieving Teamwork Through
Improved Communications
and Interpersonal Skills

Paul C. Dinsmore
Dinsmore Associates

Teamwork means people cooperating to meet common goals. That includes all types of people doing work that calls for joint effort and exchange of information, ideas, and opinions. In teamwork, productivity is increased through synergy: the magic that appears when team members generate new ways for getting things done and that special spirit for making them happen.

Teamwork offers a number of concrete benefits.

- *Teamwork enhances success.* Teamwork helps your group excel at what it's doing and boosts its chances of "winning."
- *Teamwork promotes creativity.* The team approach stimulates innovation and encourages people to try new approaches to problems.
- *Teamwork builds synergy.* The mathematical absurdity "2 + 2 = 5" becomes possible.
- *Teamwork promotes trade-offs and solves problems.* Teamwork creates a problem-solving atmosphere that facilitates decisions about schedule, cost, and performance.
- *Teamwork is fun.* Working together for a common cause creates group spirit, lightens up the atmosphere, and reduces tensions and conflicts.
- *Teamwork helps large organizations as well as small groups.* The team concept can

This chapter was adapted from Paul C. Dinsmore, "Team-Building" module, *Trainers' Workshop* (January-February 1991).

▸ *Teamwork helps large organizations as well as small groups.* The team concept can be used to involve an entire company culture as well as to stimulate a small department.
▸ *Teamwork responds to the challenge of change.* Teams thrive on opportunities to improve performance and show how they can adapt and adjust in order to win.

There are also pitfalls to watch out for.

▸ *There can be negative synergy.* When the team doesn't get its act together, then synergy becomes negative and the equation becomes "2 + 2 = 3."
▸ *There can be excessive independence.* Ill-guided or poorly built teams wander off course and start doing their own thing as opposed to meeting overall goals.
▸ *Time is needed to build and maintain the team.* If company culture is not team-oriented, a lot of time and effort is needed to create the team spirit.
▸ *Decision making is slow.* Getting a group to make a decision on a consensus basis is a time-consuming task.

Why is teamwork more important now than it has been in the past? One reason is that change—economic, societal, cultural, environmental, technological, political, and international—is taking place at an accelerating rate. And change is having a dramatic impact not only on individuals but also on organizations. Task forces, departmental teams, cross-functional teams, and project teams are replacing the cumbersome hierarchical organizational structure of the past in many organizations. Teamwork enables organizations to be nimbler, more flexible, and better able to respond swiftly and creatively to the challenge of today's competitive business environment.

Several factors have speeded this trend toward team approaches to business planning and operations:

▸ The success of the Japanese management style, which stresses employee involvement in all phases of the work
▸ The rejection by newer generations of autocratic leadership
▸ Rapid changes in technology that create a need for quick group responses
▸ Emphasis on corporate quality, which requires team effort on an organizational scale

Team building encompasses the actions necessary to create the spirit of teamwork. Research by Tuckman and Jensen[1] indicates that the team-building process is a natural sequence that can be divided into five stages:

1. Forming
2. Storming
3. Norming
4. Performing
5. Adjourning

A detailed description of the team-building process follows.

Five Classic Team-Building Stages

Stage 1: Forming

In this stage, the manager and the group focus more on tasks than on teamwork. They organize the team's structure, set goals, clarify values, and develop an overall vision of the team's purpose. The manager's role is to direct these efforts and to encourage group members to reach consensus and achieve a feeling of commitment.

Stage 2: Storming

This stage is less structured than the first stage. The manager broadens the focus to include both accomplishing tasks and building relationships. As the social need for belonging becomes important to group members, the emphasis is on interpersonal interactions: active listening, assertiveness, conflict management, flexibility, creativity, and kaleidoscopic thinking. The group completes tasks with a sense of understanding, clarification, and belonging. The manager relies not only on actual authority but also on leadership skills such as encouragement and recognition.

Stage 3: Norming

In this stage, the team-building process is more relationship-based than task-oriented. Since recognition and esteem are important for group members, the manager relies on communication, feedback, affirmation, playfulness, humor, entrepreneurship, and networking to motivate the team. Group members achieve a feeling of involvement and support.

Stage 4: Performing

At this point, the team is operating very much on its own. Management style is neither task- nor relationship-oriented, since the team members are motivated by achievement and self-actualization. The manager's role in this phase is to serve as mentor/coach and to take a long-range view of future needs. Team members focus on decision making and problem solving, relying on information and expertise to achieve their goals.

Stage 5: Adjourning

Management concern in this wrap-up stage is low-task and high-relationship. The manager focuses on evaluation, reviewing, and closure. Team members continue to be motivated by a feeling of achievement and self-actualization.

The Ten Rules of Team Building

The five team-building stages show how teams evolve over time. That process can be accelerated by applying the following ten principles of team building. Each principle helps create the spirit that gets people to work together cooperatively to meet goals

1. *Identify what drives your team.* What is the driving force that makes teamwork necessary? Is it an external force like the market? Is it internal, like organizational demands? Is it the needs of the group itself? Is the leader the only driver? Or is it perhaps a combination of these factors?

2. *Get your own act together.* Are you a bright and shining example of teamwork? Could you shine even brighter? Polish your interpersonal skills and show your teamwork talents on a daily basis.

3. *Understand the game.* All teams play games. Do you know the game and how much you can bend the rules? Each game of business is different and rules need to be rethought.

4. *Evaluate the competition.* First, know who the real market competition is. Then size it up so that your team can become competitive with a larger outside opponent.

5. *Pick your players and adjust your team.* Choose qualified players who know the basics, and teach them the skills that they don't have. Also, make sure the team players are in the right spots.

6. *Identify and develop inner group leaders.* Team builders learn to identify inner group leadership early on. If you want to develop the full capacity of your team, then delegating, mentoring, and coaching must become part of your daily habit.

7. *Get the team in shape.* It takes practice and training to get athletic teams in shape. The same is true for other teams. Start with training in the fundamentals of teamwork—things like active listening, communicating, and negotiating—and see that they are practiced on a daily basis.

8. *Motivate the players.* The only way to get people to do things effectively is to give them what they want. The secret is to discover what individuals really want and, as you deal with them, to relate to those desires—whether they be recognition, challenge, a chance to belong, the possibility to lead, the opportunity to learn, or other motivators.

9. *Develop plans.* In teamwork, the process of planning is more important than the plan. Team members must become so involved in the planning process that they can say with conviction, "This is our plan."

10. *Control, evaluate, and improve.* Knowing the status of things at any given time is important for teams to be successful. Sometimes that's a tough task. To make sure you maintain the right spirit, involve your team members in creating your control instrument.

The ten rules outlined apply throughout the five team-building phases. Greater emphasis, however, is appropriate during certain periods. Exhibit 16-1 shows the phases in which the rules tend to be most applicable.

Planning for and Implementing Teamwork

Get People Involved

The key to successful team planning is involvement: Get people involved at the outset of your team-building effort to win their personal commitment to your plan. One

Exhibht 16-1. Team-building rules and the five phases of team building.

Ten Rules	Five Phases				
	Form	*Storm*	*Norm*	*Perform*	*Adjourn*
1. Identify what drives your team.	o				
2. Get your own act together.	o	o	o		
3. Understand the game.	o	o	o		
4. Evaluate the competition.	o				
5. Pick your players and adjust your team.	o	o	o	o	
6. Identify and develop inner group leaders.		o	o	o	
7. Get the team in shape.	o	o	o		
8. Motivate the players.			o	o	
9. Develop plans.	o		o		
10. Control, evaluate, and improve.			o		o

simple technique for involvement includes a questionnaire in which team members are asked to assess the need for team building. A sample questionnaire is shown in Exhibit 16-2. In the test, team members rate the degree to which certain team-related problems appear. If the team is newly formed, the questionnaire should be answered from the perspective of anticipated problems. Then test results are tabulated and group discussion follows in search of a consensus on how to obtain team development. This consensus approach generates synergy when the team carries out the planned activities. In addition, potential differences are dealt with in the planning stage before resources are fully committed.

Group planning approaches are used in programs such as quality circles, total quality management, and participative management, as well as project management. The management skills required to make these group planning efforts effective include interpersonal communications, meeting management, listening, negotiation, situational management, and managerial psychology.

The right planning process produces a quality plan to which the parties involved are committed. Some methods that enhance the planning process are discussed below.

- ▸ *Creativity sessions.* Techniques for boosting creativity include brainstorming, brainwriting, random working, checklists, and word associations.
- ▸ *Consensus planning.* A plan reached through group discussion tends to yield a program that is well thought through, with a high probability of being implemented.
- ▸ *Decision-making models.* Formal models for making decisions can be used as a basis for planning. Some common techniques are decision trees, problem analysis, decision analysis, implementation studies, and risk analysis.

Exhibit 16-2. Team members' questionnaire.

Instructions: Indicate the degree to which the problems below exist in your work unit.

	Low			*High*	*Score*
1. Quality of communication among group members	1 2 3 4 5				_____
2. Clarity of goals, or degree of "buying into" goals	1 2 3 4 5				_____
3. Degree of conflict among group members and/or third parties	1 2 3 4 5				_____
4. Productivity of meetings	1 2 3 4 5				_____
5. Degree of motivation; level of morale	1 2 3 4 5				_____
6. Level of trust among group members and/or with boss	1 2 3 4 5				_____
7. Quality of decision-making process and follow-through on decisions made	1 2 3 4 5				_____
8. Individuals' concern for team responsibility as opposed to own personal interests	1 2 3 4 5				_____
9. Quality of listening abilities on part of team members	1 2 3 4 5				_____
10. Cooperativeness among group members	1 2 3 4 5				_____
11. Level of creativity and innovation	1 2 3 4 5				_____
12. Group productivity	1 2 3 4 5				_____
13. Degree that team perceptions coincide with those of upper management and vice versa	1 2 3 4 5				_____
14. Clarity of role relationships	1 2 3 4 5				_____
15. Tendency to be more solution- than problem-oriented	1 2 3 4 5				_____
TOTAL					_____

Test Results: Add up your scores. If the score is over 60, then your work unit is in good shape with respect to teamwork. If you scored between 46 and 60 points, there is some concern, but only for those items with lower scores. A score of 30 to 45 indicates that the subject needs attention and that a team-building program should be under way. A score of between 15 and 30 points means that improving teamwork should be the absolute top priority for your group.

You should build a team like you were putting together a puzzle. It involves:

- Individuals (like the separate puzzle pieces)
- One-on-one contacts (like pairing up matching pieces)
- Small groups (like the subsets of the puzzle)
- Large groups (like the overall picture that the whole puzzle represents)

This means that in team building, just as in putting together a puzzle, you need to view the whole range of team factors, from the characteristics and talents of the individual team members to the overall picture: the team's immediate goals and long-term objectives and how the team fits into the larger organizational scene. Some of the concrete steps that transform groups into teams are discussed below.

Set a Good Example

Here the focus is individual. As team leaders concern themselves with developing their own skills and knowledge bases, then the other pieces of the puzzle begin to gravitate and fall into place. All team leaders communicate their management philosophies to some extent by setting both overt and subliminal examples.

The manager who trusts subordinates and delegates authority to key project members can expect others to emulate that style. Likewise, an open give-and-take approach fosters similar behavior in the team and in others associated with the project under way. Through the team leader's own actions, team members' best behavior is called to the forefront.

Coach Team Members

Coaching requires some schooling in the "different-strokes-for-different-folks" philosophy, which assumes that people with different temperaments react differently to a standardized "shotgun" approach. Thus, each individual needs to be singled out for a special shot of custom-tailored attention in order for coaching to be effective.

A coaching session can be as simple as a chat with a subordinate who made a mistake about why something happened and what can be done to keep it from recurring. It can be a formal interview by the manager, who goes into the session with a tailor-made approach. Or it can be a formal appraisal session using classic management tools such as job descriptions and performance standards.

Train Team Members

Training may involve small groups or the overall group or may incorporate all the stakeholders involved in the team's efforts. Informal training sessions can be conducted in various forms, such as lectures, roundtable discussions, and seminars.

▸ *Lectures* are a one-dimensional form of training. They put large amounts of information into short time frames. Lectures given by experts can bring top-quality information to the team members. When the speaker is well known, the lecture stimulates special interest.

▸ *Roundtable discussions* are open-forum debates on pertinent subjects. They give participants a chance to air their views and present their opinions and ideas frankly. The goal may be to establish a consensus or to provide a basis for planning in-depth training programs.

▸ *Seminars or workshops* combine the informational content of the lecture with opportunities for participation offered by the roundtable. In seminars or workshops, information is dispensed in smaller doses, interspersed with group discussions and debates. Seminars are established around a longer time frame than lectures or roundtable discussions. Two- to three-day seminars are the most popular, but one-day events are acceptable, and five-day seminars are right for more in-depth coverage.

Set Up a Formal Team-Building Program

Of the approaches aimed at heightening team synergy, a formal team-building program is apt to bring the best results because:

- The longer program duration provides greater opportunity for retention of concepts as they are reworked throughout the program.
- On-the-job application of the concepts provides timely feedback while the course goes on.
- In-depth treatment can be given to subjects.
- Enough time is available to build a consensus among participants.

Effective Interpersonal Relations: The Key to Successful Teamwork

Since effective teams are all highly interactive, teamwork depends heavily on the interpersonal skills of the members. In a team setting, this personal interaction takes on a special importance because the number of relationships among members is sharply increased. Sometimes, this creates a traffic problem. Just as vehicle traffic flows more smoothly when drivers have developed their abilities, observe protocol, and behave courteously, the same is true in team situations where members have learned how to work together skillfully and cooperatively.

What are some of the skills that each team "driver" needs to operate effectively in a team situation? They include listening, applying techniques to deal with interpersonal conflict, negotiating, and influencing.

Listening

Communication, no matter how clear and concise, is wasted unless someone is listening actively to the communicator's message. When team members know how to listen actively, overall effectiveness is boosted. Here is the attitude that represents good listening:

> I am interested in what you are saying and I want to understand, although I may not agree with everything you say. You are important as a person, and I respect you and what you have to say. I'm sure your message is worth listening to, so I am giving you my full attention.

Other listening pointers include:

- Maintaining eye contact
- Not interrupting
- Keeping a relaxed posture

Good listening also requires the listener to focus on both the communicator's content and feelings and then to extract the essential message being conveyed.

Dealing With Interpersonal Conflict

Interpersonal conflict can occur whenever two or more people get together. It's an inevitable part of team dynamics. There are five basic techniques for dealing with interpersonal conflict.

1. Withdrawing (pulling out, retreating, or giving up)
2. Smoothing (appeasing just to keep the peace)
3. Bargaining (negotiating to reach agreement over conflicting interests)
4. Collaborating (objective problem solving based on trust)
5. Forcing (using power to resolve the conflict)

Application of these techniques depends on the situation. Effective team members recognize that conflict is inevitable and rationally apply appropriate conflict resolution modes in each given situation. Here are some of the applications:

1. Use *withdrawing* when you can't win, when the stakes are low, to gain time, to preserve neutrality or reputation, or when you win by delay.
2. Use *smoothing* to reach an overarching goal, to create an obligation for a trade-off at a later date, to maintain harmony, to create good will, or when any solution will do.
3. Use *bargaining* (also called conflict negotiation) when both parties need to be winners, when others are as strong as you, to maintain your relationship with your opponent, when you are not sure you are right, or when you get nothing if you don't make a deal.
4. Use *collaborating* when you both get at least what you want and maybe more, to create a common power base, when knowledge or skills are complementary, when there is enough time, or where there is trust.
5. Use *forcing* when a "do or die" situation exists, when important principles are at stake, when you are stronger (never start a battle you can't win), to gain status or demonstrate power, or when the relationship is unimportant.

Negotiating

Team members are likely to find themselves dealing with both third-party and in-house situations that call for major negotiation skills. The type of negotiation that tends to be effective in team settings is called principled negotiation. This is negotiation in which it is assumed that the players are problem solvers and that the objective is to reach a wise outcome efficiently and amicably.

Principled negotiation also assumes that the people will be separated from the problem, that premature position taking will be avoided, that alternative solutions will be explored, and that the rules of the negotiation will be objective and fair. This means focusing on interests rather than on positions and implies fully exploring mutual and divergent interests before trying to converge on some bottom line. The tenet *invent options for mutual gain*—calling for a creative search for alternatives—is also fundamental to principled negotiation.

Influencing

In team situations, individual authority lags well behind the authority of the group. Therefore, effective teams depend on the ability of members to influence one another for the good of the common cause. Influence management includes the following principles:

- *Play up the benefit.* Identify the benefit of your proposal for the other party (items such as more challenge, prestige, or visibility, or the chance for promotion or transfer). Then emphasize that benefit in conversations so that the message is communicated.
- *Steer clear of Machiavelli.* Avoid manipulation. Concentrate on influencing with sincerity and integrity.
- *Go beyond "I think I can."* Successful influence managers don't waste time questioning whether things can be done. Their efforts are aimed at how the task will be performed and what needs to be done to make it happen.
- *Put an umbrella over your moves.* Effective influencing hinges on strategic planning, to give direction and consistency to all influencing efforts.
- *Tune in to what others say.* Successful influence managers learn to identify others' expectations and perceive how given actions contribute toward fulfilling those expectations.
- *Size up your plans for congruency.* Make sure there is a fit between proposed actions, testing your plans for consistency, coherence, and conformity.
- *Remember: "Different strokes for different folks."* Be sure to adapt your approach to fit each person's individual characteristics. Size up your targets and adjust your presentation to individual needs.
- *Watch your language!* Be careful with what you say and how you say it. Screen out pessimism and other forms of negativity, putting positive conviction into what you say to increase the impact of your message.

When team members are schooled in these basics, teamwork is likely to come about rapidly. Synergy is generated as people work together to meet common goals.

Note

1. B. W. Tuckman and M. A. Jensen, "Study of Small Group Development Revisited," *Group and Organizational Studies* (1977).

References

Blake, Robert R., Jane S. Mouton, and Robert L. Allen. *Spectacular Teamwork.* New York: John Wiley & Sons, 1987.

Bucholz, Steve, and Thomas Roth. *Creating the High Performance Team.* New York: John Wiley & Sons, 1987.

Dinsmore, Paul C. *Human Factors in Project Management,* Revised Edition. New York: AMACOM, 1990.

Dyer, William G. *Team Building: Issues and Alternatives.* Reading, Mass.: Addison-Wesley, 1987.

Hastings, Colin, Peter Bixby, and Rani Chaudhry-Lawton. *The Superteam Solution.* London, England: Gower, 1986.

Heany, Donald F. *Cutthroat Teammates.* Homewood, Ill.: Dow Jones-Irwin, 1989.

Larson, Carl E., and Frank M. J. LaFasto. *Teamwork.* Newbury Park, Calif.: Sage, 1989.

Section VII

Power, Influence, and Leadership

17

Power and Politics in Project Management: Upper-Echelon Versus Conventional Project Management

Paul C. Dinsmore
Dinsmore Associates

Able politicking and skillful power brokering are key to managing projects to successful completion. Conversely, lack of focus on politics and inadequate handling of power are major causes for disaster on projects. That thesis was discussed both in papers and in the hallways at the 1988 INTERNET World Congress on Project Management held in Glasgow, Scotland. Yet in spite of references in the literature, surprisingly little has been written on this topic, which is so crucial for successfully completing projects.

The arena for practicing power and politics on projects is the project itself and its surroundings. The power to be wielded in that arena has been defined as the ability to get others to do what you want them to do. Part of that power may derive from formal authority and personality, yet politics—which has been defined as an activity concerned with the acquisition of power—is also a strong influencing factor.

Power and politics exist at all levels on projects. In this chapter, attention is focused on two specific levels: upper-echelon project management, and conventional project management.

This chapter was adapted from Paul C. Dinsmore, "Power and Politics in Project Management," *PM NETwork*, April 1989, with permission of the Project Management Institute, P.O. Box 43, Drexel Hill, Penn. 19026, a worldwide organization of advancing the state-of-the-art in project management.

Upper-Echelon Project Management

In the upper levels of management, how can politics and power be dealt with so that both company and project objectives are met? A discussion of some of the ways follows.

▸ *Matters are handled through the hierarchy.* Corporate culture may demand that all decisions be channeled through the formal hierarchy. This is effective when the company has a good track record in managing previous projects.

▸ *An appointed project sponsor (a top manager or director) takes on the task.* The sponsor in some cases coincides with the hierarchical superior but is often another upper-level manager assigned the task of giving political coverage to the project.

▸ *A project council or steering committee assumes the role.* When the project spans political boundaries (joint ventures between companies or joint efforts between areas), the steering committee is a way to apply consensus decision making to upper-echelon project management.

▸ *Project managers fend for themselves.* As a result of managerial vacuums at upper levels, project managers may find they are expected to do it all. Wise project managers (the ones who survive) work on building a political umbrella under which project work can progress.

▸ *Outside facilitators are engaged to help guide the strategic process.* To avoid political pull and tug, a neutral facilitator, conversant with both project management and the technology involved, may be called in to help make things work at the strategic level.

▸ *Experts (lobbyists, arbitrators) are called in on an as-needed basis.* This approach is corrective in nature, as opposed to preventive. It may be required when deadlocks occur at higher levels.

How should upper-echelon project management be carried out? Obviously, whatever works is right. Some approaches may actually prove inappropriate in certain cases. A steering committee could get in the way of a particularly effective project manager, or an outside party may simply muddy the waters. Company and project cultures have to be sized up to see what makes sense.

Yet the risk of neglecting upper-echelon project management is enormous. Front-end strategic and political effort must be made at the upper levels for projects to derive benefit. That takes forward thinking, early on in the project life cycle.

Conventional Project Management

In conventional project management, the responsibility rests squarely with the project manager. As the focal point, the project manager has to ensure that the project management basics are tended to. That means managing the classic areas of scope, time, cost, and performance, which in turn calls for managing communications, human resources, contracts, materials, and risks. In other words, the project manager needs to do all the things the textbooks spell out.

Power and politics, however, are complicating factors at the conventional project level. The project manager receives inevitable pressure from higher management.

The client organization also exerts itself, as do members of the project team, support groups, third parties, and outside groups. What can project managers do to enhance their power and political position at the operating project level? Here are a few standard practices.

- *Stay "tuned in" to upper management.* No matter how upper management is structured, the project manager must be closely involved with it.
- *Use strategic instruments.* The project management plan or project plan can be used by the project manager to mold strategies and policies, thus enhancing his or her power base.
- *Build a team.* Consensus management, training, interpersonal skill, conflict resolution, and group motivation are samples of what it takes to build a team, which is one of the project manager's major power bases.
- *Develop the power of competence.* It has been said that project managers are not given power, but the right to obtain it. Effective project managers build their authority bases, through competence, into legitimate managerial power.

Since at the conventional level, attention focuses on the project manager to champion the project to completion, careful selection and training of project managers would appear to meet much of the project's needs. Yet matters are not that simple. Ingrained within the project manager must be a healthy taste and inclination for project politics (as opposed to an inordinate lust for power, which hurts both the project and the project manager's own political base). Only then can the project manager hope to pull off the challenge of guiding the project to a successful close.

Pinning Down the Roles

Managing projects at the operational plateau is an art in itself, but much trickier is articulating the power game and political puzzle in the upper spheres. Whereas at the conventional levels all fingers point toward the project manager, at higher plateaus the manager may not have the political clout to be effective. Also, project managers may not see their jobs as including the role of high-level political articulators. Furthermore, conflicting perceptions as to what constitutes a successful project may confuse the issue. For instance, the project team tends to perceive cost, schedule, and quality as all-important. The client or user sees success in terms of the final result: Does the project actually meet the need for which it was designed, in spite of changes that may have occurred in the market and in technology as the project was being implemented? And finally, contractors or vendors, who often have substantial roles in managing many projects, see success in terms of "Did we make money, and will the client give us more work?" All this needs to be taken into account when striving for project success.

The Project Sponsor and Beyond

Much attention has been focused in the literature on project sponsorship, both in technical and managerial terms, and this may provide the gateway for a more complete understanding of power and politics in the project setting. Each project, however, is so peculiar in terms of culture, priorities, past experiences, and present expectations that no one response clears away the fog that hangs over the upper managerial echelons of many projects. The project sponsor role may simply fail to materialize as designed, leaving the political arena open for surprises.

Since success in managing projects hinges strongly on politics and power, and much of this takes place at the upper levels, it seems fitting that continued research be carried out on the subject. Hopefully, efforts will continue for developing an appropriate and flexible conceptual model that can help client and project organizations rise to the challenge of managing projects at the upper echelons, thus providing a foundation for more effective handling of politics and power at the project implementation level.

18

Sources of Power and Influence

Robert B. Youker
Management, Planning & Control Systems

Power (and politics) is probably the most important topic in project management but at the same time one of the least discussed. Power in the engineering sense is defined as the ability to do work. In the social sense it is the ability to get others to do the work (or actions) you want, regardless of their desires. When we think of all the project managers who have responsibility without authority, who must elicit support by influence and not by command authority, then we can see why power is the most important topic in project management.

Yet power is a neglected topic in the literature of project management. The words *power, influence,* and *politics* do not appear in the Project Management Institute *PMBOK.*[1] David Wilemon has discussed power in several of his articles, but there is general agreement in the social sciences that until recently power has not received sufficient attention. Despite the importance of power in relationships among people in project management, we seldom deal with the issue directly.

Without power, project managers can accomplish little. As organizations and projects have become more complex and as project managers become more dependent on more and more persons over whom they do not have formal authority, they increasingly need power to influence the behavior of others. There can be no argument that effective performance by project managers requires them to be skilled at the acquisition and use of social power.

The purpose of this chapter is: (1) to agree on common definitions of power and related terms such as leadership, (2) to look at a model of the sources of power, and (3) to develop practical guidelines for project managers on how to acquire and use power.

Definitions

A review of the literature in the social sciences on power quickly reveals a good bit of confusion over definitions and terms. As Cavanaugh states:

This chapter was adapted from Robert B. Youker, "Power and Politics in Project Management," Proceedings of the 10th INTERNET World Congress, Vienna, 1990. Reprinted with permission.

Since Bertrand Russell predicted that the concept of "power" would emerge as a fundamental issue in the social sciences, forty years of research and theorizing have not yet produced a single, uniform conceptualization of power. Statements such as "power permeates all human action" or "power . . . is a universal phenomenon in human activities and in all social relationships" are commonly found throughout the power literature. Bierstedt used an appropriate analogy when he asserted, "We may say about it [power] in general only what St. Augustine said about time, that we all know perfectly well what it is—until someone asks us." Like time, power is an overlearned concept deeply embedded in our culture. Individuals tend to define power in highly idiosyncratic terms. Many social science researchers operationalize the variable "power" based on preconceived notions, individual intuition, or personal dogma.

If it is acknowledged that social power is a concept embedded in our culture, its potency as an underlying force within many interpersonal and organizational relationships must also be acknowledged. However, the role of power within these interactions will be difficult to pinpoint without a more systematic means of operationalizing the concept. Unfortunately, scholars have been unable to bring clarity to the study of the phenomenon of power. The research remains "scattered, heterogeneous, and even chaotic."[2]

Nobody seems to agree about what power and control actually are. Every author has a different definition of these concepts. Therefore, one of our goals is simply to clear up this confusion by showing what these definitions have in common and where the major areas of disagreement lie. Hopefully, this exercise will provide answers to such questions as "How is power different from influence or leadership?" Let's start with several definitions.

Power

Kotter also focused on people's needs and wants when he defined power-oriented behavior as behavior "directed primarily at developing or using relationships in which other people are to some degree willing to defer to one's wishes."[3] And Mitchell called power "the ability for A to exercise influence over B when B would not do so otherwise."[4]

To more fully understand power, we need to compare and contrast power with similar terms such as *influence, authority, leadership,* and *control.* Here, Halal's analysis is useful.

> Power is defined as the potential or ability to exercise influence over the decisions of others, to determine their behavior to some degree, to establish the direction of future action. *Leadership* is the use of power for these purposes. That is, leaders employ various forms of influence to mobilize followers effectively. *Control* is the end result or objective of influence. The central concept that is fundamentally involved in these related concepts of power, leadership, and control, then, is *influence.* Influence is regarded in this framework as the underlying process through which leaders obtain

their power to control events. Leaders may derive their power from a variety of different types of influence, such as the use of physical coercion or force, money and economic resources, formal and legal authority, social pressure or status, special skills and knowledge, personal vision and charisma, and possibly other such sources.[5]

Influence

Mitchell provides a useful analysis of influence in his 1978 book. He states:

> Influence is usually conceived as being narrower than power. It involves the ability on the part of a person to alter another person or group in specific ways, such as in their satisfaction and performance. Influence is more closely associated with leadership than is power, but both obviously are involved in the leadership process. Therefore, authority is different from power because of its legitimacy, and influence is narrower than power but is so conceptually close that the two terms can be used interchangeably.[6]

Authority

The definition of authority is relatively simple. Authority is the formal power given to a person by his or her position in the hierarchy of an organization.

Leadership

Leadership has been described as "an interpersonal relation in which others comply because they want to, not because they have to."[7] Leadership is always associated with the attainment of group objectives and involves the common agreement and commitment to objectives and structuring of roles so people know what is expected of them. Another way to look at leadership is the use of power to accomplish the purposes of a group or organization.[8]

Control

Control is "the process in an organization of setting standards, monitoring results with feedback, and taking action to correct deviations."[9]

Politics

Politics has been defined as "an influence process in organizations to achieve power to change the balance of power to accomplish your goals or purposes."[10]

From these various definitions we can easily see that we have six closely interrelated terms where there is still a good bit of controversy over precise meanings and where operational definitions for rigorous social science research are not yet available. But for our purposes of discussion and action, I think we know what we are talking about.

Sources of Power

What are the sources of power and influence in addition to formal authority that are available to project managers? The classic scheme of categories was developed by French and Raven more than thirty years ago.[11] There have been minor modifications and additions, but their categorization remains the basic model used today, as shown in Exhibit 18-1. The chart lists the forms of power described by French and Raven, Mitchell, and Kotter. Some of these forms of power are self-explanatory, and some need further definition. The various forms are interrelated and do overlap. A discussion of eight forms of power follows.

1. *Rewards.* Reward power is seen as the number of positive incentives that B thinks A has to offer. Can A promote B? To what extent can A determine how much B earns or when B takes a vacation? To some extent A's reward power is a function of the formal responsibilities inherent in his or her position.

2. *Punishment.* Coercive power or punishment has to do with the negative things that B believes A can do. Can A fire me, dock my pay, give me miserable assignments, or reprimand me? These factors are again often organizationally and formally determined as part of A's position.

3. *Referent power.* In some cases, B looks up to and admires A as a person. B may want to be similar to A and be liked by A. In this situation, B may comply with A's demands because of what we call referent power. This resource is mostly a function of A's personal qualities.

4. *Expertise.* A is often an expert on some topic or issue. B often complies with A's wishes because B believes that A "knows best" what should be done in this situation. Expertise and ability are almost entirely a function of A's personal characteristics rather than A's formal sanctions.

5. *Legitimacy.* Legitimate power as a resource stems from B's feeling that A has a right to make a given request. Legitimate power is sometimes described as authority. The norms and expectations prevalent in the social situation help to determine A's legitimate power: Has A done this before? Have others complied? What are the social consequences of noncompliance?

Exhibit 18-1. Forms of power.

French and Raven	Mitchell	Kotter
Reward	Rewards	Sense of Obligation
Coercive	Punishment	Perceived Dependency
Referent	Charisma	Identification
Expert	Expertise	Expertise
Legitimate	Formal Authority	Formal Authority
	Information	
		Persuasion
	Connections	

6. *Information.* Information is often controlled by individuals within organizations. They can decide who should know what. To the extent that B thinks A controls information B wants and perhaps needs, then A has power. This information can be both formally and informally gathered and distributed.

7. *Persuasion.* This is when A tries to talk B into a course of action. It takes time, skill, and information, and B must be willing to listen.

8. *Connections.* Building alliances with influential people within the organization is an important power base for project managers who must work with and through functional personnel to achieve project objectives. Developing a variety of informal contacts can help project managers be in a better position to recognize project problems early.

The nature of power is much more complicated than a simple list. Some of the eight forms of power come from the organization (formal authority) and some from the individual (charisma). Power can be direct or indirect through someone else. Power can be possessed or merely perceived, where B thinks A can give a reward. Power can also be exercised or latent, where A has power but does not use it.

The relative use of the different forms of power also has an effect on project success and personal relationships. Wilemon and Gemmill's research indicates that the more effective project managers rely more on personal types of power, while the less effective managers are concerned with not having enough formal authority to command and punish.[12]

Kotter makes a strong case that exceptional managers understand that true organizational power is based much more on inspirational leadership than on executive rank and status. These managers have achieved their stature by establishing the power bases that are essential to the exercise of leadership. Kotter believes that the need for managers who are adept at dealing with organizational complexity will continue to grow. "A century ago," he writes, "only a few thousand people held jobs that demanded that they manage a large number of interdependent relationships. Today, millions do."[13] This fact mirrors a changing business and social environment that has grown in diversity as well as in interdependence. The resulting complexity—involving numerous goals, priorities, and constituencies—inevitably leads to conflict, which in turn can easily degenerate into bureaucratic infighting, parochial politics, and destructive power struggles. "Dealing with this pathology," Kotter writes, "is truly one of the great challenges of our time."

As shown in Exhibit 18-2, Kotter believes that the need for power is directly related to a manager's dependency on and vulnerability to others, especially where he or she does not have formal authority.

Forms of Power and Concrete Actions

How do we translate these definitions and forms of power into concrete actions by project managers? Exhibit 18-3 relates the eight forms of power to illustrative project management tools and techniques. As can be seen, specific tools and techniques allow the project manager to make use of the different forms of power.

Exhibit 18-2. Power dynamics in organization.

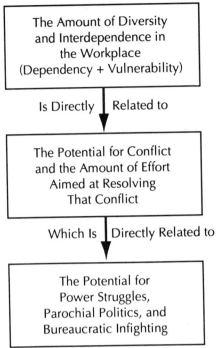

Source: J. P. Kotter, *Power and Influence* (New York: Free Press, 1985).

Exhibit 18-3. Forms of power and project management tools and techniques.

Forms of Power	Project Management Tools and Techniques
Rewards	Budget/Favors
Punishment	Personnel Appraisal
Referent Power	Team Building/Personality
Expertise	Technical Knowledge
Legitimatcy	Top Management Support/Charter
Information	Project Management
Persuasion	Plans/Meetings
Connections	Meetings
	Start-Up Meetings

Notes

1. Project Management Institute, *Project Management Body of Knowledge* (Drexel Hill, Penn.: PMI, 1986).
2. Mary S. Cavanaugh, Ph.D., "A Typology of Social Power," Chapter 1 in A. Kakabadse and C. Parker, eds., *Power, Politics and Organizations* (New York: John Wiley & Sons, 1984).
3. J. P. Kotter, *Power and Influence* (New York: Free Press, 1985).
4. T. R. Mitchell, *People in Organizations: Understanding Their Behaviors* (New York: McGraw-Hill, 1978).
5. William E. Halal, "The Legitimacy Cycle," Chapter 3 in Kakabadse and Parker.
6. Mitchell.
7. R. M. Stogdill, *Handbook of Leadership* (New York: Free Press, 1974).
8. Ibid.
9. Mitchell.
10. Kakabadse and Parker, "Towards a Theory of Political Behavior in Organizations," Chapter 5 in Kakabadse and Parker.
11. J. R. P. French, Jr. and B. Raven, "The Bases of Social Power," in Darwin Cartwright, ed., *Studies in Social Power* (Ann Arbor: University of Michigan, Institute of Social Research, 1957).
12. D. Wilemon and G. Gemmill, "The Power Spectrum in Project Management," *Sloan Management Review* 12, No. 1 (1970), pp. 15–26.
13. Kotter.

19

Effective Leadership for Building Project Teams, Motivating People, and Creating Optimal Organizational Structures

Hans J. Thamhain
Bentley College

More than any other organizational form, effective project management requires an understanding of motivational forces and leadership. The ability to build project teams, motivate people, and create organizational structures conducive to innovative and effective work requires sophisticated interpersonal and organizational skills.

There is no single magic formula for successful project management. However, most senior managers agree that effective management of multidisciplinary activities requires an understanding of the interaction of organizational and behavioral elements in order to build an environment conducive to the team's motivational needs and subsequently lead effectively the complex integration of a project through its multifunctional phases.

Motivational Forces in Project Team Management

Understanding people is important for the effective team management of today's challenging projects. The breed of managers that succeeds within these often unstructured work environments faces many challenges. Internally, they must be able to deal effectively with a variety of interfaces and support personnel over whom they often have little or no control. Externally, managers have to cope with constant and rapid change regarding technology, markets, regulations, and socioeconomic factors. Moreover, traditional methods of authority-based direction, performance measures, and control are virtually impractical in such contemporary environments.

Sixteen specific professional needs of project team personnel are listed below. Research studies show that the fulfillment of these professional needs can drive project personnel to higher performance; conversely, the inability to fulfill these needs may become a barrier to teamwork and high project performance. The rationale for this important correlation is found in the complex interaction of organizational and behavioral elements. Effective team management involves three primary issues: (1) people skills, (2) organizational structure, and (3) management style. All three issues are influenced by the specific task to be performed and the surrounding environment. That is, the degree of satisfaction of any of the needs is a function of (1) having the right mix of people with appropriate skills and traits, (2) organizing the people and resources according to the tasks to be performed, and (3) adopting the right leadership style.[1] The sixteen specific professional needs of team personnel follow.

1. *Interesting and challenging work.* Interesting and challenging work satisfies various professional esteem needs. It is oriented toward intrinsic motivation of the individual and helps to integrate personal goals with the objectives of the organization.

2. *Professionally stimulating work environment.* This leads to professional involvement, creativity, and interdisciplinary support. It also fosters team building and is conducive to effective communication, conflict resolution, and commitment toward organizational goals. The quality of this work environment is defined through its organizational structure, facilities, and management style.

3. *Professional growth.* Professional growth is measured by promotional opportunities, salary advances, the learning of new skills and techniques, and professional recognition. A particular challenge exists for management in limited-growth or zero-growth businesses to compensate for the lack of promotional opportunities by offering more intrinsic professional growth in terms of job satisfaction.

4. *Overall leadership.* This involves dealing effectively with individual contributors, managers, and support personnel within a specific functional discipline as well as across organizational lines. It involves technical expertise, information-processing skills, effective communications, and decision-making skills. Taken together, leadership means satisfying the need for clear direction and unified guidance toward established objectives.

5. *Tangible records.* These include salary increases, bonuses, and incentives, as well as promotions, recognition, better offices, and educational opportunities. Although extrinsic, these financial rewards are necessary to sustain strong long-term efforts and motivation. Furthermore, they validate more intrinsic rewards such as recognition and praise and reassure people that higher goals are attainable.

6. *Technical expertise.* Personnel need to have all necessary interdisciplinary skills and expertise available within the project team to perform the required tasks. Technical expertise includes understanding the technicalities of the work, the technology and underlying concepts, theories and principles, design methods and techniques, and functioning and interrelationship of the various components that make up the total system.

7. *Assisting in problem solving.* Assisting in problem solving, such as facilitating

solutions to technical, administrative, and personal problems, is a very important need. If not satisfied, it often leads to frustration, conflict, and poor quality work.

8. *Clearly defined objectives.* Goals, objectives, and outcomes of an effort must be clearly communicated to all affected personnel. Conflict can develop over ambiguities or missing information.

9. *Management control.* Management control is important for effective team performance. Managers must understand the interaction of organizational and behavior variables in order to exert the direction, leadership, and control required to steer the project effort toward established organizational goals without stifling innovation and creativity.

10. *Job security.* This is one of the very fundamental needs that must be satisfied before people consider higher-order growth needs.

11. *Senior management support.* Senior management support should be provided in four major areas: (1) financial resources, (2) effective operating charter, (3) cooperation from support departments, and (4) provision of necessary facilities and equipment. It is particularly crucial to larger, more complex undertakings.

12. *Good interpersonal relations.* These are required for effective teamwork since they foster a stimulating work environment with low conflict, high productivity, and involved, motivated personnel.

13. *Proper planning.* Proper planning is absolutely essential for the successful management of multidisciplinary activities. It requires communications and information-processing skills to define the actual resource requirements and administrative support necessary. It also requires the ability to negotiate resources and commitment from key personnel in various support groups across organizational lines.

14. *Clear role definition.* This helps to minimize role conflict and power struggles among team members and/or supporting organizations. Clear charters, plans, and good management direction are some of the powerful tools used to facilitate clear role definitions.

15. *Open communications.* This satisfies the need for a free flow of information both horizontally and vertically. It keeps personnel informed and functions as a pervasive integrator of the overall project effort.

16. *Minimizing changes.* Although project managers have to live with constant change, their team members often see change as an unnecessary condition that impedes their creativity and productivity. Advanced planning and proper communications can help to minimize changes and lessen their negative impact.

The Power Spectrum in Project Management

Project managers must often cross functional lines to get the required support. This is especially true for managers who operate within a matrix structure. Almost invariably, the manager must build multidisciplinary teams into cohesive work groups and successfully deal with a variety of interfaces such as functional departments, staff groups, other support groups, clients, and senior management. This is a work environment where managerial power is shared by many individuals. In the

Exhibit 19-1. The project manager's bases of influence.

Influence Base	Organizationally Derived Components	Individually Derived Components
Authority	Position, Title Office Size Charter Budget, Resources Project Size, Importance	Respect Trust Credibility Performance Image Integrity
Reward Power	Salary, Bonuses Hire, Promote Work, Security Training, Development Resource Allocation	Recognition, Visibility Accomplishments Autonomy, Flexibility Stimulating Environment Professional Growth
Punishment	Salary, Bonuses Fire, Demote Work, Security Resource Limitations	Reprimand Team Pressure Tight Supervision Work Pressure Isolation
Expert Power	Top Management Support	Competence Knowledge Information Sound Decisions Top Management Respect Access to Experts
Referent Power		Friendship Charisma Empathy

traditional organization, position power is provided largely in the form of legitimate authority, reward, and punishment. These organizationally derived bases of influence are shown in Exhibit 19-1. In contrast, project managers have to build most of their power bases on their own. They have to earn their power and influence from other sources, including trust, respect, credibility, and the image of a facilitator of a professionally stimulating work environment. These individually derived bases of influence are also shown in Exhibit 19-1.

In today's environment, most project management is largely characterized by:

- ▸ Authority patterns that are defined only in part by formal organization chart plans
- ▸ Authority that is largely perceived by the members of the organization based on earned credibility, expertise, and perceived priorities
- ▸ Dual accountability of most personnel, especially in project-oriented environments

- ‣ Power that is shared between resource managers and project/task managers
- ‣ Individual autonomy and participation that is greater than in traditional organizations
- ‣ Weak superior-subordinate relationships in favor of stronger peer relationships
- ‣ Subtle shifts of personnel loyalties from functional to project lines
- ‣ Project performance that depends on teamwork
- ‣ Group decision making that tends to favor the strongest organizations
- ‣ Reward and punishment power along both vertical and horizontal lines in a highly dynamic pattern
- ‣ Influences to reward and punish that come from many organizations and individuals
- ‣ Multiproject involvement of support personnel and sharing of resources among many activities

Position power is a necessary prerequisite for effective project/team leadership. Like many other components of the management system, leadership style has also undergone changes over time. With increasing task complexity, increasing dynamics of the organizational environment, and the evolution of new organizational systems, such as the matrix, a more adaptive and skill-oriented management style has evolved. This style complements the organizationally derived power bases—such as authority, reward, and punishment—with bases developed by the individual manager. Examples of these individually derived components of influence are technical and managerial expertise, friendship, work challenge, promotional ability, fund allocations, charisma, personal favors, project goal indemnification, recognition, and visibility. This so-called Style II management evolved particularly with the matrix. Effective project management combines both the organizationally derived and individually derived styles of influence.

Various research studies by Gemmill, Thamhain, and Wilemon provide an insight into the power spectrum available to project managers.[2] Project personnel were asked to rank nine influence bases; Exhibit 19-2 shows the results. Technical and managerial expertise, work challenge, and influence over salary were the most important influences that project leaders seem to have, while penalty factors, fund allocations, and authority appeared least important in gaining support from project team members.

Leadership Style Effectiveness

For more than ten years, the author has investigated influence bases with regard to project management effectiveness.[3] Through those formal studies it is measurably and consistently found that managers who are perceived by their personnel as (1) emphasizing work challenge and expertise, but (2) deemphasizing authority, penalty, and salary, foster a climate of good communications, high involvement, and strong support to the tasks at hand. Ultimately, this style results in high performance ratings by upper management.

The relationship of managerial influence style and effectiveness has been statistically measured.[4] One of the most interesting findings is the importance of work challenge as an influence method. Work challenge appears to integrate the personal

Exhibit 19-2. The project manager's power spectrum.

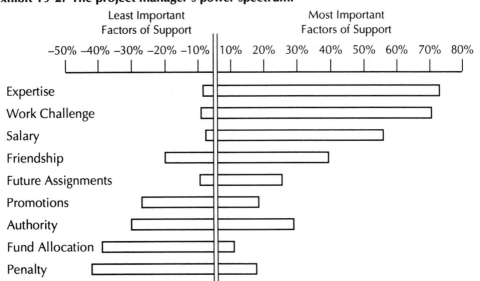

goals and needs of personnel with organizational goals. That is, work challenge is primarily oriented toward extrinsic rewards with less regard to the personnel's progressional needs. Therefore, enriching the assignments of team personnel in a professionally challenging way may indeed have a beneficial effect on overall performance. In addition, the assignment of challenging work is a variable over which project managers may have a great deal of control. Even if the total task structure is fixed, the method by which work is assigned and distributed is discretionary in most cases.

Recommendations for Effective Project Team Management

The project leader must foster an environment where team members are professionally satisfied, are involved, and have mutual trust. The more effective the project leader is in stimulating the drivers and minimizing the barriers shown in Exhibit 19-3, the more effective the manager can be in developing team membership and the higher the quality of information contributed by team members, including their willingness and candor in sharing ideas and approaches. By contrast, when a team member does not feel part of the team and does not trust others, information is not shared willingly or openly. One project leader emphasized the point: "There's nothing worse than being on a team where no one trusts anyone else. Such situations lead to gamesmanship and a lot of watching what you say because you don't want your own words to bounce back in your own face."

Furthermore, the greater the team spirit and trust and the quality of information exchange among team members, the more likely the team will be able to develop effective decision-making processes, make individual and group commitment, focus on problem solving, and develop self-forcing, self-correcting project controls. As summarized in Exhibit 19-4, these are the characteristics of an effective and productive project team. A number of specific recommendations are listed below for project

Exhibit 19-3. The strongest barriers and drivers to team performance.

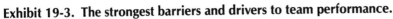
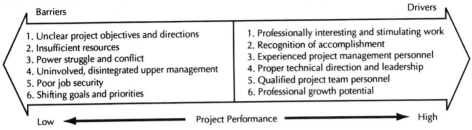

Barriers	Drivers
1. Unclear project objectives and directions 2. Insufficient resources 3. Power struggle and conflict 4. Uninvolved, disintegrated upper management 5. Poor job security 6. Shifting goals and priorities	1. Professionally interesting and stimulating work 2. Recognition of accomplishment 3. Experienced project management personnel 4. Proper technical direction and leadership 5. Qualified project team personnel 6. Professional growth potential

Low ◄—————— Project Performance ——————► High

leaders and managers responsible for the integration of multidisciplinary tasks to help in their complex efforts of building high-performing project teams.

▸ *Recognize barriers.* Project managers must understand the various barriers to team development and build a work environment conducive to the team's motivational needs. Specifically, management should try to watch out for the following barriers: (1) unclear objectives, (2) insufficient resources and unclear findings, (3) role conflict and power struggle, (4) uninvolved and unsupportive management, (5) poor job security, and (6) shifting goals and priorities.

▸ *Define clear project objectives.* The project objectives and their importance to the organization should be clear to all personnel involved with the project. Senior management can help develop a "priority image" and communicate the basic project parameters and management guidelines.

Exhibit 19-4. Characteristics of high-performing project teams.

Task

Task-Related Qualities	People-Related Qualities
•Committed to the project	•High involvement, work interest, and energy
•Result-orientated attitude	•Capacity to solve conflict
•Innovativeness & creativity	•Good communication
•Willingness to change	•High need for achievement
•Concern for quality	•Good team spirit
•Ability to predict trends	•Mutual trust
•Ability to integrate	•Self-development of team members
•Ability to anticipate problems and react early	•Effective organizational interfacing
•Synergism	

▸ *Assure management commitment.* A project manager must continually update and involve management to refuel its interests in and commitments to the new project. Breaking the project into smaller phases and being able to produce short-range results are important to this refueling process.

▸ *Build a favorable image.* Building a favorable image for the project in terms of high priority, interesting work, importance to the organization, high visibility, and potential for professional rewards is crucial to the ability to attract and hold high-quality people. It is also a pervasive process that fosters a climate of active participation at all levels; it helps to unify the new project team and minimize dysfunctional conflict.

▸ *Manage and lead.* Leadership positions should be carefully defined and staffed at the beginning of a new program. Key project personnel selection is the joint responsibility of the project manager and functional management. The credibility of the project leader among team members with senior management and with the program sponsor is crucial to the leader's ability to manage multidisciplinary activities effectively across functional lines. One-on-one interviews are recommended for explaining the scope and project requirement, as well as the management philosophy, organizational structure, and rewards.

▸ *Plan and define your project.* Effective planning early in the project life cycle has a favorable impact on the work environment and team effectiveness. This is especially so because project managers have to integrate various tasks across many functional lines. Proper planning, however, means more than just generating the required pieces of paper. It requires the participation of the entire project team, including support departments, subcontractors, and management. These planning activities—which can be performed in a special project phase such as requirements analysis, product feasibility assessment, or product/project definition—usually have a number of side benefits besides generating a comprehensive road map for the upcoming program.

▸ *Create involvement.* One of the side benefits of proper planning is the involvement of personnel at all organizational levels. Project managers should drive such an involvement, at least with their key personnel, especially during the project definition phases. This involvement leads to a better understanding of the task requirements, stimulates interest, helps unify the team, and ultimately leads to commitment to the project plan regarding technical performance, timing, and budgets.

▸ *Assure proper project staffing.* All project assignments should be negotiated individually with each prospective team member. Each task leader should be responsible for staffing his or her own task team. Where dual-reporting relationships are involved, staffing should be conducted jointly by the two managers. The assignment interview should include a clear discussion of the specific tasks, outcome, timing, responsibilities, reporting relation, potential rewards, and importance of the project to the company. Task assignments should be made only if the candidate's ability is a reasonable match to the position requirements and the candidate shows a healthy degree of interest in the project.

▸ *Define team structure.* Management must define the basic team structure and operating concepts early during the project formation phase. The project plan, task matrix, project charter, and policy are the principal tools. It is the responsibility of the project manager to communicate the organizational design and to assure that all parties understand the overall and interdisciplinary project objectives. Clear and frequent communication with senior management and the new project sponsor is critically important. Status review meetings can be used for feedback.

▸ *Conduct team-building sessions.* The project manager should conduct team-building sessions throughout the project life cycle. An especially intense effort might be needed during the team formation stage. The team should be brought together periodically in a relaxed atmosphere to discuss such questions as: (1) How are we operating as a team? (2) What is our strength? (3) Where can we improve? (4) What steps are needed to initiate the desired change? (5) What problems and issues are we likely to face in the future? (6) Which of these can be avoided by taking appropriate action now? (7) How can we "danger-proof" the team?

▸ *Develop your team continuously.* Project leaders should watch for problems with changes in performance, and such problems should be dealt with quickly. Internal or external organization development specialists can help diagnose team problems and assist the team in dealing with the identified problems. These specialists also can bring fresh ideas and perspectives to difficult and sometimes emotionally complex situations.

▸ *Develop team commitment.* Project managers should determine whether team members lack commitment early in the life of the project and attempt to change possible negative views toward the project. Since insecurity often is a major reason for lacking commitment, managers should try to determine why insecurity exists, and then work on reducing the team members' fears. Conflict with other team members may be another reason for lack of commitment. If there are project professionals whose interests lie elsewhere, the project leader should examine ways to satisfy part of those members' interests by bringing personal and project goals into perspective.

▸ *Assure senior management support.* It is critically important for senior management to provide the proper environment for the project team to function effectively. The project leader needs to tell management at the outset of the program what resources are needed. The project manager's relationship with senior management and ability to develop senior management support is critically affected by his or her credibility and visibility and the priority image of the project.

▸ *Focus on problem avoidance.* Project leaders should focus their efforts on problem avoidance. That is, the project leader, through experience, should recognize potential problems and conflicts before their onset and deal with them before they become big and their resolutions consume a large amount of time and effort.

▸ *Show your personal drive and desire.* Finally, project managers can influence the climate of their work environment by their own actions. Concern for project team members and ability to create personal enthusiasm for the project itself can foster a climate high in motivation, work involvement, open communication, and resulting project performance.

A Final Note

In summary, effective team management is a critical determinant of project success. Building the group of project personnel into a cohesive, unified task team is one of the prime responsibilities of the program leader. Team building involves a whole spectrum of management skills to identify, commit, and integrate the various personnel from different functional organizations. Team building is a shared responsibility between the functional managers and the project manager, who often reports to a different organization with a different superior.

To be effective, the project manager must provide an atmosphere conducive to teamwork. Four major considerations are involved in the integration of people from many disciplines into an effective team: (1) creating a professionally stimulating work environment, (2) ensuring good program leadership, (3) providing qualified personnel, and (4) providing a technically and organizationally stable environment. The project leader must foster an environment where team members are professionally satisfied, involved, and have mutual trust. The more effectively project leaders develop team membership, the higher the quality of information exchanged and the greater the candor of team members. It is this professionally stimulating involvement that also has a pervasive effect on the team's ability to cope with change and conflict and leads to innovative performance. By contrast, when a member does not feel part of the team and does not trust others, information is not shared willingly or openly.

Furthermore, the greater the team spirit, trust, and quality of information exchange among team members, the more likely the team is able to develop effective decision-making processes, make individual and group commitments, focus on problem solving, and develop self-enforcing, self-correcting project controls. These are the characteristics of an effective and productive project team.

To be successful, project leaders must develop their team management skills. They must have the ability to unify multifunctional teams and lead them toward integrated results. They must understand the interaction of organizational and behavioral elements in order to build an environment that satisfies the team's motivational needs. Active participation, minimal interpersonal conflict, and effective communication are some of the major factors that determine the quality of the organization's environment.

Furthermore, project managers must provide a high degree of leadership in unstructured environments. They must develop credibility with peer groups, team members, senior management, and customers. Above all, the project manager must be a social architect who understands the organization and its culture, value system, environment, and technology. These are the prerequisites for moving project-oriented organizations toward long-range productivity and growth.

Notes

1. H. J. Thamhain, "Managing Engineers Effectively," *IEEE Transactions on Engineering Management* (August 1983).
2. H. J. Thamhain and D. L. Wilemon, "Leadership, Conflict, and Project Management Effectiveness," Executive Bookshelf on *Generating Technological Innovation* (E. Roberts, ed.) in *Sloan Management Review* (Fall 1987); H. J. Thamhain and G. R. Gemmill, "Influence Styles of Project Managers: Some Project Performance Correlates," *Academy of Management Journal* (June 1974); D. L. Wilemon et al., "Managing Conflict on Project Teams," *Management Journal* (1974).
3. H. J. Thamhain, "Developing Project Teams," in D. I. Cleland and W. R. King,

eds., *Project Management* (New York: Van Nostrand Reinhold, 1988); Thamhain and Gemmill, "Influence Styles"; D. L. Wilemon and H. J. Thamhain, "A Model for Developing High-Performance Teams," 1983 *Proceedings of the Project Management Institute,* Houston (Drexel Hill, Penn.: PMI).

4. Thamhain and Wilemon, "Leadership, Conflict."

Section VIII
Quality in Project Management

20

The Essence of Quality Management

Alan S. Mendelssohn
Budget Rent a Car Corporation

The focus of quality management on projects is to control the process of executing activities to achieve customer satisfaction. In the past, control of the final results was the primary concern. Now, emphasis is placed on ensuring that the process is capable of achieving the desired results and can consistently satisfy the customer's needs. The way to make this happen is to assure the quality of each step involved in the project. The outcome of each step must be acceptable to the next person in the process (called the internal customer) until the end user (the external customer) of the project is ultimately satisfied.

The concepts of customer and process are the essence of quality management. These concepts are discussed in this chapter, with presentation of the ideas, methodology, and tools needed for implementation.

The Customer

The customer is the next person in the work process who receives the product or service. Whether a customer is internal or is the final person who receives the product depends on the perspective from which the process is viewed. Customers first have to be identified and their needs determined before they can be satisfied. This leads to developing the processes needed to satisfy those needs.

Valid Requirements

A requirement represents a need or want that the customer is looking to have satisfied. This is usually defined in specifications, through interviews with the customer, or through the manager's perception of what is desired. It is necessary to

This chapter was adapted from Alan S. Mendelssohn, "Quality—An All Encompassing Concept Critical to Project Success," 1990 *Proceedings of the Project Management Institute*. Reprinted with permission of the Project Management Institute, P.O. Box 43, Drexel Hill, PA 19026, a worldwide organization of advancing the state-of-the-art in project management.

review the requirement with the customer to be sure that it is specific, measurable, and can be provided in a satisfactory format and time frame. This may involve negotiation with the customer if the above criteria cannot be met. The requirement becomes valid only after agreement is reached that (1) the need can be satisfied, and (2) the party responsible for project management agrees to satisfy it. The same criteria apply in validating requirements for both internal and external customers.

Quality Indicators

A quality indicator measures whether a process is satisfying the customer's valid requirement, based on those things that are important to the customer—not what is convenient to measure. If the project team uses a different set of indicators from the customer, its interpretation of success may also be different from the customer's. Quality indicators are determined at the same time the valid requirements are identified. Agreement with the customer on how to measure those requirements and what targets or limits should apply eliminates misinterpretation later on.

Some valid requirements and quality indicators are given, either in a specification or as a regulatory requirement. While negotiation with the customer on these items may not be possible, it is still important to understand and agree that the requirement can be met and that compliance is measurable.

Process

When a process is to be followed on a repetitive basis, it must be controlled to ensure consistent results. Exhibit 20-1 is an example of a typical process for getting to work on time. In addition to the process flowchart, also shown are the quality indicator (the time one gets to work) and the process indicators, represented by the Q and P, respectively. Similar but more complex processes exist within the work environment itself.

Documentation of the work processes makes them visible. All the steps necessary to achieve the final product need to be shown. The flowchart for the manager should be at a level of detail which represents those activities which he or she will personally follow. Each activity block might represent a lower-level process that must also be controlled. For example, the valid requirements that engineering must meet to satisfy its customer, the purchasing department, is an equipment specification that is on time, complete, and technically correct. As shown in Exhibit 20-2, the output of this lower-level process is the input to the next customer down the line. The quality indicators in the engineering process may be the process indicators in the overall project process flow.

Process Indicators

A process indicator is used to show whether a work process is stabilized and to forewarn of problems that could impact final results. There are two kinds of process indicators. The first is used to evaluate the process itself. The best statistical tool for this is a control chart. Depending on the nature and frequency of the data collected, different control charts are used. A process can be "out of control" when data fall

Exhibit 20-1. Typical process for getting to work.

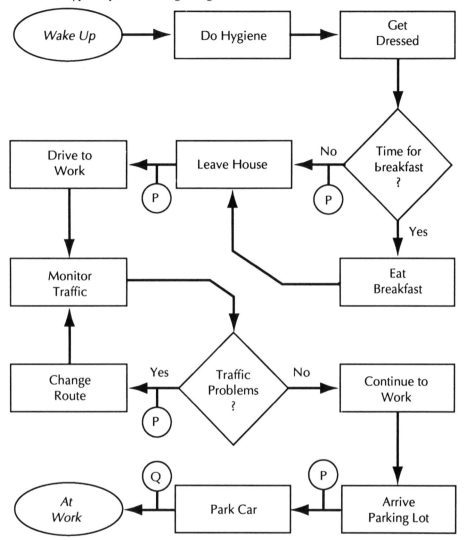

outside calculated control limits determined by established statistical models or when the trend of the data indicates an abnormality. When data fall outside calculated limits, the data must be investigated to determine if a "special cause" for this out-of-control point exists or if the problem is with the process itself. The problem-solving process, described later, is recommended for this investigation.

The second process indicator looks at the outcome of an activity and compares it with some predetermined target. If the data go outside this limit, it means that the output is unacceptable and could impact the project goal of meeting the customer's needs. To correct the situation, the problem-solving process should be used.

If the control chart shows that the process is stable but the indicators show that the targets are not being met, then the process is not capable of achieving the desired

Exhibit 20-2. Relationship of processes.

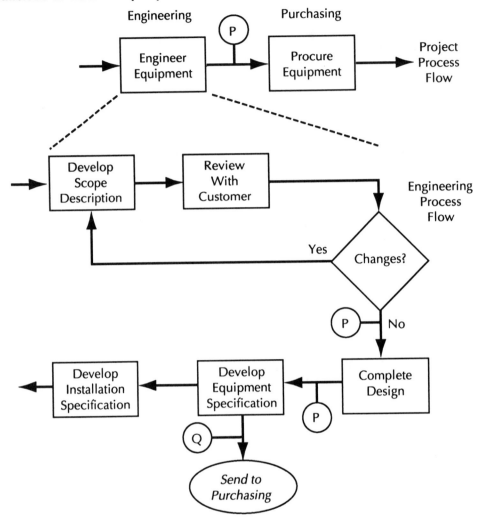

results. It must be changed in some way. The problem-solving process can again be used to eliminate common causes and identify improvements to the process.

If the indicators show that the targets are being met but the control chart shows that the process is not stable, then the project has been favored by luck. Process stability is also required for quality to be assured on a continuing basis.

Upstream Control

When a system is unstable, anything can happen, and it often does. Response to this instability is usually called firefighting. The manager must motivate team members to stabilize work processes and then give them the means to make improvements. Improved customer satisfaction comes with process improvement.

Process control requires an understanding of the relationship between the process indicators and the quality indicator. For example, in Exhibit 20-3, if the forecasted date for turnover of the equipment to the customer is the quality indicator being monitored, it is also important to follow the schedule for completion of each of the key activities. If the engineering activity is running late, this has a direct impact on the turnover date, unless action is taken to correct the situation. By monitoring this process indicator, the manager can predict whether the customer's required turnover date can be met or can take appropriate action to improve the situation before it is too late. By controlling the process upstream of the outcome, quality can be built into each step. If not, the impact is felt downstream, but not by the people who cause the problem. Correcting those things in the engineering process that cause delays may also prevent the same factors from affecting future engineering.

The manager needs to prioritize which processes should be improved first. This prioritization is based on (1) which processes contribute most to the goals of the project in satisfying the customer's valid requirements, and (2) which customer needs are not being met, based on the data currently available. As processes are brought into control and effectively satisfy the needs of the customers, reprioritization takes place as part of a continuous process improvement program.

The Problem-Solving Process

The definition of a problem is a deviation from a customer's valid requirement. In quality management, a problem is an opportunity, a chance for improvement. Any time a person downstream of an activity or process does not receive what is required, he or she is affected in some way.

Statistical tools are available to help with problem solving. These tools include such things as checksheets, graphs, histograms, Pareto charts, cause-and-effect diagrams, scatter diagrams, and control charts. Problem-solving models can also be

Exhibit 20-3. Process and quality indicators.

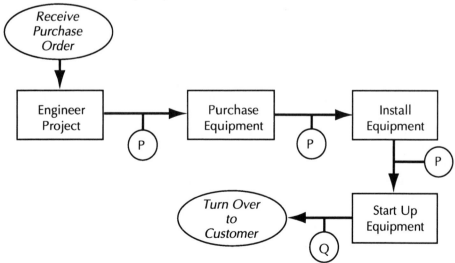

used to ensure that the real causes are found and that appropriate countermeasures are implemented. All these models have certain common elements that make them effective, which include the following:

▸ *Problem definition.* Identification of the problem in specific terms is needed before it can be solved. The data available from indicators and control charts are helpful in focusing the real problem. Pareto charts to rank problems are also useful.

▸ *Root cause evaluation.* In analyzing what the root causes are, it is necessary to keep asking the questions "Why did that happen? What causes this?" A cause-and-effect diagram is useful in this step. Once potential causes are found, it is important to verify, by using data, that these are indeed the root causes. If the real causes are not found, only the symptoms are dealt with, and the problem will likely reoccur.

▸ *Countermeasures.* After the root causes are identified, countermeasures are determined and implemented. These are aimed at eliminating the root causes. To be appropriate the countermeasures should contribute to the goal of achieving customer satisfaction.

▸ *Results.* If the results do not show the desired improvement, using the same indicators that initially showed there was a problem, it is necessary to go back into the analysis to determine if additional root causes exist or if the implementation of countermeasures was not effective. It is sometimes necessary to go through several cycles to achieve success.

▸ *Standardization.* To ensure that the problem will not reoccur, the countermeasures should become permanent. In other words, the work processes must be modified to include the improvements. This standardization of improvements in the work process leads to bettering project management approaches and eliminating firefighting situations.

The problem-solving process can be used by individuals or by teams, whatever is appropriate to solve a problem. Some common names for groups working on process improvement are quality circles, quality improvement teams, and process action teams.

The Cycle of Plan, Do, Check, and Act

Continuous improvement comes about when quality management tools and techniques are applied to work processes. The foundation for this is the Plan, Do, Check, Act (PDCA) cycle, shown in Exhibit 20-4 and also known as the Shewhart Cycle or Deming Wheel. The PDCA cycle shows that the quest for improved quality is continuous and never-ending.

Plan is the first stage of the process. Goals and objectives are set and resources allocated. *Do,* the second stage, is carrying out the plan, while gathering data about how it is going. *Check* is the evaluation stage. Did the plan work? Was it effective? What data were gathered? What does it tell? The Check stage begins as soon as data becomes available. Thus, the process of checking runs concurrent with the accomplishment of the work. *Act* means making the necessary adjustments to achieve the objectives.

Exhibit 20-4. PDCA cycle.

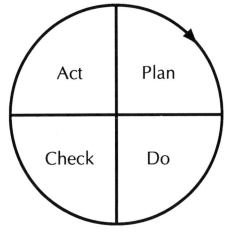

When the data in the Check stage show that a problem exists, the problem-solving process is applied. In the Act stage, the analysis is completed and countermeasures are identified. Then the cycle starts again by planning for implementation of the countermeasures. The continuous evolution from one stage to the next is called turning the wheel. If the data show that the targets are being met and the processes are in control, the Act stage still remains important. In this case, a decision must be made whether to continue with the existing process or to take action to modify it to achieve even better results.

Four Principles of Quality Management

For quality management to be an effective part of project management, four principles need to be practiced: (1) customer satisfaction, (2) the PDCA cycle, (3) management by fact, and (4) respect for people.

Customer Satisfaction

Quality management involves identifying the project's customers and communicating with them to determine their valid requirements. Then, the work processes must be designed to be sure that these valid requirements are met. While the identification part is usually easy, talking to the customer may be difficult. If the relationship is not good, it may be hard to sit down and talk things over in the spirit of mutual problem solving. On the other hand, when the relationship is going smoothly, people tend to take it for granted and don't bother to communicate regularly. As people in the organization become more proficient in implementing quality management, this communication, both vertically and laterally, becomes easier and more open.

Plan, Do, Check, Act Cycle

The PDCA cycle is the foundation for continuous improvement. As work processes are planned and implemented, it is necessary to continue to check them to ensure that they are in control and satisfying the customer's valid requirements. If not, action must be taken to change the situation and start the cycle over again.

Management by Fact

Management by fact means two things. First, collect objective data so that the information is valid. Second, manage according to this information. When people start out with the statement "I think" or "I feel," question what they are saying by asking, "What are the data that support what you want to do?" Be sure, however, that the information is in fact valid. Too often, information is accepted as fact without sufficient review to understand where the data came from and why they are good data. If a manager is going to make objective decisions, valid information must be used in this decision-making process.

Respect for People

Respect for people boils down to simple things like:

- ▸ Keeping people informed and involved, showing them how they are a part of the bigger picture
- ▸ Training people so that every individual performs at the best level he or she can achieve at the job
- ▸ Helping people communicate well so that they can do their job with peak effectiveness
- ▸ Assigning responsibility and delegating authority downward so that people are not just "doing what they're told" (even when it is wrong), but are trying to make things work better
- ▸ Providing an environment where every person has an opportunity to improve his or her work processes, and removing barriers that inhibit excessive stability in those processes
- ▸ Creating a sense of purpose in the workplace so that people are motivated to do their best

Since it is people who improve processes, it is necessary for everyone, no matter what level they operate at, to recognize and acknowledge when problems occur and opportunities for improvement exist. Continuous improvement of the processes involves more than just solving problems. When things are working well, there is a reason for it. It is also important to find what in the processes is working well and then to build on it.

References

Imai, M. *Kaizen: The Key to Japan's Competitive Success*. New York: Random House, 1986.

Ishikawa, K. *What Is Total Quality Control? The Japanese Way*. Englewood Cliffs, N.J.: Prentice-Hall, 1985.

King, Bob. *Better Designs in Half the Time*, Methuen, Mass.: GOAL/QPC, 1987.

Kume, H. *Statistical Methods for Quality Improvement.* Tokyo, Japan: Association for Overseas Technical Scholarship, 1985.

Mizuno, Shigeru. *Management for Quality Improvement.* Cambridge, Mass.: Productivity Press, 1988.

Process Control, Capability and Improvement. Thornwood, N.Y.: IBM Quality Institute, 1984.

Quality Improvement Program. Juno Beach, Fla.: Florida Power & Light Company, 1988.

Walton, M . *Deming Management Method.* New York: Dodd, Mead, 1986.

21

Quality in Project Management Services

Lewis R. Ireland
L. R. Ireland & Associates

This study of three companies providing project management services for the U.S. government focuses on the negative aspects of the quality of performance as a means of providing lessons learned. It is not the author's intention, however, to detract from the reputations of the companies or to imply that the contractual obligations were not met. These negative features are valuable lessons for others, and this study may well cause an improvement in the contracting for project management services in the future by public and private institutions. To preclude criticism of the companies or the government agencies, fictitious names are used for the companies and the specific names of the agencies are omitted.

Project Management and the U.S. Government

Project management services are not normally developed and employed on a full-time basis by U.S. government agencies. When the government requires these services for a major change in the performance of functions, such as a revision of an existing system or the construction of new facilities, it awards a contract to a private company for a specified time. Project management service contracts represent annual expenditures of several billions of dollars to enhance the government's management capability.

This study of the quality of the project management services performed for government agencies reveals weaknesses in contracting and performing these services. The study looks at a small-size company with fewer than twenty-five employees, a medium-size company with approximately 300 employees, and a large-size company with more than 16,000 employees. The author's personal involvement with the three companies gives a firsthand examination of the quality of the services and related products.

The study analyzes the services provided to the U.S. government agencies and assesses the value of such services in view of the requirement, the quality of services, and the cost of services. It highlights the shortfalls in performance and provides an assessment of the reasons for such shortfalls as lessons learned. This calls attention to those weaknesses so the omissions or errors are avoided in future contractual relationships.

Types of Project Management Services

The two categories of project management performed for the government are professional engineering services and professional technical services. Professional engineering services are performed by people trained and experienced in the physical sciences. Professional technical services encompass all other work areas performed by personnel with training in other disciplines.

Professional engineering services include studies of engineering requirements, critiques of technical documentation, logistic analyses, cost estimating, and engineering feasibility studies. Common types of professionals for engineering services are physicists, mathematicians, mechanical engineers, electronic engineers, civil engineers, chemical engineers, and hydraulic engineers. (Life science disciplines, such as medical doctors, veterinary doctors, and pharmacologists, are also contracted for by the U.S. government for project management services, but they are not included in this study.)

Professional technical services include cost estimating, cost accounting, budgeting, financial analyses, project scheduling, project planning, preparation of project communication documents, contract administration, earned value analyses, and critiques of policy and procedure documentation. The performance of the technical service tasks uses all the engineering and business disciplines, but with a concentration in the areas of business management or business administration.

Types of Contracts

The U.S. government obtains project management services using two types of contracts: a cost reimbursable contract and a fixed price/lump sum contract. These two types of contracts vary with the type of fee associated with each. Thus, the contracts can be of the following types:

- Cost plus fixed fee
- Cost plus incentive fee
- Cost plus award fee
- Fixed price plus award fee
- Fixed price plus incentive fee
- Fixed price

It is generally assumed that cost plus contracts assign the cost risk to the buyer (the government), and fixed price contracts assign the cost risk to the seller (the provider of the services). The fee associated with the contract is used to provide an incentive to the seller to meet the buyer's goals or objectives. The fixed fee associated with a cost plus contract is the seller's profit for managing the work and is usually a small percentage of the total cost. Incentive fees establish a monetary reward associated with meeting predetermined criteria, such as milestones or a percent completion of a project. Award fees encourage the seller to meet subjective goals that cannot be quantified but are developed as the project progresses. Award fee goals are deter-mined as the project moves forward, and the criteria for meeting those goals may change over time.

Sellers of Project Management Services

There are three companies in this study that provided project management services to the U.S. government in support of projects of significantly different sizes. The large company, hereafter designated Monarch Corporation, exceeded 16,000 employ-ees and had the human and dollar resources to bid for and perform on contracts with values as high as $3 billion. Monarch also had experience in managing and perform-ing on large contracts for project management services. Monarch provides project management services to the government as one of its market services, but it is primarily a hardware manufacturer for the government. As a hardware manufacturer, Monarch has been developing equipment for nearly thirty-five years.

The medium-size company, hereafter designated Swift Corporation, employed approximately 300 persons, of which the technical staff was approximately 230. Swift is a subsidiary of a parent holding company and relies upon its in-house resources for any contracted work. The holding company has no additional human or dollar resources to support Swift's contracts with the government. Swift has been a single-service (product) corporation, providing project management services to the govern-ment, for eighteen years prior to the study. The government has been Swift's only customer.

The small-size company, hereafter designated Coin Corporation, employed fifteen persons, some on contract from other companies. Coin is a single-service company with limited financial and human resources and has performed project management services for more than nine years. The history of Coin shows a rapid rise in business to employ nearly 100 persons at the six-year point, a sudden decline of contractual work in the seventh and eighth years to less than six persons, and a rebirth and building in the ninth year to approximately fifteen.

Contract Types Awarded to Companies

The type of contract awarded for each of the three companies reflects the level of risk accepted by the seller (contractor) in contracting with the government. Monarch was awarded a fixed price, award fee contract with an initial value of $684 million for a five-year period to perform project management services. This contract was awarded to Monarch after a competitive solicitation in which Monarch bid approximately $200 million less than the other contractor attempting to obtain the work.

Swift was awarded a noncompetitive, cost plus fixed fee contract for three years. This contract was awarded without competition with other contractors and provided that Swift would receive a profit fee of 7.8 percent up to the target cost of the contractual work.

Coin was awarded a noncompetitive, cost plus fixed fee contract for one year that could be modified to increase or decrease the level of effort as the work progressed. The fee was approximately 8.5 percent.

Exhibit 21-1 summarizes the three contracts and shows the type of contract, the

Exhibit 21-1. Summary of contracts.

Company	Number of Personnel	Type of Contract	Duration	Dollar Value	Project Management Sample Services
Monarch	16,000	Fixed Price, Award Fee	Five years	$684 million	Design Critiques Complex Scheduling Logistic Analyses Contract Evaluations Engineering Design Software Validation System Analyses
Swift	300	Cost Plus Fixed Fee	Three Years	$19.7 million	Design Critiques Simple Scheduling Logistic Analyses System Analyses Documentation Preparation Contract Administration
Coin	15	Cost Plus Fixed Fee	One Year	$0.7 million	Complex Scheduling

number of personnel, the duration of the contract, the dollar value of each contract, and the types of services performed.

Quality of Project Management Services

The quality of project management services rendered by each company is assessed here in terms of conformance to the requirements. The requirements for the companies were defined in the government's statements of work (SOW) and the contract data requirements lists (CDRL). The SOW defines the work to be performed and identifies limitations or special requirements. The SOW also describes the type of services, frequency of services, and scope of services. The CDRL describes the documentation, information, and software that must be delivered to the government.

Because project management services are closer to a "level of effort" than a measurable product, the most effective control that the government can exercise over a services contract is to focus on the deliverable data, including software programs as specified in the CDRL. Therefore, the evaluation of delivered plans, briefings, reports, critiques, and software programs may be the only measure of quality. The criteria associated with the delivery of these items may be the frequency of submission, the number of copies, the date of submission, and format.

Conformance to requirements means meeting the performance criteria outlined in the SOW and CDRL for the project management services contracts. Providing more than is required erodes the profit margin in a fixed price contract and could jeopardize the recovery of costs in a cost plus type of contract. To provide less than is specified and contractually required affects the level of the quality of project management services.

Monarch's Contractual Work

Government Agency A developed a request for proposal (RFP) and solicited inputs from several contractors for project management services. The development of the RFP was performed by one directorate for work required in support of six other directorates. Each directorate made inputs of its requirements to the executive directorate for the subsequent compilation and formatting into a SOW and CDRL.

All inputs were screened by the executive directorate and, to the extent possible, the wording was standardized to minimize the complexity of the SOW and CDRL, both for management of a solicitation process and for contract administration. For example, reports for schedules were required at random times by the compilation of inputs. The standardized schedule reports, however, specified the frequency of reports, the format of each type of report, and the number of copies to be delivered. In this procedure, some of the directorates believed their requirements had been changed by the executive directorate. Therefore, they would not be provided sufficient data with which to manage their work during contract execution.

The SOW and CDRL were not well coordinated by the executive directorate and a consensus was not reached on the total Agency A requirements. The directorates' expectations of quality (performance) were established as individuals and remained as individuals because the executive directorate did not inform the directorates of the changes to the requirements in the SOW and CDRL. Consequently, the formal requirements of the individual customers were not embedded into the contractual documentation.

Monarch responded to Agency A's solicitation with a twelve-volume proposal, each volume addressing a different area of the anticipated contract. A price volume was also submitted as a separate document. Monarch's technical and management proposal was evaluated for responsiveness to the requirements, and the price volume was separately evaluated (audited) to determine if the prices were realistic.

Monarch was awarded the contract and within a week was on the customer's site to start work at a low level of effort while the total force that would provide the project management services was being assembled. The directorates immediately initiated requests for project management services, but Monarch was not able to provide the services because of a lack of required skills and a shortage of personnel on the site. The perception by the directorates was that Monarch should be capable of providing the services at the start, as implied in the proposal.

Monarch experienced several shortfalls in providing the perceived level of quality the customer demanded. Examples of these are given below.

Situation #1

Requirement

A directorate requested a planner to write a computer resource management plan.

Discussion

Monarch stated that writers were not in the contract. Agency A had requested planners, which in Monarch's view were schedule planners. Thus, the planners proposed and included in the contract could not write plans. If writers were required, however, Monarch could provide those skills at an additional cost to the contract through a change of scope.

Comment

Monarch did not plan for the correct skills for the project management services. The requested work would normally be included in any type of contract of this nature.

Situation #2

Requirement

A directorate requested that a maintenance plan be written for a major system.

Discussion

Monarch prepared and submitted the maintenance plan, but it was rejected during the approval cycle. Monarch resubmitted the plan three more times and each time it was rejected. The plan was never completed by Monarch.

Comment

Monarch was not capable of preparing the plan and lacked the expertise to perform the task. Agency A acted in an arbitrary and capricious manner in continuing to reject the plan. There was little or no effort made to negotiate the requirements for the plan.

Situation #3

Requirement

Agency A requested that a greater level of effort be expended upon the job because the work was not being accomplished on schedule.

Discussion

Monarch had not anticipated a rapid start-up on the work, while the Agency A employees anticipated that a contractor would be available to assume many of the ongoing tasks. As a result, Agency A employees slowed the rate of progress just before Monarch's arrival on site. The combination of Monarch having a slow start-up period and the Agency A "saving" work until the contractor was in place resulted in nearly doubling the workload in project management services.

Comment

Monarch's solution to the problem was to double the number of personnel in the first two years of the five-year contract and reduce the staff to a minimum level for the last three years of work. This would solve the immediate problem but would leave Agency A with only a small contractor support group to implement some of the more critical aspects of the government's project. Agency A agreed to increase the scope of work for Monarch, with a resultant increase in cost.

Situation #4

Requirement

One directorate of Agency A requested that Monarch provide services to that area of the government's project, but it refused to allow Monarch's personnel into the directorate facilities. The directorate stated that the Monarch personnel did not have the requisite skills to perform the tasks.

Discussion

Under this type of contract, the government may not comment on the skills of contractor personnel, but must rely on the contractor's judgment as to the skill requirement. Only the end product and the timeliness of delivery can be raised as an issue for project management services; otherwise, the contract becomes a personal service contract. The Monarch task group that was charged with providing the services in question performed routine, in-house tasks in its area for three months and continued to charge for providing the support.

Comment

The directorate's lockout of Monarch's personnel was an interference with the performance of the contract. Agency A had to continue to pay for services that were not received. This problem should not have occurred and should have been resolved through the contract administrator, i.e., the executive directorate, when it did occur.

Situation #5

Requirement

Agency A changed the scope of the contract on several occasions.

Discussion

Agency A changed the amount of work that was to be accomplished by Monarch, in most instances increasing the amount. Changes to fixed price contracts are negotiable in that the contractor is not obligated to "sell services" at a given rate of compensation. The margins on changes to the scope are nearly always much larger than those of the original contract. Where the contract specified an award fee of up to 12 percent, any change order will have at least 12 percent, and possibly as much as 20 percent.

Comment

In reality, Agency A's changes to the fixed price contract resulted in a cost plus fixed fee arrangement. In this manner, Monarch was able to obtain more work for the same work force and at an improved cost margin.

Situation #6

Requirement

Agency A required the contractor to be fully staffed and operational at a nearby site within three months, an unrealistic requirement for a project of this size.

Discussion

Monarch assembled a project team in less than three months and established the operational site near Agency A. This rapid assembly of personnel from locations as far away as 2,700 miles caused a relocation for many families. The combination of these relocations and stress in the work environment affected the health of several key managers. Three managers were hospitalized for fatigue, and one suffered cardiac arrest. As many as six managers were reassigned because of burnout.

Comment

Agency A's forcing of a provision of the contract that required extraordinary human effort and placed a strain on the work force created problems that were greater than the original situation. Then, Agency A created a larger problem by delaying the work and deducting part of the award fee as compensation for the delay.

Situation #7

Requirement

Agency A required several functional problem areas to be resolved by Monarch. These functional areas bridged several of the directorates or were common to more than one directorate.

Discussion

In response to the requirement, Monarch established working groups for each functional area to be addressed. These groups met on a weekly basis to address the problem, the progress made toward solving the problem, and the future actions that were required. The groups held the meetings and prepared minutes of the actions, which were distributed to more than twenty key managers. Within two months, most of the groups lost their focus on the problem and ongoing actions. Individuals would not attend the meetings, and managers were too busy to read the minutes.

Comment

The working groups never fully served their purpose and tended to create more reading material for the key managers, who did not have time to read the information. The groups slowly disintegrated from lack of direction, and the initial problems had to be assigned to individuals for resolution.

Summary of Monarch's Performance

It is the author's opinion that Monarch's performance was substandard. The primary causes of poor performance and failure to meet the contract specifications are discussed below.

▸ Agency A's SOW and CDRL did not reflect the work requirements of the customers (the directorates). Therefore, Monarch could never satisfy the formal terms and conditions of the contract and meet the customers' expectations. Agency A's failure to codify the directorates' expectations or change those expectations created a situation that would always be in conflict.

▸ There was no full understanding and agreement between the buyer (the government) and the seller (Monarch) as to the wording of the contract. This should have been accomplished prior to beginning the work. This permitted Monarch to avoid legitimate work that should have been accomplished under the contract. Furthermore, Monarch was able to increase the scope of work at a cost to the government.

▸ Monarch did not anticipate the work load and plan for meeting the requirements. There was no realistic plan to staff the project with skilled personnel who could "ramp up" in a short time to meet the government's needs. The most obvious effort was just to place individuals on the job, without regard for productivity, to meet planned expenditure rates.

▸ Agency A's personnel slowed their rate of work in anticipation of an early handover of work to contractor personnel. This slowing of the work greatly increased Monarch's work load and commitment of resources. Monarch should have planned a systematic transition of work at a specified level and not accepted work that was not at the proper level of completion.

▸ Agency A changed the scope of work, often after much activity had been partially completed. This consumed resources, wasted effort, and caused major increases in cost. The lack of a unified effort in developing the SOW and CDRL had major impacts on change order requirements.

▸ Monarch did not rank the work in order of priority, but attempted to achieve work on a broad front. Work groups assigned to accomplish the work on an ad hoc basis never achieved greater than 40 percent productivity, while several of the groups detracted from the accomplishment of other functions. The focus on attempting to complete all the work simultaneously was not a successful approach with the resources available and the magnitude of the work to be accomplished.

Swift's Contractual Work

Swift had been contracting with government Agency B for eighteen years prior to the period under study. The contract, consisting of a SOW and CDRL with standard contract clauses, was evolutionary in that each renewal was only a minor change to the terms and conditions. The SOW and CDRL were seldom updated to show the actual work to be performed or the precise documents to be delivered in fulfillment of the contract. Only the number of authorized person-hours were updated to authorize the expenditure of funds at an agreed level. The updates usually resulted in increases for most of the contract work with only minor decreases.

The SOW and CDRL were general in nature and did not specify the precise type of work to be accomplished. Tasking of teams within Swift was performed by the supported Agency B personnel through oral instructions. Customer satisfaction, or quality, was subjectively measured by Agency B personnel based on responses to specific tasking. (It should be noted that the contractor-government relationship described here is close to being a personal service contract, which is prohibited by U.S. law. The law is specific: Government personnel shall not manage or direct contractor personnel in the performance of work. Work shall be performed in accordance with the written instructions of the contract, i.e., the technical specification, the SOW, and the CDRL with contractual clauses.)

Like Monarch, Swift was providing project management services to directorates, divisions, branches, and, in some instances, individuals. Each element of Agency B established expectations for the quality of project management services based on its subjective criteria because the contractual criteria were not present. Swift's management encouraged this type of subjective evaluation for two reasons: (1) evaluations based on personal likes and dislikes minimized the risk in terms of total contract performance, and (2) personal evaluations and satisfaction improved the probability of continuing work through renewal of a noncompetitive contract. Swift's management was relieved of the detailed management of the work when Agency B directed the daily tasks and conducted the evaluations on a real-time basis.

The definition of quality—conformance to requirements—in the Swift contract was not achievable at the top level. Therefore, one must assess the quality at the lowest level of performing unit within the Swift organization to determine the degree of quality in the project management services. Thus, the formal process is flawed when the contract is used as the baseline to measure the quality of the services provided to the government. Quality must be assessed by some examples of performance.

Situation #1

Requirement

A key manager for Agency B requested engineering and technical studies.

Discussion

Agency B's manager directed the work of the Swift personnel, established time frames for performance of the work, defined the format for the reports, and approved the reports. Swift's personnel performed the work and delivered the reports. The

Agency B manager was pleased with the support, and a smooth, personal relationship was maintained between the government and contractor personnel. The work was considered to be high quality.

Comment

The informal relationships, the direct tasking, and the lack of formal criteria for evaluating products places this work under a personal service contract. Agency B's position is weak in attempting to justify its payment of the contractor, if challenged, and in renewing this contract. The contractor is in jeopardy and, if challenged, may not be paid for performing such personal services.

Situation #2

Requirement

An agency B director tasked Swift with performing project management services in support of a project for expendable systems.

Discussion

Swift's supporting personnel performed to a high degree of satisfaction for the director and delivered timely and quality products, as evaluated by the director. The situation was maintained over a couple of years. The government then restructured the directorates, and Swift's project management support was aligned to meet the requirements. The new director had different expectations for Swift's personnel and different criteria for quality. It required several months for Swift to work into a smooth relationship and produce high-quality products again.

Comment

The use of subjective criteria for evaluating contractor performance to meet contractual obligations do not work well when government (buyer) personnel are changed. The expectations for quality work are based on the buyer's experiences with previous contractors. The lack of formal criteria in the contract precludes evaluation of the performance (quality) of the contractor's work from an objective baseline.

Situation #3

Requirement

The director of a group requested and received project management services in support of the acquisition of a major surveillance system.

Discussion

Agency B's director and Swift's task manager enjoyed an excellent relationship, and the quality of work was considered high. There was complete compatibility between the government and contractor personnel, and a letter was even sent to Swift praising the support personnel. There was, however, no contact between Swift's senior management and the director. Because of this poor high-level communication, Agency B lost confidence in Swift's capability to expand the work force to meet new project management requirements. Consequently, the director contracted with a second company for similar types of services, but at a lower level of effort. This slowly eroded Swift's position as a contractor providing project management services although the perception was that Swift was performing better than the new company.

Comment

Swift's senior management failed to maintain contact with the customer to obtain feedback on the customer's desires and to instill confidence in the company as the contracting entity. The second company's senior management was in contact with the director once or twice a week by personal visit or by telephone.

Summary of Swift's Performance

The Swift Corporation's performance (quality) is considered marginal because it did not work to establish criteria that should have been in the SOW and CDRL, and it failed in many instances to meet the requirements of the government. The more important causes of the weak performance are listed below.

▸ The government SOW and CDRL did not accurately reflect the work to be accomplished. Therefore, the quality of work could be assessed only on the subjective evaluation criteria of individuals. These subjective criteria varied among Agency B's managers and other individuals being supported.

▸ Agency B personnel were directing the type and quantity of work to be performed. This direction would sometimes exceed the scope of the work and often included personal services. These personal services could not be evaluated in the performance of the contractual work and detracted from the performance of professional services.

▸ Swift's senior management did not actively participate in directing the work, assessing the quality of work, managing the contract, or building the customer's confidence in the corporation. The only active position that senior management would take was discharging an employee who was criticized by the government.

▸ Agency B's view of the general nature of the SOW and CDRL, the contractual requirements, was that it provided the flexibility to manage work in a dynamic environment. It is the author's opinion that this was a comfortable position for Agency B personnel, and actions would be restricted by a more definitive contract.

Coin's Contractual Work

Coin had been contracting with government agencies for more than nine years. Only the president and two officers at Coin had tenure of more than three years at the time of this study. Coin was a subcontractor to a larger company, located approximately 600 miles from the work site. For the purpose of this study, the prime contractor was transparent to the process of managing or providing project management services. Coin maintained all customer contacts and performed all the work.

The contract between Coin and the larger company required that Coin establish an automated project scheduling system for Agency C to support a major improvement in electronic control systems. The scope of work was to be further defined by Agency C personnel during the period of performance. It was subsequently defined as a level-of-effort task that permitted the use of five persons to perform the work.

The task was to build a critical path network with task activities, groups of task activities, and a summary level schedule that depicted subordinate networks. The work was further defined as collecting information from the different departments on the task activities, the sequential relationships of the tasks, and the major groupings, and inputting the information into a computer. The computer hosted a software application program that generated graphic bar charts and tabular listings of data, which were the deliverable products.

The contract was administered by an Agency C manager, designated the contracting officer's technical representative (COTR), and who provided the detailed direction for the contract execution. The users of the reports were in other departments of Agency C. The reason for this arrangement was that the work was an add-on to an existing contract.

During contract execution, there were changing priorities for the collection of data and the development of the reports. The computer and the software were provided as "government-furnished equipment" through a separate contract with a large company.

Coin experienced difficulties with the execution of the contract for project management services for several reasons, the more important of which are listed below.

Situation #1

Requirement

Agency C directed that the scheduling information be loaded into a computer by remote terminals. The computer was located seventeen miles from the collection site and operated by the contractor for computer services.

Discussion

Problems with accessing the computer were apparent during attempts to input data by the remote terminals. The contractor operating the computer stated that the problem was with the speed of the modem transmission device, 1,200 baud versus 4,800 baud. Next, it was stated that the computer's random access memory had insufficient capacity to process the files. The situation was resolved by moving Coin personnel to the computer site to input data through a terminal with a direct connection. At that time it was learned that there were several irregularities with the computer system. The computer system contractor was preempting the computer through a priority procedure to process administrative information for another project, and the number of end users on the computer exceeded the number planned for that system.

Comment

Coin's loss of control over the computer assets created problems when the computer operators preempted the computer for processing jobs not related to the project. Coin's inability to identify and fix limitations of the computer system affected Coin's ability to accomplish the work. It is the author's opinion that the tools and personnel to do the work must be under the control of the same work group.

Situation #2

Requirement

Agency C specified that the reports of the schedule were to be in two formats, a network and a tabular listing.

Discussion

Attempts to produce the networks were frustrated by incorrect lines being drawn to connect the boxes representing activities. Connecting lines would often exit from the leading end of a box rather than from the trailing end. This gave the impression that the subsequent work started before the first activity was completed rather than that work could not begin prior to the completion of the activity. The computer services contractor maintained that the problem was the insertion of erroneous data into the menu during Coin's loading process. It was subsequently learned that this software was a beta test version that had not been fully tested prior to use. The computer services contractor was aware of this situation and failed to inform Coin of the use of a potentially erroneous software program.

Comment

The use of beta test software in a contract that requires precise reports should be avoided to limit the perception of quality problems in the input process. Moreover, the contractor responsible for the end product should be informed of the developmental status of any software program that is in use.

Situation #3

Requirement

The COTR was to coordinate the availability of managers for the collection of data with which to build the networks.

Discussion

The COTR did not work well with the other Agency C managers to obtain their support in providing Coin with the required data for the networks. This resulted in the consumers providing insufficient data to build the networks with the logical sequencing relationships. The managers responsible for providing the data assumed that the builder of the network—i.e., Coin personnel—had the knowledge with which to construct their schedules. In fact, the Coin personnel did not have knowledge of the specific network activities, but had knowledge of scheduling practices.

Comment

The knowledge for scheduling comes from the contractor while the knowledge of the specific activities and tasks with their sequential connections comes from the operational personnel—in this instance, Agency C managers. The negotiation at the time of contract award of who will provide the data would preclude such problems.

Situation #4

Requirement

Agency C had a specified completion date on the schedule reports to meet the requirements of other related work.

Discussion

Coin personnel were inexperienced in the operation of the terminals and the menus for inputting data. This inexperience dictated that the input operators receive three days of instruction. This time for the personnel to learn the computer/software applications was in the middle of the collection and input process. It was not until three months after initiation of the project that it was determined the Coin personnel were not sufficiently trained. Other computer problems masked the fact that the Coin personnel lacked the necessary skills.

Comment

Beginning a project with trained personnel assists in the rapid start of operations. Complex problems with the tools, such as those experienced by Coin, limits the identification of skill shortfalls and mitigates against the proper execution of a contract.

Summary

Coin's performance (quality) is considered less than desirable because it did not have or take action to train personnel for the required work. The government manager (COTR) made the situation more difficult because of instability in the requirements and poor coordination of data collection requirements. Furthermore, the design of the task organization with two contractors (one for development of schedules and a second for control of computer equipment) was flawed because of communication barriers through inconsistent goals. The more important causes of poor performance are listed below.

> ▸ The government's design of the remote computer operation and the control of the computer center by another contractor were not supportive of the efforts

assigned to Coin. The physical configuration and preempting of the system by the operating contractor materially affected Coin's performance capability.

▸ The contractor operating the computer center willfully accepted beta test software that had the potential for errors because it had not been previously tested for release and sale to the public. When the software program produced improper results as the end product of Coin's work, it reflected badly upon Coin as the provider of services.

▸ The government COTR was to coordinate the data collection schedule with other managers, and Coin personnel were to build the network with these data. The failure of the COTR to adequately explain to other managers the need for schedule data and the accuracy of data impacted Coin's ability to build a valid network that depicted the plan for the government's work.

▸ Coin failed to provide trained personnel for the task or to ensure personnel were trained upon receipt of the contract. Coin management's failure to recognize the skill requirements for satisfactory completion of the task was a major contributing factor to poor performance in data input and product development.

Lessons Learned

The three companies did not fare well in the execution of their respective contracts for project management services. The problems related are indications of areas to be resolved before entering into a contract, either as a buyer or seller of services. These lessons learned can be valuable contributors to the quality of performance of project management services.

▸ *Lesson #1.* The contract must provide objective criteria for the measurement of quality. When the contract is flawed by the failure to identify the work to be accomplished and how it is to be accomplished, the quality becomes subjectively judged by the buyer of services. The subjective evaluation may not be realistic or profitable. *Always ensure that quality criteria are included in the contract's SOW and CDRL.*

▸ *Lesson #2.* When performing project management services, ensure that all resources are under the control of one entity. When resources are divided between two or more sources, it is difficult to manage the cooperation between the sources. Often, two or more contractors are in direct competition for the work, and the buyer asks them to be cooperative and share information. This does not work well. *Ensure that there is unity in the resources needed for performing the work to obtain the best quality of service.*

▸ *Lesson #3.* In describing the requirements of a project management services contract, it is best to focus on the output of a contract and describe it in the CDRL. *Unless there are valid reasons for telling the contractor (seller) how to perform the work, just specify the format, the quantity, and the submission date for the deliverable documentation or reports.*

▸ *Lesson #4.* If you are the buyer of services, ensure that all affected consumers of the products are aware of the requirements and any changes that may be made to their submissions to the requirements. The single contract should be the guide for all the requirements for project management services. *Include in the contract the require-ments of all consumers, and assure the awareness of the consumers for all the individual requirements.*

▸ *Lesson #5.* The buyer of project management services often desires immediately to receive the services specified in the contract. The rapid response establishes rapport between the customer and the provider. When this is not done well, the customer has the initial impression that the performance is less than that being purchased. *Plan for an early start-up of the work, and identify the total resources required to do the job well.*

▸ *Lesson #6.* Contractors must maintain contact and develop customer relations at all levels of the project management services contract. The operative level contractor personnel may be doing extremely well in providing the quality services, but the customer's decision makers may not have visibility into that process. *Plan for customer interfaces at all levels of the contractual work.*

▸ *Lesson #7.* Fixed price contracts appear to be an attractive situation for the buyer of services, but this is misleading when the contract's SOW and CDRL are not definitive enough to limit the number of changes. Change orders place the buyer at the mercy of the seller for the pricing of changes. The options are usually limited to buying the services at a cost plus fee or obtaining the services from another contractor. *Change orders to fixed price contracts are expensive options and must be controlled. The definition of the work should dictate whether the contract is awarded at a fixed or cost plus price.*

▸ *Lesson #8.* Level-of-effort (LOE) contracts should focus on the end products—i.e., the deliverable data or services—during the preparation of the CDRL to ensure the LOE is controlled through objective criteria. LOE contracts are difficult to control because the usual criteria is time spent on the job and not productive hours spent. *Use the end product as the objective criteria for measuring LOE types of contracts.*

▸ *Lesson #9.* A buyer's interference with the seller's ability to perform work, such as a lockout of personnel or a failure to provide information, usually takes place at the buyer's expense in fixed price and cost plus contracts. *Buyers must plan to provide sellers with access to areas and to information so that sellers have no reason not to complete the contractual obligations.*

▸ *Lesson #10.* Unlawful or poorly worded contracts inhibit the proper execution of the work. Both the buyer and seller of services have a vested interest in ensuring the full understanding of the contractual requirements so the work may proceed with the least disruption. *Buyers and sellers of project management services need to fully agree on the contractual requirements prior to the seller's beginning work.*

Conclusion

Contracting for project management services, from both the buyer's and the seller's perspective, should be well planned and mutually understood as to the requirements of the work. This forms the basis for determining the quality of services, any changes to the scope of work, and a baseline for evaluating the performance of services. Planning the work requires setting goals, often stated in terms of expected results, and defining the scope of work. The buyer, in preparing the contract, should avoid instructions that describe how the work will be performed and with which skills, instead focusing the descriptions on end products to be delivered at specified times. The buyer should plan to be in a monitoring role during the contract implementation and become involved in the processes by which products are developed only when the contract is not being fulfilled.

The seller of project management services is obligated to understand the requirements and provide the skills that can best meet those requirements. The requirements, defined in the contractual documentation, set the standard for all work to be performed. A mutual agreement between the buyer and seller as to the terms and conditions of the contract is the baseline for the seller to achieve customer satisfaction. Flawed or faulty contracts that do not promote agreement with the actual requirement limit the opportunities for customer satisfaction in project management services.

References

U.S. Government, Federal Acquisition Regulations (FAR), Washington, D.C.

U.S. Department of Defense, Defense Acquisition Regulations (DAR), Washington, D.C.

U.S. Department of Transportation, Acquisition Regulations, Washington, D.C.

U.S. Department of Defense, DOD Instructions 5000.1 and 5000.2, Washington, D.C.

U.S. Public Law, Competition in Contracts Act of 1984, Washington, D.C.

Part II
Project Management Applications

Section IX

Project Management and Change Management

22

Managing Change Through Projects

John R. Adams
Western Carolina University

The purpose of this chapter is to analyze the change process in an effort to understand the part project managers play in implementing changes within the organization. The change process itself is examined first, from the standpoint of its effect on both the organization and the individuals who make up that organization. Next, the project management process is reviewed to analyze its impact on the organization that supports it and to document the relationships between project management and the change process. The requirements for successfully implementing projects and planned organizational changes are shown to be essentially identical. In this way, the role of the project manager is shown to include the tasks of the "change masters," with all of the pressures and responsibilities that the term and the concept implies.

The Change Process

Three separate states exist to bound the change process. These states are presented in Exhibit 22-1. The first state is the present, representing what currently exists in the organization: its structure, its human resources, and the physical resources it uses to produce its products or services. The second state represents the future: the set of conditions that are to exist at some point to come and toward which we wish to modify the current organization. The third state represents a process of transition from the present state to the future set of predicted conditions. To proceed through the transition phase may require extensive adjustments to the current organization, including its structure, the available human and nonhuman resources, the processes used by the organization, and even the objectives that the organization is trying to achieve. As these adjustments take place, the culture of the organization also changes, affecting the way in which work is accomplished as well as the type of work that is performed.

Exhibit 22-1. Stages of the change process.

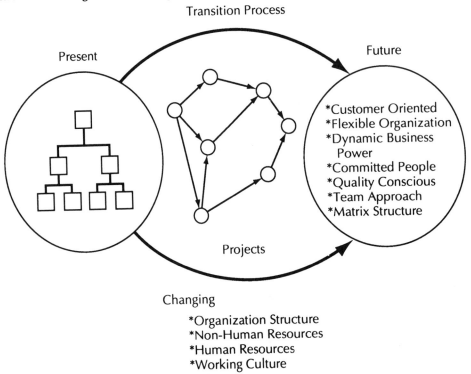

Projects and Organizational Change

Since most modern organizations wish to survive for a long time, their choice must be to manage the change process, making every effort to adapt as an organization to the changing needs they are attempting to serve. The result is that organizations must use a process for defining the needed changes, developing plans for implementing those changes, and then implementing those plans with the objective of modifying the organization to meet predicted future needs.

There is common agreement that project management is a goal-directed activity. That is, the basic definition holds that a project combines human and nonhuman resources for the purpose of achieving some specified goal. Project management is thus a set of management practices designed to accomplish a specific goal. Project management theory adds to this basic definition by indicating that the goal should be accomplished within specified funding and resource limitations through the development of a formal or informal temporary organization brought together for the express purpose of accomplishing that goal. In short, project management can be considered a specified management process with the express purpose of achieving a defined goal at some specified time in the future.

Projects thrive in an environment of change. They are generally established by some level of management senior to those implementing the work; that senior level provides a goal or objective that the organization is to achieve. In effect, senior management has reviewed the future of the company and defined the future state it wishes to achieve. The project is established to take the organization from its present condition to what is projected to be needed in the future. In short, project management implements the transition state of the change process. It is clear that the extent to which the project is successful determines the extent to which the organization is able to adjust satisfactorily to the conditions its management foresaw would exist in the future. Thus, project management can be seen as the means by which the activities needed to achieve the future goal are defined, scheduled, implemented, and accomplished, while the project can be seen as the means by which the needed change is planned and implemented. Project management is crucial to the change process in that it is the means by which organizations can control or manage their adaptation to projected future requirements.

The Individual's Response to Change

Change implemented within an organization is implemented through people and affects the way some or many people go about their work. For example, the construction of a new work facility may require people to change their working location, the way they travel to get to that location, the conditions within which they work at the facility, and even the location of their home, since most need to live relatively close to where they work. A new computer program may require managers to change the way in which they make decisions, since new reports with new information may be available to them. Others must collect different items of data and enter them into the computer in new ways. Still others have to learn the program and be able to maintain, support, and modify it to meet the changing needs of the organization. The development of a new product requires changes in production workers' jobs, while marketing personnel need to learn the new products and perhaps develop new marketing techniques and advertising programs. Since the company may enter new markets and may have to build new production plants and develop new production methods for dealing with the new product, a successful new product development may lead to many additional projects affecting many hundreds of people throughout the organization.

Through all this, project managers are the catalysts for implementing change, and as such they are targets for the resistance and anger that often accompanies the introduction of a change process. In addition, as the project is implemented through its life cycle, the project itself is subject to change. Schedules and budget requirements change. Personnel may leave the project, as their particular services are completed, while others may join the project as their skills are required. The very goals of the project may be adjusted as senior management clarifies its needs or as further changes occur external to the organization. In this way even members of the project team must deal with the change process as it affects them and the jobs they are performing. If the project managers are to implement changes of this magnitude, it is appropriate that they understand the process individuals must go through to adapt to the changes imposed upon them.

The basic process by which an individual recognizes and adapts to change is demonstrated in Exhibit 22-2. Most individuals prefer stability. They enjoy being able to predict what they are likely to be doing in the reasonably near future. Thus, most individuals prefer to work in the same location from day to day, or to draw a paycheck on a regular basis, or to have a consistent set of friends with whom to socialize. The

Exhibit 22-2. Individual process of change.

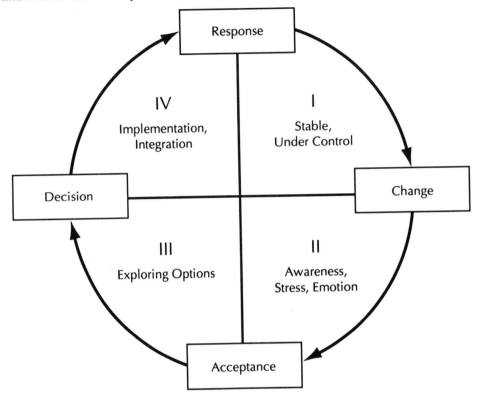

Source: Reprinted from *An Organization Development Approach to Project Management* with permission of the Project Management Institute, P.O. Box 43, Drexel Hill, Penn. 19026, a worldwide organization of advancing the state-of-the-art in project management.

condition of stability is represented in Quadrant I of the exhibit. During this period, individuals should be examining their work environment for potential sources of changes, so that they may predict how their behavior may have to change in the near future. Most, however, fail to recognize this necessity. Nevertheless, at some point in time, some event occurs that imposes itself upon individuals as a change in the way they work or live.

Quadrant II represents individuals becoming aware of a change being imposed upon them, and the reactions that are likely to occur. Individuals typically do not approach change in a logical manner, at least not initially. People react to significant change emotionally. The more significant the change, the more emotional resistance is likely to be demonstrated. They place blame. ("It's Bob's fault: He's been late with those reports so many times that it was obvious the boss would have to put controls on us! If it weren't for him, I wouldn't have to spend the next two months developing a new reporting process.") Or they seek justice. ("Well, it's not my fault. My work's been done on time and regularly. I've met every deadline the boss has set for me in the last two years, even though I haven't been recognized for it much.") Generally, individuals work through the stress and anger that typically follows the announcement of a significant change, and then they begin to consider how the new process or technique may help them. Eventually, most come to understand and accept that the change will take place. Depending on the magnitude of the change and its impact on them, however, this emotional reaction could take a long period of time to work through, with the attendant reduction in both commitment and productivity. Only when the point of acceptance is reached can progress be made in implementing the change.

At this point, individuals can begin logically evaluating the impact of the change on them and how they can best react to it. This is represented in Quadrant III, where a problem-solving process is used to determine the individual's possible options for implementing as appropriate a response as possible. In this quadrant, it is feasible to implement a logical decision-making process for identifying and examining the options available and for selecting the most appropriate option for the individual and the organization concerned. Once an alternative is selected—that is, once the decision is made—it is time to implement that decision.

Quadrant IV represents the process by which the necessary activities are defined and assigned to those who must accomplish them, and the new methods, processes, or products are integrated into the normal work flow of the organization. Such implementation activities finally result in the actual response to the need for change that was originally defined. The organization can now settle into a new period of stability—that is, until the next need for change is identified, and then the process continues.

Every individual in every organization must go through this process each time a change is implemented. Some individuals proceed through the process rapidly, while others may agonize over their response to a change for seemingly endless periods. There are many reasons for this difference, not the least of which is the magnitude of the change itself, the impact that change is likely to have on the individual, and the criticality of that change to the individual's job. It is clear, however, that high levels of stress and anxiety are associated with this change process. The levels of stress and the expressed resistance to change are increased dramatically as the time available to react is reduced.

This implies some clear guidelines for managers involved in implementing change, particularly the project managers who must cope with the individuals affected by the change they are implementing. The manager must first provide the time necessary for individuals to work through the emotional phase of accepting the change. More important, time and effort must be committed to developing a sense of trust and the supportive working relationships that help individuals proceed rapidly through Quadrant II. From the project manager's standpoint, productive work cannot be accomplished until the individuals affected by the changes have completed their transition through Quandrant II and can begin to look at alternative methods and techniques for adapting to the change. A cooperative and supportive working environment can speed the individuals' adaptation to the required change, but it cannot eliminate the need for dealing with the emotional reactions to change that will exist.

The Project in a Bureaucracy

Traditional bureaucratic organizations were developed with the concept of stability in mind. The basic idea was to develop the best and most appropriate approach to conducting repetitive work in an efficient manner. The basic assumption of the industrial revolution was that work is repetitive and can be broken down into very small logical segments, and individuals can be specialized to doing their repetitive tasks very well and very swiftly. One result of using the process of breaking tasks down into smaller and smaller increments has been high levels of productivity per worker. Another result has been the automation of many tasks, in some cases entirely eliminating the need for the worker. In this situation, the organization needs to train its people carefully, ensuring that they master the limited skills necessary to accomplish each task. Further, since one task depends on the previous work accomplished, it is imperative that the work accomplished at any specific workstation be precisely the same from one day to the next, even though the individuals doing that work may change. To accomplish these ends, the organization develops detailed rules, regulations, and work procedures that are reviewed and learned by any person placed into that job. Individuals become highly skilled and highly productive at their individual tasks.

With this perspective, it is easy to see how an organization that has been successful in developing such a bureaucratic structure would strongly resist the need for change by either the organization or the individuals within it. Change in this environment is something perpetrated by troublemakers. It results from poor planning, since appropriate planning would have developed the best approach for doing the job in the first place. Since change disrupts the status quo, it may affect the efficiency with which the organization produces its products, and therefore it is to be avoided. If a change must be implemented, then it must be controlled rigidly and implemented quickly to avoid unnecessary disruption of the work. This view of change may be very appropriate in an environment where change does not occur frequently. Unfortunately, such stable and predictable environments are quickly disappearing from the society in which we live.

The drawbacks to such an organization's structure have been documented thoroughly over the years. Perhaps the best summation is provided by Harold Kerzner in his book *Project Management for Executives*. The essence of his view is summarized in Exhibit 22-3. Kerzner draws upon the well-known difficulties of communications, both vertically through the structure and horizontally across functions, to define "islands of operations" within which individuals can work together and understand each other easily. The difficulty of vertical communications deals with the differing experiences and perspectives of the individuals at different levels of the organization, as well as the power differentials among these levels. When combined, these issues make it difficult for individuals lower in the organization to report problems and concerns accurately and concisely to senior-level management. It thus becomes difficult for the senior levels in the organization to know what is going on at the lower levels. It is equally difficult to communicate across functions within the organization. Each function is narrowly defined, individuals within the function are narrowly educated in the fields the functions support, and each function has developed its own terminology and perspective of the organization as a whole. Since the jobs themselves are narrowly proscribed and job descriptions are tightly defined, communications across these functions become increasingly difficult to understand as we proceed lower in the organization. The overall results are communications and coordination difficulties, which in turn make implementing change a very difficult and time-consuming process.

Exhibit 22-3. Islands of operations in a bureaucratic organization.

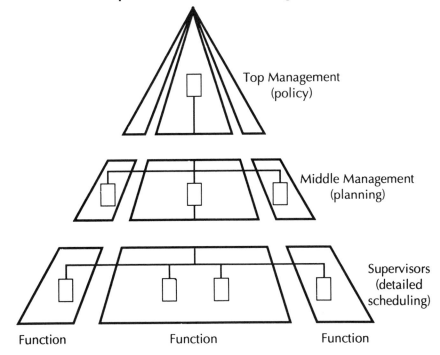

Top Management
(policy)

Middle Management
(planning)

Supervisors
(detailed
scheduling)

Function   Function   Function

Organizations that are more receptive to the issue of change take an entirely different view of the process. Generally, such organizations have not developed tall, narrow, rigid bureaucratic structures, but rather they strive for organization that is relatively flat and flexible and can adapt quickly to changes. In such organizations, change is seen as an inevitable process resulting from the interaction of the organization with its environment. It is seen as the natural result of evolution and growth and is looked forward to for its beneficial contributions toward helping the organization survive. Change is seen as often providing beneficial results, providing for challenge, growth, and the long-term survival of the organization. It is recognized by such organizations that change should be managed to optimize the positive results. Specific goals are established that must be achieved by changing some aspect of the organization, and a specific process for accomplishing that goal is also defined. In other words, such organizations are likely to make extensive use of project management as a means of managing the change process itself.

Organizations of this type have made conscious efforts to limit the number of bureaucratic levels and to enhance communications across functions. The primary method used to implement change is demonstrated in Exhibit 22-4. Here, although Kerzner's islands of operations still exist, the project manager is installed with the specific responsibility of cutting across the organizational boundaries for the purpose of implementing projects (i.e., to communicate among the operational islands and coordinate their efforts toward implementing the change represented by their project). The project manager's most critical "right" is the ability to cut across organization lines to whatever function and whatever levels are necessary to resolve difficulties in implementing the project.

Exhibit 22-4. Coordination between project manager and islands of operations.

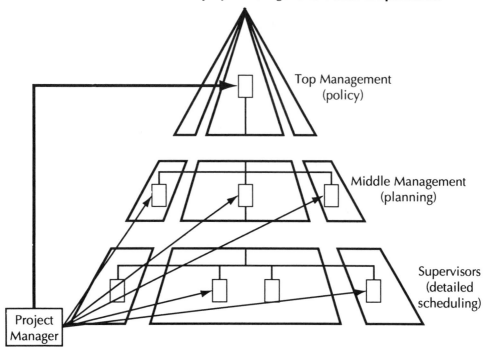

The net result is to implement change within a bureaucracy that is designed for stability. Modern management concepts for expediting this procedure include reducing the levels in the organization and emphasizing the balance of power between project and line managers. These concepts enhance the basic philosophy of project managers implementing change while line managers support stability by increasing the flexibility of the organization.

Change in Project Management

Our view of change has emphasized the strategic planning process, where goals are defined by senior management for implementation by the project manager. In most organizations, the support for senior management is absolutely critical to the institutionalization of any proposed change in the organization's structure, resources, and culture. The way in which senior management implements change is depicted in Exhibit 22-5. Here, senior management identifies a new direction that it feels the organization must pursue. As with anyone else, senior managers had to work through accepting the need for change before deciding how to implement the change. Senior management's implementation, however, involves notifying the next level of management that change will be necessary, and providing sufficient direction for that level of management to begin planning for implementing the change. Middle management, of course, must also work through its emotional resistance and decide how to implement the desired change. It in turn introduces the change to the next level of the organization. The point is that the change process flows down through

Exhibit 22-5. Organizational flow of change.

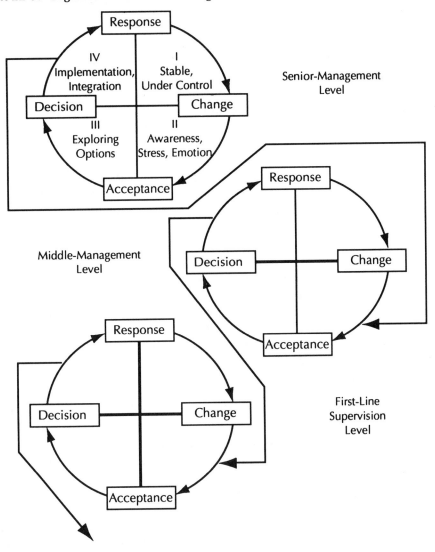

Source: Reprinted from *An Organization Development Approach to Project Management* with permission of the Project Management Institute, P.O. Box 43, Drexel Hill, Penn. 19026, a worldwide organization of advancing the state-of-the art in project management.

the organization, with personnel on each successive level having to work through their emotional resistance and accept the fact that the change will occur, and then decide how best to react to that change as individuals. Only after going through this process can any level of management begin implementing the change. Thus, change takes time to progress through the organization. The right of the project manager to coordinate across operational islands becomes invaluable in expediting the flow of the change through the organization.

The implications of this flow process for implementing and institutionalizing change within an organization are summarized briefly below.

▸ *Permanent change requires top-down agreement.* Change can be initiated in a number of ways. It can result from pressure arising from subordinates, or a lead department of the organization can document the need and support the implementation of the change. Either of these approaches is likely to be temporary without the support of top-level management. Planned organizational changes must necessarily begin with those senior executives who establish policies and goals. The change process therefore involves managing the accomplishment of these goals through project management "change masters."

▸ *Emotions must be managed, along with actual events.* The change process is more than a series of technical activities implemented in sequence over a period of time. It involves both the organization and the individuals who constitute that organization. If a change is to be permanent, it must deal with the attitudes, the needs, and the culture of the people who work within the organization and are affected by the change.

▸ *Implementation of more than one change within specified time or constraints requires a strategy.* In today's environment, most organizations are undergoing many changes at any one point in time. Much of the difficulty in implementing these changes results from the fact that they are frequently not coordinated or integrated into a cohesive plan that can be communicated to the participants. This makes it even more difficult for the individual to accept emotionally the need for changes, particularly when they seem to conflict with each other and fail to support some common goal. The change process can proceed much more smoothly if it is coordinated through senior management and communicated to the organization as an overall strategic plan of what the organization is trying to achieve.

▸ *The management of change requires dynamic leadership as opposed to evaluative management.* The functions of most line managers involve close control of the resources allocated to them, careful evaluation of those who work for them, and the allocation of rewards for the accomplishment of improved efficiency. Unfortunately, this approach is not conducive to the implementation of change. Project managers must deal with the emotions of those involved in the change and provide a dynamic leadership that emphasizes what the organization and each of the individuals participating in the change have to gain from implementing the change in a cooperative way. There is no substitute for the personal enthusiasm and leadership demonstrated by a project manager who is committed to creating a new way of doing work.

▸ *Organizational resources must be provided in a timely and systematic manner.* Change does not come free. Projects must be provided with the appropriate resources at the appropriate points in their life cycle to accomplish the objectives that have been established. For most projects of this type, the resources may be "borrowed" from line organizations since they will be needed for relatively short periods of time. Funds, of course, should be based on realistic budgeting estimates and controlled by the project manager. Sufficient flexibility must be provided to overcome the unexpected disruptions that are bound to arise as the project progresses. While projects may consume both money and resources, the real losses occur when we have failed to adapt to the changing needs of our clients. Such losses reach to the very lifeblood of our organizations.

▸ *Rewards and reprimands must be linked to change management.* The project manager typically does not provide formal organizational rewards to the participants in the project. Such rewards are provided by line managers. However, it is inconsistent and damaging to the change process if the organization's rewards are provided to those championing stability while being denied to those striving to implement change. Some form of cooperative understanding between the project and line managers must be developed that will allow those individuals who have demonstrated outstanding support for the project and the changes it represents to be rewarded in appropriate measure for their efforts.

Conclusion

Change is inevitable in our society, and it is clear that those organizations that refuse to adjust will fail to survive in the long run. In particular, if business, services, and government organizations are to survive, prosper, and meet the needs of their clients, they must plan for and implement change as a recognized part of the organizations' strategic plans. The individuals within the organizations must also be considered in any such change process. They must be provided with the time to accept the fact that the change is necessary, develop any new skills that may be required, and participate in the change being implemented.

Project managers who are capable and dynamic leaders must be selected and developed specifically for their skills in implementing change in a cooperative and nonthreatening manner. Such an approach will not ensure the survival of the organization or the cooperation of the individuals within that organization. No one can assure that the organization can successfully adapt to whatever unknown changes may be required of it. However, failure to take this approach and allow both senior and project managers to provide the concentrated management attention needed to assure goal accomplishment will ensure that the organization will fail. It will simply not be capable of meeting the needs of its clients in the long run. As the environment within which the organization functions becomes more dynamic (as predicted by practically all futurists in our society), and as the costs of adapting become greater, the well-developed, capable, and committed project manager will be ever more critical to the success of the organization.

Bibliography

Adams, John R., C. Richard Bilbro, and Timothy C. Stockert. *An Organization Development Approach to Project Management.* Drexel Hill, Penn.: PMI, 1986.

Kanter, Rosabeth Moss. *The Change Masters.* New York: Simon & Schuster, 1983.

Kerzner, Harold. *Project Management for Executives.* New York: Van Nostrand Reinhold, 1982.

23

Planning for Change

Stephen D. Owens
Western Carolina University

M. Dean Martin
Western Carolina University

The project-management organizational approach is suited to deal with environmental change, both internal and external to the project. However, the management of change does not automatically occur with the use of project management techniques. Rather, change stimuli must be analyzed on a systematic and consistent basis or the need for change is not detected, and corporate as well as project goal accomplishment suffers. Environmental screening and corrective action are an innate part of strategic planning. This is especially true as organizations become more involved in the international arena. Such an attitude and practice must permeate each organizational entity, including the project organization. For this to occur the project team must be included in the strategic planning system. Thus, planning for change becomes an organizational goal. Of necessity, the human element must be recognized and integrated into the change management system.

Some speculate that resistance to change is an inherent human characteristic; however, the authors don't entirely accept this premise. This chapter posits that there are ways to design and develop a change management system that motivates the project team to be innovative and competent when analyzing the inevitable change elements that are involved in project implementation. Moreover, the chapter investigates the basic nature of change in the project environment and examines the elements that must be considered when designing and developing an effective strategic planning process.

The Nature of Change

Definitions of change often deal with the process of alteration, modification, or transformation. Organizational change has been succinctly defined as the adoption of a new idea or behavior by an organization.[1] Failure to plan for turbulent change

This chapter is reprinted by permission from AACE International (formerly the American Association of Cost Engineers), 209 Prairie Ave., Suite 100, Morgantown, W.Va. 26505.

Exhibit 23-1. Organization of stimuli leading to change.

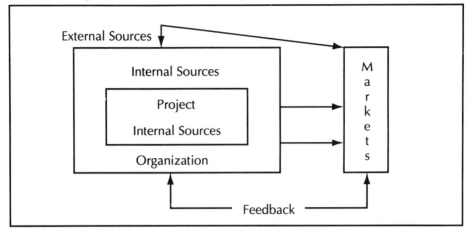

Source: M. D. Martin and S. D. Owens, "Management Change in the Project Environment," *Proceedings of the 32nd Annual Meeting of the AACE*, New York, 1988. Reprinted by permission from AACE International (formerly the American Association of Cost Engineers), 209 Prairie Ave., Suite 100, Morgantown, W. Va. 26505.

can and often does lead to the demise of the organization. Toffler examines the rapidity of technical changes specifically and shows how even advanced industrialized nations "find it increasingly painful to keep up with the incessant demand for change. . . ."[2] To illustrate, he points out that if the last 50,000 years were divided into approximately 800 lifetimes each consisting of sixty-two years, the human race has spent 650 of those lifetimes as cave dwellers. Most of the technology that the modern project manager takes for granted has existed for a single lifetime or less.[3]

The project management organizational approach is theoretically well suited to deal with environmental change, both in response to stimuli from internal as well as external sources. However, project managers must be aware of the diverse sources of change and be able to detect and deal with change effectively.

Origin of Sources for Change

A stimulus for change may originate from a source internal or external to the organization and the project. External sources are generated by activities in the organization's macro environment. This situation is reflected in Exhibit 23-1.

External Sources

The project team has little if any control over external change forces. Early Detection may provide an opportunity to take action, but these external sources are basically uncontrollable. These sources often include the following:

- ▸ *Political and legal.* Federal, state, and local governments frequently pass laws that impact the organization and the way it operates.
- ▸ *Economic.* Factors such as increased competition, inflation, high interest rates, and material shortages may require project cost revisions.
- ▸ *Social.* Project demand is a derived demand. Changing consumer tastes, attitudes, values, and needs may necessitate project changes.

- *Technological.* Project plans may envision the use of certain materials. Improved composites and metal alloys may require project redesign or even abandonment.
- *Ecological.* Increasing concern for the physical environment has led to operational restrictions. Most construction projects typically involve the need for an environmental impact evaluation.
- *International.* Competition has become increasingly global in scope. This development has required project managers to become familiar with the cultures of countries very different from their own.

Internal Sources

As the external sources are detected and plans for them are formulated, changes internal to the project must also be examined. Troublesome internal sources often include the following:

- *People.* It is easy to see that corporate management succession, project manager replacement, and other human resources actions can create conditions that necessitate the need for change management.
- *Management.* A change in management philosophy may necessitate a change in organization structure, i.e., the change from a functional organization to some variant of project management. A formal organization development program may be necessary to implement the new management philosophy.[4]
- *Processes.* New technology has required many changes in both manufacturing and management processes.
- *Policy.* The need for cost, schedule, and quality control has led many organizations to question their policies in terms of how project managers are assigned, appraised, and compensated.

Such variables, while not totally controllable, can be managed more than those from external sources. These illustrations should suffice to establish the fact that the project environment is very complex and is fraught with the potential for changes to develop and impact both the overall organization and the project. The key becomes one of detecting the need for change. This is best accomplished by understanding the role of the strategic planning process.

The Strategic Planning Process

Planning in its purest form is really problem solving that involves a series of decisions oriented to future actions. Effective implementation of long-range (strategic) planning has been described by Drucker: "Long-range planning should prevent managers from uncritically extending present trends into the future; from assuming that today's products, services, markets, and technologies will be the products, services, and technologies of tomorrow; and, above all, from dedicating their resources and energies to the defense of yesterday."[5]

The importance of planning for change cannot be stressed enough, and of equal importance is the need to involve the project manager and team in the strategic planning process. Exhibit 23-2 depicts this process as a structured algorithm involving a series of annual plans that address a long-term time frame. The annual activities include the planning, programming, and budgeting cycles.[6]

As shown, the strategic planning process contains several key steps. Step 1 involves the formulation and dissemination of general planning guidelines to the major project level based on data obtained from continuous environmental scanning. Optimally, much of the data would have been gathered by the organization's project managers and forwarded to the strategic planning group throughout the preceding year for consolidation, analysis, and evaluation. Included would be information relative to potential opportunities and threats both in the context of the corporation and the project environments.

During Step 2, project personnel develop detailed plans for the next operational year. In addition, the subsequent strategic years are analyzed in the context of the information about environmental change that has been provided.[7] Step 3 involves the evaluation of projects in terms of financial and business risks, the desired rate of returns, criticality to the company survival, and a variety of related factors. It serves to integrate the project and corporate modes of thinking.

In Step 4, top management decisions are evaluated. Should an appeal relative to a specific project decision seem justified, action is initiated. Otherwise, project personnel proceed to identify and delineate the basic resources. Step 5 involves top management in the process once again, this time to review the revised project plans and the related programming recommendations. Step 6 requires project personnel to develop operational budgets in the context of funding and priority constraints as imposed by top management.

In Step 7, top management reviews, approves, or modifies the proposed project budgets. The targets as established serve as control points so that effectiveness and progress may be assessed at periodic intervals. This consolidation of plans, programs, projects, and budgets becomes the central core of the overall strategic plan. Finally, in Step 8, the completed strategic plan is disseminated to all levels of the organization. Distribution of the plan completes the cycle; however, feedback and environmental scanning may well require revisions before the plan is implemented. Since change is

Exhibit 23-2. Strategic planning process model.

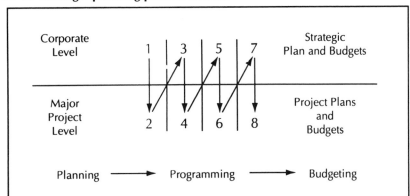

Reprinted by permission from AACE International (formerly the American Association of Cost Engineers), 209 Prairie Ave., Suite 100, Morgantown, W. Va. 26505.

a constant that must be managed continuously, an essential ongoing activity to mitigate the effects of change is that of environmental screening.

Environmental Screening

Project managers must screen the environment for possible opportunities and threats. Information about environmental variables must be identified, monitored, evaluated, and disseminated to key persons within the project. Screening the environment must occur to avoid surprises and monitor factors that impact future project success or failure.[8] Essentially, then, roles must be created in the project organization to process information, to coordinate the project with key persons in the organization, and to represent the organization to the environment.

These activities must be performed in a manner that actually spans both the macro and micro environments. The dynamic variables that interact within these two domains are depicted in Exhibit 23-3. The micro environment is concerned with the culture of the parent organization. Each project must compete for resources with other projects and depends on other organizational elements for support. The macro environment is structured by inputs external to the company and the project organization. These factors require the planners to screen the external environment to assess opportunities and threats that fall into one or more of these categories. For example, the construction of an electrical power-generating plant involves the development of an environmental impact statement and negotiations with various regulatory agencies on the federal and state level.

A key issue in this area is the assessment of project uncertainty. Environmental uncertainty for a project can relate to cost, schedule, or performance. For a large

Exhibit 23-3. The project and its environments.

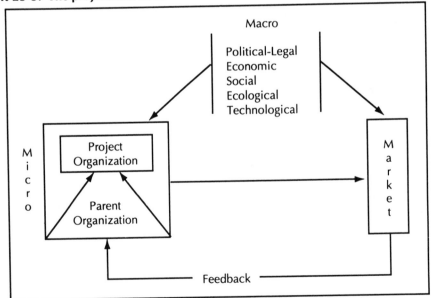

Reprinted by permission from AACE International (formerly the American Association of Cost Engineers), 209 Prairie Ave., Suite 100, Morgantown, W. Va. 26505.

company with multiple projects, the use of a permanent team to assess and measure uncertainty as related to the micro and macro environments is a possible organizational alternative.

Relationship of Project Planning to Strategic Planning

Project planning is an output-oriented activity or process, concerned with determining in advance specifically *what* should be done, *how* it should be done, *when* and *where* it should be done, and *who* should do it. Planning, pure and simple, is the process of preparing for change and coping with uncertainty by formulating future courses of action. Planning can also be viewed as a form of decision making and problem solving. The process involves establishing project objectives, premising, determining alternative courses of action, evaluating alternative courses of action, and implementing the alternatives.

Theoretical issues as to the types of plans, preoccupation with the process itself, and a short-term focus quite often lead project managers to the conclusion that planning is a simple function. This form of planning myopia can be counterproductive to the individual and the organization. The key is that planning must be accomplished. It must deal with strategic planning (involving time frames in excess of one year), with operational planning (the one-year budget), with activity planning (weekly or monthly), and with daily managerial planning. For each company and its projects, some balance between the various types of plans must be attained. It's important that project managers not focus on operational and activity planning and ignore the need for strategic planning.

Planning as such is a line function. Yet managers are generally too busy to activate and implement the planning process. As a consequence, many companies have a staff activity to initiate the cycle and to coordinate the many activities that must be accomplished to complete a planning cycle. An additional complication is that in any given time period, actions must be completed that deal with all four types of plans. However, the major difficulty derives from the nature of change and its accelerating rate.

This high rate of change creates environmental uncertainty. Few companies and fewer project managers are prepared to deal with uncertainty whether it relates to cost, schedule, or performance.[9] The company and the project exist as part of a system (as shown in Exhibit 23-3). Environmental forces emanate from political, economic, technological, ecological, and sociocultural domains. These changes directly impact the company, the project, and the cost, schedule, and performance parameters.

Conclusion

The rate of change in our complex environment is increasing at an explosive rate. Constantly changing conditions require the project manager to detect and track events occurring in both the macro and micro environmental areas. Environmental screening is thus an essential task for project managers. Effective screening results in the design and development of proactive responses to the diverse changes buffeting the project environment.

An integral requirement for predicting and dealing with incessant change is the organization's ability to plan. Planning has been identified as the primary management function. However, many project managers do not participate in their organization's strategic planning system and are not rewarded on the basis of their planning effectiveness. However, the strategic plan for a company serves as a road map for managers at all levels, including the project manager. The project staff must be involved in the development of the strategic plan and must understand its premises and assumptions. The basic idea through this process is to identify opportunities and threats and to assess accurately the organization's strengths and weaknesses so that objectives can be attained or revised accordingly.

In order to participate in planning, project managers must understand the strategic planning process. This process typically follows a logical series of steps included in the planning, programming, and budgeting cycles. Unfortunately, project managers are generally so busy dealing with crisis situations of an operational nature that they frequently fail to become involved in or even to understand the company's strategic planning. Many times they are not allowed access to the company's strategic thinking. Further, most project managers see no reason why they should be concerned with the long-range strategic plan.[10] However, project managers must be active participants in long-range planning. They have the unique opportunity to screen the external environment and identify those trends that could either generate new opportunities or require changes in corporate objectives to meet emergency threats. Unfortunately, poor planning and an unwillingness to deal with foreseeable change continue to plague projects. A more structured planning effort involving team members can help to ensure both project and organization success.

Notes

1. R. Daft, *Organizational Theory and Design*, 2nd ed. (St. Paul, Minn.: West Publishing, 1986).
2. A. Toffler, *Future Shock* (New York: Bantam, 1971), p. 9.
3. M. D. Martin and M. McCormick, "Innovation and Change in the Project Environment," 1984 *Proceedings of the Project Management Institute*, Philadelphia (Drexel Hill, Penn.: PMI), p. 110.
4. J. Adams, R. Bilbro, and T. C. Stockert, *An Organizational Development Approach to Project Management* (Drexel Hill, Penn: PMI, 1986), pp. 7–8.
5. P. Drucker, *Management: Tasks, Responsibilities, Duties* (New York: Harper & Row, 1974), p. 122.
6. M. D. Martin and S. D. Owens, "Management Change in the Project Environment," *Proceedings of the 32nd Annual Meeting of AACE*, New York, 1988, p. 6.3.
7. M. D. Martin and P. Cavendish, "Product Management in the Matrix Environment," in D. Cleland, ed., *Matrix Management Systems Handbook* (New York: Van Nostrand Reinhold, 1984), p. 172.
8. T. L. Wheeler and J. D. Hunger, *Strategic Management and Business Policy*, 2nd ed. (Reading, Mass.: Addison-Wesley, 1986), p. 90.
9. J. R. Adams and M. D. Martin, "A Practical Approach to the Assessment of Project Uncertainty," 1982 *Proceedings of the Project Management Institute*, Toronto, Canada, October 4–6, 1982 (Drexel Hill, Penn.: PMI, 1982), pp. IV–F, 1–11.
10. J. Adams and M. D. Martin, *Professional Project Management: A Practical Guide* (Dayton, Ohio: U.T.C., 1987), pp. 43–44.

24

A Process of Organizational Change From Bureaucracy to Project Management Culture

Robert J. Graham
R. J. Graham and Associates

This chapter relates a process followed by one organization in an attempt to change from a bureaucratic-oriented culture to a project management culture. The organization involved flourished in the bureaucratic mode with limited competition and stable products and services. However, it found itself in the intensive world of deregulated financial services. As more and more projects were developed to respond to the new environment, the company executives discovered that their project management practices were reflections of their bureaucratic past rather than of their project management future.

Attempts to teach managers the basics of project management were not successful. The newly trained people found that the practices necessary for successful project management were not supported by the departments in the organization. From this experience, company executives came to realize that the culture needed to change in order to respond effectively to the new business environment. The process they followed in order to achieve that change is outlined here. This process is presented as an example of the steps needed to install sound project management practices into a business organization.

An Organizational Change Model

Research on organizational change indicates that most people in organizations will not change their behavior unless they see a clear need for such a change. Some people come to realize the need for change because their culture is not consistent with their business strategy. However, just realizing this does not bring it about. What is needed is a planned and directed organizational change effort that has the support and involvement of senior management.

The components of an organizational change effort are depicted in Exhibit 24-1. In general, they can be summarized as follows:

Exhibit 24-1. Components of an organizational change effort.

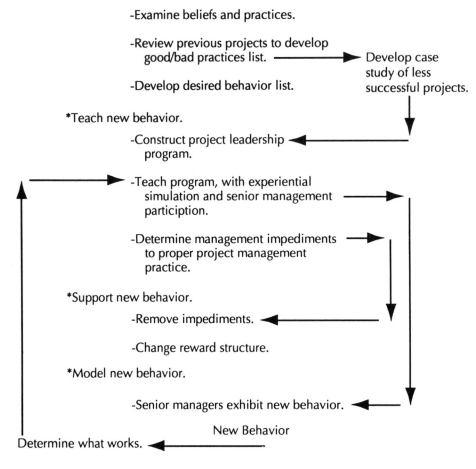

▶ *Define new behavior.* The senior managers must lead the move toward new behavior by clearly defining what the new behavior should be and what it should accomplish.

▶ *Teach new behavior.* Once the new behavior is defined, it must be taught. This means that management development programs must be designed and developed to impart the knowledge as well as the feeling of what life will be like in the future organization. Senior managers must be a part of this program so that they understand the new behavior that is being taught. In addition, the program should incorporate feedback from participants to help to refine what works in the organization.

▶ *Support new behavior.* Development programs have little effect unless they are supported by senior management. In addition there often needs to be a change in the reward system to ensure that the new behavior is rewarded and thus supported.

▶ *Model new behavior.* Management development programs are reinforced by a combination of top management support and effective role models. This means that senior managers must exhibit the new behavior that is being taught and thus become effective role models for other organization members.[1]

An organizational culture has been defined as "the environment of beliefs, customs, knowledge, practices, and conventionalized behavior of a particular social group."[2] So any change effort toward a project management culture must begin with a serious examination of the current beliefs and practices that caused projects to be less than successful. One way to achieve this is to compare successful and unsuccessful projects to determine what practices seemed to be present in the successful projects. This comparison could be augmented by practices that have been proven successful in other organizations. The result of this examination should be a description of the new, desired behavior.

Once this is determined, the new behavioral patterns must be taught. The lessons from the examination above should be put into a case study for use in the training program. At a minimum, the case study of the least successful project could become an indication of the types of assumptions and behavior that are not wanted.

An Organizational Example

The organization described in this section will be referred to as OE (Organization Example). This organization is used to illustrate the types of problems typically encountered by bureaucratic organizations. It is also used to illustrate how the change process described in the previous section can be applied for organizational change.

OE's business began with a series of local offices selling consumer financial services. As the business grew, it became necessary to develop a general procedure's manual so that offices across the country would run according to the same principles and procedures. This manual was developed to such a degree that placement of everything in the office was defined so precisely that any manager could walk into any office and know exactly where everything was. A highly structured organization grew up to support these procedures, and OE flourished as a result.

With such standardized procedures and with everyone going by the same book, it became part of the OE culture that people were interchangeable. That is, it was assumed—and it was true—that any manager could run any office. This assumption of interchangeable parts, such an asset in earlier years, later proved to be quite an obstacle to proper project management. The assumption led to the practice of continually moving people from project to project and changing the compositon of the team as the project progressed. As this was common practice in the past, many managers failed to understand that in the project management world, people are not as interchangeable as they were in the past. Some of the general differences between a bureaucratic culture and a project management culture—which OE experienced—are summarized in Exhibit 24-2.

OE went through a tumultuous change as a result of the deregulation of the financial services market. Suddenly there were more competitors and fewer people on staff. This combination generated a sudden increase in the number of "special projects" in the organization. Most of these new projects involved computer technology, so that projects and project management became associated with the computer department. As there was little history of project management in the organization, it

Figure 24-2. Bureaucratic culture vs. project management culture.

Bureaucratic Culture	Project Management Culture
Many standard procedures	Few, new procedures
Repeated processes and products	New process and product
More homogenous teams	More heterogenous teams
Ongoing	Limited life
High staff level	Low staff level
High structure	Low structure
People more interchangeable	People not interchangeable
Little teamwork	More teamwork and team building
Positional authority	Influence authority
Departmental structure	Matrix structure

seemed natural that the project managers should come from the computer department. This assumption proved to be another obstacle to proper project management.

The basic problem was that the person managing the project was not from the department that initiated the request. As such, the project manager had little formal responsibility and accountability other than making the product work technically. He or she had no formal responsibility to make certain that the product performed the way that the initiating department had envisioned.

"Accidental" project managers thus arose from the technical departments, and procedures evolved somewhat haphazardly. Each department involved mostly responded to requests and were content to do only as requested. They did not share ownership of the final product. As the project manager was not ultimately responsible for achieving end results or benefits, the role evolved into one of project coordinator. As such, project success depended more on informal contacts, as there was little formal methodology. The role of project manager was highly ambiguous and thus not an envied position.

In addition, there was little concept of a continuing project team. People were often pulled onto a project as needed, and they were just as often pulled off a project in the middle of their work. As the project was identified with the computer department, contributing departments did not feel it necessary to keep people on a project for its duration. Thus, team membership was fluid, and there was often loss of continuity.

Despite all of these problems, there were some OE projects that were decidedly successful. However, there were others that were definitely unsuccessful. After a few of these failures, upper management decided that it was time for a change. This is the normal procedure with any decision about change. Any group will hold onto a set of procedures for as long as the procedures do not cause problems. One failure is usually not enough to change people's minds. After a few failures, the need for change becomes clearer.

Developing the New Project Management Culture

This section utilizes the organizational change model in Exhibit 24-1 and shows the actions of OE executives as an example.

Step 1: Define New Behavior

To begin the change toward better project management, a conference of senior managers was arranged to examine what was right and what was wrong with project management practices at OE. At that conference the managers listed those projects that were deemed to be most successful and those that were judged to be less successful. One division president became extremely interested when he realized that most of the failures were from his division. This realization was a fortunate occurrence as he then became the champion for the management development program that was later developed.

From the analysis of the "winners and losers," it became fairly clear what behavior patterns had to be modified. The senior management team then began the task of defining the new behavior, at least in outline form. Some of the changes in behavior defined were as follows:

▸ The project manager should be a defined role. The project manager should be designated from the user department and held accountable for the ultimate success of the project. It is up to the user department to define the specifications and see that they are delivered.

▸ A core team of people from the involved departments should be defined early on in the existence of major projects. The people on the core team should, as far as is possible, stay on the team from the beginning until the end of the project. The project manager is responsible for developing, motivating, and managing the core team members to reach the ultimate success of the project.

▸ A joint project plan should be developed by the project manager and the core team members. This project plan should follow one of the several project planning methodologies that were in use in the corporation. The specific methodology was not as important as the fact that the planning was indeed done.

▸ A tracking system should be employed to help core team members understand deviations from the plan and then help them devise ways to revise that plan. The tracking system should also give good indications of current and future resource utilizations.

▸ A postimplementation audit should be held to determine if the benefits of the project were indeed realized. In addition, the audit should provide a chance to learn lessons about project management so that projects could be better managed in the future.

These points formed the basis of the project of instilling a project management culture in OE. A case study was also developed, based on a project failure, for use in the subsequent training program for the new project managers. This case study highlighted how things went wrong in the past and what behavior needed to be changed for the future.

Step 2: Teach New Behavior

Defining new behavior is not all that difficult. Realizing the new behavior, however, is quite a different matter. At this point the people from the management development area began to determine development needs. They began to ask the question of how to teach this new behavior throughout the organization.

This posed significant problems. In order to implement project management, the role of the project manager had to be redefined. In addition, people throughout the organization had to understand the new role of the project manager. This person was no longer to be just a coordinator but a leader of a project team. This person had to do more than just worry about technical specifications, but rather, had to see to it that new changes were actually implemented. That is, the project manager had to lead a project team that would develop changes in the way that people in the organization did their business. Thus, the person also had to manage change.

These additional aspects redefined the role from that of project manager to that of project leader. The emphasis was then changed to developing a program on the role of project leadership. The program was aimed not only at the project leader, but also at the other people in the organization who had to appreciate the new role.

In addition to developing an appreciation of the new role, the development program also had to develop an appreciation of the use of influence skills rather than reliance on positional authority. In a bureaucratic culture there is a higher reliance on positional authority, but the increased responsibility of the project leader was not matched with increased authority. This is usually the norm in project management. Sometimes the project is identified with a powerful person so the project manager can reference that person and get referent authority. That is, the project manager can say "the CEO wants this done" and wield authority based on the CEO's position. But in general, project leadership requires that the person develop his or her own abilities at influence and not depend so much on referent power. Therefore, the development program had to impart this idea in a usable form so the future project leaders would become more self-sufficient, more self-reliant, and more entrepreneurs than simply project coordinators.

These concepts are easy to talk about but difficult to teach—and maybe more difficult to learn. The project leadership role can be defined and put on paper, but it is not really meaningful until it is experienced. Thus, it was imperative that the training program be experiential, so that people could have a better idea of what the project leadership role would be like in the future. In addition, it was important that others on the project team, as well as others in the organization, experience what it would be like dealing with the new project leaders. It was thus decided that a simulation experience, involving all layers of management personnel, would be the best management development tool.

Using Simulation to Teach New Behavior

The simulation chosen was "The Complete Project Manager," developed by the author. It was designed as a computer-based in-tray exercise where teams of people assume the role of project leaders for a new software product. The simulation was used as a part of a learning process to put people "in the moment" making decisions about project leadership. The idea is that it is easy to teach the principles of leadership and project management, but when managers are in the moment of a decision, they often forget these new principles and rely on old patterns of behavior. The idea of the development program was to change those old behavior patterns, so the program was designed to first teach the new behavior and then put people in simulated situations where they learn to apply the new concepts. There is thus a large component of feedback in the simulation, which indicates if the simulation participants used old procedures rather than the new concepts. The simulation model is shown in Exhibit 24-3.

In the simulation, teams are presented with a variety of situations where they must solve problems that arise during the simulated project. Most of the problems have a behavioral orientation and deal with such areas as team building; obtaining and keeping resources; dealing with requests from clients, top management, and budgeting personnel; and generally living in a matrix organization. Each situation encountered has a limited number of offered solutions, and the team members must agree on one of the possible choices. During the normal play of the simulation, participants are scored on their ability to develop an effective project team and deliver a quality product while satisfying the often conflicting demands of top management, clients, accountants, and other important project stakeholders. The simulation presents situations that emphasize developing skills in the areas of building the project team, motivating the project team, managing diverse personalities on the project team, developing influence to achieve goals, developing a stakeholder strategy, and managing to be on time.

The simulation was used to give people some experience in a different world. It purposely did not simulate their current experience as the idea was to get them ready for new organizational expectations. The simulation experience thus helped to clarify what the role of the project manager would be in the future and gave people some brief experience in this role. Potential project team members also received benefit as

Exhibit 24-3. Simulation model to teach new behavior.

Project Leadership
Principles

Decisions made
"in the moment":
What should we do?

Discussion:
What practices
should we change?

Feedback:
How did we do?
What did we do right/wrong?

they experienced the problems of project management from the point of view of the project leader. They thus obtained a better understanding of what a project leader does and why they do what they do. This allowed them to become much better and more understanding project team members.

Step 3. Support New Behavior

Many organizational change efforts seem to die from a lack of senior management support. That is, people are trained to practice new behavior, they get excited about the benefits of the new behavior, but then they return to their departments and find that senior management still expects and rewards the old behavior. When this happens, the net effect of the management development program is to cause frustration for all concerned. Thus, effective change strategies require constant interaction and communication between the training function and senior management to ensure that there is support for the behavior that is being learned.

The senior management at OE worked to ensure this communication and support. To begin, one of the division presidents sponsored the program and was physically present to introduce most courses and discuss why they were being offered. This sent a message to course participants that the move toward a project management culture was serious and supported by senior management.

The development program included a top management review of the perceived impediments to changing behavior in the organization. People in the development program often saw the benefits in changing behavior but sometimes felt that there were impediments in the organization, usually assumptions on the part of upper management that favored old behavior. Each group in the development program thus developed a list of those behaviors that they felt they could change themselves and those where they felt there were organizational impediments. These lists of impediments were then collected from the participants and presented to senior management. The senior management team then worked to remove the impediments and thus helped to support the change.

Step 4. Model New Behavior

Proper project management requires a discipline on the part of project leaders in the areas of planning, scheduling, and controlling the project, as well as dealing with the myriad of other problems that arise during the project execution. One aspect that senior managers may sometimes fail to realize is that it requires a similar discipline on their part. That is, in order effectively to ask subordinates to follow certain procedures, senior managers must be ready to follow those procedures themselves, or subordinates will not take the requested changes seriously.

In effect, this means that senior managers must be role models for the changes that they want others to implement. This requires a number of behaviors on their part. Senior managers must:

> ▸ *Enforce the role of project plans.* Project management requires planning. However, if senior managers never review the plans, project leaders may not take planning seriously. In addition, project leaders should know how their project fits into the overall strategic plan for the organization. It is thus important that upper manage-

ment work with the project leaders to review their project plans and show them where the project fits into the overall strategic plan.

▶ *Enforce the core team concept.* Project management requires a core team of people that stays with the project from beginning to end. Most everyone in organizations believes that this is true, but adopting this approach limits senior managers' ability to move people at will. Upper management must thus model the behavior of not moving people off core teams unless there is an extreme emergency. If they do not adopt this posture, the core team concept will fail.

▶ *Empower the role of project leader.* Project management requires that the end-user department takes responsibility for the project. The project leader needs to be empowered from that user department. This means that the senior manager from the user department also takes responsibility for all projects in his or her department.

▶ *Hold postimplementation audits.* Project management requires that postimplementation audits be held to determine if the proposed benefits of the project were indeed realized. In addition, audits should be used to help members of the organization to develop better project management practices by reviewing past project experiences. The audit should be seen as a unique chance to learn from experience, and the results of audits should be reviewed by senior management.

Notes

1. Robert J. Graham, *Project Management as if People Mattered* (Bala Cynwyd, Penn.: Primavera Press, 1989).
2. David I. Cleland, *Project Management: Strategic Design and Implementation* (Blue Ridge Summit, Penn.: Tab Books, 1990), p. 352.

Section X
Engineering and Construction Concerns

25

Administrator–Engineer Interface: Requirement for Successful Contract Award

George C. Belev
General Electric Company

The role of the engineer is significant in a build-to-print, specification, or research and development procurement. It is a role that directly and critically impacts the resultant procurement inclusive of complete failure of the vendor to provide the necessary supplies or services. The engineer has the ultimate responsibility for accomplishing the technical work of an organization, whether for internal research or for external government or other clients. But in fulfilling this responsibility, the engineer cannot and does not function alone. During some or all of the engineer's program work, contact with a purchasing administrator is required—contact that can be characterized by adversariness or alliance. The relationship between contract administrators and engineers during the early phases of a project exerts a strong influence on the final product's quality and cost. The contract administrator's technical knowledge and people skills play a key role in the success or failure of this contract administrator–engineer interface.

There are three key elements of the procurement process in which this is particularly true.

1. Development of the initial acquisition strategy and formulation of contracting methodologies
2. Development of the request for proposal
3. Proposal evaluation and order award

Development of the Initial Acquisition Strategy and Formulation of Contracting Methodologies

This element is perhaps the most important in the procurement process, yet it is the one given the least attention by engineers. Being detail-oriented, engineers tend to focus on the immediate, giving less emphasis to the big picture. But the tone and perspective of the entire procurement, as well as its probable success, is a function of the initial acquisition strategy. It is during this initial stage that the integrated procurement plans, funding profile, source selection procedure and criteria, and type of contract are established. The engineer's involvement in this stage can spell doom or success down the road. If one compares the funding process to zero-based budgeting, then planning deficiencies or unworkable contracting methodologies can result in a vulnerability to outside influences attacking the viability and legitimacy of the strategy.

The Integrated Procurement Plan

The total program requirement must be developed, understood, time-phased, and communicated by the engineer to all involved in the procurement process. Proposed hardware deliveries must be realistic, technically feasible, consistent with the known capability/capacity/certification status of anticipated vendors, and based on the engineering cost estimate. Data (software) requirements must be delineated, with submittal timing supporting the overall program and consistent with potential vendors' process need. Test plans and procedure, test performance, and data availability must be logically sequenced and support program schedules. And how the procurement is to be funded must be clearly established. Will the funding be for the total program or incrementally? Is the funding type (capital equipment, operating, general plant, etc.) and source (private, government, financed) known and committed? Are contract line item deliverables affected by the funding source or type?

The integrated procurement plan is not a true technical document and, as such, the engineer must work closely with the contract administrator in its formulation. The pricing received with the vendor's proposal reflects the way that the vendor intends to meet the requirements of the specification. If there is any change in this plan, the pricing proposed could change. If the engineer is not sensitized to the direct relationship among such factors as proposal pricing, vendor deliveries, vendor election to detail relative to meeting requirements, and other programmatic relationships, then the engineer's overall program can be jeopardized before it begins. The contract administrator can assist by providing the focus necessary to ensure that there is a clear relation among the technical work, the sequencing envisioned, the specification developed, the bidding instructions issued to the prospective vendors, and the engineering cost estimate for the entire program.

The Source Selection Plan

The engineer must determine how the vendor will be selected during the procurement process. Often a selection based upon technical merit, rather than price, is in the best interest of the overall program. In this case, the engineer must (1) determine the procedures for evaluating vendor proposals (setting up a rating system and preproposal conference, and making preaward visits to vendor facilities); (2) establish the evaluation criteria (i.e., go/no go minimum qualification, and relative importance/ relative weight definition); (3) convene a source selection board (entailing member selection, with program requirements clearly and concisely defined); and (4) obtain approval of the source selection plan and the minimum qualification and evaluation criteria. The engineer must drive the whole source selection process to ensure closure, selecting the most technically acceptable proposal, while maintaining the timing of the overall program schedule.

While source selection—resulting in the most technically qualified vendor proposal—seems like a straightforward activity, it is subject to many potential problems. By definition, the process is subjective. As such, there is need for greater scrutiny of the review from a procurement standpoint. In the engineer's search for the best, most technically qualified proposal, it is often forgotten that the rules of competitive procurement still apply. The contract administrator must ensure that during the proposal evaluation stage, there is no change to the evaluation criteria that were originally communicated to the vendors prior to submittal of the proposals. Thus, the proposal review team must include a member from the contract administration function to ensure that all proposals are fairly evaluated, using the original criteria, in a manner that will not result in a protest from an unsuccessful vendor.

Contract Type

The needs of the program, as defined by the technical specification, directly impact the contract type considered for the procurement. This relationship is not always obvious. In an attempt to control the overall cost of the program the engineer attempts to get a firm fixed price contract with a vendor. A firm fixed price contract sets a dollar ceiling that is not related to the vendor's actual costs expended in performance of the contract work. However, such an arrangement is not always in the best interest of the engineer and his or her program. The type and complexity of the requirements, the degree of control over the performance of the work desired by the engineer, and the confidence that the engineer has in the ability of any vendor to meet the requirements must all be considered in the selection of contract type as well as in the drafting of the technical requirements.

The contract administrator makes a critical contribution at this point, since the problems associated with the wrong type of contract usually do not surface until after the order is placed and administration begins. A wealth of prior history of contract performance problems associated with the wrong type of contract can be brought to bear. What must be considered is not only the degree of control desired by the engineer, but how that control can adversely or negatively impact the contract, shifting the risk of loss or potential for a claim for additional costs to the engineer. Also, how good are the design and performance requirements contained in the specifications? The contract administrator must make it clear to the engineer that the engineer warrants that a model, provided with the specification, meets the requirements of the specification. The engineer warrants the correctness and reasonableness of the design specification. It is not contractually easy to shift the responsibility for a bad procurement to the vendor. When a controversy is raised between buyer and seller, the courts interpret the specifications against those who drafted them.

The Funding Profile

Nothing can derail a technical program faster than overlooking the critical part that the funding profile plays in the overall procurement process. Engineers are not accountants and usually do not care what the source of funds are, as long as there are funds to spend. But this is not always all that needs to be considered. In any business—commercial or government, internal or external—funding comes from a budget. The amount contained in the budget has been approved for expenditure in a certain manner. It may be unrestricted, it may be dedicated (e.g., only for capital or plant equipment, or only for construction), and so on. If the engineer fails to appreciate the distinction between these various "colors of money," the program can find itself unfunded, with little to no time to get the right "color" of funding.

The engineer has a good understanding of the nature of the work contained in the technical specification, and the contract administrator has a good knowledge of funding sources and the restrictions that often accompany them. Together, the engineer and contract administrator must reach a mutual understanding on the source of funds very early in the formulation of the acquisition strategy to permit development of the appropriate contracting methodology.

Program Control

The degree of program control that the engineer desires must be consistent with the technical specification and administrative requirements proposed for inclusion in the contract, the procurement regulations governing program controls, the payment schedules, and the contract type being proposed. Consideration must be given to how best to structure the purchase order relative to the line item deliverables. This not only provides for the timely receipt, acceptance, and utilization of the items being procured, it permits the vendor to invoice, receive payment at reasonable intervals, and maintain a positive cash flow position. Discrete, separate deliverable items should be described and listed in the purchase order, with acceptance criteria defined for each deliverable item. The engineer must be sensitive to the financial position of the vendor selected to perform the work; the fact that a fixed price contract has been placed is of little value if a cash flow problem forces the vendor into extreme financial difficulty.

The engineer is responsible for monitoring the vendor's progress during performance of the work, to ensure that the vendor is on a schedule that is consistent with the delivery requirements of the order and expending the funds at the rate appropriate to the estimated costs in the order. Often, the vendor is required to submit cost reports to the engineer, the detail of which is agreed upon prior to placement of the contract.

The more detail that the engineer requires in the cost report, the higher the vendor's cost to compile and submit it. The contract administrator can provide the engineer with guidance on the details required in a cost report and how this information should be used in monitoring the vendor's cost performance. Often the contract contains clauses that require the vendor to notify the contract administrator when the cost level is at (or about to exceed) a certain percentage of the estimated cost of the order. The contract administrator should encourage the engineer to put in place an informal cost monitoring system, regardless of the contract type incorporated into the order. As noted above, the fact that a fixed price contract has been placed is of little value if a cash flow problem forces the vendor into extreme financial difficulty. Measurable milestones should be established by both the engineer and the contract administrator that serve not only to monitor performance of the actual work but are used by the contract administrator as "flags" for projecting overruns of the contract funding.

Development of the Request for Proposal

The engineer often takes for granted development of the request for proposal (RFP), believing it to be the routine function of the procurement department and not fully understanding the whole process. There is a tremendous reluctance on the part of the engineer to change the engineering documents (specifications, drawings, materials, and lists) solely to facilitate the procurement process. The truth is, there is very little that the contract administrator can do without support from the engineer. A request for proposal, far from being a routine procurement document, is the sole piece of paper that communicates to the outside world. It is all that the vendors have that tells them that something is being procured and a proposal being sought. In addition to the technical specification, the RFP contains the proposed contract type, the delivery requirements, the method of payment, the terms and conditions of purchase, socioeconomic and other certifications required for government procurement, and many other important, if not purely "technical," items.

   While the contract administrator has the final responsibility for the final vendor list (since the contract administrator is the sole person empowered to contract for the company), the engineer must have performed sufficient market research to support the choice of vendors, to ensure full and open competition, or to justify a restricted or limited list of potential vendors. The engineer should prepare a detailed cost estimate to assist in establishing the appropriate terms and conditions of purchase, as well as supporting the contract type selected.

The Vendor List

The vendor list is the place where the engineer can really damage an otherwise good procurement. By specifying a restricted or limited vendor list, the engineer can limit competition. This can have a negative effect since the best prices generally can be obtained by full and open competition among qualified vendors. All vendors capable of performing the work must be given the chance to compete for the work, being advised of the qualifications that they must ultimately meet. They should not be excluded. The engineer must realize that by virtue of the way it is written, the technical specification can effectively restrict the vendors. For example, writing the specification around a specific product, or identifying that the item desired must be "identical to" a brand name item, is a sure method restricting the vendors. The contract administrator's review of the specification should ensure that "brand name or equal" designation contains the minimum, essential, salient characteristics of the item being procured, thus removing the apparent restriction.

   The contract administrator can be of great assistance to the engineer in developing the vendor list. Often the engineer's market research has been limited to familiar vendors or those that have provided similar work in the past. However, the contract administrator is skilled in utilizing sources such as the *Thomas Register, Nuclear News Buyers Guide,* and existing and prior purchase order information, which will provide the engineer with a significantly increased vendor base from which to select the vendor list for the specific procurement.

The Cost Estimate

The engineering cost estimate is almost as important as the technical specification in the procurement process, and the engineer must take its preparation seriously. Initially, the cost estimate is the basis for the funding request, and it can influence the acquisition strategies, depending upon its magnitude and the actual availability of funds for this and other programs. During the proposal evaluation process, the cost estimate is used to establish the negotiation objectives. Finally, it can be used as the basis for award. Government regulations, for example, permit award based upon a favorable comparison to an engineering cost estimate. Often, little to no science is put into preparation of the cost estimate, thus making it very difficult to use it for the establishment of negotiation objectives and as a basis for award. An inadequate cost estimate can cause the need for repeated requests for additional funds or an overcommitment of funds that could be used elsewhere.

As the chief negotiator, the contract administrator must have the best information at his or her disposal, inclusive of the cost estimate. Anything less can (and often does) result in an unacceptable procurement. Either too high a price is paid and there is inequity between the work performed and its intrinsic value, or too low a price is paid and the work performed is not what the engineer desires (you often get what you pay for). In both cases, the procurement is not in the best interest of the engineer, the contract administrator, or the vendor.

In addition, the cost estimate must be "independent"; that is, it must be arrived at by the engineer in such a manner as to permit its use as a basis for award. It must be made very clear to the engineer that presolicitation price discussions with a vendor as a basis for the engineering cost estimate can result in that vendor having an unfair advantage, since such an estimate is not independent.

Proposal Evaluation and Order Award

Once the proposals are received by the contract administrator, the engineer exerts pressure to get the order awarded and the program started, provided that there are sufficient funds available. And why not? Isn't the placing of the contract the whole reason for this time-consuming process? It must be emphasized, though, that this is not the end of the process. Errors made at this stage can delay the order award, which could result in vulnerability to loss of the funds for this program by their diversion to a program that is ready for order placement. During the proposal evaluation and order award process, both the engineer and the contract administrator must also take care to prevent the potential of a protest by one or more of the unsuccessful vendors. While most engineers recognize that a fair price must be agreed upon, they are not as sensitive to the concept of benefit to the government, equity, or justification of what constitutes a fair price. The result might not be the best obtainable under those circumstances.

Failure to reach mutuality—whether contractually (under terms and conditions of purchase), price-wise, or technically—can be fatal to the engineer's program. It is crucial that the contract administrator and the engineer evaluate the proposals, both for technical conformance to the specification requirements and reasonableness of the effort proposed, in terms of labor, materials, and subcontract items. The engineer must also assess the schedule proposed for consistency within itself and within the engineer's integrated procurement plan that was prepared at the initiation of this process. A negotiation objective must be mutually established, and the basis well understood by both the engineer and contract administrator, to permit the conducting of meaningful negotiations.

During the negotiation process the contract administrator and the vendor must clearly establish how all communications during the life of the contract will be handled, as well as how documents will be reviewed and controlled, how nonconforming conditions will be dispositioned, and what measures will provide for interface and change control. Once this negotiation process is concluded, the engineer must make any revisions to the technical specification that were agreed upon and form the basis for mutuality between the contract administrator/engineer and the vendor. If the final price is not close to the engineering cost estimate used as the basis for establishing the negotiation objective, the engineer must prepare a technical evaluation of the final price, to permit the contract administrator to establish equity and benefit to the client.

Negotiation

Negotiation is often a very exasperating procedure for the engineer. It was bad enough to write and rewrite the technical specification because the contract administrator required modifications to assure that all bidders were being treated fairly. Now the engineer is being called upon to defend his or her cost estimate and justify the technical adequacy and conformance of the vendors' proposals being evaluated.

Perhaps nowhere else in the process is there more of a need for teamwork and mutual understanding than during negotiation. Since most manufacturing costs are approximately 50 percent material and 50 percent labor, it is impossible to effect any meaningful decrease in the price proposed without challenging these items directly. Without the "smarts" of the engineer to permit meaningful and realistic fact-finding, the best the contract administrator can hope for is negotiation of labor rates and indirect expense (burden) rates. The result will be far from the best obtainable and certainly not in the best interest of the client or the engineer's overall program.

The Program Plan

A careful review by the engineer of the program plan proposed by the vendors is crucial to the success of the program. Often, the engineer has provided the contract administrator with an unrealistic manufacturing or performance schedule, since it was developed by fitting the work into the available time span. A vendor, not wanting to appear unresponsive during proposal evaluation, may indicate without any further elaboration that it intends to meet contract schedule. The contract administrator must ensure that the overall program plan is broken down by the vendor into its constituent elements and that the engineer thoroughly evaluates each element for sequence correctness, realism, and attainability. Elements that must be reviewed include the test program, material ordering and delivery, document submittals, subcontract placements, and any qualifications never done before. There is nothing worse for the success of the program on the part of a vendor than to agree to a schedule that cannot be met, just to receive the work, expecting that something can and will be worked out later on during contract performance.

The Order Award

Finally, the contract is placed and the work can commence. Can the engineer relax and get about his or her business, leaving contract administration to the contract administrator? Absolutely not! The proof that there was meeting of the minds and mutuality as to the work being performed can be demonstrated only during the actual execution of the contract requirements. Since much of the direction and success of any program takes place during the early initiation stage, it is highly desirable that the engineer and the contract administrator visit the vendor's facility to participate in a kickoff meeting. During this meeting all parties concerned can review the technical specification and the vendor's plan for meeting the requirements, as well as discuss plans for obtaining the necessary materials, subcontract support, qualification of processes/personnel, and the schedule for documentation submittal. The person loading and machine/facility resource profiles to support the proposed deliveries and intermediate program steps can also be discussed. Milestones can be developed to permit the monitoring of the vendor's progress and its attainment of program objectives. Cost control and reporting methods and formats should be clearly defined, as well as the content and depth of information to be provided in any cost reports called for under the contract. Both the engineer/contract administrator and the vendor should leave the kickoff meeting feeling that there are no obvious misunderstandings, that trust is developing, that the program can be successfully completed, and that there is nothing that is left to the imagination of either party. Now, the work can begin!

Conclusion

Since the contract administrator is usually given the responsibility of ensuring vendor conformance to contract requirements, it is necessary for the contract administrator and the engineer to develop a partnership beginning with development of the initial acquisition strategy and formulation of the contracting methodologies through order placement. A successful contract administrator–engineer interface exerts a strong influence on the finished product's quality cost, and delivery. An unsuccessful relationship, on the other hand, can seriously jeopardize the acquisition process and result in the failure of the total program.

26

Managing to Avoid Claims: A Design Engineering Perspective

Irving M. Fogel
Fogel & Associates, Inc.

Design professionals are spending more of their time and money—and their insurance carriers' money—defending themselves against claims being made by owners, contractors, casual passersby, and third-party users such as passengers in elevators and tenant employees. Usually, the design professional's exposure to losing when defending against these claims results from something other than technical failure. It results instead from the failure to manage properly. The design professionals fail to manage or administer their efforts properly during the predesign and design process, they fail to manage and administer their work properly during the bidding process, they fail to manage and administer their responsibilities properly during the construction phase, and/or they fail to manage and administer properly the postconstruction or closeout phase of the project.

Design professionals think of themselves as professionals skilled in the application of aesthetic, functional, and scientific principles to achieve pleasing and practical results. They often lose sight of the fact that in the process, they must manage contracts in order to try to avoid claims and to be prepared to defend themselves if and when claims are made against them. A claim or lawsuit resulting from the failure to manage or administer properly is no less grievous than one resulting from a design error. The design professionals must never forget that they are also contract managers—managers of contracts with clients, consultants, and others. The management and administration of the contracts is no less important than the management and administration of and performance of the design and, where they act as construction administrators, the management and administration of the construction process to ensure the successful completion of the project.

The design professionals' contracts usually define the phases of a project as the study and report phase, the preliminary design phase, the bidding or negotiating phase, and the construction phase. For administrative and management purposes, there is also a preprofessional service contract phase.

The Phases of a Project

The Preprofessional Service Contract Phase

Although no services are being performed as yet, the foundation for many disputes is often laid during the preprofessional service contract phase of the project because of poor communication and the lack of proper documentation. The contract usually includes language outlining and limiting the scope of services and responsibilities. It also contains provisions for the arbitration of claims and disputes that arise from differences in the interpretation of the language. We must try to eliminate the need for activating the provisions on dispute resolution.

In order to avoid the costs that result from arguing over what is meant by the contract, the professionals must try to communicate as clearly as possible during the negotiation phase what they intend to do and what they intend not to do. In addition to communicating, they must also document their understanding of their scope of services document with the same care that they devote to their design calculations. Too often, people honestly believe they hear what they would like to hear, when in truth something else is promised. The contract can't cover everything, and professionals have certain responsibilities that are never covered or eliminated by contract.

The Study and Design Phases

Again, during the study and design phases, "consultation with the owner" is a major consideration. To avoid disputes, we must consult, communicate, and document.

Agreements with consultants must detail, *in writing*, the duties and responsibilities of the parties. The work performed by consultants must be reviewed for conformance with the agreements. Lines of communication must be established so that all concerned are kept informed of changes and/or other facts that may affect their work.

During these phases, as a result of the development of the design, factors affecting the cost of the project must be communicated to the owners to allow them the privilege of determining, in advance, if and how their money will be spent. Letting the owners decide in advance whether they want to pay for something and properly documenting the decisions or agreements reached can help prevent the oft-heard argument, "If I would've known, I wouldn't have gone ahead with it or I would've done something different."

Design professionals regularly rely on representations made by others who are "supposed" to know. The design professional has a responsibility to document the representations and at least check whether the oral representations made are in conformance with the published literature. Many disputes result from the acceptance of oral representations that are contrary to the literature published by the organization being represented.

The professionals responsible to the client for the total package have the responsibility for coordinating their work and that of all consultants. This responsibility must be diligently managed and administered. "My consultant made a mistake" *may* be a valid defense. You don't, however, want to get to the point where you have to defend yourself. The cost of a defense and vindication may ultimately be greater than paying without defending.

Standard specifications are truly standard. They are, however, neither all-inclusive nor valid for all projects. They must be checked and conformed to the particular project for which they are intended, and the drawings and specifications must be conformed to eliminate conflicts.

The design professional usually has the responsibility to advise the client of any changes in the original cost estimate for the project. A procedure must be established to track the estimated cost of construction as it relates to the originally established construction budget. This tracking process can also help determine conformance with the original concept: overdesign or, possibly, underdesign. In either case or in neither case, the relationship between the current estimated cost of construction and the preliminary estimate will be known.

The Bidding or Negotiating Phase

Many design professionals believe they can relax once the bid package is complete and that there really isn't much to do until construction starts. This is not true. They have many responsibilities during this phase of the project, most of which are basically managerial or administrative.

There are differences between contracts that are let by competitive bidding and those awarded as a result of negotiation. It is not true, however, that the services during the bidding phase of a publicly bid contract that nominally will be awarded to the lowest responsible responsive bidder are strictly of a pro forma nature. At a later date, many things can either come back to haunt or protect us: conducting prebid meetings, conducting prebid site conferences, answering questions, provisionally approving substitutions, and recording what is done and what is said by the proper issuance of addenda, or the lack thereof.

The design professionals are usually required to assist the owner in evaluating bids or proposals. When analyzing a bid, the professionals must verify that all the conditions are met and that all the documents required to be submitted have been submitted. Before certifying that a contractor is "capable" or "competent," you as the professional must verify that the contractor is, in fact, whatever it is you are certifying, and you must document what you did to satisfy yourself. When you certify that a bid is "reasonable," you may be taking on a lot more responsibility than you wish. Remember that a bid is based on an estimate, and an estimate, by definition, is an estimate. There is at least one instance where in support of the validity of his "excess" costs or damages, one of the contractor's major arguments was based on the fact that the engineer had "verified" the estimate as valid and all-inclusive.

The Construction Phase

The professional's responsibilities during the construction phase of a project are more subject to interpretation than his or her duties and responsibilities during any other phase of the project. This is truly the phase during which the perceived responsibilities may be greater than the actual. Also, paraphrasing an attorney discussing the subject, "if you have the right, you have the duty."

During this phase of the project, in addition to the responsibility for coordinating with his or her own consultants and client, the design professional may have the responsibility for dealing with the constructor. There may be additional managerial and administrative responsibilities relating to other consultants, to inspecting organizations, and to testing laboratories that have been contracted with directly by the client.

In addition to the engineering competence required to judge technical compliance with the contract, to review shop drawings, to review schedules, and to review proposals for substitutions and/or modifications, the design professional may have both technical and administrative responsibilities relating to the contractors' applications for payment and change orders. In addition, depending on contract and/or perception, the design professional may have many other rights, responsibilities, and duties that require management.

The Postconstruction or Closeout Phase

Although contracts do not usually identify a closeout phase, per se, it's a distinct phase requiring its own management. Before certifying completion—by whatever title—in addition to the "punch list" efforts that may be required, the professional must assure that all the administrative aspects of finalizing the contract are met. This includes but is not limited to filing certificates with governmental agencies; issuing certificates to the contractor or contractors; verifying "as-builts"; ensuring that all the operating manuals and warranties that are called for are in fact received; and documenting that all the contractual responsibilities have been complied with.

Claims Prevention

Most management failures result from errors of omission and not errors of commission. One of the simplest and yet most efficient ways to minimize the probability of missing something is to prepare a checklist for each project, no matter how small. The checklist can be based on a generic list used by the engineer for all projects, but the list must be modified to include the requirements of that specific project.

Since most claims arise as a result of errors of omission on the part of the professional, a good place to start is to follow through on each of the following action items:

- Check drawings for proper coordination between technical specialties.
- Check to see that the information on the drawings conforms to the written word of the specifications.
- Read the boilerplate language to see that it conforms, specifically and uniquely, to the project under consideration.
- Enter into written agreement with consultants detailing exactly what their responsibilities are.
- Review the work performed by consultants for conformance with agreements.
- Check the finalized program against the estimate or budget to determine the current validity.
- Communicate properly with consultants so that a change wrought by one that affects the work of another is properly accounted for.
- Include owners in the communications process to permit them the privilege of determining, in advance, how their money will be spent.

- Establish a reasonable time frame for review.
- Establish reasonable durations for implementation.
- Specify scheduling using one of the many available network scheduling techniques.
- Review the specifications to determine whether items specified are still available (or, for that matter, whether they have been available for the past X number of years).
- Check whether the information given by a sales representative or sales engineer is valid or in conformance with the specifications sheet prepared by the very company he or she represents.
- Check the bids, quotations, or proposals for conformance with the contract documents.
- Review the insurance requirements of the contract documents to assure compliance.
- Review the schedule carefully, and react in a properly and timely manner.
- Establish and adhere to an orderly system of controlling or keeping track of the documentation.
- Retain the backup information or supporting data for the approval, modification, or rejection or payment requests.
- React in a timely manner to requests for clarification or interpretation of the project documents.
- Monitor the progress of the project and report objectively to the owner as required.
- Take responsibility for discrepancies and/or omissions in the project documents.
- Issue clarifications and instructions in a timely fashion.

Reacting to a Claim

If confronted with a claim, management reaction must be prompt and positive. Attorneys and insurance carriers must be notified and assisted, without reservation, in mounting a defense. Delay in mobilizing both information and resources for contesting the claim results in weakening the defendant's position, even in relationship to unfounded claims.

27

Construction Claims: Entitlement and Damages

A J. Werderitsch
Administrative Controls Management, Inc.

Joseph S. Reams
Administrative Controls Management, Inc.

Construction claims present a sad but real dilemma for the construction industry. Claims establish an "us-versus-them" attitude when what is required is a team approach to accomplish a project. Finger-pointing accusations from unknowledgeable and uninvolved owners, above-it-all architects and engineers, and underhanded contractors continue to cast a pall over complex, technological projects. Lessons learned often end in an attempted one-sided contractual arrangement rather than a solution to the root causes of claims.

Construction claims are a reality; as such, each new project must be prepared for the eventuality of a claim. Reports and other project documentation, which in the past have represented management practices, are now being prepared with an eye to building cases. The stakes are high; change orders anticipated to total 5 percent of contracts may now be influenced by alleged claims ranging from 30 percent to 100 percent of the contract amount.

Delay and acceleration are complex issues from an entitlement determination and cost quantification viewpoint. This chapter presents a review of items to be considered in the cause-and-effect relationship of delay and acceleration. The chapter is intended to provoke additional questions and provide a basis for solutions for readers faced with the possibility of preparing or defending against claims for delay and acceleration.

Background

The contract documents are the foundation of construction claims analyses that focus on establishing entitlement and proving damages. Construction contracts generally contain certain clauses to facilitate the execution of changes to the intended scope of work. These clauses define the responsibilities of the parties, allow for changes to the work, provide for time extensions, define the methods for pricing the changes, provide for contract termination (convenience to the owner or default by the contractor), and stipulate the means of resolution.

The contract documents may be the source of major disputes centering on the impossibility of the specifications. Constructive changes during the execution of the work often result in claims. These claims may result from contradictory or ambiguous language and specifications, errors or omissions, or work that is impossible to perform according to the documents. In the case of obvious errors, it has been found that the contractor bidding the work has the responsibility to call the error to the attention of the owner.

Other issues resulting in claims include disputed change orders, differing site conditions, apparent authority, and overzealous or improper inspections. Construction claims result from misinterpretation and improper administration of the contract documents during project implementation. They also occur because of misunderstandings concerning the rights and responsibilities of parties to the contract. This often leads to the waiving of one's rights as provided for by the contract.

The most difficult issues to resolve in construction claims are those associated with delay and acceleration. They are difficult to resolve because they usually involve several complex issues. Adding to this complexity is the assessment of whether an issue is excusable or nonexcusable. Further complicating this assessment is whether an issue occurs independently, concurrently, or as a serial result of one or a combination of excusable or nonexcusable issues. For example, an entitlement analysis of the total delay may result in the finding that the delay was partially excusable and partially compensable. In this case, only a part of alleged time and compensation requested by the contractor would be warranted. The issues may sometimes be so complex that separate hearings are convened first to determine entitlement and then, based on finding entitlement, to determine the damages.

In the event of a delay, to establish entitlement to time extensions and delay damages, it must be proved that the delay impacted the contract completion date. The cause-and-effect relationship must be identified, quantified, and supported by contemporaneous documentation.

Having established entitlement, alleged damages must be proved. Actual damages supported by project records are the best substantiation. For example, liquidated damages must be shown to represent an estimate of the owner's anticipated damages, or these damages may be interpreted as a penalty and not enforceable. Actual owner damages must be supported by proper documentation. Contractor's delay damages—such as field indirect costs, general conditions, home office, and administrative expenses—must be itemized and documented. Damages associated with inefficiencies resulting from impact, such as work resequencing and stacking of trades, must be supported. Industry data studies may be used; however, contemporaneous project records identifying project conditions and realized productivity are superior documents.

As-planned and as-built schedules are also used to assess inefficiencies. These schedules are also used to analyze entitlement and calculate the number of days for the assessment of either owner or contractor delay damages.

The purpose of the following discussion is to present basic principles regarding entitlement and damages for delay issues. A basic familiarity with these principles will allow contract parties to understand their own as well as the other party's positions. Understanding the complexities provides an incentive for the parties to resolve their differences equitably without going to court.

The comments presented are based on the assumption that a lump sum contract for general contractor work exists and that the contract contains standard clauses for addressing changes, differing site conditions, time extensions, and liquidated damages. It is also assumed that time is of the essence and that there is no no-damage-for-delay clause.

Entitlement

Entitlement to contract time or sum adjustments resulting from delay is usually found in the contract clause pertaining to time extensions. Most clauses provide for a time extension if the cause of the delay is attributable to actions or inactions beyond the control of the contractor. Labor strikes, severe weather, acts of God, and delays to the work within the control of the owner are generally items considered for time adjustments. The changes clause may also address time extensions by specifying that the contract time be adjusted as a result of change orders.

A direct relationship must be established between the change, the delay, and the contract completion date. When this relationship becomes difficult to establish or is nonexistent, a dispute arises that often results in a delay claim. The dispute becomes more difficult to resolve when several delay issues are present.

It is also necessary to determine the cause of the delay when analyzing delay entitlement. The cause is defined as an issue and must be supported by contemporaneous documents. The treatment and classification of these delay issues are generally not defined in the contract documents. By *treatment*, it is meant whether the contractor is entitled to a time extension and no compensation, to a time extension plus compensation, or to neither. Delay issues are generally classified as follows:

- *Excusable compensable delay.* This delay is within the control of the owner and provides for a contract time extension and compensation to the contractor.
- *Excusable noncompensable delay.* This delay is beyond the control of the owner and the contractor. The treatment provides for a contract time extension. However, the contractor is not entitled to compensation, and the owner is precluded from assessing delay damages for this time period.
- *Nonexcusable delay.* This delay is within the control of the contractor. The contractor is not entitled to a time extension or compensation. If the contract completion date is exceeded, the owner's liquidated or actual damages are assessed against the contractor.

Classifying delays is not as simple as applying the above definitions. The delay may be such that the owner and the contractor are each responsible for delaying different activities during the same or overlapping time periods. Both of these activities may be critical to the completion of the project. The overlapping delay period is treated as excusable noncompensable and is considered a concurrent delay. A time extension may be granted, but not compensation.

The same applies when an excusable compensable delay is concurrent or overlaps with an excusable noncompensable delay. For example, if the resolution of a differing site condition (excusable compensable) is concurrent with a labor strike (excusable noncompensable), time extensions would be granted to the contractor only for the period of time these two issues concurrently delayed the project.

Complexities in resolving delay entitlement are further increased when the serial effect of a delay is considered. For example, if work that was planned to be completed before a strike is actually performed after the strike as a result of an earlier excusable compensable delay, the delay resulting from the strike could be argued as compensable. If the work in question was delayed by an earlier nonexcusable delay, the argument that the contractor is not entitled to a time extension would exist.

Establishing Entitlement

Entitlement analysis is usually based on the identification and quantification of excusable delay issues. The reason for this apparently one-sided approach is that project documentation is fairly consistent between both the owner and contractor regarding an excusable delay. The project impact associated with an excusable delay can be quantified.

It must be determined, however, whether a nonexcusable delay is concurrent with an excusable delay or by itself impacted the contract completion date. This step may have a tremendous effect on the outcome of a delay analysis.

Generally, once identifiable delays have been quantified, the difference between the resulting adjusted contract completion date and the actual contract completion date is viewed as a nonexcusable delay.

Project Documentation

Contemporaneous project documentation is used to identify and assist in quantifying delays. Project documentation includes, among other documents, the contract bid documents, correspondence, meeting minutes, daily reports, photographs, change orders, field orders, bulletins, submittal logs, payrolls, and cost and accounting records. Interviews with key project personnel provide direction in identifying which project events and activities to focus upon.

Potential delay issues are identified from these interviews and the documentation review. Chronologies for these issues must be prepared. They concentrate on activities occurring prior to, during, and after the time period at issue. Analyses of the project's planned and actual activities, including the delay issues, are used to quantify the project impact.

Documenting and proving impact to the contract completion date are critical to supporting entitlement to time extensions. This documentation and proof require cause-and-effect analysis. Using prepared project documents and issue chronologies, a schedule delay analysis is performed. The party having a thoroughly researched and documented position is more likely to prevail in seeking or refuting entitlement.

Generally, one of the primary requirements for entitlement is written notice. The notification requirement provides the notified party with the opportunity to review the condition and take action to resolve or mitigate its impact. In the absence of formal notification, project documentation may be the source to prove knowledge of the issue, thus waiving the written notification requirement.

Documents such as meeting minutes, internal memorandums, and daily job records may provide the proof that both parties were aware of and working toward mitigating the delay.

A suggested presentation of an entitlement position includes a brief description of the contract scope of work, a summary of the breached contract clauses, and discussion of the issue or issues in dispute. Each issue is developed in a clear and concise chronology of the events. Both parties' positions should be defined from the project chronology. Positions should provide references to specific actions or inactions resulting in impact to the contract completion date. This impact must further show that material damage was incurred. Damages should be treated separately and supported by the entitlement position.

Damages

Damages for delay, like entitlement, include many complex items which in themselves may be the subject of dispute. It is also important to understand the theories of damage recovery that have in several instances been upheld by the courts. The following discussion addresses both owner's and contractor's damages.

Owner's Damages

The contract documents formulate the basis for the recovery of damages. Owner's damages regarding delay may be specified in the agreement or contract form. Frequently, owner's damages are defined as liquidated damages and are assessed against the contractor for each day the contractor finishes beyond the contract completion date. In lieu of liquidated damages, actual damages may be stipulated and include special damage considerations.

Generally, if the contract documents stipulate liquidated damages, they cannot contain a provision to seek recovery of actual or other consequential damages. An exception may occur when specific limitations have been placed on the limits of the liquidated damage clause as to what damages are specifically included and what damages are specifically excluded in the clause.

Liquidated damages are defined as an agreed-upon amount of dollars, usually represented as a daily amount. The amount represents the estimated cost to the owner of not having the contract completed on time. Stipulating the amount of predetermined liquidated damages in the bidding process minimizes an additional item to be disputed.

It is important that the amount of liquidated damages represents a reasonable attempt at estimating the real damages. To be valid and enforceable, the estimate must be prepared at the time of contract execution and represent foreseeable damages. For example, a list should be prepared for the estimate, including the expense to continue with resident engineering and inspection services; contract administration services; anticipated loss of revenue; temporary rental facilities; differential costs for utilities, maintenance, security, and financing; and other damages that would be incurred if the contract completion date is not met.

The owner attempting to assess liquidated damages who is the cause of the delay in whole or in part will find that its assessment will not be upheld. The assessment period must exclude all delay attributable to excusable issues resulting in an amended contract completion date.

Generally, the assessment period ends when the project is substantially complete, unless stated otherwise. Substantial completion—the point at which the facility is sufficiently complete so the owner can occupy or utilize the work for its intended purposes—is usually chosen, because it is often difficult to determine when the project is 100 percent complete.

Liquidated damages may not be enforceable if it is proved that the owner did not suffer actual damages because of the delay. The same principle applies to liquidated damages that have been set too high.

Clauses providing for actual damages to be paid to the owner require the owner to itemize and substantiate its claim for such damages. The itemization and substantiation includes providing records of the costs that were incurred as a result of the delay. Because of the difficulty in identifying, itemizing, and substantiating these costs plus their being the subject of additional disputes, the liquidated damages provision is more often used.

Contractor's Damages

Allowable contractor damages for delay are usually not specified in the contract. Contract change clauses provide for the direct cost associated with the change. Contract time extensions may provide for sum adjustments, but the specific inclusions for these sum adjustments are not defined.

Contractors seeking recovery for delay damages may include impact costs such as loss of efficiency and extended general conditions. Efficiency losses are the result of work disruptions, resequencing and stacking of trades, and performing work in weather and other unanticipated conditions. General condition costs claimed for the delay period include extended site supervision, management, construction equipment, site offices, change houses, fabrication facilities, and monthly site operating costs such as utilities, cleanup, maintenance, and similar items. Reimbursement may also be sought for contractor general office overheads and administration expenses for the delay period.

Generally, the claim to these damages is presented in one of two ways: (1) total cost, or (2) an itemization of specific costs including impact. The total cost position is one of comparing the bid or estimate amount to the total contract cost incurred. The total cost claim is usually not upheld by courts because it does not take into account inherent inefficiencies attributable to the contractor. Additionally, the total cost position does not quantify the delay issues. It is usually based on the premise that the total delay period was excusable and compensable.

Seeking recovery of damages by identifying specific cause-and-effect relationships requires a greater effort by the contractor but provides a firm basis for the contractor to argue the merits of its claim. By developing this itemization, the contractor is in a better position to support its claim and the owner is in a better position to review its merits. This is important if the primary objective is one of resolution and equity.

To recover the costs of lost labor efficiency requires the contractor to: establish the progress it expected to achieve with its use of anticipated resources; substantiate the cost required to achieve the actual progress; and prove that the increase in costs is related to a compensable delay issue. This effort requires the contractor to develop and use schedules of its work plan including relationships, durations, and anticipated resource requirements. In addition, the contractor must keep records depicting the actual progress and impact of the delays.

Several industry trade studies have been prepared to quantify efficiency losses. These have addressed losses resulting from significant numbers of change orders, adverse weather conditions, overtime, multiple shifting, and other project conditions affecting productivity. These studies must be viewed in the context of how they apply to the specific issues being disputed.

A more effective approach to establishing the extent of efficiency losses is to show what productivity was realized on the project during periods of no disruptions or other impacts. This is then compared with the productivity realized during the period in dispute.

Other specific costs associated with efficiency losses, such as the utilization of additional foremen to direct crafts and supervision to coordinate activities, must also be itemized.

The contractor must also substantiate its damage claim for extended general conditions. This includes the itemization of site management and office personnel and other expenses required during each delay period. This should not reflect the peak contract period but should represent the delay period. If this period cannot be isolated, it may be necessary to determine the costs for general conditions for the project duration and use an average daily rate.

The contractor may also be entitled to seek recovery for its office overhead and administrative expenses. The theory applied in this situation is that during a work suspension that resulted in a delay period, the contractor was required to maintain its overhead expenses while not receiving expected contract revenue. This is viewed as an unabsorbed overhead during times of work suspension. The theory has been applied to delay periods as well as suspension periods. This consideration for overhead and administrative expense is the subject of recent court rulings, and the outcome has varied.

One method used in allocating this overhead cost is known as the Eichleay formula. The formula assumes that overheads are fixed and evenly distributed during the course of the contractor's operations and provides for the computation of a daily amount of overhead for the project delay period.

Acceleration

Claims for acceleration can be classified into two types: (1) actual acceleration, and (2) constructive acceleration. Actual acceleration is experienced when the contractor is directed by the owner to complete the work earlier than the contract completion date. Constructive acceleration exists when: (1) a delay existed that was excusable and warrants a time extension; (2) the time extension request was refused by the owner; (3) the contractor performs in an accelerated method as a result of the owner requiring such; and (4) the contractor incurs additional costs as a result of accelerating its work.

The entitlement to acceleration costs is dependent upon which party was responsible for the project delay at the time acceleration is required or directed. For example, if it is determined that the contract completion date will not be met, the owner may direct the contractor to accelerate its work and meet the contract completion date. If the owner is responsible for the delay resulting in the completion date not being met, then the acceleration is viewed as compensable to the contractor. If, on the other hand, the contractor has caused delay to the contract completion date and the owner then directs the contractor to accelerate its work, the costs associated with the acceleration are against the contractor.

The costs of acceleration may include premium pay such as shift differential and overtime, added foremen and supervision, loss of efficiency, and other costs for equipment and administration. The proof of these costs is also a requirement for recoverability and includes certified payrolls and identification of added supervision and expenses.

The issue of acceleration entitlement is similar to the analysis of the delay issues. It is a cause-and-effect study to determine whether it is excusable or nonexcusable.

References

Hohns, H. M., et al. *Deskbook of Construction Contract Law.* Englewood Cliffs, N.J.: Prentice-Hall, 1981.

Lambert, J. D., and L. White. *Handbook of Modern Construction Law.* Englewood Cliffs, N.J.: Prentice-Hall, 1981.

Levin, P. *Claims and Changes.* Silver Springs, Md.: Construction Industry Press, 1981.

McDonald, P. R., and R. Lamb. *The Mechanical Contractors Handbook of Claim Avoidance and Management.* Reston, Va.: Reston Publishing, 1986.

Nixon, M. A. "Legal Rights." *Project Management Journal* 18, No. 1 (March 1987): 22–25.

Rubin, R. A., et al. *Construction Claims.* New York: Van Nostrand Reinhold, 1983.

Simon, M. S. *Construction Law: Claims and Liabilities.* Butler, N.J.: Arlyse Enterprises, 1989.

Stokes, M. *Construction Law in Contractors' Language.* New York: McGraw-Hill, 1977.

Sweet, J. *Legal Aspects of Architecture, Engineering and the Construction Process.* St. Paul, Minn.: West Publishing, 1985.

Werderitsch, A. J. *Construction Disputes: A Negotiated Resolution.* Morgantown, W. Va.: AACE Transactions, 1986.

Werderitsch, A. J. "Delay Analysis—An Automated Approach." 1987 *Proceedings of the Project Management Institute.* Drexel Hill, Penn.: PMI.

Werderitsch, A. J., and S. Firoozi. *Construction Delay Claims—Assessment Defense.* Morgantown, W. Va.: AACE Transactions, 1983.

Section XI

Information Systems and Software Projects

28

Managing Software Projects: Unique Problems and Requirements

William H. Roetzheim
Booz-Allen and Hamilton, Inc.

As senior project manager for Tetra Tech Services (a Honeywell subsidiary), I specialized in managing software development projects. During an airline flight, I enjoyed a lively debate with a project manager specializing in power plant construction. He was convinced, in his words, that "project management is project management, no matter what the specific nature of the project." I argued the point (and, I think, won) that software management really was different, especially in the area of project planning. I thought it might be worthwhile to use my notes from the flight (scrawled on an airline napkin) to argue this case in a more public forum.

On the Surface, There Is No Difference

At the top level, I must agree that the tasks performed by a software project manager are identical (in name) to the tasks performed by any other project manager. All project managers are responsible for planning, tracking, controlling, and reporting. As shown in Exhibit 28-1, the planning process can be further broken down into the following five steps:

1. Decomposing the project into tasks
2. Defining dependencies between tasks
3. Estimating resource requirements for each task
4. Performing a risk analysis
5. Scheduling the project

Looking at these five planning steps, I believe that the first significant difference between software project management and other project management is subtly present. Nonsoftware project planning emphasizes the dependency definition and

Exhibit 28-1. Five steps of project planning.

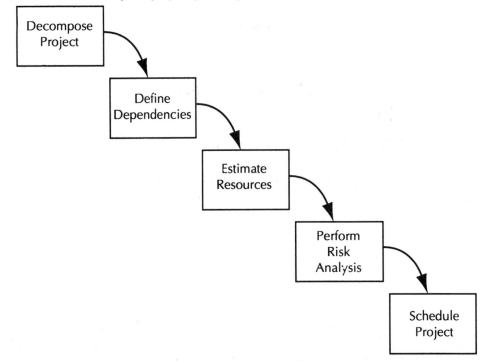

scheduling steps. Just look at most "project management" computer software on the market for evidence of this emphasis. This is true because:

- ▸ The schedule is very much dependency-driven.
- ▸ Given an adequate task decomposition, resource estimation is straightforward (albeit tedious).
- ▸ In general, risk analysis can be dealt with on a high level.
- ▸ The detailed task scheduled is a driver of project success.

Effective software project management, on the other hand, emphasizes the resource estimation and risk analysis steps. Let's look at each of the five steps in the project planning process in more detail to understand better both this relative emphasis and other factors that set software project management apart.

The Steps in the Project Planning Process

Decomposing the Project Into Tasks

Software projects are unfortunate in that a relatively significant amount of the project work (perhaps 30 percent) involves deciding what to do. I'm not referring to subtle points of implementation, but major design decisions on a par with "Should we have the power plant burn oil or use nuclear reactors?" Imagine being required to come up with a detailed task list *before* this decision was made. Experienced software project managers solve this dilemma by preparing three task decompositions:

1. The *concept-oriented decomposition* provides a rough, largely generic outline of project requirements and is used for ballpark estimates and schedules (perhaps plus or minus 50 percent).

2. The *capability-oriented decomposition* is prepared after analysis is complete and describes delivery of functionality to the customer, but it makes no attempt to describe how this functionality will be achieved. Time and budget estimates at this point are normally valid within approximately plus or minus 25 percent.

3. Finally, the *implementation-oriented decomposition* is prepared after the software design is fairly well advanced. For the first time, the project manager knows how the project will be accomplished, and tasks will have some correlation with deliverable items (software modules). It is only at this point that close estimates of time and budget are possible.

Another significant difference is that it is difficult to measure completion of tasks. You know when a building foundation has been poured and can mark that task as complete with some confidence. But software project managers never really know when most tasks are complete. Even a module that is marked as complete can (and often does) still require additional work to correct hidden defects, allow it to integrate with other modules, or meet clarified/modified requirements.

Somewhat related is the fact that actually building the software (coding) is a relatively small percent of the project effort—perhaps 10 to 15 percent. The bulk of the effort and difficulty comes from testing the "completed" modules and trying to put them together (integration). Worse yet, the very nature of testing and integration tends to push them to the later stages of the project, when schedule/cost changes are difficult and time is short.

Finally, the scope of software tasks varies widely with interpretation. I can literally meet the exact same set of requirements with software whose costs and complexity vary by a factor of ten. The bulk of software costs are used to add capabilities that are difficult to quantify and measure such as user friendliness, quality, and exception handling (which involves anticipating and coding for unusual situations).

Defining Dependencies Between Tasks

In my experience, software dependencies are always of the partial-finish-to-start variety. This type of dependency relation says that "Task A must be XX percent complete prior to the start of Task B," with XX varying from 0 to 100. Note that if we substitute 100 for XX, we have a traditional finish-to-start dependency. For most software tasks, the proper number for XX is between 25 percent and 75 percent. This aspect of the dependency definitions obviously complicates defining the dependencies and discourages their use.

Software dependencies are also uniquely characterized by a degree of rigidity. Very few software dependencies are rigid requirements ("Task A *must* be done before Task B"). More often, they are preferences ("It is more economical to do Task A before Task B," or "The customer would prefer that we do Task A before Task B"). These dependency relations can neither be ignored nor dogmatically followed if the project is to be successful.

Perhaps most important of all, software dependencies do not generally arise from the physical nature of the tasks. Instead, they originate within the people doing the work and the problem being solved. Each person working on a project has unique talents and limitations, implying task dependencies in the scheduling of tasks so that the right person can work on a particular task. Similarly, the unique characteristics of the problem being solved often drive the sequence in which tasks should be completed in order to support partial deliveries, prototyping of key areas, risk reduction, etc.

In the end, most software project managers (1) do not attempt to do formal dependency definitions, (2) do the definitions at a sufficiently high level that they are both correct and useless, or (3) do the definitions once to meet a customer or company requirement, and then ignore them.

Estimating Resource Requirements for Each Task

I believe that when compared to other projects, the process of estimating resource requirements for software projects is totally different and much more difficult. Perhaps the single most important reason for this difference is that software costs are nonlinear while other project costs are roughly linear. For example, let's suppose that a particular type of building costs $50 per foot to build. This number can then be used to estimate the cost to build a 10,000-square foot building, a 100,000-square foot building, or a 1,000,000-square foot building simply by multiplying the number of square feet by the cost per square foot ($500,000, $5 million, or $50 million).

For software, the relationship between cost and "size" is not nearly so simple. The cost per line of software grows roughly linearly as long as the same number of people can do the work (i.e., going from 100 lines of code to 1,000 lines of code), but it makes nonlinear jumps as you must add new project personnel. This nonlinearity (and lack of predictability) results because the bulk of the cost for large software programs can really be attributed to communications costs among the project participants.

There are other factors that contribute to the unique nature of software resource estimation.

- ▸ Software requirements and related factors (the target computer, for example) are often changed during the project, with accompanying wide variances in resource estimates.
- ▸ As mentioned earlier, software costs are largely driven by hidden factors such as quality.
- ▸ Project scope, and hence costs, are only really known relatively late in the project.
- ▸ Software project managers have very limited long-term historical information to assist them in preparing resource estimates.
- ▸ Software productivity varies widely, often by a factor of ten or more, from one individual (or one team) to the next.

Although the resource estimation picture painted thus far sounds rather bleak for the software project managers, we do have one ace in the hole. The vague and changing nature of the requirements combined with the inherent flexibility of software are ideally suited to a "design-to-cost" mentality. Successful software project managers invariably ask (or otherwise determine) how much the customer wants to spend, then tailor the entire development process around that figure.

Performing a Risk Analysis

I've already claimed that risk analysis is significantly more important to software project managers than to other project managers. The reason is obvious when you examine the nature of software. Every software project is doing something new and different. If the project was the same as an earlier project, you would just use the code you developed earlier! Furthermore, most software projects of any consequences are pushing the state of the art in at least one area. This is an inevitable result of the relative newness and rapid pace of advance of our science. State-of-the-art development always involves significant risks that must be dealt with, and software is no exception. Software project managers who downplay risk analysis soon disappear when one of their projects fails to deliver anything useful at all.

Successful software project managers look not only at projectwide risk areas, but they also perform a risk analysis for each task in the work breakdown structure. This task-level risk analysis is used for risk avoidance (e.g., prototyping risky tasks, assigning top talent to the more risky tasks) and contingency planning (e.g., scheduling risky tasks early to allow recovery time, budgeting additional funds for high-risk tasks, developing strategies to replace/redesign risky components). Software project managers often estimate and report on five distinct types of risk for each task.

1. *Technical risk.* Failure to complete the task to a required degree of technical excellence
2. *Schedule risk.* Failure to complete the task within the estimated time
3. *Cost risk.* Failure to complete the task within the estimated cost
4. *Network risk.* Risk related to the dependency network linking various project tasks
5. *Overall risk.* A composite of all risk factors

For each of these five risk factors, the project manager looks at both the likelihood of failure and the consequence of failure. Obviously, tasks with a high likelihood of failure *and* a high consequence of failure are the most worrisome.

Scheduling the Project

If a detailed and accurate software schedule is maintained during a project (which is often not the case), it is only possible with continual revisions to the initial schedule. Simplicity in changing the schedule is paramount in any scheduling technique used. One factor that contributes significantly to this is the fact that developments later in the project often necessitate the addition of new tasks and/or cause tasks that were completed earlier to become "uncompleted."

One additional difference between software scheduling and other project scheduling is the close interdependency between scheduling and costing experienced by software project managers. More than any other single factor, software costs for a given project are driven by the project schedule. A project that is initially scheduled to take four years can be accelerated to three years (or additional requirements can be added to achieve the same type of schedule compression even with the original four-year deadline). Some researchers estimate that software costs increase with project schedule compression as an inverse to the fourth power relationship! For example, there is some evidence that cutting a schedule in half (or doubling the delivered functionality without increasing the schedule) doesn't double the cost, but rather increases it by a factor of sixteen.

Some Differences During Tracking and Control

Although the most clearcut differences come out during the planning process, there are additional (although more debatable) differences during the tracking and control phases as well.

▸ *Technical awareness is more important* on software projects. To be successful, a software project manager *must* understand top-level aspects of both the application being coded and the general software development process. This is true both to maintain adequate channels of communication and to facilitate proper scheduling and design-to-cost decisions.

▸ *Quality control is one of the most important jobs* of the software project manager. Recall that software modules can vary widely in terms of hidden defects and built-in functionality. The software project manager must control the nature of the code being produced to ensure that the number of defects and underlying functionality of the code is appropriate for this particular project.

▸ *The software project manager must manage the customer* throughout the project. Virtually no customer starts the project with a clear, specific idea of exactly what the finished software will look like when it is delivered. The project manager must mold the customer's expectations during the project to match the software that will eventually be delivered, ensuring a favorable reception for the finished product.

But, in Conclusion, a Counterargument

I won the debate on the airline flight about the uniqueness of software project management, but my victory was perhaps the result of my opponent's failure to make the right counterargument. We spent considerable time (then and in this chapter) discussing the process and mechanics of project management. I am convinced that these are unique for software projects. Perhaps this focus on the mechanical aspects of project management falls into the technology trap so prevalent in technical writings and in the marketing hype surrounding project management tools. Down deep, I realize that project management is really the management of people. It is the process of coaching, cajoling, manipulating, leading, and molding a diverse group of people into a team with a common goal, then letting the team charge straight at that goal! After you achieve this, the job simply involves staying out of their way (and keeping others from getting trampled). This is the case in all types of project management—software project management as well as the rest.

29

Implementing Project Management in Large-Scale Information-Technology Projects

Rainer A. Otto
Southern California Gas Company

Jasjit S. Dhillon
Decision Management Associates

Thomas P. Watkins
Decision Management Associates

Project management is receiving more attention and emphasis in information systems (IS) departments. IS projects are becoming more challenging to deliver on time, within budget, and with the functionality desired by the user. Their high cost poses a great deal of financial risk to the company if they are not managed properly. This is being caused by business and technology trends that are increasing the importance of IS projects to the success of the company. Thus, IS departments are recognizing that project management can help lead to improved project success as it has in other industries such as construction and aerospace.

Impact of Business Trends on Information Systems Projects

New computer systems that businesses need today tend to be larger and more complex than those in the past. These systems have typically served the needs of one

This chapter was adapted from Rainer Otto, Jasjit S. Dhillon, and Thomas P. Watkins, "The Project Management of an Information System," *Project Management Institute Seminar/Symposium*, Calgary, Alberta, Canada, October 1990. Reprinted with permission of the Project Management Institute, P.O. Box 43, Drexel Hill, Penn. 19026, a worldwide organization of advancing the state-of-the-art in project management.

department and dealt with the automation of transaction-oriented processes. Examples of such systems include:

- An accounts payable system for the accounting department
- A materials management system for the central warehouse
- An employee information system for the human resources department

For the most part, these were batch, paper-oriented systems which, while challenging projects, were generally accomplished with more informal project management approaches.

The need for companies to become more competitive through increased sales or controlling costs has precipitated a rise in the need to share data among departments. Thus, new systems need to serve the requirements of multiple departments and divisions. For example, a marketing department needs timely access to the customer order department's detailed information on customers, as well as product sales information in order to better target sales and new product development efforts. To reduce costs and material order lead times, all departments require access to new purchasing systems to submit purchase requisitions and obtain status information. Often this means that the new system must satisfy competing and sometimes conflicting needs and involve many more users, thus resulting in significantly larger projects.

This, in turn, has resulted in businesses' growing acceptance of the need to prepare a strategic information systems plan that facilitates corporatewide data sharing. This introduces significant interproject dependencies as each project is building part of a corporatewide architecture. Thus, a project to construct a materials management system can no longer be viewed as a stand-alone project. It must be integrated with the purchasing, accounts payable, cost reporting, and employee systems.

Impact of New Technology on IS Projects

The use of new technology has considerably increased the complexity of IS projects because of the specialized skills required to use and implement this technology. Almost all new systems are on-line systems that require more specialized skills than batch systems. A new challenge is the use of cooperative and distributed processing, which splits the processing and data between personal and mainframe computers. This and other kinds of new technology saddle projects with many unknowns, complicate the design of the system, and call for skills that are in very short supply.

This trend has led to increased specialization of the project team members needed to build a new computer system. This makes a project manager's job more challenging because resources are less and less interchangeable, requiring better project planning and management. Previously, most team members could design files, but now database design specialists are required. Because this skill takes considerable training and experience to develop, it is often organized in its own group which provides services to the project when required. Communications, personal computer, and data security have also become specialized skills—resources that are needed on every project.

IS projects are often key to company success. There are an increasing number of examples where the success or failure of IS projects has had a profound impact on the success or failure of a company. The use of information systems to achieve a competitive edge is an often-cited fact in today's business literature. The American Hospital Supply Company's use of information systems to increase its competitive edge by facilitating the inventory and ordering process of its customers was fundamental to its success. American Airlines' Sabre airline reservations system achieved significant profits for the company when compared with those of its basic business, airline operations.

Software development projects have also had significant problems that have had serious consequences on companies. Bank of America's abandonment of a multimillion dollar development project was a serious setback. Ashton Tate's inability to deliver a bug-free version of Dbase IV has significantly eroded its market share in database products. Finally, IBM's laggard performance in the early 1990s has been attributed to its inability to deliver software to utilize the powerful computers it is building.

IS departments are therefore under the gun to deliver larger and more technically sophisticated systems in shorter times. They are recognizing that the use of sound project management techniques can sometimes make the difference between success or failure. On their journey to improved success, IS managers realize that they must cross the same bridge as other industries that implemented formal project management in the past.

There are many aspects of IS project management that are the same as those of its predecessors. However, there are some distinct differences. We will now discuss these aspects.

How IS Projects Are the Same as Projects in Other Industries

Information systems project managers have argued that project management for IS projects is different. The fact is, however, that project management for IS projects has many of the same characteristics as project management in other industries.

Product Similarity

Zachman[1] has compared the products produced during the construction of a building to that of a computer systems project. Exhibit 29-1 summarizes the similarities between the products of the two industries. As with construction projects, the first phase of a computer systems project requires the project manager to define the objectives of the project and the scope of work to be completed. Once the scope is agreed to by the user group (client) and the project team, the business is modeled so that the analyst can have a complete understanding of how the user views the business environment. The architect's drawings are used in the same manner as they illustrate the building as seen by the owner.

After the models are developed to show the user's view of the business, models are constructed to show how the information system is seen by the designer. The architect's plans are similar in concept as they portray the building as seen by its designer. The technology model used for systems projects has equivalent objectives

Exhibit 29-1. Similarities between products of construction of a building and a computer systems project.

Buildings	Computer Systems
Architect's Products	Computer System Equivalents
Bubble Charts Gross sizing, shape, spatial relationships	Objectives—Scope Gross sizing, scope
Architect's Drawings Building as seen by the owners	Model of the Business System as seen by the user
Architect's Plans Building as seen by the designer	Model of the Information Systems System as seen by the designer
Contractor's Plans Architect's plans as constrained by nature and available technology	Technology Model Information system's model as constrained by available technology
Shop Plans Description of parts/pieces	Detailed Representations Description of parts/pieces
Functioning Building	Functioning Computer System

to the contractor's plans. Both take into consideration the constraints put onto the project by available technology. The contractor must also be concerned with the outside environment.

Finally, the systems projects require detailed representations that provide detailed descriptions of the parts and pieces of the new information system. The shop plans are the equivalent building product. They also provide descriptions of the final parts and pieces of the building.

As illustrated in Exhibit 29-1, both industries require similar products throughout the life cycle of the project. Thus, the project manager of a systems project must manage the development of these products in much the same manner as the project manager of a building construction project.

Life Cycle Similarity

Systems projects are broken into phases that are similar to the phases of the building construction industry. Exhibit 29-2 lists the analogous life cycle phases for projects in both industries. First, both systems projects and construction projects have a concep-

Exhibit 29-2. Similarities in life cycle phases of construction of a building and a computer systems project.

Construction	Computer Systems
Concept/Feasibility	Conceptual
Planning	Planning
Engineering Studies	Definition
Detailed Engineering	Design
Construction	Implementation
Testing	Conversion
Commission	

tual stage in which the feasibility of the project is determined. The costs versus benefits are measured, and the project is ranked with other potential projects to determine its value to the company.

The objectives of the planning stage are also equivalent in both industries. The primary objective is to determine the scope of the project and gain agreement from the user (client). The most effective strategy to accomplish the objectives is also determined. During the definition phase of a systems project, the requirements of the user (client) are documented, and the current system is modeled so that the objectives of the new system can be clearly defined. Engineering studies have similar processes in a construction project.

The design effort of a systems project and the detailed engineering of a construction project are also similar. Both detail the requirements of the new system and provide for technical plans that will be used in the final construction/implementation of the product. Finally, the implementation phase of a systems project consists of the final coding and testing before the new system is converted into full-time use. The management of this phase is very similar to the management of the construction and testing phases of a construction project, which result in the commission of the new building.

Similarity in Management Functions

The management functions of the systems project manager are virtually the same as the management functions of the building construction project manager. Though the organizational structure used for many information systems departments is a weak matrix, the primary responsibility of the project manager is still to ensure that the project is completed on time, within budget, and at the project's objective quality level.

The following management functions can be expected of the project manager in both the building construction industry and the information systems industry:

- Planning
- Organizing
- Scheduling
- Monitoring
- Directing
- Integrating
- Controlling
- Reporting
- Negotiating
- Resolving conflicts

In addition to the above functions, the project manager of systems projects is usually the supervisor in charge of many systems analysts and programmers. This provides the project manager with the added function of staffing some of the project's resource requirements. This has some advantages and disadvantages that will be discussed in more detail later in the chapter.

How IS Projects Are Different From Projects in Other Industries

Information systems projects present some unique challenges to the application and implementation of classical project management principles and techniques. Additionally, there are specific areas of emphasis that differentiate information systems project management from that of other industries.

Some of the principal challenges facing IS departments attempting to implement project management include difficulties in scope definition and management, the intensive multiproject environment, inflexible organizational structures, and rapidly evolving development technologies and methodologies. The following sections highlight some of these issues with particular reference to our experiences in the Southern California Gas (SoCalGas) Company's development environment.

Scope Definition and Management

In classical project management, scope definition and management is very critical to the success of a project, from a schedule, resource, and cost management perspective. The scope statement defines what business functions are under consideration for automation. It is just as important to define what is to be excluded from consideration as well as what is to be included.

In traditional information systems development, project scope definition has been a very fuzzy and ill-defined area. This is the result of a number of different reasons, some of which are:

- The interrelationship of business functions, causing more automation than originally planned
- The use of text to define scope, which often leads to misinterpretation of what is actually in the scope
- Difficulty in defining the end deliverables
- Frequent changes in business requirements during the project life cycle

The Multiproject Environment

In most large corporations there are a multitude of systems development efforts taking place simultaneously. These efforts are sponsored by various customers (users) within the organization and are carried out by the information systems department. The principal challenges in IS project management are as follows:

- There is a finite resource pool to draw upon for systems development efforts.
- Specialized technical resources are often required and need to be shared across multiple projects.
- Cross-utilization of resources leads to conflicts in resource allocation, which in turn causes schedule delays and cost overruns.
- Resource management needs to be done on a real-time basis to control project costs.

Organizational Structures

The project organizational structure is another differentiating factor in information systems project management. The structure adopted by SoCalGas is a hybrid matrix. In such a structure, the project manager has dual roles: that of a project manager as well as that of a functional manager. This has resulted in a weak matrix with the following organizational facets:

- Project managers are also the functional managers of many of the project team members (systems analysts, programmers, etc.).
- Project managers can staff many of their projects with their own functional staff members.
- Project managers don't have enough authority as compared to project managers in the construction and aerospace industries. This situation is improving as project management implementation matures within SoCalGas.
- Interface management is easier because of the fact that many project team members are also functional subordinates.
- There is faster reaction time to project requests among direct reports.
- There is more control over direct subordinates.
- Project managers have more formal authority over project team members. This, in turn, enhances team motivation because the project manager has both position and reward power.
- Conflicts within the project team are more easily resolved.
- The project managers do not have enough time to do either their project or functional tasks well.
- There is often a conflict of interest in setting priorities because of project priorities versus functional priorities. Project priorities often suffer.

Exhibits 29-3 and 29-4 describe the involvement and contribution of the various information systems departments at SoCalGas prior to the implementation of project management and after the implementation of project management. It is clearly evident when the two exhibits are compared that the involvement of various departments has increased in the entire project life cycle as a result of the decision to

Exhibit 29-3. Involvement and contribution of information systems departments prior to implementation of project management.

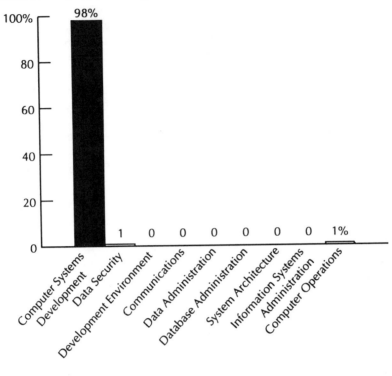

Exhibit 29-4. Involvement and contribution of information systems departments after implementation of project management.

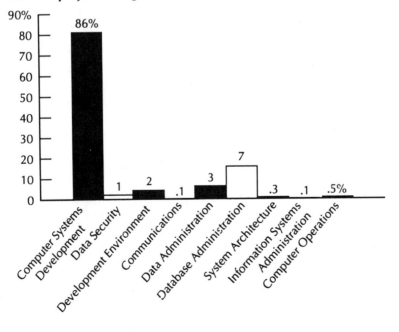

implement project management in the systems development process. Exhibit 29-4 shows that there are now six groups participating in a project that did not participate previously. The project manager has to spend a disproportionate share of his or her time dealing with these project team members.

Rapidly Evolving Technologies and Methodologies

Systems development projects have been—and in the majority of cases, still are— very labor-intensive undertakings. Essentially speaking, systems developers take a list of requirements from customers (end users) and using their intellectual know-how, convert these requirements into functional software applications.

To alleviate the labor-intensive facet of information systems development, a class of development productivity enhancement tools has emerged. These tools can significantly shorten the development life cycle as well as reduce overall cost.

However, this class of productivity tools is evolving at such a rapid pace that the majority of management information systems/data processing organizations do not have the ability to keep up with the new technology. This has led to a reliance on the tried and true (and inefficient) methods of systems development, which are labor-intensive and less risky. Consequently, project management has also been viewed as part of the new technology/methodology, and there has been significant resistance to its implementation.

Note

1. J. A. Zachman, "A Framework for Information Systems Architecture," *I.B.M. Systems Journal* 26, No. 3 (1987).

30

Project Management for Software Engineering

Lois Zells
Lois Zells & Associates, Inc.

Software engineering is the term applied to all aspects of information processing systems development and maintenance. The term *engineering* is used to indicate that the procedures used in software projects are comparable to the scientific method rather than to random artistic endeavors.

The study of software engineering management is broken into people issues and process issues. Although the people issues are very important, they are not within the domain of this chapter. On the other hand, the process issues will be covered in depth. The procedural side of software engineering management is further divided into work that is done to build the system and work that is done to manage the project. When practitioners do work to build the system, their efforts result in software specifications. When they do work to manage the project, their efforts result in estimates and plans. Even in a construction project, these two separate types of work occur, usually simultaneously. For example, the cement subcontractors may be pouring the foundation (building work), while the project manager is planning the construction of the walls (project management work).

Furthermore, the best project management skills alone do little to overcome deficiencies in the software engineering management process—without an equivalent level of mastery in building the system. If the project is on time and within budget and it solves the wrong problem, it is not likely to be of much use to anyone. Furthermore, until planners understand the deliverables that are produced while building the system, they will be hard-pressed to develop a thorough and all-inclusive plan. Identifying what deliverables are to be produced, then, requires a complete understanding of the phases of development.

Portions of this chapter have been excerpted from Lois Zells, *Managing Software Projects: Selecting and Using PC-Based Project Management Systems* (Wellesley, Mass.: QED Information Sciences, 1990). Used with permission of the publisher. (1-800-343-4848). © Lois Zells, 1991; all rights reserved.

Traditional Development Phases

In any kind of a project—even a project to build a simple birdhouse—there are at least four phases.

1. Analysis: The builders must first determine what is to be constructed.
2. Design: The builders must then create a blueprint for the construction.
3. Construction: The product must actually be built.
4. Installation: The product must be qualified and put into use.

Distilled down to their most fundamental components, software projects also must complete the analysis, design, construction, and installation phases.

1. Analysis: The software engineers must first define the business problem the software will ultimately solve.
2. Design: The software engineers must then create a blueprint for the software solution.
3. Construction: The software engineers must write the code.
4. Installation: The code must be tested and accepted.

Actually, before *any* phases are initiated, it is necessary to evaluate the justification for software systems services. A quick assessment is made to determine the justification of the request. Many projects, perhaps even 50 percent, do not survive this initial screening.

The Analysis Phase

During the first phase, the developers must determine what business problem is to be solved through the installation of the software. This is called business requirements analysis. This analysis effort is driven from the business perspective of the customer (sometimes called user, client, etc.). Answering the question "What would be the problem if this were 1901 and there were no computers?" helps to identify the correct business requirements. During this process there may also be some limited technical aspects that need to be taken into consideration. Thus, it would be useful to think of analysis as 90 percent business-driven and 10 percent technically driven.

Preanalysis

The early part of the analysis phase of most software projects is typically somewhat chaotic. Project participants may not know one another and may be unsure of themselves; customers may have a hard time conveying what they want; meetings may go astray; and the whole project may seem ungovernable. Furthermore, one of the most serious difficulties that continues to plague software systems developers is getting a clear understanding and agreement of who's in, who's out of the project effort and what's in, what's out of the product effort. This definition is called the *domain of study*. Furthermore, it is essential to develop a concise declaration of what's important to the product and the project. In other words, the agree-upon priorities must drive the project.

To crystallize these requirements, today's more enlightened software organizations have added an introductory phase to the project development process, called the preanalysis phase. Preanalysis is an orientation and screening phase that helps to: (1) identify and resolve problems before the analysis and design stages; and then to (2) identify the operational features and procedures necessary to complete the work successfully; and finally to (3) diffuse any issues that will become obstacles.

Many of the current software specification techniques are weak from the perspective of not being able to capture and address the questions of who the customer really is, what's most important to the customer, and which customers should have the highest priority. Lack of a clear definition of these elements is a significant contributor to the creeping commitment that often destroys any success potential a project may have.

During this preanalysis phase, customers are identified; their high-level wants, needs, and tastes are captured and prioritized; and the customers themselves are prioritized with respect to who should drive feature and functionality decisions. Customer requirements are prioritized by customer area. A very important aspect of this process is the resolution of conflicts in customer priorities.

Partititioning Analysis

Most software engineering authorities now agree that analysis, as a single phase in all but the smallest software systems projects, is simply too big. Therefore, expert practitioners often take a spiral approach, dividing analysis into more than one go-round. This technique employs the concept of *controlled iteration*: for example, a high-level analysis, an intermediate-level analysis, and a detailed analysis. Some or all of the specification development is executed concurrently—with each successive iteration becoming more and more detailed—until all of the requirements have been accurately and completely captured.

The high-level analysis is an orientation and screening effort that, most importantly, confirms the domain of study. It also provides a cursory evaluation of the business requirements, confirms the priorities, and describes the value of each required feature.

During the intermediate-level analysis, the high-level specification is expanded, a project management agreement is written, and the team drives to get a handle on how big the project really is. If the group is able to ascertain that the risk is too high to try the project as it is currently defined, its members may reduce the domain of study and the proposed system scope before proceeding any further. (The true definition of scope is the part of the system, in a software engineering project, that will be committed to automation.)

The third analysis iteration is the time to dissect the business problem completely. It is during this effort that the real job of analysis is completed. The most significant deliverable of this effort is the verified requirements definition, which establishes the specifications for building the system. It describes in thorough detail what the system must do in order to be deemed a success. Most failures to deliver the correct system can be traced to the fact that even by this stage there was still no unambiguous agreement between the developers and the customers about the system's requirements. Emphasis, then, must be on the document's completeness and accuracy.

Postanalysis

At the conclusion of the business analysis, it is necessary to designate which features (or parts of features) will be automated and which will remain as manual operations. Additionally, the parts elected for automation should be mapped into hardware and software requirements. Decisions are made regarding batch processing, on-line processing, distributed processing, database requirements, or any other technical approach. These decisions serve as input to the selection of one or more purchased package solutions and/or to the design of the automated portion of a new system.

Although the domain of study must be specified at the beginning of the project, it is not until the process of carving out the boundaries for automation has been completed that the final decisions regarding scope are made. Therefore, the scope is not truly defined until the end of this postanalysis phase. Subsequent changes to the scope of the system are subject to the change management procedures described later in the chapter.

The Design Phase

This phase provides the transition from the selection of a solution to the ability to construct a reliable, high-quality product. The objective is achieved through systematic software design methods and techniques that are applied to the chosen automated solution from the prior phase in order to obtain an implementable computer system. The design phase is partitioned into three types of work: (1) the design of the technical architecture of the system, (2) the external design, and (3) the internal design.

Design of the Technical Architecture of the System

The system is partitioned into pieces that will ultimately become groupings of source code instructions. These groupings, usually called subsystems or programs, are in turn divided into modules, routines, subroutines, etc. How these groupings interface with one another is called the technical architecture of the system. It is analogous to the blueprint for a construction project and, as such, may be graphically represented in one of the many acknowledged design diagramming techniques that are used by software engineers. The technical architecture declares the basis system design, the control subsystems, and the data structure control interfaces for intermodule communication.

External Design

External design—so-called because it considers design from the outside of the system (that is, the customer perspective) without regard to the internals of the modules, programs, etc.—addresses such issues as design of input screens and forms, hierarchy of screen menus, and design of output reports. In a prototyping environment, some of the external design may have been done much earlier in the project. If so, the external design (to the extent that it was not completed in the earlier phases) is finished now. Many of the deliverables in this subphase will be direct input to customer procedure guides and manuals. Therefore, since external design is so closely related to the documentation factors, these tasks must be closely coordinated with the individual(s) responsible for customer documentation.

Internal Design

The internal design provides the detailed directions for module design, program design, database design, and so on. These internal specs will be used, during the coding phase, to create source codes in one or more compiled programming languages. Team members are assigned the responsibility for designing each module (generally less than or equal to 100 source code instructions) or program (group of modules, routines, or subroutines). The specifications include the name, purpose, language, calling parameters, calling sequence, error routines, algorithms, module logic, and restart and recovery procedures. The database design—complete with names, descriptions, values, size and format of fields, data usage statistics, the distinction between stored and derived data, keys, access relationships and methods, and backup and retention criteria—is also finalized.

The Construction Phase (Coding)

It is during this phase that the code is actually written from the design specifications that were developed for the program modules and databases. Programming considerations are influenced by the type of language (e.g., third or fourth generation), the choice of the language itself (e.g., COBOL, C), and the installation of productivity aids (e.g., code optimizers, application generators). The units coded during this phase are also tested.

The Installation Phase

During the installation phase, all of the activities carried out during the project finally come to a climax. Characterized by the integration of software development, hardware installation, documentation, testing, training, and conversion, this last phase of the project life cycle marks the ultimate joining of all of the deliverables from each of these efforts. During systems testing and acceptance testing, the successful integration of these outputs and the smooth operation of the system are verified, and the final decisions regarding implementation are made.

Doing Things Right

There is a saying in the software engineering community that quality is built in and really cannot be tested into a system. Yet it is alarming how many software managers still cling to the mistaken belief that more testing as well as improving testing skills will bring quality to their systems.

If practitioners have the skills to develop a complete and comprehensive set of test cases, and if they can then measure the time and effort involved in executing those test cases one time, those onetime measurements represent the true cost of testing. Almost every minute spent after the first execution of those test cases is *not* being spent on testing! Instead, time is being spent on work that *should* have been completed in the earlier phases. Examples of work being done at the wrong time are specification reexamination and correction, redesign, recoding, and retesting.

Since the fastest, cheapest, highest quality way to build software is never to make any mistakes during development and never to do any job more than once, it is a good idea to learn how to do **the right things right—the first time!** Thus, good systems development techniques are the essential requirements for improved quality and faster project completion times, and they may not be ignored.

Furthermore, to the surprise and chagrin of those who look for their productivity solutions in code generators, they are looking in the wrong place. The greatest improvements come not from the coding process, but from robust analysis and design specifications. Experts in software engineering management now acknowledge that 40 to 65 percent of the errors in delivered requirements arise from poor analysis and design. Proper analysis and design, then, are crucial to effective testing of the system and the ultimate delivery of a good product. Not fully appreciating this, participants in traditional project development rushed through the early phases in order to ensure that they would have enough time for testing. At a maximum, they spent 25 to 40 percent of the software development effort on analysis and design. Consequently, programmers spent the majority of their time fixing errors that were carried over from the early phases. Of course, what they were really doing was the analysis and design that ought to have been done earlier in the project. This is a very poor approach, because errors discovered during testing cost fifteen to seventy-five times more to fix than those that are discovered during analysis. Sooner or later, analysis and design will be done! It's not a question of whether they *will* be done, but a question of *when* they will be done and *how much* the organization is willing to pay for them.

Simply stated, this means front-loading the effort for analysis and design. This concept requires organizational acceptance that the project team will spend 40 to 65 percent of the project effort during analysis and design. That is, they will shift the distribution of their effort to the beginning of the project.

But what a change in the mindset of the organization this kind of an approach requires—because many people believe that project teams are not doing anything meaningful until they're writing code. People are just not used to spending 40 to 65 percent of the project time before they start coding—but that is what it takes to get a better idea of project size, to get better estimates, and to build quality software systems.

Similarly, to provide quality software project management, organizations have to divorce themselves from their construction project notions and embrace new ways of addressing the management issues. Unlike construction projects, which have a heavier distribution of effort during the implementation phase, in a systems project, 60 percent of the project may be expended before any coding starts.

Managing Changes to the Domain of Study and the System Scope

It is also in the early stages that unknown requirements start to emerge, both the domain of study and the scope start to enlarge, target dates begin to slip, groups begin to make compromises, and the project often starts to fall apart.

The organization must have a way to respond to changes in the domain of study and/or the scope of the system. Many people try to freeze the specifications, but that often only leads to: (1) the discovery that people change their minds anyway; (2) animosity when the system users feel they didn't understand what they were signing off to; or (3) an "on-time" system that doesn't fulfill the customer requirements.

It is not possible to control change, but it is possible to manage it. Changes are initiated through a change request that is assigned a number and entered into a change management log that keeps track of the current status of the request. An analyst assesses the costs, the benefits, and the impact in terms of time, money, and people. The change is then scheduled for consideration by a group of change management decision makers. The change management decision makers consider the impact and prioritize the request: accepted, rejected, or postponed until the next release. The necessary parties are notified of the decision and its impact on the time, money, and resources of the project(s).

The Difficulty of Managing by Phases Alone

Early project management concepts introduced the idea of gaining control by partitioning the project into phases. Because it was moving in the right direction, this was a good step, but it didn't solve the total problem. As practitioners have come to recognize, using the disciplines, methodologies, and development techniques did not automatically guarantee project success. Those early project developers found that the phases could be very long and that they still couldn't determine if they were on schedule. So they tried breaking the phases into major milestones, with each milestone representing a significant project event.

Again, the use of milestones was a move in the right direction, but it was still not the total answer. The significant events were hard to identify, and progress was hard to monitor. Milestones were very far apart, and estimators had a difficult time sizing up the effort it took for completion. Long periods elapsed before the project manager could evaluate status; consequently, valuable time would be wasted before the problems were recognized and corrective action could be taken. There was no really effective way to evaluate progress, so status was reported as a function of percentage against hours used (e.g., if a job was estimated at forty hours and the worker had spent twenty hours on it, the job was reported as 50 percent completed). This is one of the ways projects got to be 90 percent complete so quickly, while the last 10 percent took another 90 percent of the time.

A better approach is to partition each milestone into smaller pieces. Commonly referred to as *inch-pebbles,* these bits and pieces afford better control of the unknowns and easier monitoring of progress. The sum of many small estimates is more reliable than one large estimate and is also harder to shave down during scheduling negotiations.

To begin, inch-pebble jobs can be assigned to one person, making status easier to determine. Similarly, status is easier to report when the state of a job can only be binary: The job is either 100 percent complete or 0 percent complete; no other status is meaningful. This approach diffuses the impact of the subjective reporting of fractional percentages of completion, which are often expressed simply as a function of how much of the original effort has been consumed. Using smaller estimates and reporting binary status also reduces the possibility of the last 10 percent of the project taking another 90 percent of the time.

With smaller jobs, status is reported more frequently. If progress is poor, the manager knows it right away. Corrective action may be taken sooner, thus helping to avoid the wide differential between expected progress and actual progress. And finally, the smaller the estimate, the smaller the interval between the extremes. The smaller the confidence interval (the range between the longest and shortest estimates), the higher the level of statistical accuracy in the estimate.

Thus, the secret to successful project management is to partition the project into pieces of pieces of pieces until a statistically reliable level is reached. For example, the project can be divided by phase deliverables. The phase deliverables, in turn, are separated into their significant milestone deliverables. The milestone deliverables are then partitioned into major deliverables, and the major deliverables are broken into individual deliverables. Inch-pebbles are statistically reliable and are usually found at the individual deliverables level. It takes the completion of a significant number of inch-pebbles to produce a major deliverable. A fair number of major deliverables contribute to the completion of a milestone. And, of course, every phase has a certain number of milestones.

Implementation of Inch-Pebbles

How Small Is Small?

But what is the size of an inch-pebble? How small is small? Each of the inch-pebbles must be small enough so that:

- A reasonable estimate may be figured for its completion.
- The estimate reflects reality.
- The confidence interval will be small.
- The organization may be comfortable about the level of "accuracy."
- It will be hard to intimidate the estimator into reducing the estimate.
- The 100 percent completion level can be reached rather quickly.
- Managers know they're in trouble before disaster descends upon them.
- When the job is done, there is a meaningful and verifiable deliverable.

An inch-pebble thus represents a work unit that cannot be meaningfully subdivided and is best completed without interruption. In addition, to afford effective partitioning, estimating, scheduling, and status reporting, a unit of work (an inch-pebble) produces a meaningful and tangible deliverable that can be verified, is commonly assignable to one and only one person, and is usually completed in from four to forty hours.

Identification of meaningful deliverables is an area that causes lots of confusion when trying to partition the development of specifications. For example, if an analysis specification is to be produced across the span of several phases, it may be prepared at a high level in a Phase 1, an intermediate level in a Phase 2, and a detailed level in a Phase 3. One could then say that it will not be completed until the end of Phase 3. However, this would make status reporting and management of each phase very difficult. A better approach would be to partition the development of each specification into a job that can be worked on as an inch-pebble and later designated as 100 percent completed when it is finished. For example, an administrative system deliverable could be (1) the high-level specification of payment processing, (2) the intermediate-level specification of payment types, or (3) the detailed specification of backdated payment processing.

The implementation of the inch-pebble concept allows organizations to achieve many of the goals they are attempting to satisfy. It also helps them to recall that many small estimates added together have less margin for error than a single large estimate; therefore, they may more quickly realize their ambition for "accurate" estimates. Additionally, "one job–one person" combined with status of "done–not done" dramatically simplifies status reporting and thus the management of the project. (Remember: "one job–one person" is a rule of thumb and, as such, there are always exceptions. For example, meetings and reviews are inch-pebbles that, obviously, are assigned to more than one person.)

Setting a forty-hour maximum on inch-pebbles creates an environment in which a number of jobs are being completed every week. As a result, crises are frequently identified soon enough to avert disaster. Not every inch-pebble, however, is exactly forty hours long. Many are less than that and some may even be greater. Therefore, not every job starts on Monday morning and finishes on Friday evening.

At last, since most organizations have few to no experts in estimating, the discipline of getting down to the confidence intervals of four to forty hours goes far to diffuse the novice effect.

Resistance From Many Groups

To identify inch-pebbles of four to forty hours is not a trivial task. Although they are never faced at the same time, there may ultimately be as many as 2,000 inch-pebbles in a medium-size project. Frequently, people balk at what appears to be just so much overhead.

It is important to determine what makes sense in the organization, what information is needed, how often it is required, and how reliable it must be. Organizations should decide:

- How much estimating expertise is on the team—and its effect on the accuracy of the total plan
- If the range that is selected is small enough to support a high degree of confidence in the accuracy of the estimate
- If the range that is selected gives the status data soon enough (that is, how long the group members can comfortably wait before knowing if they're in trouble)
- How much risk can be borne

This approach has been implemented in many enlightened companies. Those that accept this concept buy into certain givens. It is agreed that the project team members will be allowed the time to plan, in the first place. Furthermore, since it is impossible to identify all of the inch-pebbles for the entire project at one sitting, only those inch-pebbles in the short term will be included in the plan. Then, after completion of a preselected and limited number of inch-pebbles, it is agreed that the team members will be allowed to use their newly acquired knowledge (and be given the time) to plan the next short-term effort. It is also agreed that this process may be repeated more than once for each milestone, phase, or project, depending on its size and complexity.

The Implications of Replanning

Furthermore, it is also accepted that, during each replanning exercise, the new knowledge that is gained may necessitate the implementation of one or more of the following project management strategies:

- ‣ Extending the finish date
- ‣ Adding more resources
- ‣ Eliminating features
- ‣ Risking (sacrificing) some degree of quality and/or reliability and/or performance
- ‣ Finding a low-risk method of improving productivity.*
- ‣ Even canceling the project.

These appear to be the only six choices. For example, the date may be locked in and the project must not be cancelled (because of a valid business requirement); but then, some combination of the second through fifth choices must be selected.

Realize that there's no free lunch! There is often a disconnect between making the target date of the current project and the costs of maintaining the system after it's put into production. Of course, no one advocates risking quality (and so on), but sometimes, it is the default decision. If—in order to save time during the project—quality, reliability, and/or performance are unintentionally (or consciously) sacrificed in order to make a critical target date, then operational costs are likely to be increased later during maintenance. Many organizations are either not aware of this obvious state of affairs or they just refuse to acknowledge it. The result is that, unwittingly, they often choose unrealistic strategies that, by default, simply lead to the ultimate sacrifice of quality. There are enough sorry practitioners around (who remember burning the midnight oil while trying to maintain a poor-grade system) who can attest to the results of such choices.

On the other hand, sometimes projects must be managed with a fixed date to completion (for example, because of regulatory requirements and strategic product

---

*There are efficiencies to be gained in both the project management process and in the development techniques. The introduction of new methodologies and/or technologies may, in the long run, improve productivity. However, in the short term, the associated learning curve may actually appear to reduce productivity and will certainly extend the dates. On the other hand, this learning curve may be offset by "buying the expertise"—either by reassigning in-house experts or by hiring outside consultants.

development). When groups do not have the luxury of moving the date, they simply integrate the other management strategies of adding more resources, descoping, introducing productivity measures, or canceling the project. If canceling the project is not an alternative, then teams are obviously left with the first three choices. If the regulatory requirements or strategic product development absolutely drive the date, then sacrificing quality may be the only choice. But that choice is made while consciously acknowledging the trade-offs.

Estimating

Some people would insist that accurate estimates in the software industry are impossible. It even seems contradictory to put these two words together. To the contrary, in some organizations there are groups that consistently give good estimates. Yet the skill does not seem readily transferable; and sadly, many people do give very poor estimates. Careful investigation, however, has surprisingly shown that it isn't the estimate that has been so wrong. The problem often stems from the fact that the bulk of the effort required to complete the job is simply overlooked during the estimating process. In other words, it's what is left *out* of the estimate that usually gets the estimators into trouble. Thus, the first challenge lies in finding an estimating method to ensure that everything that needs to be included in the estimate is recognized. As a group, though, the software engineering community has been unable to agree upon one commonly accepted estimating technique. Because this discipline is still so new, no models have yet emerged as the standard.

Statistics for Project Management

The use of statistical theory can provide a foundation for: (1) providing estimates earlier in the project life cycle than many of the traditional lines of code and function point techniques; (2) overcoming the uncertainty experienced in estimating software projects in general; and (3) addressing the noncode-related aspects of project management. The science of probability theory allows managers to substitute numbers in place of their hunches or conjectures.

The Navy Special Projects Office, Lockheed Aircraft, and Booz-Allen and Hamilton employed statistical theory in estimating and managing the Polaris missile submarine project way back in 1958. Specifically, they applied the concept of uncertainty, the beta (β) distribution, and a formula for expected effort. They called their process the Program Evaluation and Review Technique (PERT). This PERT estimating method was quickly adapted in many commercial sectors, such as the construction industry. Similarly, use of PERT estimating concepts for assessing lines of code was employed as early as 1976. Unfortunately, because of our tireless search for the silver estimating bullet, the concept was usurped by other lines of code formulas and such. To our chagrin, there is still no such thing as mindless estimating.

Estimating in Uncertainty

In software projects, team members are, in truth, usually trying to estimate in uncertainty. In estimating in certainty, it may be possible to derive acceptable results by using just one estimate. But if there are unknowns that may influence the estimate, it is advisable to provide a range of estimates instead of one predictor, to compensate for the uncertainty or lack of knowledge. By providing estimates for: (1) the optimistic, (2) the pessimistic, and (3) the most likely, we may come up with an acceptable range for the formula to compute effort.

In analyzing these three estimates, it is expected that the pessimistic and optimistic estimates would occur least often. Based on a formula called the beta (β) distribution, the formula for expected effort is:

$$\frac{\text{(1 times the optimistic estimate)} + \text{(4 times the most likely estimate)} + \text{(1 times the pessimistic estimage)}}{6}$$

This weighted average simply gives more importance to the estimate about which the estimator is most certain (the most likely). It assumes that the most likely estimate will be true four times more often than either of the other two estimates. At the same time, it biases the results so that the expected effort falls closest to the side of the greatest uncertainty (either optimistic or pessimistic). Thus, it also allows for some compensation due to that uncertainty.

Section XII
Research and Development Projects

31

Managing High-Technology Research Projects for Maximum Effectiveness

William N. Hosley
All-Tech Project Management Services, Inc.

Research and development is the engine that generates sales and profit growth for corporations, creates competitive advantage for entire countries, and begets quality of life benefits for all people. It is virtually a matter of life and death for all stakeholders (owners, customers, employees, the government—in fact, the entire general public) that R&D *does the right things* and *does things right*. This is especially true of the high-technology environment, where advances require the skill of post-doctoral training and experience in such fields as electronics, pharmacology, high-energy physics, computer design, photography, and biochemistry. Since R&D is a project-by-project endeavor, doing things right is the equivalent of good project management.

Some Opinions on R&D Project Management

In 1950, Dr. C. E. Kenneth Mees, founder and director of the Eastman Kodak Research Laboratories, was asked to describe his technique for good project management. He replied, "Simply hire the best people you can find and get out of their way."[1] There is considerable wisdom in this. Creative, highly educated people typically resent and hold in contempt "bean counters," schedulers, and others who are bothered by the ambiguity of the research environment and try to tidy things up with budgets and rules and regulations. The highly intelligent, motivated person readily understands what needs to be done, establishes goals for his or her work, and pursues those goals until they are reached and surpassed as quickly as possible. Asking such a person to abide by a plan created by a staff person with only a superficial understanding of the technology is likely to be considered insulting and counterproductive.

Is that all there is to R&D project management? Of course not! While Dr. Mees's view may be appropriate in the small, highly personal, well-funded laboratory, it would be a disaster in today's large-team, applied R&D efforts in the competitive pharmaceutical, computer, defense, and communications industries. Companies in these industries have staffs of thousands and annual R&D budgets in the hundreds of millions of dollars with corresponding complexity. In these cases, an across-the-board laissez-faire approach to R&D output is not practical. While many researchers proclaim that you can't schedule invention, this may simply be an attempt to reduce the pressure to produce results.

Certainly one cannot plan chance discoveries. (However, it is important to have an environment where serendipity can happen and bloom.) But most large-scale, mission-oriented R&D is not dependent on a chance "Eureka." It is, instead, based on numerous planned experiments that expect to converge on a few preferred solutions to a well-defined problem that is further tested before advanced-process and quality-assured production is implemented. These are team efforts, not solo performances. To be effective, teams must be like an orchestra playing one tune, not a group of cacophonous prima donnas trying to drown each other out.

The Merck Model

Merck & Co. provides an example of R&D success that others would do well to emulate. Like Dr. Mees, when asked about good project management, Dr. Roy Vagelos, CEO of Merck, said, "Hire the best, provide the best training, and encourage professional growth." Noted management expert and author Peter Drucker placed Merck "among those companies that have mastered the rules of research." For four years in a row, in a survey conducted among 8,000 executives by *Fortune* magazine, Merck was voted America's most admired company largely for its highly successful R&D effort, which now involves over $750 million per year with 4,000 professionals at sixteen research sites worldwide.[2]

What is Merck's secret? The answer is project management with an emphasis on coordination and planning. Reporting directly to the president of the Merck Sharp & Dohme Research Laboratories is a senior vice-president of planning who has a staff of eight coordinators who support 400 research projects. These coordinators oversee the development of detailed project plans using advanced software. Liaison among research, marketing, manufacturing, and all functional groups is provided by the coordinators. Project progress is monitored by regular status reports and meetings.

Project planning and management at Merck Sharp & Dohme uses several techniques to keep management informed of the status of product development and to guide the project teams toward development of a new drug to be approved and used. The process consists of:

- Organizing project teams, which form objectives and plan regular meetings.
- Constructing critical path timelines and schedules to:
    1. Synthesize compounds thought to be medically active
    2. Screen the compounds
    3. Confirm their biological activity
    4. Identify the lead candidates
    5. Determine the safety of the drug

6. Develop formulation of the drug
7. File an investigational new drug approval with the Food and Drug Administration
8. Determine worldwide interest in and market potential for the drug
9. Scale up the pilot plant
10. Determine and document human safety of the drug
11. Determine and document the drug's efficacy
12. File for new drug approval with the FDA
13. Scale up production of the drug
14. Introduce the new product

‣ Estimating program cost and resource requirements

‣ Conducting regular program reviews and taking action on critical activities that are late

‣ Coordinating preparation of development proposals and filing activities

‣ Coordinating research response to market need[3]

The duration of the drug development process is five to ten years. There is a great deal of urgency to the process, both for the sake of curing human illnesses and to maintain competitive advantage and help the company's bottom line. The relaxed freedom implied by Dr. Mees's comments doesn't fit very well with today's global competition and aggressive march forward.[4]

At Merck, there is considerable individual freedom in the research process, but on a full-time basis, the privilege is limited to those who have shown that they use the freedom wisely. On the other hand, an opportunity is given to everyone to use at least a small portion of their time for personally chosen investigation. This is a way to let serendipity surface.

Another lesson that can be learned from Merck's example that applies to all high-technology R&D efforts is the structuring of a "standard" timetable of sequence of events. Whether it be drugs, computers, aircraft, or whatever, there probably is a logical sequence of events that leads from initial concept through development and production scale-up to product introduction. The steps along the way should be well defined and synchronized so that the elapsed time for their completion is minimized. It should be obvious that the less time consumed in going from concept to market, the more competitive the company and the sooner and greater the human benefit from the new product.

SmithKline Beecham's Strategy

The merger of SmithKline Beckman and Beecham created one of the world's largest drug companies with an annual research budget in excess of $500 million. In developing a company strategy, the managers stated goals that probably should be adopted by all progressive, research-based companies. In the vein of doing the right things and doing them right, they have an eight-point strategy:

1. Focus on the core business
2. Build on competitive advantages

3. Stimulate growth through investment in new products and improved productivity
4. Accelerate new product flow
5. Improve efficiency to be a low-cost producer
6. Design a responsive organization
7. Develop a strong global presence with local sensitivity
8. Be market-driven

Regarding the acceleration of new product flow, the policy of SmithKline Beecham can be summed up by the following company statement: "With shorter effective patent life and growing generic competition, research-based companies need to generate a consistent flow of new products. Once new ideas emerge from the laboratory, required resources are devoted to ensure that safe, effective products reach the market as quickly as possible. Ways to shorten the time between concept, research, product testing and trials, and submission of data to regulatory agencies for marketing approval must be found. This research has led to the development of a set of investment priorities, a structuring of development plans and clinical trials, and worldwide coordination of regulatory submissions."[5]

A Standard Process

Every company that depends on R&D for its growth should define a standard development timetable rather than improvise a timetable for each new product that enters the pipeline. With a well-defined process in hand, efforts can then be applied to streamline it for maximum R&D effectiveness.

Although the specific process would be different for each industry and company, a bare skeleton common to many companies would include the following six phases[6]:

- *Phase I:* Preproject Conceptual Development
  - Identify the need for the new product or service
  - Generate creative ideas to fill the need
  - Study the technology
  - Conduct experiments to prove effectiveness
  - Conduct patent literature search and apply for a patent
  - Test ideas to uncover potential problems
  - Consider ethical issues
  - Select the most promising alternative configuration
  - Conduct a business analysis
  - Define the project
  - Submit the project proposal to sponsor/management
  - Obtain sponsor/management approval to proceed

- *Phase II:* Establishment of Project Organization
  - Appoint a project leader
  - Prepare the project plan and critical path schedule
  - Determine resource requirements

- ‣ Prepare the preliminary design
- ‣ Estimate the project cost
- ‣ Estimate the market demand and revenue
- ‣ Refine the business case
- ‣ Obtain sponsor/management approval to proceed

‣ *Phase III:* Establishment of Feasibility

- ‣ Define the project team requirements
- ‣ Recruit and organize the project team
- ‣ Develop the detailed design
- ‣ Consider product quality, reliability, value, and manufacturability
- ‣ Conduct an analysis of competitive action
- ‣ Refine the business case
- ‣ Build a product sample or service simulation
- ‣ Conduct a performance evaluation
- ‣ Conduct potential problem/risk analysis
- ‣ Obtain vendor quotes
- ‣ Develop the marketing plan
- ‣ Finalize the design and business case
- ‣ Obtain sponsor/management approval to proceed

‣ *Phase IV:* Development

- ‣ Modify the design (if necessary)
- ‣ Refine cost estimates and update the business case
- ‣ Design tooling and manufacturing facilities
- ‣ Design packaging/presentation materials
- ‣ Order tooling and sample quantities of materials
- ‣ Recruit and train development personnel
- ‣ Produce testing quantities
- ‣ Conduct usage trials
- ‣ Prepare advertising and promotion literature
- ‣ Obtain sponsor/management approval to proceed

‣ *Phase V:* Production/Implementation

- ‣ Install tooling
- ‣ Order/receive pilot quantities of materials
- ‣ Produce the pilot lot
- ‣ Certify production process and qualify the product
- ‣ Produce promotional materials
- ‣ Train marketing and customer service personnel
- ‣ Obtain sponsor/management approval to announce product, scale up production, take orders, ship product, and initiate service

‣ *Phase VI:* Project Termination

- ‣ Evaluate acceptance of the product or service
- ‣ Solve initial field problems
- ‣ Document the project
- ‣ Reassign the project team

Of course, any specific application will differ from this outline. However, in a successful organization, this step-by-step process will be clearly defined, with target times for each step. The target times should represent "stretch," but the goals should be attainable. Ideally, upon completion of a successful project on time and within budget, there should be bonuses for the project team members who have contributed to achieving the goals.

Streamlining the Process

Achievement of stretch goals not only involves attentive coordination of activities with prompt action when delays are threatened; it may also mean taking risks. The main purpose of frequent reviews of project progress in relation to the project timetable is to obtain early warning of problems. Some factors that could upset the timetable are results of experiments that reveal unexpected technical problems, loss of key personnel, delay in receiving critical materials or equipment, and postponement of meetings with key people. The project leader must be resourceful and take action to overcome such problems.

Some additional ways of accelerating development time and streamlining the process are:

- Wherever possible, conducting activities simultaneously rather than sequentially
- Applying extra resources (i.e., additional people or overtime) to activities on the critical path
- Incurring the risk of starting a successor activity before the predecessor activity is complete (if possible)
- Engaging more highly skilled people
- Subcontracting certain activities
- Expediting management reviews

Risk Management

On occasion, the project leader must take risks to keep the project on schedule. That is to say, he or she must act with insufficient information to make a good decision. The risks taken should be calculated risks, not blind ones. In other words, the information that is missing to make a good decision is clearly recognized and is either too costly, too time-consuming to obtain, or simply unavailable. The outcome of experiments and tests are typical examples. In these situations, whenever possible, there should be a contingency plan or fallback position in case the needed information, when it finally becomes available, is negative. Of course, if the risk is still too great to tolerate, then the project should be aborted or at least modified.

Unknowns that can turn into unpleasant surprises include: technical solutions that don't work as expected; experiments and tests that fail; unanticipated side effects or by-products; loss of key people; materials that do not arrive on time; being eclipsed by an unanticipated, superior product announcement or patent application by competitors; market research indication of a lack of customer acceptance; greater-than-estimated development or product costs; and reliability, quality, or produceability problems.

Although having standard times to execute a standard process is an important project management tool for planning R&D projects, it would be foolish in many cases to expect rigid conformity, especially where uncertainties are involved. To have realistic expectations, it is useful to simulate the project schedule network using one of several simulation techniques. A project simulation should indicate the minimum, most likely, and maximum times a project should take along with a time probability distribution. GERTS, SLAM, and the All-Tech Project Simulator are available software packages that can simulate project duration time distributions.[7] Also, many project planning software packages have the capability of answering "what if" questions posed in the form of input variations.

In planning R&D projects, it is important to identify risks—that is, to define the technical, cost, and market elements. Included as part of the project activity list should be efforts to obtain missing technical, cost, and market information. If, as indicated above, this information is unknowable, then steps should be taken to mitigate the risks.

In the R&D environment, one way to mitigate risks is to conduct redundant development paths with the thought that if one approach doesn't work, perhaps the other will. There can be multiple redundancies. Of course, this approach costs more, but it may be worth it for the sake of reduced risk and elapsed development time. One of the simulation approaches mentioned above could indicate the value of redundancy.

R&D Effectiveness Measurement

How does one measure R&D project management effectiveness and know whether it is good or bad in a given instance? The answer is that it is not done with precision. One way is to determine how well each project team adheres to the standard times of the standard process. In all honesty, however, most surprises are negative, not positive, so adherence to the standard process is likely to be exceptional and on the "good" side of what's to be expected. The more uncertainties there are in the R&D environment, the more exceptional standard adherence will be. On the other hand, it is likely that the more uncertainties there are in the R&D environment, the greater the possibility of being unique and perhaps more profitable. Bold but well-conceived ventures should produce dramatically profitable results. That's the way it has been at the leading drug, computer, and electronics companies.

Truth is found in the bottom line. A company can put lots of money into research, but if the effort does not enhance sales growth and profitability commensurately, it can be concluded that the money has not been well spent. Conversely, the high-technology company whose sales and profits are growing faster than the competition's has to have more effective R&D project management. Their people are doing more right things and doing them right. Of course, one year doesn't tell the story. A fair appraisal requires at least a five-year span.

Project Leadership

Studies have shown that the critical success factors in project management are leadership and planning. Some aspects of planning were addressed above. As for leadership, it is often discussed but not well understood because there are no formulas and few reliable guidelines. Yet leadership is readily recognized when present or absent. It has been said that leadership is the wise use of personal power. To many, the word *power* is distasteful. Yet in project management, personal power is very important in getting things done. If project leaders are perceived as unimportant, they have difficulty in getting their fair share of resources as well as team cooperation.

Power has been described as several kinds: (1) assigned power, or power by virtue of position or ownership; (2) reward power, or power to give raises and promotions and grant favors; (3) connective power, or access to powerful people; and (4) coercive power, or power to punish or withhold resources. These are kinds of positional power. There are also some kinds of personal power regardless of position: (1) expert power, exerted by a recognized authority on a particular subject; (2) informational power, by one who possesses special information; and (3) charm or charisma, by someone with an irresistible personality.[8]

Most project leaders have to depend on personal power to propel the project. Often a project leader does not have reward or other types of positional power. The mere assignment as project leader will not win the cooperation of research people if the project leader is not respected as a person. Disgruntled team members have countless invisible ways of getting even with a disliked leader. In other words, the project leader must have sufficient technical expertise to understand and make intelligent decisions with regard to technical issues. He or she must possess or have access to needed information, as well as a charismatic personality, especially if deficient in the other two attributes. The leader's personality must be one that inspires excitement, and he or she must be a person whom others like to please (or are afraid not to). On the other hand, just as there are many different routes to heaven, probably no two successful leaders' styles are exactly alike.

As an example, James Watson, codiscoverer of the DNA molecule and Nobel Prize winner, was made project leader of the $3 billion, fifteen-year, international Human Genome Initiative, the project to catalog all human genes. Obviously, Dr. Watson has the technical credentials. However, he has been characterized as a perfectionist with a low tolerance for ordinary mentalities and has been described as having "carried petulance to a high art." So, charisma comes in unusual packages.

Normally, a good R&D project leader, in addition to being technically competent, has the following characteristics. He or she:

- Expresses enthusiasm
- Is a good communicator and keeps the team informed
- Is a good listener
- Makes decisions promptly
- Has and follows project plans
- Expresses urgency
- Builds team spirit
- Has a vision of the outcome of the project that is communicated to the team members and gets their commitment
- Anticipates problems and is a good problem solver
- Knows how to obtain needed resources
- Does not change project goals capriciously[9]

This is a list of project leader "dos." There are also some "don'ts." A good project leader (and project sponsor) tries to prevent any "start-stop-start-stop" handling of research project activities. Often company management or other project sponsor is not sure what it wants the project to achieve and may wish to modify or postpone some aspect of the project after it's under way. While perfectly understandable in many situations, it should be realized that such action is very disruptive and demoralizing to the research worker who is deeply committed to the project. So whenever possible, the mission should be clear from the outset and remain that way until the project is complete. It is recognized, however, that discoveries along the way may call for a change in mission definition. Also, discoveries elsewhere can raise the priority of other projects that will compete for the same resources.

Good project leaders also do not ignore the project timetable. If they do, others will conclude that they needn't give the schedule much attention either. Research workers would prefer not to have their "feet to the fire" to produce results, so they tend to resist timetables and schedules. Yet if accelerated product introduction timelines are to be achieved, a high level of schedule discipline is essential. Good project leaders support this idea.

Project Planning Software

Project planning software has changed the way projects are managed. This has been the case for many years in the construction industry and among defense contractors. It is now also the case in the research laboratory. There are a number of packages available that are valuable in the laboratory environment. Mouse-driven PC packages (MacProject) are useful for conceptualizing single projects of up to forty activities. Other PC packages (like Super Project, Microsoft Project, or Project Workbench at the low end and Primavera at the high end) are useful for planning and tracking larger projects and allocating the time of research personnel working on several projects. A mainframe system (like Artemis) is needed to plan, track, and allocate resources appropriate for a large multiproject environment.

The use of project planning software formalizes the planning process. Detractors claim this rigidity is one more threat to the laissez-faire environment necessary for creativity. This is an ever-present danger, but that threat is balanced by a better response to competitive pressure overall. Better planning of experiments and tests, which constitute the bulk of R&D effort, should help to speed up the R&D process.

The heart of project planning and a requirement of every software package is the compilation of a project activity list. This list, arranged in sequence with a critical path calculated together with elapsed and working time estimates, defines the scope of the project in an unambiguous way. The schedule also enables an optimum allocation of resources to projects. The standard process described above provides the framework for compiling the activity list.

But every project has its special concerns and potential problems. These should be "smoked out" at the outset. There is a problem-solving set of activities that is applicable to almost any potential problem. These activities should be made part of the plan. Again, the formality demanded by software use helps assure the inclusion of these problem-anticipation-solution activities in the plan so that problems don't arise as unpleasant surprises. Letting project software provide accurate, comprehensive, and timely status reports results in uncovering problems while they are small, leading to more prompt remedial action and quicker completion of the project.

Doing the Right Thing

While project management focuses on leadership and planning, the topic of managing research projects for maximum effectiveness would not be complete without consideration of the process for selecting projects for R&D. Doing the right thing should be compatible with the strategic plan of the company. A step-by-step process for compiling an R&D project list is as follows:

1. Define where the company is now in relation to its major goals (such as total sales, profits, and share of the market).

2. Define where the company will go over the next ten (or more) years if there are no new products.

3. Define where the company should go in the next ten (or more) years. (The difference between the results of Step 2 and Step 3 is the *gap*.)

4. Compile a large list of possible projects that capitalize on the company's strengths, together with an estimate of potential sales, required investment, and probable success. This is an intensely creative process that should have the input of marketing, customers, and manufacturing as well as research. A conference to generate these ideas should be held at least annually. New product ideas should be safe, ethical, and represent a new, good value for consumers.

5. Prioritize items from the list so that the *gap* is filled year-by-year. Easily achieved ideas, projects already under way, and very promising breakthroughs should be given top priority. The prioritization process should also have input from a variety of sources.

6. Initiate new projects. These would be the highest priority items identified in Steps 4 and 5. More projects than will fill the *gap* should be initiated because a percentage of the projects may fail or take longer than expected.

Notes

1. Eastman Kodak Co., *Journey: 75 Years of Kodak Research* (Rochester, N.Y.: Kodak, 1989).
2. Merck & Co., *1989 Annual Report* (Rahway, N.J.: Merck, 1990).
3. Stephen S. Hall, "James Watson and the Search for Biology's 'Holy Grail,'" *Smithsonian* (February 1990).
4. R. G. Henry and D. M. Erb, "Worldwide Research Project Management," 1989 *Proceedings of the Project Management Institute* (Drexel Hill, Penn.: PMI).
5. SmithKline Beecham, *1989 Annual Report* (Brentford, Middlesex, England: SmithKline Beecham, 1990).
6. PMI Standards Committee, *Project Management Body of Knowledge* (Drexel Hill, Penn.: PMI, 1987).

7. Bernard W. Taylor III and Laurence J. Moore, "R&D Project Planning With Q-GERT Network Modeling and Simulation," *Management Science* (January 1980).

8. Douglas Peters, *Cross Functional Teamwork* (Mound, Minn.: Douglas Peters Assoc., 1986).

9. Hans J. Thamhain and David L. Wilemon, "Anatomy of a High-Performing New Product Team," 1984 *Proceedings of the Project Management Institute* (Drexel Hill, Penn.: PMI).

32

R&D Project Management: Adapting to Technological Risk and Uncertainty

Lee R. Lambert
Lee R. Lambert & Associates

Achieving a sensible, beneficial, and cost-effective application of project management in the research and development environment can be as difficult and challenging as the technical problems the researcher is attempting to solve.

Senior management, with a focus clearly on the business aspects of the task at hand, looks to the project management process for assistance in "controlling" the research and, along with it, the cost and schedule associated with the project. Unfortunately, especially for these business-driven managers, the use of project management does not provide the panacea for the problems that historically rear their heads when dealing in an environment of uncertainty and risk. Any effort given the distinction of being classified as an R&D project is, by definition, filled with uncertainty and its accompanying risks. This condition is a given. Otherwise, it wouldn't be called an R&D project.

In assessing the applicability of using the project management process and in determining the degree to which the process is implemented, the amount of uncertainty and risk associated with the specific project must be thoroughly understood. Project management can't be applied in the same way to all R&D projects. The greater the level or degree of uncertainty, the more carefully the utilization of project management techniques must be evaluated. Once this applicability assessment is complete, the project management tools and techniques selected must then be conscientiously implemented and monitored to assure that the maximum benefit-to-cost ratio is realized and maintained throughout the life of the project.

Selecting the most appropriate project management tools for R&D is no easy chore. It is clearly a misnomer to view R&D as a single component process. Realizing the maximum benefit of project management requires the user to recognize the subtle but critical differences between the R and the D. The life cycle of an R&D project can realistically be divided into three distinct phases, two of which are research and one of which is of development. The Phase I research (R) phase is exploring, or "basic."

The Phase II research (R) phase is feasibility, or "applications." Phase III—the development, or D, phase—can best be described as refinement, or "optimization."

As further clarification, when considering the many variations of R&D project management applications, the potential user must understand that there are considerable differences in the technical scope and management needs depending on the type of project being undertaken. There are two major types. Type 1 involves product-oriented R&D projects, which are conducted in support of the development of a new product or to facilitate the improved performance of an existing product. Type 2 involves information R&D projects, which are initiated to gather, manipulate, and analyze data; support conclusions; and eventually produce a formal report for publication as information for private organizations or government agencies.

Although the Type 2 example does clearly produce a product—a report—the output itself rarely passes beyond Phase I of the process. However, the contents of this R&D-generated report may well serve as a catalyst for additional R&D targeted at product development or product improvement.

Type 2 projects realize benefits from selective application of project management techniques. Caution must be exercised to avoid overapplication. Any extensive or rigid use of project management techniques, beyond that which will be discussed for Type 1–Phase I activity, most likely will prove counterproductive and could actually impede Type 2 progress, rather than expedite it.

The consideration and selection of appropriate project management tools and techniques for application on Type 1 R&D projects and the associated phases are the primary focus of this chapter.

Application Considerations

The world of research and development is a stimulating and exciting place to spend a career. Brilliant minds produce a constant flow of bright ideas—ideas that promise products that improve the environment in which we live and at the same time generate huge profits for corporations. The flow of ideas seems to be endless. Unfortunately, only a few of the seemingly great ideas are able to survive the challenge of moving through the product development flow cycle. As depicted in Exhibit 32-1, idea input is relatively unrestricted: Any good idea is usually accepted into the cycle. The role of an R&D project is to bring realism to the process and to substantiate which ideas are truly feasible and will, in fact, have significant social and financial impact on the marketplace.

Since it is critical not to stifle creativity by limiting the number of ideas that are allowed to enter the process, it is imperative that the evolution of each idea is carefully managed to assure proper balance of resource utilization and timely decisions regarding the idea's advancement to the next phase of the project. Using the project management process improves a manager's chances of "turning off" the idea faucet at the appropriate time, therefore maintaining focus on those few ideas that present the highest return-on-investment (ROI) opportunities.

As the traditional life cycle of an R&D project progresses from an idea to an actual new or improved product, it passes through the three distinct phases cited earlier. The benefits realized from utilizing project management techniques increase rapidly as a function of, and in direct proportion to, the reduction of uncertainty.

Exhibit 32-1. Product development flow cycle.

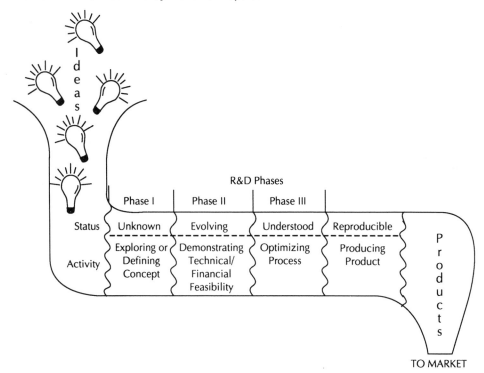

(See Exhibit 32-2.) It should be recognized that the project management process is founded on the concept of fundamental structure and disciplines—two words that literally send chills up the spine of most research professionals. Experience shows that when the use of project management concepts is suggested to a researcher, likely responses are "Project management doesn't really apply. My project is unique," or "Project management is too constraining. It stifles creativity."

Those comments often are made with limited understanding and appreciation of the powerful benefits of properly used project management tools. But for those researchers spending the majority of their time investigating ideas in Phase I or pre–Phase I, these or similar project management application disclaimers may have merit and should be properly considered. However, it has been demonstrated that even the most basic research effort, with its associated high levels of uncertainty, can realize important benefits from selective and common-sense–based use of some of the elementary project management tools and techniques—specifically, work breakdown structures (WBS, of vertical or hierarchical relationships) developed to the third level and network logic flow diagrams (horizontal or work flow relationships) without critical path considerations, but with third-level WBS efforts' dependent work input-output relationships established.

Phase II and Phase III both realize substantial returns from the use of a project management approach. Clearly, Phase III (development) stands to realize the highest returns as the level of uncertainty typically reaches its lowest point in this later phase.

Exhibit 32-2. Benefits of utilizing project management techniques.

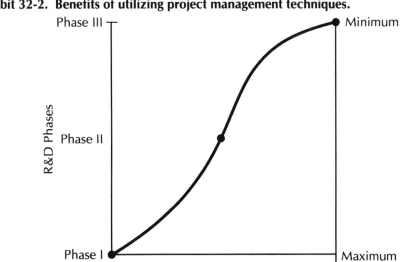

Applications in Phase III have proved that the effort devoted to developing project structure and using management discipline begins to pay big dividends.

The type and sophistication of the application of project management to any R&D project is often dictated by the form of project organization structure (POS) being employed by the organization undertaking the project. Many POS variations exist, but two specific approaches seem to be most popular and suitable for the R&D environment. The first approach is the multidisciplined/functional project team with a strong marketing representative serving as project manager. This approach can be defined as market-driven or product-focused.

The second organizational approach frequently used is again a multidisciplined/functional team, but with the most critical or challenging technical area representative filling the role of project manager. This approach is best described as functionally driven or technology-focused.

Both of these organizational options have proven effective, although recent experience has shown that the balance has begun to shift to the market-driven approach. Because the basic content of the project substructure is the same for both approaches—that is, the same technical areas of R&D are involved and the technical contributors face the same challenges—the responsibility for achieving a smoothly operating and productive project team falls squarely on the shoulders of the assigned project manager.

In either configuration, the project manager must possess excellent communications, negotiation, and influencing skills. In most cases the project is conducted under the restrictions that come with operating in a matrix environment. The project and its contributors often fall victim to the dreaded "two-boss" syndrome, where perceived or actual higher priority technical challenges or "pet" projects threaten to impact the original project's resource commitments. History indicates that most technical researchers assigned to support a specific project continue to respond to their "home" functional organization manager's request for contribution. Oftentimes, this "back home" support is provided at the expense of the project to which the researcher is assigned. Project managers must be aware of this condition and take steps to minimize its impact on the project. These steps include holding regularly scheduled meetings with the team member's functional boss to discuss performance and contribution as well as perceived personal and professional development needs; obtaining agreement for formal input into the assigned professional's performance review and suggested salary adjustment; and obtaining agreement to discuss any planned or actual change in commitment level as early as possible.

A third project organizational configuration—although used much less frequently on R&D projects because of the significantly higher cost associated with this approach—is that of a stand-alone, dedicated, multidisciplined project team or, as some call it, task force. In this case the theories of product- and technology-driven projects become one. The project manager for this task force approach may be drawn from any part of the parent organization, with the selection criteria emphasis being on project management experience and/or hierarchical position. The project manager on a task force effort must have the organizational clout or reputation to facilitate productive cooperation from the various factions of the parent organization.

Making the Process Work

Regardless of the project organization employed, the types of project management tools or techniques selected, or the sophistication of the project management implementation, ultimately two factors hold the key to how big a contribution project management makes to the R&D project: (1) clarity and understanding of the project's goals and objectives, and (2) the commitment to and understanding of the project management process by people—the users of the process.

Perhaps more than any other type of project manager, those charged with the duty of managing R&D projects walk a precarious tightrope, constantly adjusting to maintain the delicate balance between technical, time, and cost considerations, in hopes of avoiding a potentially fatal fall. The importance of establishing well-defined technical objectives early in the R&D project can't be overemphasized. The number of failures resulting from poorly defined goals and objectives is second only to the number caused by inability to solve critical technical problems. The early objectives for the R&D project are oftentimes generated by the marketing organization. It is imperative that before these early objectives (including performance criteria and physical characteristics) are finalized, the appropriated technical experts have ample input opportunity as well as thoroughly review and concur. Agreement or buy-in by the technical staff that will be held responsible for delivering the final results must be gained very early in the process. Failure to obtain this buy-in results in a condition of catch-up from almost the first day of the R&D project.

Everyone recognizes how important it is to freeze project scope. In R&D projects this is extremely difficult to accomplish. As research is undertaken and results analyzed, the scope of the project requires adjustment to accommodate the findings. Project management *does not* eliminate this condition. However, the project management process does allow the project manager to recognize the need for scope change and provides the ability to assess the potential impact of any scope change much sooner than would have previously been possible. In R&D projects, as illustrated in Exhibit 32-3, the sooner the better when it comes to modifying the project scope!

Once the project's objectives, target time, and cost constraints have been clearly defined and understood by the appropriate team members, the project management process should provide the mechanism or conduit for moving forward. As stated earlier, the role of project management in Phase I is limited. However, as the project enters the late stages of Phase I and prepares to move into Phase II, the project management process begins to play a bigger role.

The efforts to assure that maximum advantage is realized from using the project management process on R&D projects focuses on six key areas.

1. Refinement and expansion of the Phase I WBS. All required work tasks must be identified and the appropriate responsibility assigned. This expansion effort includes a clearly defined scope of work for each detailed WBS element (approximately five to seven levels) and the time and resources required to complete the scope of work assigned at those lowest WBS levels.

2. Refinement and expansion of the Phase I integrated work flow diagram. The detailed work tasks identified in the expanded WBS must be incorporated, and there must be development and incorporation of time estimates for each working level WBS element. This produces a critical path schedule for the project. Where possible, the work flow should be optimized through the use of overlap or lead/lag dependent relationships, but on R&D projects, utilization of the overlap or lead/lag scheduling technique should not be overdone. While the approach can result in notable projected

Exhibit 32-3. Assessing the impact of scope changes.

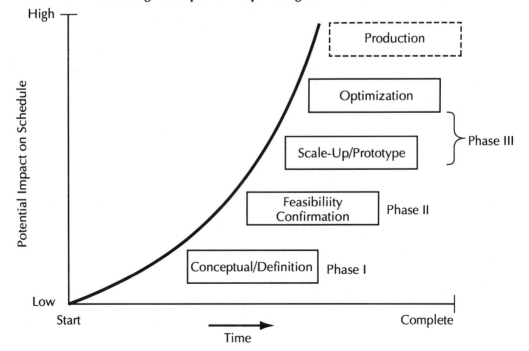

time savings, it often significantly increases the risk associated with starting one task before another task is completely finished. In R&D projects the uncertainty factor can have a major impact on the actual value or contribution of this technique.

3. Identification of all organization/technology interface dependencies where any form of input-output relationship exists. Any critical decision points that may have significant impact on the smooth flow of work on the project must also be isolated. The integrated network diagram is the most effective project management tool for accomplishing this important activity. These interface points and key decisions must be closely managed throughout the life of the R&D project. The result of technical breakthroughs, technical problems, and the accompanying actions taken should be analyzed in regard to these interface and decision points.

4. Development of fallback or contingency plans and approaches in those areas where the initial planning process indicates that a high level of uncertainty exists or a great deal of technical risk is obvious. These contingency plans should be developed *now*—not when the problem actually presents itself. Too often in R&D projects there is no attention given to anticipating problems and making allowances for dealing with the little problems early so they don't become big problems later. This contingency planning method may actually result in some redundancy in the project. Parallel research efforts should be considered when the project can't afford the loss of time associated with investigating research options in a linear mode. If two or more promising solutions to the same technical problem exist and none clearly has a better chance of success, simultaneous research may be warranted with the potential outcomes of each option carefully considered in the planning and analysis of the total R&D project.

5. Establishment of a comprehensive material and equipment needs list in the first few weeks of the project. The ordering and obtaining of special materials are two of the most important activities supporting a successful R&D project. Wherever possible, obtain backup materials with similar technical characteristics. To the extent financial resources allow, procure spare material and equipment as reserve in the event some material is out of specification, equipment failure occurs, or the need to repeat research investigations is required. The lead times for achieving this material and equipment procurement must be factored into the planning process. Overlooking or ignoring the potential impact of not having the required material or equipment are common shortcomings of R&D project managers and have resulted in numerous project failures.

6. Preparation of a schedule for the various technical reviews that are necessary during the life of the project, once the WBS has been expanded and the logic network diagram has been completed, including the identification of a critical path. In addition to the normal technical reviews that occur on an R&D project, internal and occasional external or third-party peer reviews should be incorporated into the plan. The pride of ownership or closeness to the research being conducted often results in tunnel vision on the part of the researcher. These independent reviews and the comments that result serve as a sanity check for those deeply involved in the research process. Effective use of this peer review approach facilitates the early warning mechanism that is so critical to achieving quality R&D output within the most reasonable time and cost considerations.

The world of business is understandably cost-driven. However, in R&D the overemphasis on planning and managing costs can lead to less than quality R&D output. Granted, the reality of organizations precludes what was once known as the blank check mentality, where research essentially said, "Tell me what you want and when I'm done I'll tell what you get." Money was not a major factor. Those days are gone forever. But R&D project managers (and business managers) must remember that you can't control innovation and creativity. You can put some boundaries around R&D, but you can't, with any confidence or semblance of reality, provide precise estimates of time, resource, and budget needs.

With this fact in mind, the R&D project manager should consider range estimating whenever possible. This technique suits the R&D environment very well. This range estimating approach is effectively used for planning project cost or time requirements. The normal range estimate is plus or minus 10 percent of the base estimate, but as the degree of uncertainty or technical difficulty increases, the range expands to account for the unknown.

Business managers within organizations performing R&D projects should recognize the value of allowing this range estimating approach. Essentially, range estimating provides an opportunity to incorporate contingency into the R&D project plan. If this contingency consideration is not addressed and clearly stated, experienced R&D project managers simply bury it in the estimates that are provided for business management use. This lack of visibility prevents realistic management of the range and results in less than effective utilization of money and time. Additionally, the ability to recognize problems and take early corrective action is seriously compromised.

Technology-Based Earned Value

The concept of earned value (EV) has become extremely popular in the project management environment. The EV approach comes from the cost/schedule control systems criteria (C/SCSC) and is normally applied to large projects where management can use dollars as the common denominator for planning, statusing, analyzing, and forecasting the work tasks required to accomplish project objectives.

Projects with substantial R&D content have often found the use of the traditional dollar- or cost-based EV techniques too cumbersome, too restrictive, and considerably less than effective. Despite the relatively bad experience with EV on R&D projects, there is a modified EV approach that has demonstrated the capability to provide realistic, accurate, and timely technology-based information for R&D project managers and task managers without relying on dollars as a data element.

The technology-driven EV approach relies on developing and combining three independent "point value" data elements to generate the project's technical performance measurement baseline (PMB). The three critical components of the R&D EV methodology are: (1) the position of each task on the project's integrated critical path schedule; (2) the technical difficulty of each research task, as assessed by the individual responsible for achieving the specific technical objectives; and (3) the task's relative risk to the successful and timely completion of the project, as assessed by the managers of the respective technical expertise areas involved.

The assignment of total EV point values for each task is determined based on the following factors:

FI. *Position on the Critical Path Schedule*

- ▸ on critical path   30 points
- ▸ ≤ 10 days off critical path   25 points
- ▸ ≥ 11 days off critical path   15 points
- ▸ ≥ 50 days off critical path   10 points

FII. *Technical Difficulty*

▸ Phase I: Exploring	The high level of uncertainty associated with Phase I research severely limits the benefit of using an EV approach here.
▸ Phase II: Applications	3–5 points
▸ Phase III: Optimization	2–4 points
▸ Production (if included)	1–3 points

FIII. *Project Risk*

- ▸ All project tasks   0–5 points

To determine any task's EV point value, the formula is very simple: FI(FII + FIII) = EV points. Using this formula, the maximum value for any one task is 300 EV points, and the minimum for any one task is 10 EV points.

When the proper values have been determined for each task, the point values are assigned to the calendar month in which the task is scheduled to be completed. It should be noted that since EV is awarded only when tasks are completed, the shorter the individual task duration, the less distortion of the plan-to-actual comparison database. Subjectively determined EV "progress points" can be awarded as work proceeds, but before actual completion. Although possible, this approach is not highly recommended unless the use of intermediate progress measurement milestones are incorporated into the plan. Once all task point values have been properly assigned to a planned completion month, a project PMB curve (similar to a cost plan curve) is generated as shown in Exhibit 32-4.

As technical tasks are completed, value is earned. The total EV for the individual or current month, or the total for the cumulative-to-date period, can be determined and then compared to the expected achievement point value represented by the PMB.

These EV plan-to-actuals comparisons can be generated and analysis conducted for the project total or any subdivision of the total R&D project, i.e., by individual task, by technology or functional group, by product component, or even by individual responsible research investigator.

This unique application of EV to R&D projects provides management information that is, by its very derivation, clearly consistent with planned technical work and that work that has been accomplished. Obviously, the EV integration of planned effort and actual accomplishment relies heavily on input from the project research professional. The R&D project manager serves as the catalyst for the development of the EV data and as a coordinator and/or integrater of the EV data at the various project

Exhibit 32-4. Performance measurement baseline.

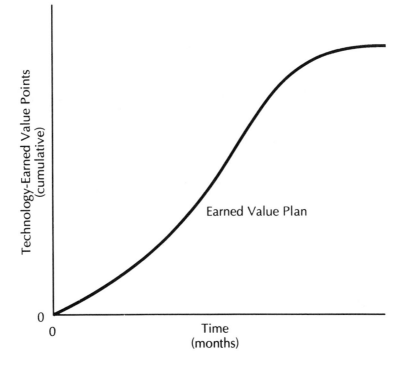

summary levels. To realize the full range of benefits from this EV approach, it is imperative that the WBS is properly structured and carefully numbered to facilitate the many different "information sorts" requested for management use.

Two years of experimental use of technology-based earned value was conducted on a sophisticated R&D project accompanied by the author. This application has validated the process and repeatedly demonstrated its versatility in the R&D environment. During the two years of use, the EV data generated have been extremely accurate in illustrating the true status of the project and reflecting the impact of problems and corrective action taken.

33

The Behavior of Knowledge Workers on R&D Projects

Jacques Marcovitch
University of São Paulo

Antonio C. A. Maximiano
University of São Paulo

R&D activities offer a fertile terrain for the use of project management techniques. This is so because most R&D activities begin and end within a planned frame of time and cost and are aimed at solving specific problems involving various degrees of investigation. However, project management techniques do not apply directly from other types of activities to R&D projects, because R&D projects are different. And they are different for many reasons. One reason is R&D people themselves, and they are the major subject of this chapter.

R&D People: Are They Really Different?

The behavior of knowledge workers, as R&D people are often called, is perhaps the most fascinating and controversial theme in the field of R&D project management. It arouses the interest of behavioral science scholars, R&D managers, and above all, the professionals themselves. From a management point of view, this interest is related to the need to understand R&D professionals, their attitudes, and their career aspirations in order to implement the correct human resources management policies and to ensure the best of the R&D workers' potential contribution to the company's effectiveness.

Some of the reasons why R&D people are said to be different to manage from other work groups appear to lie in the difference between so-called college offer and organization demand. By *college offer*, we mean the peculiar set of attitudes that technical schools influence their students to develop. By *organization demand*, we mean the requirements of professional organizations, encountered once those students leave school and enter the work world.

The College Offer

The personality traits that most scientists and engineers have in common, the values that they share, and the ways in which they are trained to think and work account for peculiar behaviors that have been studied and reported by many authors.[1]

The following remarks are propositions rather than conclusions reached on the behavior of professionals—specifically, young electronic engineers—in a study on Brazilian R&D projects. Whether these propositions hold true for other countries or even other R&D settings remains a matter of investigation and discussion. It must also be understood that these comments are the authors' interpretations of answers to questions made to R&D directors and project managers.

▸ *Professionals tend to value a product's technical merit rather than its organizational and business implications.* This means that technical people are genuinely interested in making products with the highest scientific and technological quality possible; other considerations come later, if at all. The higher the quality of the schools from which the students graduate, the stronger this attitude is. In addition, individuals of great intellectual ability who hold degrees from excellent colleges tend to be demanding toward themselves, their colleagues, and their work. In other words, the greater the demands imposed upon them during their college years, the more demanding they become in professional life.

▸ *Professionals tend to value individual solutions.* This appears to be a consequence of the selection and teaching methods that are used in good quality college education. Since the student is individually requested to accomplish highly complex academic achievements, what counts is the personal solution that he or she gives to the problem and the extent to which this solution reflects a personal and not a group actualization. The more challenging the problem, the more pressing the search for the solution. This reinforces the spirit of the artisan in the technical professional, which makes him or her willing to leave his "technical fingerprint" on the end result. As a possible undesirable outcome, some R&D people may develop an attitude of refusal to accept other people's ideas and points of view, especially when they come from "uneducated" people.

▸ *Professionals are methodical, analytical, and rational.* This is the attitude that results from being trained to translate every problem into manageable variables and parameters, and to try to solve problems with formulas and techniques that maintain a cause-and-effect relationship. (This is a behavior trait that scholars can greatly benefit from, since R&D personnel tend to be extremely receptive to self-analysis when requested to engage in it. However, this trait does not help to solve "people problems," only to understand them better.)

▸ *Professionals may develop an introspective behavior that may be a consequence of their artisan attitude and of the complexity of problems.* It is not unusual for a student studying to become a scientist or engineer to work for days with little rest until a problem is understood or solved. Students and R&D people accordingly train themselves to concentrate on problems with little possibility of being diverted. One cannot say that this helps people to become extroverted. In addition to this, professionals may also develop specific languages that both reflect the need for precision and are a means of excluding people from the "inner circle."

The Organization Demand

Once graduated and in the market, professionals are confronted with the need to comply with the requirements of life in organizations, as well as with the needs of organizations that have a survival drive and often an orientation toward effectiveness or profitability, regardless of their being public or private. Business organizations, however, tend to give more emphasis to the requirements described below, which we call organization demands. The question addressed in the specific cases presented below is whether "organization demand" and "college offer" are convergent.

▸ *Products with business merit.* Organizations require products that have been developed taking into account a market, a client, and the client's needs, as well as being profitable—which does not necessarily mean projects with the highest technical quality or the proper motivational appeal from the professional's point of view. The professional's and the management's concept of what project to work on and on the schedules and resources needed to attain a satisfactory solution to the project problem do not always coincide. These are not only potential sources of conflict but also serious problems in the organization of project teams, since R&D people are able to exert a great degree of self-direction in the choice of which projects to work on.

When there is no possibility of choice, the alternative may be the "smuggled project." This is what R&D people call experiments and even larger projects that have not been authorized by management, but that R&D workers undertake from mere personal curiosity or because they think the projects should be undertaken in the company's interest. "When we do not succeed in convincing management that the project is important, we 'smuggle' it into someone else's project, often a client's project," says one engineer, "and sometimes management pretends not to see." Good management policy? Hard to say. After all, not all companies can afford to budget basic research, which would solve this problem.

▸ *Group solutions to problems, within time and cost limitations imposed by the organization's budgets and schedules and commitments to clients.* Organizations generally have little use for individual and independent solutions. Instead, business organizations require collective solutions that are conducive to products that reflect many individual contributions. These must take into account several aspects of their operation, especially the production-marketing-service cycle.

▸ *Sensitivity to the emotional dimension of human behavior.* Organizations are above all "people systems" that emphasize the requirements of life in common. Consequently, professionals are required not to abandon their rational attitude, but to complement it with the ability to estimate and deal with the impacts of their own decisions and behavior on their colleagues and subordinates. This is especially so when people are in management positions.

▸ *Initiative and expression.* It is unlikely that a person without minimum communications skills would be able to live within any organization, much less effectively perform a managment job. These skills are required in any organization, be it public or private, and not only business organizations with an R&D function. Therefore, the ability to move toward this profile is required of anyone willing to start an organizational career. This is a much greater need for someone taking a management position, not only because this person must reason within a new frame of reference, but must also induce his or her subordinates to do the same.

The Transition to Management

Good project managers with technical backgrounds are not hard to find; otherwise there would not be so many scientific and technical achievements coming from so many public and private organizations. However, the transition from the professional to the managerial role is not always easy to accomplish.

In addition to a possible difference between college offer and organization demand, there are some other peculiar problems in this transition. Among them are the following:

▸ *Lack of management knowledge and tools.* This is the most obvious drawback that makes difficult the transition from professional to manager. It is not uncommon for a person to be promoted to a management position without having been properly prepared. To help to solve such a problem in its earlier stages, the University of São Paulo and many other Brazilian colleges offer one semester of "Fundamentals of Management," in order to provide future professionals with at least an understanding of organizational requirements and the business environment. And of course, there are always R&D management development seminars, which are a very popular trend in Brazil as well as in other countries.

▸ *Fear of loss of technical identity.* Managerial activity invariably brings about all but a termination of technical activity. In lower-level management jobs, the person may still be partically a technician, but as he or she climbs the ladder, more likely management absorbs the total work time. Along with the fear of being unable to stay up-to-date, the person may actually be rejected by those whom he or she is supposed to manage.

It is not proposed here that management and technical professions are in totally separate worlds. As a matter of fact, the contrary may be true, as suggested by the experience of many notable organizations that have first-class scientists at their top management positions. Unfortunately, most people and organizations still seem to experience difficulty in balancing the two.

▸ *The ghosts of old projects.* Frequently a new manager is haunted in his or her day-to-day managerial activities by the old projects in which he or she had a technical assignment. This may make the manager feel the temptation to continue working as a technician and prevent him or her from properly concentrating on the new managerial duties. Many newly appointed technical managers also have an inherent difficulty in abandoning the professional, specialized role. They are likely to lose sight of the "big picture" and try to interfere in technical details of the tasks of project personnel—much to the latter's resentment.

▸ *Lack of motivation.* Some other problems in R&D projects occur in the staffing function. Among them is the fact that scientists, engineers, and even technicians find it difficult to take part in projects that they consider involve obsolete technology. They typically prefer to be assigned to state-of-the-art projects and may even refuse servicing "old" projects in the field. This may not be a problem in Europe or the

United States, where technical staffing power abounds, but it poses a major setback in the process of team building in a country where there is short supply of this kind of personnel.

It may be difficult in some cases to find people to fulfill management positions, since some professionals are specialty-oriented and may have little if any organizational orientation.

Special Problems of R&D Projects

In addition to the distinctive features of their human resources, R&D projects usually pose some other very special management problems to their direct supervisors and to people at other decision levels. Among them are the following:

▸ *Which activities are projects?* It is not uncommon that R&D managers and personnel find it difficult to distinguish projects from other types of activities and consequently to have problems making the decision as to whether or not to use a project management approach. The only solution is to come to an agreement on a certain number of criteria to tell real projects from projectlike activities that are to be managed along the functional lines of the organization. These criteria have been the subject of other writings.[2]

▸ *How do you link laboratory and factory?* R&D projects demand a strong linkage between laboratory people and factory people, which is not always the case. Sometimes, however, good solutions come by accident. In one computer company, the story is told of a production supervisor who took sick leave and had to be replaced by a project manager, who had developed the project that was just entering the factory phase. "Things worked amazingly well," said the engineering vice-president, "so we decided to make it a policy of appointing R&D project managers as supervisors of initial production."

Types of R&D Projects

R&D projects are different not only in that their people pose special problems, but also because they may lead to nothing. Let us take a closer look at this concept, focusing on the division of R&D projects into two major categories along the science and technology spectrum.

Research-Oriented Projects

Research-oriented projects are the open-ended projects at the science end of the spectrum. They are open-ended to the extent that the project manager and team do not know what they are going to find—or whether they are going to find anything at all. Medical research, space and marine exploration, research into subatomic particles, and the search for superconductive materials and their potential uses are examples of this kind of project.

Since the search for knowledge and development of new technologies are the end products, the key feature of these projects is uncertainty. Therefore, failure may be a measure of success, because failure shows that a given path of investigation has proven ineffective and that something else has to be tried. The widely publicized descriptions of how the Swiss IBM team reached their formula of superconductivity is a very good example of the trial-and-error method that is often employed in similar undertakings.

Consequently, projects of this type are better evaluated when their long-term results are considered. And the result is often the development of technical capabilities instead of material products. This does not mean that management-type control of schedules and budgets is not important in these projects, but it is harder to accomplish and has only secondary effects.

Development-Oriented Projects

New product development and engineering projects are different from research projects. In research projects, people have a greater degree of certainty about what they want to accomplish, and the project is a way of going from a known problem to a little-less-than-known solution that depends on the employment of available technology. On the other hand, in development-oriented projects, the problem may be the attainment of a new state of technology.

The degree of familiarity that goes along with these closed-ended projects, at the technology end of the spectrum, does not imply an automatic condition of success as a result. Factors such as the ability to understand the problem correctly and interpret input data from potential end users usually interfere either positively or negatively with the strategic level of project planning, which is the definition of the end result to be achieved. The quality of operations planning, specification and procurement of parts, and assembly tends also to be a critical factor. This was dramatically shown in the U.S. space program with the *Challenger* shuttle accident and the Hubble space telescope fiasco.

Notes

1. F. L. Harrison, *Advanced Project Management* (Hants, England: Gower, 1981).
2. S. P. Blake, *Managing for Responsive Research and Development* (San Francisco: Freeman, 1978); Patrick L. Izanhour, "How to Determine When Project Management Techniques Are Required," *Project Management Quarterly* 13, No. 1 (March 1982), pp. 31–38.

Section XIII

Launching New Products and Build-to-Order Projects

34

Faster New Product Development

Milton D. Rosenau, Jr.
Rosenau Consulting Company

Companies introduce new products in a variety of ways, ranging from the chaotic to the systematic. While successful results are obviously the payoff, it is unwise to rely on luck to salvage an unorganized procedure. Although you can also obtain your new products from external resources, if you do so you usually must share some of the expected profits.

Unstructured Approaches

Unquestionably, any new product development effort must be preceded by or initiated with an idea for a new product. This idea can range anywhere from a vague notion to a specific and detailed construction. Exhibit 34-1 reveals two sources of ideas: a real need and technological capability. When the idea for a new product is generated because someone has devised a solution to a market problem (market pull), you are more likely to have a commercial success. In this case, you find or create a solution to a sharply targeted goal. For example, many products created in response to market pull are incremental improvements over existing products. Ideas derived from a technological capability (technology push) are less likely to be commercially successful. In this case, you have a solution looking for a problem, and you must search for potential users whose unmet needs can be satisfied at acceptable cost. If you can find or create such an unmet need, your technology push product can sometimes have great market success, as demonstrated by 3M's Post-it Notes.

Generating this idea may require time and effort, but in this chapter I intend to deal only with the process and time following the articulation of an idea. Theodore Levitt has observed that you can put inexperienced people together in a brainstorming session that produces exciting ideas that show how little importance new ideas themselves actually have. Nevertheless, there are companies that mistakenly believe

Exhibit 34-1. Two sources of ideas.

A Real Need	Technological Capability
Market-driven External orientation Better success rate	Technology-driven Inward orientation Higher failure rate

that an idea will easily become a successful new product. Thus, once a superficially attractive idea has been articulated, such a company pushes ahead, but it forgets or overlooks required steps and slips from its desired schedule. Sometimes unstructured development leads to seizing the opportunity to demonstrate an early prototype at an important trade show; later, the company is unable to manufacture production quantities quickly, which can invite a more nimble competitor to beat it to the market.

Another problem with the chaotic or random approach is that it fosters changes in the new product's specifications every time anyone has an embellishment. Without a formal structure in which to freeze specifications and evaluate changes, creeping elegance often runs amok and nothing is ever introduced because the far-off hills always look greener.

New Products From External Sources

You can introduce a new product quickly if another company (or individual) has already completed its development and sells it to you. You might use licensing, a joint venture, outright purchase, or some subcontracting arrangement to obtain the rights or the product itself. However, there are two problems with this.

First, the other party must have already spent time on the development. That time is still a part of the limited window of opportunity in which the product is feasible. Although your own involvement may be short, this does not necessarily speed up the entire process. Second, the most important reason to introduce new products is to increase your company's profits. When you obtain a new product from an external resource, you have to share some of the profits, so unless the procured new product offers you some synergistic leverage, you're unlikely to make as much profit as you would with an internally developed new product.

In the development partner approach, the other company may have people you lack, its people may have pertinent experience, or it may have faster equipment. Conversely, it requires time to locate a development partner, and using one does not increase your own capability. Even with a strong internal new product development, you should not forgo this external route entirely. In fact, a proactive search for products that you can acquire is normally worthwhile.

General Characteristics of Phased Approaches

Phased approaches are widely advocated for the development of new products. A phased approach can improve comprehension, provide a sharp focus for the work, improve speed, and reduce risk. It can also help maintain challenge and motivation in an inherently lengthy new product development effort, since there may be several major intermediate milestones on which to focus. Nevertheless, it is important that the phased approach you adopt (there are a number of them) be tailored to your business to avoid problems such as excessive detail. Any new product development process should include some intermediate reviews to try to ensure that the corporation's resources are being deployed in the most effective manner.

Most phased approaches to new product development have time sequences, as depicted in Exhibit 34-2 under (a) and (b). In these illustrations, there is a time gap between phases (whatever their specific content). Exhibit 34-2 (a) illustrates the so-called relay race, in which a baton is passed from one runner to the next. Here, the transfer is from one department to another, which exacerbates the cross-functional conflict. The other four situations in the exhibit depict the use of multifunctional teams from beginning to end, which I will stress in more detail later in the chapter. It is clear that eliminating dead time between long phases, as shown in Exhibit 34-2 under (c), is an improvement over the first two approaches.

Recently, even overlap of several phases has been advocated, as shown in Exhibit 34-2 (d). In this new product simultaneous work is carried on by several departments (such as marketing, engineering, and manufacturing). It is claimed that this approach is much faster than other approaches. This is probably true in the special case where

Exhibit 34-2. Five phased new product development concepts.

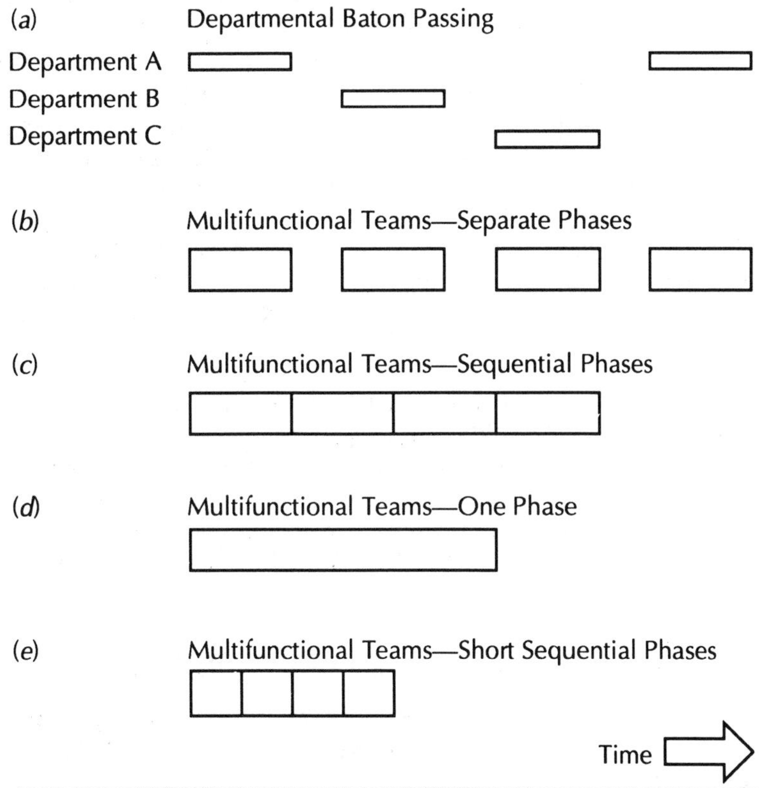

(a)   Departmental Baton Passing

Department A

Department B

Department C

(b)   Multifunctional Teams—Separate Phases

(c)   Multifunctional Teams—Sequential Phases

(d)   Multifunctional Teams—One Phase

(e)   Multifunctional Teams—Short Sequential Phases

Time

the new product is similar to a previously developed product and where the same experienced team is available. However, that is a rare situation.

No rapidly growing company can afford to dedicate its most experienced people to working on only one new product at a time; in fact, these people are likely to desire career growth, in which case they would subsequently want to head their own new product development efforts. If the experienced team is not available or if the product being developed is unique, there is greater risk that activities will be overlooked in the mad scramble to finish. The cost of correcting a runaway new product development project can be enormous.

Part of the alleged attraction of new product rugby is the absence of strangulating procedural obstacles that sometimes accompany a phased new product development procedure. However, no one has to erect unnecessary paperwork hurdles, and it is possible to have a simple phased new product development policy.

Any new product development project (or any other corporate activity) will be delayed by the need to prepare an elaborate presentation, conduct a lengthy review, or await a tardy decision. The problem is with the elaboration and tardiness, not with the phased approach. Reviews have to be thorough, not elaborate, and the resultant decision has to be made promptly. Despite the allure of new product rugby, especially the cooperative teamwork (which I strongly support), I am not aware of anyone who favors unsystematic, unmonitored, unchecked, unplanned, or undirected new product development—quite the reverse. As a practical matter, if you must play new product rugby, be sure to have some brief intermissions in which to review the effort so as to lessen the risk.

In distinction from the first four concepts illustrated in Exhibit 34-2, I propose shortening the total new product development process by having short, sequential phases as illustrated in Exhibit 34-2 *(e)*. By analogy to rugby, this can be thought of as a soccer or a basketball game (without a halftime recess) in which a cooperative team moves together toward a goal. This offers lower risk than overlapped phases. I eliminate (or minimize) dead time between phases to shorten the total process. Most companies will find that the shorter phases, in which the required work is completed very quickly, are realistically achievable.

Finally, I propose separating the feasibility work and the maintenance work from the time-critical new product development process. These two activities are important, but the first, feasibility, cannot be rigidly scheduled. The latter, maintenance, cannot start until the new product is introduced.

The specific practices in different companies with which I am familiar apply various portions of phased procedures. In one industrial product company, the steps or phases are: (1) idea, (2) feasibility phase, (3) specification phase, (4) breadboard phase, (5) engineering prototype phase, (6) pilot lot phase, (7) production, and (8) follow-up. In one customer product company, the approach is as shown in Exhibit 34-3. A process business might use laboratory feasibility, process development, pilot plant, semicommercial or midsize batch, and full-scale commercial production phases.

Three Reasons for Using a Phased Approach

There are three important reasons why you should use a phased approach for your new product development efforts: (1) improved understanding, (2) greater urgency, and (3) reduced risk.

Exhibit 34-3. Five-stage approach used by a consumer product company.

Stage 1: Ideation
- Idea generation
- Preliminary criteria screening
- File search and secondary data investigation

Stage 2: Concept testing
- Concept and alternative product positioning
- Concept evaluation

Stage 3: Product testing
- Prototype development
- Consumer product testing

Stage 4: Test market
- Marketing plan
- Test marketing and evaluation

Stage 5: Commercialization
- Market expansion

---

1. *Improved understanding.* Comprehension of the participants is improved when you use a phased approach. It is much easier to understand a short-term program and the steps involved in it than to understand a much longer and necessarily more complex program. In a short phase it is possible to start out with all the steps you have to undertake explicitly articulated and identified. In addition, you can easily list the required steps that comprise the new product development process in their time sequence. Then, your development team is not likely to be suddenly surprised by the requirement to undertake some development activity for which they had not made allowance. Exhibit 34-4 illustrates that an ambitious new product development goal must necessarily have some initial uncertainty about the exact objective and when it will be achieved. In a single phase, however, you only have to accomplish certain things, not the entire totality of steps required to introduce a new product. Distraction is reduced because you don't have to deal with unrelated future activities. Thus, a short phase is easier to understand than the entire new product development process. To put this differently, a specific near-term goal is easier for people to understand than a long-term, and thus somewhat imperfectly defined, goal. The target is both more precise and less remote.

2. *Greater urgency.* Not only are the participants more likely to have a better schedule plan for a fairly short phase, but they are also less likely to let the clock run without making progress. There is a greater sense of urgency. It is hard to let the first month of a three- or six-month phase slip by without making progress. Conversely, participants can all too often exhibit low schedule urgency at the start of a three-year product development effort.

3. *Reduced risk.* Short phases have lower risk. Not only is the schedule risk less, but the financial risk is also less. You approve only small development increments at

Exhibit 34-4. Phases of a new product.

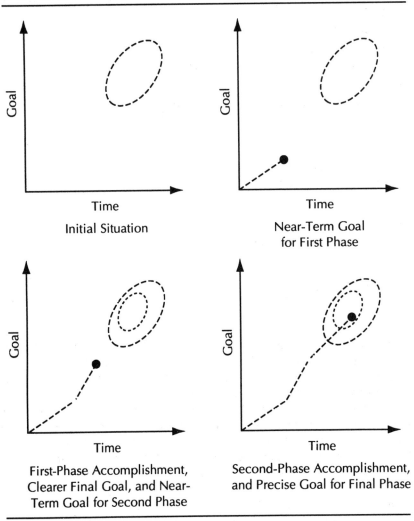

Initial Situation

Near-Term Goal
for First Phase

First-Phase Accomplishment,
Clearer Final Goal, and Near-
Term Goal for Second Phase

Second-Phase Accomplishment,
and Precise Goal for Final Phase

any given time, so these are inherently less costly than the entire development effort. This obviously limits risk. (Also, you have approved only a limited, specific effort, so there is less temptation to change specifications during a short phase.)

Approving a phase does not guarantee that anyone must approve the subsequent phases. Clearly, one does not approve a phase without an expectation that one will approve subsequent phases. However, if the goals of an approved phase cannot be achieved, then you do not have to approve subsequent phases. The goals of a specific phase on a particular new product development effort might in fact be achieved satisfactorily, but approval of the next phase can still be withheld to reallocate resources onto a higher priority or more promising new product development effort. In approving the entire development project at the beginning, there is both a long period of time for the entire development cycle as well as a large amount of money. Consequently, management has less assurance that the time and money will be efficiently used.

Conversely, in a phased approach, where each incremental work package is itself relatively small, there is less opportunity to use resources aimlessly and ineffectively, especially since the approval for additional, subsequent work is made only after milestones are successfully achieved. You can stop work in the middle of a phase if an unexpected, revolting development occurs. Similarly, one of the benefits of any phased approach is that you can discontinue less promising efforts even if they are progressing in a fully satisfactory way. This allows your corporation to concentrate its limited resources on the few most promising new product development efforts. It is much better to produce a few successful new products than to work with great energy on many and produce none.

Overview of Approach

The general phased approach that I favor is neither a rigid straightjacket nor a magical solution to the complex process of developing a new product, but it does avoid many of the common pitfalls that can needlessly delay the new product development process.

In broadest overview, there may be three activities involved with the introduction of a new product: (1) feasibility, (2) development, and (3) maintenance. Obviously, an idea for a new product, which may range anywhere from a vague notion to a specific and detailed construction, must precede or initiate this sequence of activities.

Exhibit 34-5 lists these three activities and also shows four development phases: (1) optimization, (2) design, (3) preproduction, and (4) production. These four phases are illustrative, not prescriptive. You must have optimization to establish firm specifications; and this can be followed with one or more phases leading to routine new product shipment. These four phases, or others better suited to your business, divide the total development activity, which is often lengthy, into short periods, each of which has a specific, limited goal, as the exhibit shows. Thus, each phase involves only a portion of the work required to introduce a successful new product. The total budget for all development activities in the company is its new product development budget less those amounts reserved for feasibility and maintenance activities. (The new product development budget is often called the research and development budget, even if very little research is truly included.)

A more general view is shown in Exhibit 34-6 (in which the specific numbers at the bottom depicting the number of ideas and relative cost are meant to be conceptual rather than exact). This highlights four other aspects of my phased approach.

1. While it should be easy to initiate a development activity, you filter out less promising efforts as you move progressively through the phases, which helps you concentrate your company's limited resources on the better opportunities. (Or, to put it differently, you have to kiss a lot of frogs to find one prince.)

(text continues on page 417)

Exhibit 34-5. Activities and development phases involved in the introduction of a new product.

Activity = Phase =	Feasibility	Development				Maintenance
		Optimization	Design	Preproduction	Production	
Start point	Start with possibility.	Start with product idea and proven technology.	Start with specification.	Start with complete documentation and breadboard.	Start with prototypes and debugged documentaion.	Start with problem.
Goal	Goal is proof of technology.	Goal is to put specifications in "concrete."	Goal is to prove specifications can be met.	Goal is to prove documentation is complete and accurate.	Goal is routine shipment of product.	Goal is to solve problem.
Some typical activities	*Technology critical* Laboratory experiments, breadboards, analysis. *Process critical* Bench and pilot scale trials. *Market critical* Exploratory market research.	Secondary market research and test marketing or primary market research completed. Musts and wants clearly defined. Market segments and competition understood. Technical trade-off studies, including crude production cost estimates.	Product's promotion basis developed. Preproduction prototypes built or pilot line operated. Production cost estimates and schedule completed. Discounted cash flow analysis.	Final product name selected. Advertising to trade and users planned. Sales and distribution plans completed. Completion of designs, parts list, scale up, formulas, quality assurance plan, technical service requirements, test specifications, and vendor qualifications. Obtain final regulatory compliance, if required. Order long-lead tooling.	Initiate production. Complete service and training manuals. Complete all sales support materials, advertising, and other promotion.	Limited quick fixes where cost or quality justified.

Key decisions	Continue to invest in or drop exploration.	Select most attractive combination of product attributes for initial market introduction of product.	Whether production is justified.	Production methods, tooling design, and vendor selections.	Production rates, inventory levels, and similar issues.	Authorization of a new product (improvement) development program, when justified.
End point	Output is report plus bench model, chemistry, analysis, software module, or similar conclusive demonstration.	Output is approved specification and critical path schedule for development.	Output is complete production documentation, working breadboards, and critical path schedule for preproduction.	Output is production of prototypes, final production documentation, and production schedule.	Output is product.	Output is minor revision and/or new idea.
Schedule	Typically 1 to 24 months.	Typically 1 week to 3 months.	From critical path network diagrams			Typically 1 day to 6 weeks.
Management authorization	Approve only 3 months at a time.	Approve entire phase	Approve entire phase; review quarterly.	Approve entire phase; review quarterly.	Approve entire phase.	Approve entire project.
Market introduction	No product plan, but efforts must support strategy.	Product introduction date only approximate.	Product introduction quarter set.	Product introduction month set.	Product introduction date set.	
Budget	Total budget perhaps 5–10% of NPD budget.	Total budget is 100% of NPD budget less amounts dedicated to feasibility and maintenance.			Standard factory cost.	Requires 10–25% of NPD budget.

(continues)

Exhibit 34-5. (continued)

Schedule vs. cost-risk trade-off options	Can authorize procurement of long-lead items for design without commitment to undertake design.	Can authorize procurement of long-lead tooling and other items for production without commit- ment to undertake preproduction.	Can authorize procurement of long-lead tooling and other items for production without commitment to undertake produc- tion.

General notes on the phased approach:

1. Some products may not fit the normal procedure and must be exempted from the details (but not the spirit).
2. The start of any phase is not a commitment to initiate the next phase.
3. For every production phase project, there might be:
   1.1 Preproduction phase projects
   3 Design phase projects
   10 Optimization phase projects
4. Maintenance phase work should be assigned to a separate sustaining engineering group or else the people working on new products should not be scheduled for more than 75–90% time effort.
5. Feasibility phase projects should be limited to some preset fraction of the new-product development budget. The reports on each project must be circulated widely within the corporation.
6. Reviews between and within phases must be prompt, and go/stop decisions must be rendered promptly.
7. The approval authorization levels to initiate phases must be established to be consistent with other assigned responsibilities.
8. Checklists for specification ingredients should be established for use in optimization phase projects.
9. If the specifications are obvious, the optimization phase can be shortened to a one-day meeting of the triad team for approving it and creating the critical path schedule for the design phase.

Exhibit 34-6. General overview of phased concept.

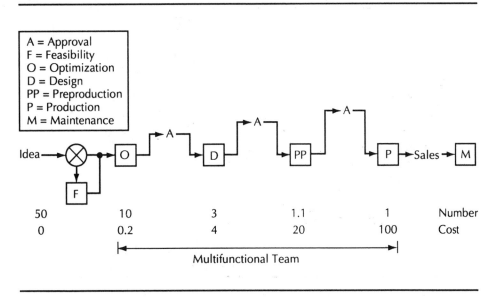

2. You can afford this selectivity because the earlier phases have much lower costs than the later phases.
3. All departments or functions should be involved in each phase.
4. Approvals require higher levels of management as the cost risk increases, which often induces companies to search (unsuccessfully, as far as I know) for algorithms and quantitative devices to try to replace qualitative judgments.

Three other points are also illustrated.

1. Ideas can arise anywhere.
2. You might (although rarely) kill a new product effort that was in the production phase.
3. There can be a short (or long) gap after the development activity ends and a maintenance project starts.

A fast new product development effort is one in which the allowable schedule for each of the four development activity phases is as short as possible and where there is no (or a very short) time gap between the end of one phase and the start of a successor. This was previously illustrated in Exhibit 34-2 *(e)*. To put this somewhat differently, one of the activities during a phase is to ensure that appropriate management personnel are suitably aware of the project's status. It then requires only one management meeting both to approve the end of one phase and to authorize the initiation of the successor.

Exhibit 34-7 provides a partial picture of the new product development work that might be under way in a corporation during an interval of time. Authorization of a feasibility activity is not a commitment to launch a new product or even to undertake

Exhibit 34-7. Example of new product development work under way in a corporation.

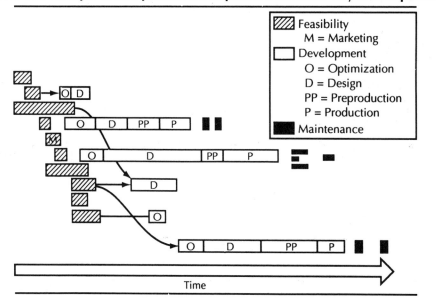

any development activity, as illustrated by many feasibility activities that end without any direct follow-on effort. While feasibility activity work is normally done by a technology department (such as engineering, R&D, or software), sometimes it might be done by the marketing department to investigate a totally new market, as suggested by the M in one feasibility activity bar in the exhibit. In other situations, feasibility work might be done by the manufacturing department to investigate a new production process.

The optimization phase must be separate from and precede the design phase because it is impractical, if not impossible, to make a schedule or budget for the design phase until the product specifications have been set, as illustrated in Exhibit 34-7. It is clearly possible to omit the optimization phase if the product specifications are obvious and you do not require market research before initiating the design phase, as illustrated by one project in the exhibit that commences with the design phase. Undertaking the optimization phase is normally, but not necessarily, a commitment to undertake the design phase. However, undertaking the design phase does not constitute a commitment to produce the new product, even though there may be a schedule for a proposed market introduction. The preproduction activity normally is a commitment to produce; however, you can stop a development activity in the preproduction phase (or even in the production phase). You might do this, for instance, if you learn that a competitor has just introduced a similar or better product at a selling price lower than your intended price.

You will have a better track record meeting your new product development objectives if you recognize that feasibility efforts and maintenance efforts must be allowed for but made separate from the time-critical new product development efforts themselves. Feasibility and maintenance commonly require the same human and physical resources that the new product development activity requires. The three new product development activities in Exhibit 34-7 that reach completion all illustrate subsequent maintenance activity. If your company does not recognize that reality, then you will find that schedules for new product development efforts are not met. There are two reasons for this, and they are different depending on whether you look at feasibility or maintenance.

If there are no separate feasibility efforts allowed for, then new products that require new technology or move into totally new markets require inventing on schedule—which, in fact, does not occur on schedule. The feasibility activity, as important as it may be, may require an invention or technical breakthrough that cannot be scheduled; thus, the most that can be done here is to identify that requirement, provide resources, and develop a sense of urgency. To put this differently, the goal of feasibility efforts is to give you a stockpile of proven technologies in the form of breadboards, bench-scale chemistry demonstrations, completed analyses, or, perhaps, new debugged software algorithms. Or, you may have feasibility activity efforts to evaluate unknown markets or to experiment with new manufacturing technology.

After you start to sell a product, maintenance activity may be required. Typically, a user, a customer, or perhaps the sales department discovers that there is some problem. When this happens, you must solve the problem immediately. In many cases, the people who did the original product design can solve the problem most quickly. Unfortunately, this is especially true when the problem arises due to a software defect (or bug), because the documentation is often defective or nonexistent. If you have not allowed for this reality, then your next new product development effort will suffer because the people who work on it must go back to firefighting on the prior product's maintenance problems. Realistically, therefore, you must either have a separate maintenance group (commonly called sustaining or continuing engineering), or you must not schedule the development effort of subsequent new products on the assumption of 100 percent availability. You should examine your own company's historical record; but, as a guideline, only about three-fourths to four-fifths of the time of your development people is available for development if they must also do maintenance work.

Finally, when you establish a phased approach such as this, you must always permit an escape clause if the new product itself can't fit this exact procedure. For instance, you can extend or recycle any phase, although, as a general rule, this may be a danger signal suggesting that the new product development effort is seriously offtrack. Similarly, you can omit these phases. In your own company, because of your market position, competition, or corporate culture, you can combine or divide these phases differently to provide a procedure that is most useful in your own organization. There is no single right way to carry out new product development. In fact, you may want to have different procedures for different kinds of new product development efforts (for example, totally new to the world, minor revision, and so on). You can create a summary table (such as Exhibit 34-5) for whatever procedure(s) you do adopt, but you have to decide which characteristics and phases to define. From time to time specific cases may require a deviation from your company's general procedure, which is acceptable as long as the key people understand clearly why it is happening. As an example, you can exempt some very small projects from many of the detailed reviews normally given to a larger new product development effort. Obviously, the risk of lack of control for exempted projects is much greater, but that

Exhibit 34-8. Unnecessary delays in new product development.

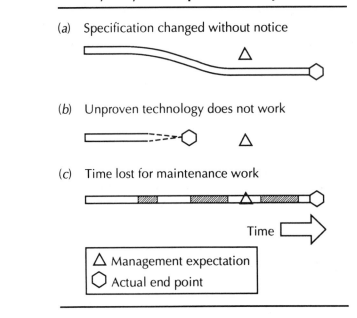

(a) Specification changed without notice

(b) Unproven technology does not work

(c) Time lost for maintenance work

Time

△ Management expectation
◯ Actual end point

risk may result in less expected cost than the certain cost of subjecting very small projects to even a simplified new product development procedure.

Avoiding Unnecessary Delays

There are three frequent problems with new product development as it is commonly practiced which result in delayed market introduction. By adopting the phased approach, you can avoid all three of these.

1. Where they exist, unphased efforts tend to wander, and upper management is invariably surprised that the resulting new product is both later than and not the same as its original expectation. Exhibit 34-8 *(a)* illustrates this unfortunate result.

Obviously, if you install a phased procedure but the product specification is not rigid, the same type of surprise is common. I have heard many senior executives complain that products are frequently introduced late with some key attributes (for instance, the factory standard cost) that are not what they were previously led to expect. One of the reasons this happens is that the specifications are changed during the development effort. However, in a typical case where this occurs, top management is not aware of the changes in the specifications because no flag went up. Thus, there is no visible signal that the development project now has a different goal than it had when it was originally authorized. Therefore, my approach starts with clear specifications that are cast in concrete during the optimization phase. If it is necessary or desirable to change the specifications at some later time during the development effort, then the development team should stop (or kill) the initial development effort. This requires the concurrence of top management. You can then start a new effort, preferably with a new title. The new effort might start at a later phase of development effort, because good work should not be thrown away when you discontinue the original effort. However, unless the specifications at which the effort is aimed are clearly understood, many people will lose time by working in counterproductive ways.

2. New product development efforts sometimes take much longer than anyone wishes because the effort depends on an invention. Unfortunately, inventions cannot be produced on schedule. In some cases, the inventions just don't occur at all, as illustrated in Exhibit 34-8 *(b)*. Although the work within any feasibility activity effort is scheduled, successful results are not guaranteed. That is, you authorize people to do laboratory or market research work for short periods of time (typically three months) consistent with and in support of corporate strategy, but you do not rely upon success. New product development activity may be difficult, challenging, and even lengthy, but it starts only when there is a belief that no problems having unknown solutions will arise. If there are significant unknowns, however, the schedule becomes unpredictable, and feasibility work should be undertaken rather than development.

3. You may have established a reasonable phased schedule for the new product effort. Then, an urgent maintenance problem on a previously introduced product requires work by some of the development team. Exhibit 34-8 *(c)* illustrates the delay caused by this fire fighting, which unfortunately is a common occurrence in many companies.

Compressing the Schedule of the Phased Approach

Phased approaches for new product development have existed for many years. These were adequate in an era where product life cycles were long. Today, we have to salvage and make productive use of the good ideas available in a phased new product development concept, but we must eliminate unnecessary lost time. How do we do that? To start, we strip away the three worst features that delay the conventional approach. That is, we first eliminate lost time between phases, as shown in Exhibit 34-9 *(a)* and *(b)*. I propose the following ground rules to overcome this problem:

▸ The multifunctional triad leading the development team (discussed below) must schedule the end of phase review one month before phase completion; normally, the member from the marketing function on the leadership triad is primarily responsible for this. Then, management has one day to render a stop or go decision; the absence of a stop decision is to be taken by the development team as a go decision. The advantage of this ground rule is that it focuses attention on a success-oriented program, but it gives management the right to redirect or terminate the new product development effort if appropriate.

▸ Each phase is itself made as short as possible. Exhibit 34-9 *(b)* and *(c)* illustrate this.

▸ We preclude the traditional baton-passing problem that occurs when phases

Exhibit 34-9. Avoiding wasted time in new product development.

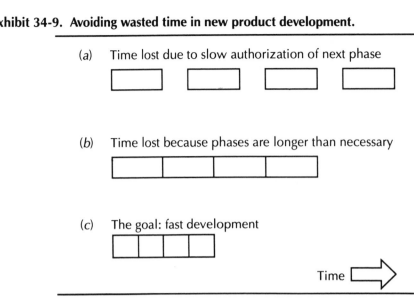

(a)   Time lost due to slow authorization of next phase

(b)   Time lost because phases are longer than necessary

(c)   The goal: fast development

Time

are organized to be run like a relay race. This classic problem with phased new product development arises when one department is responsible for one phase of work. When that department is finished, it hands off its completed work package to the next department, which is then responsible for the following phase of work. The second department naturally blames the first department for doing an incomplete job (whether or not this is the case). Similarly, the first department criticizes the second department for either failing to appreciate the good work that it did or for destroying it. This baton-passing approach diminishes interdepartmental harmony rather than promoting it. This is a very serious and unfortunately prevalent problem in many companies that have phased new product development procedures. However, it is not inherent in any phased approach and can be entirely avoided by involving every functional department in each phase.

Leadership by a Multifunctional Triad

Because of the problems with baton passing and interdepartmental disharmony, I advocate that each new product development effort be managed by a multifunctional triad consisting of a key person from the marketing, technology (which includes research, development, and engineering), and manufacturing departments. The first among equals should normally be the person from the marketing function. He or she must have superb people skills to ensure that the other two triad team members are proactively cooperative.

Although a multifunctional triad provides the leadership for all work, the amount of work done by a particular department does tend to vary from one phase to another. For example, most feasibility activity work is done entirely by the R&D department (or the research department, if it is separate from the development department). However, the feasibility investigation of an entirely new market could be primarily a marketing department effort, and the investigation of a totally new manufacturing process or technology could be primarily a manufacturing department effort.

Unfortunately, there is a practical problem, as one observer puts it: "My experience with manufacturing causes me to doubt how useful they can be in traditional business organizations in feasibility activities, including evaluating new manufacturing processes or technology. Typically, manufacturing doesn't want to do anything that will divert attention from ongoing production." This attitude is prevalent. In one company, a member of the manufacturing department said: "We don't want to spend time working on new product development activities that aren't going to get to manufacturing." The result, of course, is that they also do not work on or contribute to those others that eventually do reach manufacturing. This normally causes the designs to be difficult to manufacture or of high factory (standard) cost. In many cases the design has to be done again, causing a painful delay. There is a solution, which is to treat manufacturing engineering work as a development expense (which is really what it is on a new product development effort), rather than a manufacturing (overhead) cost. If you do this, you are able to hire more manufacturing engineers to participate in the early phases of new product development, thus saving a lot of subsequent waste.

The most crucial phase for equal participation by all functional departments is optimization. Even market research, a primary responsibility of the marketing function, is of better quality if both the technology and manufacturing functions also participate. Conversely, the technology departments, especially engineering, do most of the work in the design phase; however, extensive participation by manufacturing engineering helps. In the preproduction phase, manufacturing engineering is the department most actively involved, and, obviously, the manufacturing department is primarily involved in the production phase. Nevertheless, the entire development is led by a multifunctional triad to ensure that nothing is done to create avoidable problems.

Maintenance activity is similar to feasibility activity in that one department may be almost entirely responsible. This is obvious if a separate substaining engineering department is established. However, some maintenance problems can be most quickly solved by another department. For instance, the marketing department could change advertising claims or lower the product's price if several buyers complained that some features were not as specified. This might be a quick fix until engineering and manufacturing introduce a product modification to overcome the shortfall. Thus, every phase of the new product development effort involves the participation of all the key departments, and it becomes a joint responsibility.

35

Innovative Program Management: The Key to Survival in a Lethally Competitive World

David Gordon
University of Dallas

J. Royce Lummus, Jr.
General Dynamics Corporation

As the world becomes smaller and more economically interdependent, corporate survival is rapidly becoming more and more dependent upon successfully competing with worldwide competition for market share. In this lethally competitive environment, innovative program management is the key to survival by allowing organizations to: (1) select the right programs to pursue using sound financial and programmatic success criteria; (2) execute these programs competitively, using methods like integrated product development to speed the development and reduce costs of new products; and (3) help to instill the cultural change of total quality management that allows these methods to work.

The Problem: Lethal Competition for New World Markets

As the world gets smaller, trade barriers are diminishing, and corporations from all over the world are competing for the same key lucrative markets. The Eastern Bloc represents an example. There, rapid change in the political climate means the opening of new markets for which there will be intense competitive pressures. The message is clear. As new markets are created—either from innovative new products or services producing new demands, or from new markets for existing products—the shrinking world will be a battleground for stiff international competition. Survival in this demanding market environment means selecting the right products to pursue. It also means reducing product development cycle times so as to get more new products to the market first, with high quality so that they continue to sell.

Corporations have long understood that the first entrant to a market can often control the market for some time. By the early 1980s, progressive corporations were beginning to understand that to destroy competition, getting to the market first on a consistent basis, especially on high-tech products, might even be more important than performing on budget. Honda used this strategy in the early 1980s against Yamaha in the "motorcycle wars," when it replaced 113 models in eighteen months, the equivalent of turning over its product line twice. This totally devastated Yamaha, which could not match this blitzkrieg because it had not prepared or structured for time-based strategy.[1] Since then, Honda and a number of other industry-leading corporations are using this strategy effectively to control markets. Honda cut new car development from five to three years (and has led the new car market in the United States); AT&T cut phone development from two years to one; Navstar cut truck development from five to two and a half years, and Hewlett-Packard cut computer printer development from four and a half years to twenty-two months.[2] Not only are these corporations reducing the time to market, they are also achieving reduced production costs on the manufacturing floor with less rework—and they are turning out higher quality products to boot.

A research report[3] supports the notion of the value of reducing time to market even at the expense of budget considerations. The report indicates that high-tech products coming to market six months late but on budget earn 33 percent less profit over five years than those that come out on schedule. However, products coming out 50 percent over development budget but on time earn only 4 percent less profit than those that come out on time and on budget. By contrast, overrunning production costs by only 9 percent results in 22 percent less profit over the life of the product. Clearly, it is critical to get to market first with a high-quality product! In a recent *Harvard Business Review* survey,[4] fifty major U.S. companies put time-based strategies at the top of their strategy lists and expect it to be one of their most powerful competitive tools in the 1990s. Industry leaders are achieving substantial competitive advantage by selecting the right products and implementing methods to reduce the time and cost to market. To compete, program managers must learn to employ these techniques effectively.

Innovative Program Management Solutions

Selecting the Right Programs to Pursue

There must be a rational evaluation, screening, and selection process for determining which new program opportunities the corporation should pursue. The program manager must understand and utilize this process to select the program to pursue and to gain the support of corporate management. Many successful corporations use a process similar to that shown in Exhibit 35-1. The exact formulation of the process is not as critical as the inclusion of all of the critical elements in the evaluation of the program's potential success.

The suggested process for financial evaluation and selection of new business programs that fit corporate strategic product line ground rules is as follows:

Exhibit 35-1. Program evaluation and selection process.

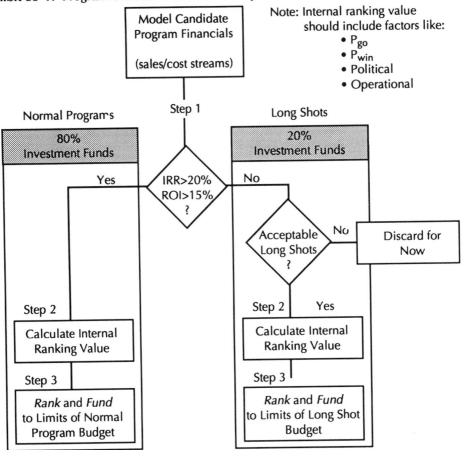

- ▸ *Step 1:* Evaluate internal rate of return (IRR) of potential program by modeling the initial costs and net cash flow stream
- ▸ *Step 2:* For the program with IRR ≥ 20 percent (or the corporate accepted screening value), calculate:
  - ▸ NPV: The net present value assuming a realistic cost-of-capital during program
  - ▸ P_{Go}: The probability of the program being funded and achieving the IRR and NPV
  - ▸ P_{Win}: The probability of winning the program if it does go
- ▸ *Step 3:* Rank and select programs from Step 2 by highest internal ranking value (IRV). IRV = $P_{Go} \times P_{Win} \times NPV$

Consideration of Important Long Shots

Some programs do not pass the financial screening but may still deserve further evaluation. This is primarily due to their potentially high direct or indirect benefits to the corporation despite their inherent cost and risk factors. Some percentage of available new business funds (e.g., 15–20 percent) should be allocated to pursue "long shots." To maximize the likelihood of success, such programs should compete among themselves for long shot funding. It should be noted that approved long shot programs require even more management involvement than those programs passing the normal financial screening.

The program evaluation and selection process is equally important in expansive and regressive corporate climates. In an expansive climate, ample investment capital is available to sponsor new products. However, failure to sponsor the high payoff programs dilutes corporate efforts to penetrate or dominate a market even if the corporation can afford the financial risk. In a regressive climate, investment capital in future programs is very limited, and maximum leverage must be achieved from every investment dollar.

Cutting Costs and Time-to-Market Through Integrated Product Development

Once the program has been selected on the basis of an acceptable predicted probability of success, the program manager faces the critical problems associated with the execution of product development and insertion into the market. As previously noted, one of the most critical of these problems is getting the product developed quickly and to the market first without compromising quality. Building cost-cutting features into the development and manufacturing processes is also key to achieving and sustaining future market share.

The Challenge in Product Development

The traditional product development approach is shown in Exhibit 35-2. This process is made up of a linear series of consecutive steps: market research to develop customer requirements; product design (including research into process design and engineering); manufacturing; testing; and sales and distribution. In each step the work is performed largely in a vacuum by the controlling functional department for the particular stage of development. Traditional functional turf boundaries are strictly observed. The work is handed off to the next step with little or no involvement or communication between the groups upstream or downstream in the process. As a result, the problems that either failed to be solved in the current stage, or that may be catastrophic for subsequent stages, are pushed downstream. Problems eventually must be solved by costly redesign or rework. The work must be returned to the step (group) required to solve the problem.

The result is a very high-cost, time-consuming, inefficient process with many cycles of redesign, scrap, and rework. Product quality is inherently low, and a product may take several passes through the process to meet acceptable quality standards. Not only is the cycle time for the process both costly and long, it also fails to involve the customer effectively in the development process. Another major problem with the traditional process is a failure to provide leverage for solving problems in the early "think-work" conceptual phases of product development, in which most (approximately 70 percent) of the life cycle cost is rendered unchangeable for a given product design.

Exhibit 35-2. Traditional product development process.

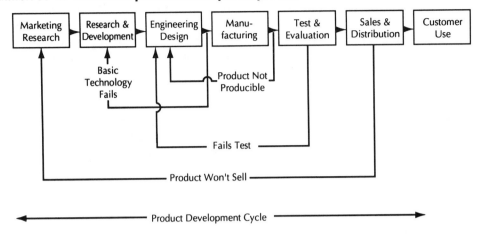

The Solution: An Integrated Process for Product Development

To respond rapidly to customer desires and competition-driven market demands, a new organizational structure and approach is required that signficantly reduces the development cycle time while continuing to reduce costs and improve product quality. Exhibit 35-3 shows such a structure. This parallel process approach to product development requires that all developmental steps prior to manufacturing be performed concurrently by multidisciplinary cross-functional teams. This approach to product development has been called by a variety of names, such as concurrent engineering, design for manufacturability, integrated product development, and fast cycle-time teams. Depending on the nature of the product, applications may differ somewhat in their emphasis but not in their intent: the simultaneous involvement of those disciplines that have an impact on the total cycle time required for product development.

The Need for Total Quality Management

What is required for the cross-functional teams to be effective in achieving integrated product and process development? To achieve their goals effectively, the cross-functional teams must operate within a corporate environment that is dedicated to a total quality management (TQM) philosophy and is committed to the changes in organizational structure required to allow the teams to function effectively. The teams themselves must also be empowered and operate within some basic tenets that have been found necessary for success. These are outlined below.

Establishing the TQM Environment

The corporation dedicated to a TQM philosophy rapidly adopts the use of the cross-functional team approach because the aims and mechanisms agree. TQM is an

Exhibit 35-3. Integrated product development process.

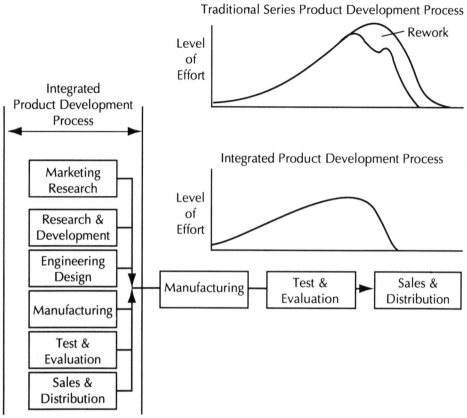

approach to managing that continuously seeks to improve the quality of goods and services by the participation of all levels and functions of the organization. TQM (like the cross-functional teams) recognizes that poor quality results from voids or overlaps of responsibility; solutions are sought by identifying and resolving these voids or overlaps. This commitment to quality means establishing a clear picture of the corporate mission and conducting an analysis of the organization's processes—including its structure, policies, procedures, functions, relationships, resources, products, services, and suppliers—in light of its desire to provide customer satisfaction to both internal and external customers. In addition to a management commitment to achieving a cultural change permeating all levels in the corporation, several key components usually attributed to TQM are:

- ▸ Achieving higher quality products (with rapid response to customer needs and concerns
- ▸ Gaining both internal and external involvement, including that of customers and suppliers
- ▸ Utilizing concurrent engineering and just-in-time practices

- Achieving continuous improvement of products and processes through education and critical process teams
- Utilizing improved methods of analysis like statistical process control and shared databases

The cross-functional team approach is in fact an inherent outgrowth of TQM, in which the critical process teams come together from multifunctional disciplines to solve a specific process problem within the organization, while the cross-functional teams similarly come together to produce a specific product. Total quality management promotes a corporate mindset that continuously questions the value of everything that is being done to see if it adds value. Culturally, TQM means an open door where turf wars and infighting are unacceptable. The commitment is to being jointly responsive and competitive.

Following the Three Principles

Three major principles must be followed if cross-functional team implementation is to achieve an improved competitive capability in a TQM environment.

Principle 1: Follow an Integrated Management Approach

Integrated management literally means that all functions share in the process of managing the product's development.[5] The concept of "upstream and downstream" will fade because all functions are integrated, beginning with concept definition and extending through product development. Accomplishing this level of integration requires significant organizational responsibility changes. For example, if equal importance is attached by the customer, engineering must accept producibility and supportability requirements as equal in importance to performance requirements. Manufacturing, marketing, logistics, materials, distribution, and quality must take proactive roles up front in the design process. In short, equal emphasis should be given to both product development and product process development.

Integrated management also means empowering and facilitating the cross-functional teams. Team leaders must be appointed by management. The team leader does not adopt the role of management decision maker in the traditional sense, but acts as a facilitator to help the team arrive at and implement its decisions. Senior management must be very careful to empower the team, set checkpoints for it, and then step back with the goal of influencing without directly managing the team. Management watches the team's progress and consults with the team's leader, but the team actually works to manage itself to a large extent. In addition, team members should be trained in group process and cycle time analysis. Their training should support them as they perform the systems engineering functions of translating the customer requirements into product requirements, defining team goals and roles, problem solving, and conflict resolution.[6]

Principle 2: Follow the Integrated Product Development Process

A key precept of integrated product development is to create robust, high-quality products that are affordable, producible, reliable, maintainable, and supportable. In this context, *robust* means that the product has built-in flexibility for product evolution or market extensions.[7] As previously illustrated, product and process development should begin during the concept phase, since maximum leverage exists during this segment of the product's life cycle for effectively influencing the quality of the product. The product design and producibility are largely locked in during the early phases with the ability to make changes virtually eliminated by the time the production phase is reached. To further enhance this process, cross-functional teams should not only be empowered; their members should be located together in an area dedicated to the product team. This fosters a team spirit by breaking down functional barriers and speeding the process of interdependence among team members.

Principle 3: Make Customer and Supplier Interactions With the Cross-Functional Team Primary Objectives

The ultimate goal of the cross-functional team should be to develop a product that satisfies the customer. Consequently, customer satisfaction is the ultimate measure of quality.[8] At the outset it is mandatory that the team clearly translates the customer's requirements into product requirements. It is the team's responsibility to seek agreement with the customers on these requirements.

The Success of Cross-Functional Teams

Cross-functional teams have provided real competitive advantage for many corporations. These corporations have learned that cross-functional teams can overcome some of the chronic problems associated with the traditional approach to product development. The use of cross-functional teams and the integrated product development approach provides the following advantages:

- ▸ Reduced time to market with new, higher quality products
- ▸ Reduced total costs because the product is better designed and more producible with less rework
- ▸ A more affordable product that ultimately proves to be more reliable and thus sustainable in the field
- ▸ Early involvement by the customer and suppliers in the design and development process, which builds in market acceptance while simultaneously achieving requirements and schedules

Industry leaders in many varied development and services markets have adopted the integrated product development approach with time-based philosophy at the heart of their business strategy. Users of this concept include Sony, Toyota, Toshiba, Honda, Benetton, Federal Express, IBM, Domino's Pizza, McDonald's, General Dynamics, and Atlas Door.[9] This strategy has enabled some of these companies to virtually eliminate their competition in their respective markets. These companies are not only applying the principles of cross-functional teams to product development, but to sales and distribution improvements as well. For example, Toyota used the process to reduce the time from ordering to delivery of a new car in Japan from six weeks to just eight days.

Notes

1. Christopher W. Musselwhite, "Time Based Innovation: The New Competitive Advantage," *Training and Development Journal* (January 1990).
2. Ibid.
3. *Hewlett-Packard and Engineering Productivity.* Hewlett-Packard report (May 1988).
4. George Stack, Jr., "Time—The Next Source of Competitive Advantage," *Harvard Business Review* (July-August 1988).
5. *Critical Process Team Report on Concurrent Product Development.* Unpublished internal report, Research and Engineering Department, Fort Worth Division, General Dynamics Corp. (Spring 1990).
6. Christopher Meyer, "Reducing Cycle Time for Sustained Competitive Advantage," *Vision/Action: A Journal of the Bay Area OD Network* 8, No. 2 (June 1989).
7. *Critical Process Team Report.*
8. Ibid.
9. *Hewlett-Packard.*

36

Product Development Challenges in the Telecommunications Industry

Sri Sridharan
Alcatel Network Systems

In the business of new product development, the most critical factor is getting to the market quickly. Historically, products that entered the market early with adequate quality and price have proven more successful than products that got to the market later with better quality or price and with more bells and whistles. The idea is to gain market acceptance of a simple version, get the customer response, and then establish enhancement directions. This is not a new idea. Ford's concept of "any color you want as long as it is black" has a similar basis.

The telecommunications market poses additional unique problems. The customers in the telecommunications market have definite procurement cycles and it is critical to meet these needs with the right product at the front end of this cycle. The network is not totally standardized, to allow modular procurements that operate routinely. Systems engineering effort is required on the part of the customer to make the procured systems operational. This leads to a requirement to minimize variations in equipment in order to minimize the systems engineering effort. Therefore, most telecom operating companies select one or two vendors and stick to them as long as the products are functional and the costs are reasonable. The challenge the vendors have is in becoming the candidates for qualification when the customers are ready. This is a moving target depending on customer needs and the status of competitors. Missing this qualification opportunity is just as bad as missing the whole market window. This emphasizes the fact that whatever we in the telecommunications industry do, it better lend itself to reduced cycle time.

Telecommunictations products have evolved over time to become more and more

This chapter was adapted from Sri Sridharan, "Managing Changes in Telecommunication Product Development," *Project Management Institute Seminar/Symposium*, Calgary, Alberta, Canada, October 1990. Reprinted with permission of the Project Management Institute, P.O. Box 43, Drexel Hill, Penn. 19026, a worldwide organization of advancing the state-of-the-art in project management.

complex, requiring higher technology and more integration. The products, therefore, take a longer time and larger investments to develop. However, at the same time the life of products in the field is getting shorter. Microwave radio products in the 1970s and early 1980s had a useful life of eight to ten years before becoming obsolete, but recent products have a much shorter life as a result of the pace at which technology is changing. The cost pressures faced from customers and competitors are also intense. In a nutshell, this means developing high-technology products with high investments in a short period and being able to survive short payback periods and intense price wars.

The objectives are clear: Reduce cycle time. Reduce cost. Extend product life. And in trying to achieve these objectives, don't disrupt ongoing projects.

Meeting the Challenges

This chapter focuses on meeting the challenges of shortening the development cycle, reducing product cost, and extending the life of the product. Approaches to minimizing the impact these might cause on the organization and ongoing projects are also discussed.

Shortening the Development Cycle

Most product development R&D organizations have a product-oriented structure. High-technology product development efforts are normally driven by technical experts who generally do not have project-oriented management skills. The challenge is in creating this project management focus and yet not compromising on quality or technology. The logical answer is getting a project manager to worry about project-related issues. The challenge remains in placing the project manager appropriately. In most construction projects and government-related development projects, the project or program manager heads the whole operation exclusively or in a matrix fashion. But in a high-technology development project that demands just as much technical direction as it does project direction, a creative organizational structure may be required to strike the balance.

Research on project management suggests getting a project manager and giving him or her as much authority as the organization's culture permits. Irrespective of where the project manager is placed and what his or her authority is, there are some significant top-down directives that can be provided to enhance the project focus and to help shorten the development cycle.

- ▸ Develop the schedules with an emphasis on deliverables.
- ▸ Provide the greatest visibility possible to the schedule milestones with focus on near-term goals.
- ▸ Monitor the milestones closely.
- ▸ Celebrate making the milestones.
- ▸ Encourage team effort to minimize and make up schedule slips.

It is important to recognize that there is no good or bad organization structure. The structure evolves from the culture of the organization and the strength and weaknesses of the people available. Some structures are more conducive to functional excellence than the structures associated with project management. When it comes to performing the balancing act between promoting functional excellence and maintaining project focus, it takes leadership and imagination in setting the priorities and providing clarity in mission.

The structure is important. Changing the structure for improving effectiveness is important. The suggestion here is to make a number of small changes over time to position the organization toward success. While living with the nonideal structure, provide the leadership to gain control of the mission, which is to shorten the product development period.

Reducing Product Cost

Design Approach of Developing a Common Platform

Developing an architecture that can be reused to serve future products reduces product cost as well as development cycle time. This requires developing requirements for a product family beyond the first product and developing a common platform that can serve as a base for the entire product family. This might be possible in niche product areas where the growth of the product family can be clearly defined. In speculative markets, defining the direction of a product family can be difficult. Thus, developing the structure for a whole family of products might require doing more work upfront and designing a nonoptimum architecture for the first product. This can have development cost/schedule and product cost implications. But future products will have a definite advantage, not only in development cost and schedule, but also in market acceptance. This is particularly attractive when the product operational in the field can be upgraded with minor swaps and plug-ins. The customers feel they are being benefited when the growth progression is clear, assuring nonobsolescence.

This architecture decision depends entirely on the probability of growth in the product family. If there is high probability of logical expansion of the product family, it pays to develop a platform that will survive the future needs. This is quite evident in the area of personal computers where the power supplies are overdesigned to handle add-on accessories, and expansion slots are provided for memory expansion and interfaces. Computer vendors offer entire product lines that are growable as needed.

This is much like the factors a newlywed couple might consider when planning their first home: make the foundation strong enough to accommodate a second story in the future; include the kids' rooms for the near future; buy large enough heating/cooling units to meet potential growth; route the plumbing and wiring such that the backyard can be adapted to having a pool. All of these cause higher initial investments in time and money, but the life cycle costs and the utility and upgradeablity of the product will more than offset these initial investments.

The challenge here is balancing the short-term objectives of schedule and cost of the product being developed with the long-term objectives of strategic leveraging of the product into a product family by creating a platform with the handles and hooks to accommodate logical growth. The benefits are speedier and cheaper incremental development and a higher probability of market acceptance. The risks are greater initial effort. There is also another possible risk of having to live with an outdated platform and having to be compatible with that platform in all future development. These factors have to be evaluated carefully before making the architecture decisions. It should be noted that making architecture changes during development or building from a nonoptimum must be avoided as much as possible.

Application Specific Integrated Circuits

Application specific integrated circuits (ASICs) have been part of telecommunications systems since the mid-1970s. ASICs are miniature discrete circuits that can be mass-produced economically. The potential cost reduction is great because of the mass production. They help in reducing the space, improving the performance, and improving the reliability of the products. In high data-rate circuits, ASICs are required to perform the operations at very high speed.

The main problem faced is the time it takes to develop the ASIC and the risk involved in making it work in one turn. Identifying and undertaking the ASIC effort early on in the project cycle is important to minimize this risk and retain the cost-reduction directive. There are a number of ASIC development tools available that improve development time. Some help in simulation and testing and can improve the probability of first-time success. Identifying these tools, evaluating the tools for meeting the desired criteria, integrating them into the development process, creating the procedures, and training the users are no trivial tasks. It is recommended that this effort be decoupled from any product development–related activities and managed as a stand-alone project.

Like any other project, this ASIC process improvement project requires resources, time, and money. This should be viewed as an investment in the future and must be undertaken with a definite plan, a set of deliverables, and a detailed schedule. Once the improved ASIC development processes are established and verified, the product development projects are ready to integrate them into their plans. This approach applies to any effort on improving processes that are a significant part of the product development cycle. Combining such major efforts with ongoing development projects ends up compromising both efforts and must be avoided.

All contingency actions must be considered to reduce the risk relating to such custom component development in a project. In addition to simulation, breadboarding and second-sourcing may be used. Parallel effort on achieving the ASIC's functionality using discrete components may be considered for initial product release. Adequate resources must be applied to ensure thorough planning, design, testing, integration, and documentation of the component. The ASICs must be defined in their entirety as early as possible so that a redesign does not delay the entire program. Reuse of already available ASICs with proven performance must be encouraged. The ASIC vendor's capabilities, capacity, and strategic orientation must be thoroughly researched prior to signing the contract. A number of intermediate milestones must be defined in the ASIC fabrication process to enable progress measurement. A detailed test plan must be developed and executed so that there are no surprises while integrating the ASIC to the product.

Extending Product Life

Developing a base product on a hardware platform and initial load of software and then progressively developing variant software to customize or enrich the features proved to be a great way to extend the life of telecommunications products in the past. In the mid-1980s, the software effort on a transmission product was less than 5 percent. Today, the same type of product is designed with software representing about 50 percent of the total effort. This provides the flexibility required in today's products to extend product lines. Also, implementing a given feature using software instead of hardware might reduce the product cost, since in the telecommunications field, fixing software problems is perceived to be easier than fixing hardware problems. If all this sounds too good to be true, it is because getting there is not easy.

There is significant systems engineering effort required in partitioning hardware and software at the systems level, and then integrating and testing the system as a whole. There are gaps in skills that must be recognized and filled in order to perform these tasks. For instance, in the area of telecommunications transmission product development, the systems engineers had always been hardware-oriented, and the software systems types rarely had adequate experience in transmission products. This forces the creation of a new breed of "requirements"-type engineers and "integration"-type engineers. These groups must be developed from the existing base of systems engineers, and this might require some training in software development areas. Even after crossing this bridge, there are lingering problems in synchronizing the efforts. Partitioning into hardware and software can never be clean and complete in reality, particularly when the product evolves through development. Therefore, software development normally has a tendency to wait for the more physical hardware development to gel and become completed. This puts the software development always behind schedule.

Another problem faced is having to produce and maintain a number of hardware prototypes in order to develop the test-bed or platform where the ongoing versions of software can be tested. Therefore, although higher software content lowers the product cost, the development cost can be significantly high. This change of product content translates into changing the skill-mix of the engineering organization and developing a number of new procedures to manage the process. This can be traumatic if it is not planned carefully. Retraining selected engineers, forming the "requirements" and "integration" groups, defining the contents of the documents to be created, and managing the test-beds and the integration process are difficult tasks requiring attention to details. But the transition has definite promise for enhancing the product life.

Conclusion

Telecommunications product development as a whole is facing new challenges. The lead times are getting shorter as a result of unpredictable market windows. Development costs and cycles are greater because of the complexity and flexibility of the products demanded by the market. Product life is getting shorter because of the pace at which technology is changing. There is intense competition in the U.S. market with a number of international vendors creating price wars. To survive these challenges, several changes must be made in the way we in telecommunications do our business.

We must review the organization structure to identify opportunities to bring better project focus and reduce development cycles. Technological solutions like ASICs should be used to bring down product cost. And we must develop a flexible product architecture that can adapt to future requirements, thus extending the useful life of product in the market. These changes are difficult, requiring leadership and vision, careful planning, and strategic implementation. Changes must be phased to minimize the pain. Achieving the final solution might require making a number of small changes in the right direction.

The customers in the telecommunications field are no longer excited about a high-tech gizmo that meets a niche application. They demand a network solution that integrates various types of equipment, supports multiple applications, and will stand the test of time without becoming obsolete. This clearly indicates the need for long-term planning. A living strategic plan that is well understood and established as the basis for defining all projects can do wonders in meeting market needs in a timely manner.

Section XIV
International and Cross-Cultural Projects

37

Managing International Projects

Larry A. Smith
Florida International University

Jerry Haar
University of Miami

As international projects proliferate, the need to identify, distinguish, and respond effectively to a distinct set of managerial requirements is the foremost challenge facing international project managers. Consequently, it is necessary to understand the project management system and consider the unique attributes within the international setting. It is within this framework that this chapter is developed showing an overview of international project management.

Plans

International project management plans are subject to the same threats and opportunities as domestic ones. However, there are a number of additional constraints that shape objectives, goals, and strategies. Basically, foreign environments are more complex. Factors such as political instability and risk, currency instability, competition from state-owned enterprises, pressures from national governments, and nationalism can all interfere with project management planning. Strategy development, therefore, requires that the company:

- Evaluate opportunities, threats, problems, and risks
- Assess the strengths and weaknesses of its personnel to carry out the job
- Define the scope of its global business involvement
- Formulate its global corporate objectives
- Develop specific corporate strategies in the organization as a whole[1]

Recognizably, no prescription can be ironclad. Moreover, the human dimension in project management is of the utmost importance in international projects. Many projects that are technically, financially, and organizationally strong have failed as a result of cross-cultural factors—that is, the inability of project managers and supervisors to comprehend and respond appropriately to foreign environments. As Copeland and Griggs state, project managers and others working around the world must be sensitive to these factors.

> In Asia, the Arab world, and Latin America, a manager needs a warm, personalized approach, demonstrated by appearing at birthday parties and soccer games, walking through the work areas often, recognizing people by name, talking to workers and—even more importantly—by listening to them. In Latin America and China, it is important to drop in periodically for social visits with workers inquiring about their health and morale without mentioning work problems. Without singling out an individual, the group should be complimented liberally to give everyone "face." Evenings out are an integral part of business, most notably in Japan. Plan your schedule so that plenty of time is regularly invested in these personal contacts. Don't depend on memos. Don't be too busy.[2]

With this attitude of requiring greater time for socializing and small talk, time estimates require slightly different input considerations than in the United States. Managers must plan accordingly.

Communications and Information Systems

Time, cost, and performance vary considerably within the international arena. Time is a communications system, just like words and language. For example, Western culture views time as a resource: "time is money." Eastern and Middle Eastern cultures view time quite differently, as do most Mediterranean peoples. Consequently, concepts such as schedules and deadlines, which are essential to project management, are not held in the same regard and, therefore, are not followed as conscientiously as in Western, industrialized cultures.[3]

Western project managers, in particular, demonstrate very little patience for and tolerance of tardiness. The lack of punctuality or obsession with time (depending on one's cultural perspective) can severely affect not only project timetables and deadlines, but also interpersonal relations between home country managers and host country personnel.

Performance information varies as well, since different monitoring devices are used in international settings. Additionally, changes in the external environment can affect the limits of possible performance, which in turn could require a change in performance standards. Consequently, the information reporting in international projects differs in both kind and format, in many instances, from that which characterizes domestic projects.

As Copeland and Griggs point out, in the United States, "information is usually generated outside and flows in to a manager. The system works because responsibility is delegated and initiative is valued." But in Europe and South America—where authority is centralized—the situation is different. It is the manager who must "take the initiative to seek out information and personnel take less responsibility to keep managers informed." A foreigner who fails to understand how information flows in a given culture might not be informed of important decisions.[4]

Another communications factor to be considered is directness. In the United States, one is direct and gets straight to a point. In other words, "we like facts while others like suggestions. We specify while others imply."[5] In fact, in other cultures, the direct route is avoided and even disliked. Sometimes this is because the foreign cohort wishes to establish a relationship before getting down to business and concluding a deal.

Arabs, Europeans, and Asians do not go straight to a point. In France, this might mean that an American attending a business meal must wait for his or her French colleague to enjoy dinner first, without mentioning business. It might also mean that "an American will write a detailed letter with all the facts and plans and a sense of completion and finality. The Frenchman will write quite a different letter. It will be the first in a series, full of subtleties that will be elaborated upon in future correspondence."[6]

Control Systems

Basic to any project management system is a control subsystem comprised of standards, comparison, and corrective action. Control and its associated problems in international projects are much more complex than in domestic ones as a result of cultural, economic, political, and legal environments. Geographic distance, language barriers, communications habits, culture, and differing frames of reference all influence the control subsystem.[7] For example, a lack of understanding and acceptance of a group's cultural values could well impair a manager's ability to evaluate information accurately.

Criticism and how it is expressed can seriously affect managerial control; detailed reporting and tight controls are not accepted in some cultures. For example, in the Japanese culture, maintaining group cohesiveness is more important than reporting a problem to a superior; supervisors tend to solve problems at the group level before referring them to upper management.[8] Essentially, the astute manager is able to negotiate a successful balance between project control imperatives and the reality of the cultural milieu in which the project operates.

Techniques and Methodologies

One of the authors spent five months in China trying to implement project management systems. Before visiting China, he asked the Chinese whether PCs and project management software were available. A firm "no problem" meant that there was a PC *somewhere*, but it was not necessarily working. The Chinese added that if software was brought into the country, they would have no problem making copies since copyright protection did not exist.

This illustrates the fact that inadequate education and training in the international setting results in a group of managers who do not understand and, therefore, cannot learn the technical aspects of project management. Not only in China, but elsewhere, successful project management requires extensive and intensive training in techniques and methodologies of project operations. In fact, proper diagnostic and learning readiness assessments are required prior to the training activity. Essentially, it requires a lot of creativity to develop a working level of project management techniques and methodology, particularly in non-Western and less developed environments.

The use of scheduling, costing, modeling, and programming techniques and methodologies should be much the same in large international projects. However, because of variations in education and the availability of hardware and software, adjustments must be made in project management systems. Inappropriate technology limits project efficiency and effectiveness, to be sure; however, it may well be the only option available to the company.

Organization

Authority, responsibility, and accountability vary by project, culture, and the company's preference. For example, highly technical and security-sensitive projects tend to be more centralized and more tightly controlled. Group decision making seems to work well in Japan and is being promoted in the United States, but it is not as prevalent in other societies.[9] For example, French companies show more autocratic behavior, while large and experienced companies in the United States and the rest of Western Europe exhibit the highest levels of management delegation.[10]

These findings are germane to project success. For while there are many reasons for the failure of projects in the international environment, the most significant is the inability to get maximum performance out of people. Each culture has different expectations of the boss-subordinate relationship.

The definitions of responsibility, authority, and accountability vary from country to country. In many countries authority in business and government is inherited. Thus, one notes the difference between respect that has to be earned, as in the United States, or respect that is assumed due to lineage, family, birth, etc. All too often in some countries, management and policy-making jobs are awarded to individuals based upon status and position rather than merit. Consequently, Western project managers in many cases must deal with individuals whose professional competence is not always high.

Position, rank, authority, and respect are supported in many foreign countries by informal and formal codes of dress, behavior, and attitudes. It is generally well understood who is in charge. Leaders and senior executives in some of these countries do not do their own shopping, drive their own cars, or mix with the masses.

While delegation and participative management are promoted and practiced in the United States, this is not the case in many foreign countries. Clearly, these organizational and operational patterns significantly affect project management staffing, planning, and implementation overseas.

Cultural Ambience

Unquestionably, cultural factors—values, attitudes, tradition, beliefs, behavior—are the principal factors influencing the successful management of projects. What specifically do we mean by culture?

Culture is the distinctive lifestyle of a particular group of people. It is composed of an interrelated set of systems: kinship, educational, economic, political, religious, health, and recreation.[11] As Harris and Moran state, "A cosmopolitan manager, sensitive to cultural differences, appreciates a people's distinctiveness and seeks to make allowances for such factors when communicating with representatives of that cultural group. He or she avoids trying to impose one's own cultural attitudes and approaches upon these 'foreigners.'"[12]

Not surprisingly, most problems that managers living abroad face stem from the value orientations of different cultures.[13] The most frequent problems center on individualism, informality, materialism, attitude toward change, and orientation toward the concept of time. Some of the more germane dimensions of value structures that can influence the conduct of business (and, of course, project management) in a cross-cultural setting are listed in Exhibit 37-1.

Human Subsystems

Human subsystems in international project management—motivation, communications, negotiation, conflict—are by their very nature far more complex and complicated than in the management of domestic projects.

Self-esteem and the social status of most Americans are derived from professional accomplishment. With little job security and modest social security, U.S. workers are motivated to work hard in order to earn money. But motivation varies widely by country and culture. To the French, quality of life is what matters most. While appreciative of the industriousness of the U.S. worker, the French value free time and vacations to a higher degree. In Eastern Europe, on the other hand, bonuses for salaried workers are emphasized strongly, since there are fewer other motivational options.[14] In Japan, society and company come first, and workers are motivated by permanent or lifetime employment, bonuses, and fringe benefits based upon the company's performance as a whole. In many developing countries, career and personal development are key motivations in scientific and technological areas.[15]

Exhibit 37-1. Cultural value orientations.

U.S. Culture	*Contrasting Cultures*
Individualism	Collectivism
Precise time reckoning	Loose time reckoning
Future-oriented	Past-oriented
Doing (working, achievement)	Being (personal qualities)
People controlling nature	Nature controlling people
Youthfulness	Old age
Informality	Formality
Competition	Cooperation
Relative equality of sexes	Relative inequality of sexes

Source: Gary P. Ferraro, *The Cultural Dimension of International Business,* © 1990, p. 115. Adapted by permission of Prentice-Hall, Englewood Cliffs, New Jersey.

Turning to communications, this subsystem is a dynamic verbal and nonverbal process.[16] Body language, dress, and other nonverbal gestures contain messages, whether intended or not. Word choice, tone of voice, and inflection can significantly affect work relationships in project management. Criticism or sharp disagreement with native managers in the presence of others can permanently undermine work relationships in both the Arab and Latin worlds. As for symbols, an American manager who brings yellow flowers to his French colleague's wife is unintentionally conveying infidelity. This all means that:

> In Asia, the Middle East, or Africa, Americans need to read between the lines. We need to know the context of a communication to understand it, because that's where much of the information is. The anthropologist Edward T. Hall calls these cultures "high context." The opposite are "low context" cultures, such as Switzerland, Germany, and Scandinavia, where information is explicit and words have specific meanings."[17]

Exactness and precision guide conversations and discussions just as they reflect a nation's accomplishments in science and technology.

Negotiations within the international context are made all the more difficult by differences in culture, trade customs, and legal order. Language barriers can complicate negotiations: Interpreters can slow the pace of negotiations and/or take the unwanted active roles. There is substantial difference in bargaining style across cultures,[18] and in many cases "yes" and "no" do not mean what we understand these terms to be. For example, the Chinese don't like refusing your request, so instead of saying "no," they use expressions like "no problem" or "we'll look into it." Legal language, the sanctity of contracts, and even the validity of certain clauses (e.g., the Arab boycott on doing business with Israel) are not irrevocable.[19]

The successful negotiator in international project management sees and understands the world as others do; manages stress and copes with ambiguity; sells the merits of the proposal in meaningful terms that express ideas clearly; and demonstrates cultural sensitivity and flexibility.[20]

Ensuring Success in International Project Management

Given the many differences, complexities, and uncertainties that distinguish international project management from domestic project management, a set of guidelines to ensure success would be most desirable. Unfortunately, this is exceedingly difficult—in fact, unrealistic. Nevertheless, recommendations can be made that enhance the likelihood of success. By no means comprehensive, they can produce significant effects.

▸ Establish a risk assessment system that evaluates the political, economic, social, technological, and regulatory environments of the project, and use it to monitor the project.

▸ Develop and implement a corporate social responsibility program that involves the company in the community in a positive, noncommercial way.

▸ Involve senior management in the selection and utilization of project management personnel who are proficient in both the technical and decision-making requirements of projects. Additionally, the personnel selected should be trained by the company. There should be follow-up to keep the project management personnel abreast of both conceptual and practical new information in the field.

▸ Make sure that information systems—specifically, reporting and network planning systems—along with accompanying techniques are appropriate, dynamic, and exceedingly user friendly (particularly if projects are located in less developed countries). These systems should also permit quick and effective corrective actions, as needed.

▸ Clearly define and properly delegate planning, programming, budgeting, control, and readjustment functions. Accountability and performance evaluation should be emphasized. Time estimating, scheduling, and work control budgets should be carried out by individuals who are eminently qualified to perform these tasks.[21]

Notes

1. Arvind V. Phatak, *International Dimensions of Management* (Boston: Kent Publishing, 1989).
2. Lennie Copeland and Lewis Griggs, *Going International—How to Make Friends and Deal Effectively in the Global Marketplace* (New York: Plume–New American Library, 1986).
3. Robert Levine and E. Wolfe, "Social Time: The Heartbeat of Culture," *Psychology Today* (March 1985), pp. 29–35.
4. Copeland and Griggs.
5. Ibid.
6. Ibid.
7. Phatak, *International Dimensions*.
8. David Clutterbuck, "Breaking Through the Cultural Barrier," *International Management* (December 1980), pp. 41–42; Arvind V. Phatak, *Managing Multinational Corporations* (New York: Praeger, 1974).
9. B. M. Bass et al., *Assessment of Managers: An International Comparison* (New York: Macmillan, 1979).
10. Ronald E. Berenbeim, *Operating Foreign Subsidiaries: How Independent Can They Be?* (New York: Conference Board, 1986).
11. Philip R. Harris and Robert T. Moran, *Managing Cultural Differences* (Houston: Gulf Publishing, 1979).
12. Ibid.
13. Phatak, *International Dimensions*.
14. Harris and Moran.
15. Joseph A. Bello, "Behavioral Problems of Operational Research Implementations in Developing Countries," in Ukandi G. Damachi and Hans Dieter Seibel, eds., *Management Problems in Africa* (New York: St. Martin's, 1986), pp. 232–269.
16. Larry A. Samovar and Richard E. Porter, *International Communication: A Reader* (Belmont, Calif.: Wadsworth, 1976).

17. Copeland and Griggs.

18. John L. Graham, "The Influence of Culture on the Process of Business Negotiations: An Exploratory Study," *Journal of International Business Studies* (Spring 1985), pp. 81–96.

19. Parviz Asheghian and Bahman Ebrahimi, *International Business* (New York: Harper & Row, 1987).

20. Pierre Casse, *Training for the Cross-Cultural Milieu* (Washington, D.C.: SIETAR, 1979).

21. Harold Kerzner, *Project Management: A Systems Approach to Planning, Scheduling, and Controlling* (New York: Van Nostrand Reinhold, 1989).

38

The Negotiation Differential for International Project Management

M. Dean Martin
Western Carolina University

The Influence of Culture

Culture has been defined as the distinctive way of life of a people.[1] As Terpstra indicates, it is difficult to define and is certainly no simple subject. He lists seven specific elements of culture:

1. Material culture
2. Language
3. Esthetics
4. Education
5. Religion, beliefs, and attitudes
6. Social organization
7. Political life

Culture is both created by humans and environmental. It is transmitted from one generation to the next through the family, school, church, and other agencies. The elements of culture are the stimuli encountered in given situations. There are two conditions with which the project manager should be familiar in approaching another culture: the self-reference criterion, and culture shock. These two conditions must be thoroughly understood and constantly guarded against.

As a consequence of the self-reference criterion,[2] the individual has a tendency to evaluate the values of people from other countries and cultures in terms of his or her own value system. People are led to judge the actions of foreigners in terms of

This chapter is adapted from M. Dean Martin, "The Negotiation Differential for International Project Management," 1981 *Proceedings of the Project Management Institute*. Reprinted with permission of the Project Management Institute, P.O. Box 43, Drexel Hill, Penn. 19026, a worldwide organization of advancing the state-of-the-art in project management.

what is right or wrong. Project managers who fall prey to this condition are setting up barriers that hinder communication and cause conflict to increase, thereby making it impossible for the managers to negotiate effectively with people from other countries. An example is the attitude that often develops relative to food. The project manager who criticizes and refuses to partake of the food of a foreign country may offend the people of that nation and thereby set up a barrier to understanding and communication.

A closely related condition is what is commonly known as culture shock. This condition occurs because the individual is away from the known and familiar and is faced with differing customs and ways of doing things. Project managers should be concerned with getting the job done, rather than with trying to teach people how to do the job their way. There is always more than one way to do a job.

Understanding these two conditions should enable project managers to develop an awareness of the need to understand cultural differences and to permit the charting of a safe course through unknown waters. We now turn to an examination of the seven elements of culture.

The Elements of Culture

Material Culture

Material culture refers to the physical objects created by people or the results of technology.[3] Each cultural element is impacted and to an extent shaped by the other elements. Thus, the project manager planning a technical approach to the construction of a bridge in a foreign country must take into account the types of tools that are normally used and the construction techniques employed, as well as such factors as the skills of local workers, their attitudes toward work and time, and their work habits. The manager needs to know this information to plan for negotiations. To assume that the bridge will be built in a foreign country exactly as it would be in the United States may be fallacious. Also, what is acceptable from a technological standpoint may be impacted by religion, educational level, and a myriad of other factors. For example, the introduction of television into Saudi Arabia in 1965 was permitted by the Ulema (an established group of theologians) only after King Faisal convinced them that here was yet another tool to spread religious doctrine.[4]

Language

Language has been called a cultural mirror.[5] To know the language of a culture is to know the people. Language is the primary communications medium, but language can be tricky: Words or expressions in one language do not mean the same in another. To assume an equality of meaning can lead to disaster for project managers in negotiation meetings. Miracle and Albaum state that there is no substitute for learning a language as a way to understand another person's beliefs, way of life, and point of view.[6] The importance of language to a people is such that it behooves the project manager to try to learn the foreign language. Observation has shown that the people of foreign countries appreciate the efforts of others to learn their language.

You may be corrected and receive quite a few smiles for your efforts, but the understanding and rapport that often accrue are well worth the tedium.

The author once conducted a negotiation in Italy using a combination of gestures, French, English, and Italian. The author knew English, French, and some Italian. The Italians knew Italian (of course), some English, and some French. It was an interesting experience. The results turned out to be very satisfactory, and the contract was completed without insurmountable problems.

If learning a foreign language is not an acceptable option, then translators can be used in an effective manner. Regardless of the approach, language must be an important consideration for the project manager.

Esthetics

The art, music, dance, and other such customs of a foreign country do not directly influence the success of the project in most cases. However, an appreciation of these features can enrich the time that the project manager and project staff spend in a given country. Thus, while not critical, attending the theater in London or an opera in Milan or visiting the Louvre in Paris may facilitate an awareness of language and the other cultural elements. It often provides a topic of conversation with the foreign hosts and might even be useful to design engineers planning a bridge or other structure.

Education

The cultural variable of education deals with the transmission of knowledge through the process of learning. It determines in large measure how the people of a culture approach problems, how they relate to other peoples, and how they approach and view foreigners. Some negotiators to Iran and other Arabic countries have commented on the ability of the average Iranian or Arab to focus very effectively on the details, yet not be able to conceptualize quickly the totality, of a project. Such knowledge can be beneficial in planning an approach to negotiations with these individuals. Again, a knowledge of the educational system of a country and the values that are transmitted by it can lead to a better understanding of that culture.

Religion, Beliefs, and Attitudes

Religion is often termed the mainspring of culture, influencing each of the other elements in a pervasive manner. It affects dress and eating habits. For example, it is taboo to eat beef in India, and in Arab countries women must wear a veil. The basis of both of these customs is to be found in religion.[7] Religion can also influence the attitudes of workers to a work site. Construction on roads, dams, and other projects has often been delayed because workers felt that some spirit inhabited the area. Only by working through local political and religious leaders have such situations been resolved. In some cases roads have had to be rerouted at increased cost as a consequence of this type of belief and the inability to resolve the problem quickly.

Religion also influences attitudes toward work and time. Pastner spent some time studying a Baluchi fishing village in Pakistan.[8] He found that problems arising in work situations often were ignored and not immediately solved as the villages felt that the problems arose because of "God's will." If God wanted the situation to be different, then it would not have happened. Since Pastner was not a believer, he often felt the need to take action. When he did, he found his actions criticized and approved by different groups of villagers, criticism being the majority reaction.

Studies by Hall indicate that different cultures have different attitudes toward time.[9] In the United States, promptness is valued and norms generally do not permit positive reactions to tardiness. On the other hand, in some cultures, appointments cover a general time interval and do not denote a specific point in time. Foreign managers thus often keep project managers waiting until they have finished the business at hand. The foreign managers do this not to keep people waiting for the sake of waiting, but because they want to give the project managers their undivided attention and cannot do so if they are distracted by unfinished business. The specific time set for the appointment is of less importance.

There are countless illustrations that reflect the differences in values caused by religion, beliefs, and attitudes. The important point is that the project manager should be aware that culture can and does affect these critical variables and that an understanding of this fact is required to communicate effectively with individuals for negotiation and management purposes.

Social Organization

This cultural element deals with the organization of individuals into groups and the structure of activities by these groups to accomplish goals and objectives. The family is one such group. Family relationships can affect attitudes toward business and, as such, negotiations. The individual in his or her culture is also a member of many other groups, including labor unions, social clubs, and other societal reference groups that influence attitudes and values. Social organization also relates to social classes in a society. In the United States there are social classes but they are not always clear-cut. In some countries, however, social mobility is not as prevalent as in the United States. This type of stratification places limits on who can negotiate and deal with whom. The Simmons Company found its entry into the Japanese bed market hindered because it hired salespeople of a certain class and had them trying to call on managers of a higher class.[10]

A knowledge of social organization permits the project manager to be more productive in terms of business contacts and time scheduling and provides an understanding of the formal versus the informal in terms of how to conduct negotiations. During one two-week negotiation in Paris, the author encountered extreme difficulty making progress in negotiations during the day at formal meetings. However, evenings at cocktail and dinner functions were highly productive and permitted a tough negotiation finally to be completed.

Political Life

Most foreign governments get involved in the business dealings of their companies and nationals with foreign companies entering their market. This seems to be even more prevalent with the growth of multinational corporations.[11] The foreign government in many cases wants to influence the way the project is to be performed. The government's concerns relate to the treatment of its people by the foreign company, the number of jobs created, the magnitude and scope of financial transactions, safety considerations, the amount of profit the foreign company is making, and a host of other factors. By its actions the government can delay the importation of equipment, materials, and supplies; can approve or disapprove the issuance of certain licenses and permits; or can in various ways make the project manager's job extremely difficult. Often, the question of ethics arises in terms of whether or not to bribe local officials.

In some cases the foreign government wants to have a representative at the negotiation meeting, depending on factors that include the nature of the contemplated work, the magnitude of the dollars involved, the level of technology involved, and the level of government support that will be required. Thus, one can again see the impact of culture on negotiations.

The Impact of Culture on Negotiation

The negotiation process as such is the same whether the arena is the domestic or the international market.[12] The project manager in both cases is concerned with cost, schedule, and performance. The differentiating factor is culture. The remainder of this chapter examines the negotiation process and the impact of culture on each phase. The negotiation process is displayed in Exhibit 38-1.

The Prenegotiation Planning Phase

The prenegotiation planning phase involves a problem-solving mode. The project manager has a requirement that needs action. For example, he or she may be bidding on the construction of a road, bridge, or dam in a foreign country. He or she knows the product, the company capabilities, and the other factors that the company will bring to the negotiation table. The need is for a plan that delineates the manager's approach to the negotiations. The project manager needs to know his or her opponent and that person's environment to develop a contingency plan; to decide on whether to take an individual or team approach; to designate a team leader; to develop strategies and tactics; to develop cost, schedule, and performance objectives—both minimums and maximums; and to identify give and take points.

The first step is to perform a thorough cultural analysis of the country where the project is to be activated. This analysis should include data relative to the seven cultural elements previously discussed. The author had the occasion to talk to an individual who had gone to China in the 1970s on the first U.S. trade mission to that country since the revolution in 1949. He confided that he was amazed at how well prepared the Chinese negotiators were. They possessed many details about his company and his family and were very knowledgeable about the costs involved in his

Exhibit 38-1. The negotiation process.

Prenegotiation Planning	→	Negotiation Meeting	→	Postnegotiation Critique

line of work. He, however, did not know the same about them and was in general unprepared for the negotiation in terms of cultural knowledge. The end result was that he found himself in the position where it was impossible to negotiate terms and conditions of sale that were acceptable to his management. Hall states that many of our difficulties in dealing with the Chinese is our lack of understanding of the difference between our two cultures[13]—something that is crucial in conducting successful negotiations.

The information for the cultural analysis can be obtained by personal observation (a visit to the area), by conducting studies and surveys in the country (an approach that is often not practical), and by reference to secondary data sources, such as reports and government studies. After the information is gathered, it should be analyzed and evaluated. The arrayed information then forms the basis for the preparation of the plan described above. The risk in the situation needs to be assessed and should form the basis for the formulation of detailed strategies and tactics.* Strategies relate to cost, schedule, and performance variables, whereas tactics relate to the actual negotiation meeting and how the negotiator should react to and deal with the opponent.[14]

The Negotiation Meeting Phase

All the planning, analysis, and evaluation culminates with the negotiation meeting. The meeting involves five distinct stages:

1. Protocol
2. Probing
3. Tough bargaining
4. Closure
5. Agreement

The first stage involves protocol considerations. The length of this stage depends on the participants. It is during this stage that the participants get acquainted, decide on the type of table and the seating arrangements, and so on. The cultural analysis by the project manager and project staff provides the information as to how the protocol stage should be approached. Generally speaking, it is best to let the meeting evolve and not try to rush things.

The second stage is that of probing. It is during this stage that the two sides actually start communicating with one another. Eye contact, voice tone, gestures, posture, and other actions become meaningful. Verbal communication is the obvious dimension for the meeting.[15] The individual needs to exude confidence and to speak with fluidity.

The other dimension in the meeting is the nonverbal aspect of communication, sometimes called body language. One aspect, eye contact, is important to convey your message.[16] It tells your opponent that you are attentive and in control of the situation. However, Hall states that your eyes can betray you.[17] Studies have shown that the pupil of the eye is a very sensitive indicator of how people respond to a

---

*C. L. Karrass includes an excellent discussion of the various strategies and tactics in his book *The Negotiation Game* (New York: World Publishing, 1970). This area is also covered quite well in N. W. Beckmann, *Negotiations* (Lexington, Mass.: D. C. Heath, 1977).

situation. When an individual is interested in something, the pupil dilates, and when a person dislikes something that is said, the pupil contracts. Hall then describes how Arabs use this information to read mood changes in their opponents. They also try to deny this information to their opponents by wearing dark glasses, even indoors. In addition to factors relating to the eyes, managers should know that Arabs have a different concept of body space than Americans. They have a tendency to sit close to those they are negotiating with and at times to place their hand on their opponent's knee or leg—something that a person from a culture with a different concept of body space can find quite disconcerting. Regardless, the probing stage involves the two sides feeling each other out, hopefully to identify weaknesses, areas of interest, or urgency. It is a time for validating the adequacy of one's strategy or for falling back on contingency plans that have been developed.

The third stage is that of rough bargaining. This means knowing the points that you must take and going after them with confidence and decisiveness. This approach has been validated by studies as being the most successful one in negotiations.[18]

At some point, the key issues of cost, schedule, and performance are pretty well settled; this marks the entry to stage four: closure. This stage generally involves a summary of the agreements reached on individual issues. When this has been completed without objections, then stage five, agreement, has been reached. This stage is characterized by discussions relative to when the work should actually start and a consideration of other side issues, including when you hope to meet again. This is a good time to review key phrases that are to be included in the contract, as different words have different meanings for different people, and the communication that you thought existed may not have been effective.[19] Not surprisingly, negotiations have on occasion been reopened at this point. A key consideration is to permit your opponent to save face (this is assuming you won). Face as a concept is most aptly illustrated by the Arabs[20] as involving a perception that relates to an individual's value of self-worth. For negotiation, it means that both sides were "winners." (Your side just won more.)

The Postnegotiation Critique

This phase of negotiation provides feedback as to how well the project manager did in planning.[21] It reveals what facts were needed that were not available. During this phase the agreement is generally reduced to writing. This recording of the agreement may take the form of a contract or a memorandum;[22] the mode of recording depends in large measure on the country involved. In order to fix the country whose laws will govern, the project manager should ensure that a jurisdiction clause is included.

As a general rule, it is not good practice to discuss the course of the negotiation at this point with your key adversary and his or her staff. You may want to negotiate with them again and there is no need to risk some chance remark that might antagonize the other side.

Notes

1. V. Terpstra, *International Marketing* (Hinsdale, Ill.: Dryden, 1972), p. 83.
2. R. Kahler and R. L. Kramer, *International Marketing*, 4th ed. (Dallas: South-Western Publishing, 1977), p. 123.

3. V. Terpstra, *The Cultural Environment of International Business* (Dallas: South-Western Publishing, 1978), p. 176.

4. P. A. Iseman, "The Arabian Ethos," *Harper's* (February 1978), p. 55.

5. Terpstra, *The Cultural Environment of International Business.* p. 2.

6. G. E. Miracle and G. S. Albaum, *International Marketing Management* (Homewood, Ill.: Richard D. Irwin, 1970), pp. 8–9.

7. E. W. Fernea and R. A. Fernea, "A Look Behind the Veil," *Human Nature* 2, No. 1 (January 1979), p. 68.

8. S. Pastner, "A Nudge From the Hand of God," *Natural History* 87, No. 3 (March 1978), pp. 32–36.

9. E. T. Hall, *The Silent Language* (Greenwich, Conn.: Fawcett, 1959), pp. 128–145.

10. D. A. Ricks, M. Y. C. Fu, and J. S. Arpan, *International Business Blunders* (Columbus, Ohio: Grid, 1974), pp. 20–22.

11. L. T. Wells, Jr., "Negotiating With Third World Governments," *Harvard Business Review* 55, No. 1 (January-February 1977), pp. 72–80.

12. P. R. Cateora and J. M. Hess, *International Marketing*, 4th ed. (Homewood, Ill.: Richard D. Irwin, 1979), pp. 134–135.

13. E. T. Hall, "How Cultures Collide," *Psychology Today* (July 1976), p. 66.

14. J. R. Adams, S. E. Barndt, and M. D. Martin, "Planning for the Project," in *Managing by Project Management* (Dayton, Ohio: U.T.C., 1979), pp. 64–73.

15. J. A. Hall et al., "Decoding Wordless Messages," *Human Nature* 1, No. 5 (May 1978), pp. 70–72.

16. J. Fast, *Body Language* (New York: Pocket Books, 1971); D. Goleman, "People Who Read People," *Psychology Today* (July 1979), pp. 66–78.

17. E. T. Hall, "Learning the Arabs' Silent Language," *Psychology Today* (August 1979), p. 45.

18. "Show You're Tough, Then Ask the Price," *Psychology Today* (October 1979), p. 116.

19. R. Plutchik, "A Language for the Emotions," *Psychology Today* (February 1980), p. 71.

20. Iseman, pp. 43–44.

21. Harold Kerzner, *Project Management: A Systems Approach to Planning, Scheduling, and Controlling* (New York: Van Nostrand Reinhold, 1989), p. 168.

22. T. A. Warschaw, *Winning by Negotiation* (New York: McGraw-Hill, 1980), p. 266.

39

Challenges in Managing International Projects

Paul C. Dinsmore
Dinsmore Associates

Manuel M. Benitez Codas
M. M. Benitez Codas

A backhanded "V for Victory" sign is an uncomplimentary gesture in Australia. In Brazil, the American "A-OK" sign is also offensive. These are lessons that presidents, diplomats, and businesspeople have learned the hard way. Awareness of such cross-cultural subtleties can spell success or failure in international dealings, whether in diplomatic relations, general business, or the project arena.

Projects conducted in international settings share these sometimes embarrassing communications pitfalls and others as well. They are subject to cultural, bureaucratic, and logistical challenges just like conventional domestic projects are. In fact, project management approaches to international ventures include the same items common to domestic projects. Under both circumstances, successful project management calls for performing the basics of planning, organizing, and controlling. This also implies carrying out the classic functions outlined in the Project Management Institute's *Project Management Body of Knowledge (PMBOK)* of managing scope, schedule, cost, quality, communications, human resources, contracting and supply, and risk.

The primary factors in cross-cultural settings that call for special attention and an "international approach" are: functional redundancy, political factors, the expatriate way of life, language and culture, additional risk factors, supply difficulties, and local laws and legislation. Of the items pinpointed, some offer particular challenges from the viewpoint of the *PMBOK*. Some comments on these critical topics follow. These are the subjects that require special care to ensure that the internationally set project meets its targeted goals.

▸ *Functional redundancy* means the duplication or overlap of certain functions or activities. This may be necessary because of contractual agreements involving technology transfer requiring "national counterparts." Language or organizational complexity of the project may also be responsible for creating functional redundancy. Special attention is called for, therefore, in managing the project functions of human resources and communications.

▸ *Political factors* in international projects are a strong influence and are plagued with countless unknowns. Aside from fluctuations in international politics, project professionals are faced with the subtleties of local politics, which often place major roadblocks in the pathway of attaining project success. In terms of classic project management, this means reinforcing the communications function in order to ensure that all strategic and politically related interactions are appropriately transmitted and deciphered.

▸ *The expatriate way of life* refers to the habits and expectations of those parties who are transferred to the host country. This includes the way of thinking and the physical and psychological needs of those people temporarily living in a strange land with different customs and ways of life. When the differences are substantial, this means making special provision for a group of people who would otherwise refuse to relocate to the site, or, if transferred on a temporary basis, remain highly unmotivated during their stay. The basic project management factors related to the expatriate way of life include communications, human resources, and supply.

▸ *Language and culture* include the system of spoken, written, and other social forms of communication. Included in language and culture are the systems of codification and decodification of thoughts, beliefs, and values common to a given people. Here all the subtleties of communications become of special importance.

▸ *Additional risk factors* may include personal risks such as kidnapping, local epidemics, and faulty medical care. Rapid swings in political and economic situations, or peculiar local weather or geology, are also potential uncertainties. These different risk factors require analysis and subsequent management to keep them from adversely affecting the project. The obvious basic project management tenet in this case is risk management.

▸ *Supply difficulties* encompass all the contracting, procurement, and logistical challenges that must be faced on the project. For instance, some railroad projects must use the new railway itself as the primary form of transportation for supplies. In other situations, waterways may be the only access. Customs presents major problems in many project settings. A new concept in logistics may need to be pioneered for a given project. Contracting and supply on international projects normally calls for an "overkill" effort, since ordinary domestic approaches are normally inadequate. This usually requires highly qualified personnel and some partially redundant management systems heavily laced with follow-up procedures. Heavy emphasis is needed in the areas of contracting and supply.

▸ *Local laws and legislation* affect the way much of business is done on international projects. They may even affect personal habits (such as abstaining from drinking alcoholic beverages in Muslim countries). Here the key is awareness and education so that each person is familiar with whatever laws are applicable to his or her area. In this case, the project management tenets that require special attention are communications and supply.

It is apparent from Exhibit 39-1 that in terms of classic project management, special emphasis is required on international projects in the areas of communications, contracting and supply, human resources, and risk. Since all of the project management areas—including the basic areas of managing scope, schedule, cost, and

Exhibit 39-1. Relationship of internationally sensitive factors to the basic concepts of the *PMBOK*.

PMBOK Areas	Internationally Sensitive Factors						
	Functional Redundancy	Political Factors	Expatriate Way of Life	Language and Culture	Additional Risk Factors	Supply Difficulties	Local Laws and Legislation
Scope							
Schedule							
Cost							
Quality							
Communications	X	X	X	X			X
Human Resources	X		X				
Contracting and Supply			X			X	X
Risk					X		

quality—are interconnected (a communications breakdown can affect quality, for instance), extra diligence is called for in managing communications, contracting and supply, human resources, and risk. It must be assumed that a conventional approach to managing these areas will be inadequate for international projects.

A Model of Intercultural Team Building

The challenge in international team building boils down to creating a convergence of people's differing personal inputs toward a set of common final outputs. This means developing a process that facilitates communication and understanding between people of different national cultures. Making this process happen signifies the difference between success and failure on international projects.

People's inputs are things like personal and cultural values, beliefs, and assumptions. They also include patterns of thinking, feeling, and behaving. Expectations, needs, and motivations are also part of people's inputs into any given system. The outputs are the results or benefits produced by a given system. They may be perceived as a combination of achievements benefiting the individuals, the team, the organization, and the outside environment. The outputs are the object of the efforts generated by the inputs.

The secret is to transform the way people do things at the beginning of the project into more effective behavior as the project moves along. This transformation initially involves identifying the intercultural differences among the parties. Once this is done, a program of intercultural team building is called for in order to make the transformation take place. The result of the team-building process is to influence the behavior of the group toward meeting the project's goals. Intercultural team building thus calls for developing and conducting a program that will help transform the participants' inputs into project outputs.

Some Global Considerations

Globalization affects all areas of endeavor, including how projects are managed. It affects the internationally sensitive factors mentioned earlier in this chapter and reinforces the need to create teams that are capable of dealing with the dynamics of globalization.

The groundswell toward globalization stems from a number of factors, from advances in transportation and communications technologies through international trade agreements such as the U.S.-Canada free trade agreement, the General Agreement on Tariffs and Trade (GATT), and the European Common Market. New international standards, replacing national standards that impeded the movement of goods and services, also open doors toward a more globalized economy.

While the trends toward globalization of project management and related technologies such as the construction industry are apparent, there still remain basic differences in the way business is performed from one land to the next. A contrast between the United States and Japan appears, for instance, when examining the relationship between general contractor and architects. This relationship is traditionally adversarial in the United States, as is reflected by the habitual finger pointing that goes on at the end of contracts, sometimes resulting in litigation. In contrast, in Japan these relationships are much more cooperative in nature; there is a certain congeniality between design and construction. Also in contrast, mutual risk taking between contractors and clients is a more common practice in Japan than in the United States. It is a common practice in Europe as well. Meanwhile, partnering—one form of mutual risk taking—is a known concept in the United States, but it is almost routine procedure in Japan and Europe.

The way technical information is developed and transferred also affects how business is performed, and consequently, how projects are managed and implemented. Various systems or models are in place for generating and transferring knowledge in different parts of the world. In very general terms, the basic models may be called the European, the North American, and the Japanese. (These terms are used only to identify trends, as all three models can be found in most countries.) The characteristics of the models are as follows:

▸ *The European model.* In Europe, there are highly structured, formal, and centralized national systems for generating and disseminating technical knowledge. Responsibilities are clearly defined, with specific national organizations charged with generating research, while other organizations take care of transferring the result to industry. The Swedish system is a typical example, with the National Swedish Institute for Building Research responsible for knowledge generation, and the Swedish Institute for Building Documentation responsible for dissemination. National systems in Europe are often jointly financed by government and industry.

▸ *The North American model.* The system in North America is less formal than in Europe. There is, in fact, little coordination in the construction research effort in North America. In contrast to the European model, advanced construction knowledge is mainly generated at the university level. The dissemination to industry is largely performed by broad-based engineering or trade associations such as the American Society of Civil Engineers. The technical work is carried out in these associations by committees made up of volunteers.

▸ *The Japanese model.* In the Japanese model, research is concentrated in the Big Six integrated companies that dominate Japanese construction, where technology development is considered a significant competitive tool. Therefore, as much as $100 million is invested annually by the Big Six in research, which is considered proprietary and subject to commercial confidentiality. Companies invest in research to attain competitive advantage.

In spite of these differences in philosophy and style, globalization is evident at every level of the construction industry—from material, through manufactured goods, to services. The general trend in international industrial research and development is toward strategic alliances and joint ventures to reduce the risk factor and share the spiraling costs.

Governments are now changing previous policies aimed at achieving regional goals in favor of sponsoring research and development at the multinational level. Examples are projects such as Airbus and the jointly funded R&D programs such as ESPRIT and RACE underwritten by the European Community. While there is sharing going on, which points to increased globalization, the fight for the competitive edge is still under way.

Another factor that influences managing projects internationally is the increasingly active role being taken by the owner organizations in the management of their projects. In the case of developing countries, this often reflects a national policy aimed at attaining greater managerial and technical capability so as to be less dependent on the developed world. Owners in such countries have a need for contracting services toward getting their project completed as well as transferring experience to their own organizations.

The globalization of project management information and know-how takes place through independently published literature and through two major internationally recognized organizations that are dedicated exclusively to the field of project management—PMI (the Project Management Institute) and INTERNET (the International Association of Project Management)—both of which are affiliated with numerous other organizations with related interests. PMI is based in North America. INTERNET is a federation of project management associations, primarily European. Another association with significant published literature in project management is the AACE (the American Association of Cost Engineers).

Integrating Two Cultures

While globalization is an ongoing influence on the management of international projects, success depends primarily on giving the proper emphasis to those factors that are particularly vulnerable in cross-cultural settings and on building a team capable of dealing with the challenges presented.

This discussion is drawn from the experience of co-author Codas in the management of "binational projects" in South America that involved the merging of cultures of projects jointly owned by the governments of two countries bordering rivers of staggering hydroelectric potential.

It is common practice in binational projects to have formal authority shared by two people, one from each country. This shared authority ranges from an integrated partnership of managers to a lead-manager/backup-manager situation.

Binational projects are products of hard political processes that involve long and difficult negotiations. In most cases each side has a different perception about the adopted solution, and during the project phase each side may try to "win back" some of the points initially "lost" at the negotiating table. The final diplomatic agreements are lengthy texts that are usually rich in political rhetoric and poor in operational and technical considerations. This sets the stage for conflict during the implementation phase of the project. The need for strong communications management becomes immediately evident in such a setting. An additional complicating factor is the fact that diplomatic documents contain writing "between the lines" and are consequently not easily decipherable by project managers and engineers.

Most binational agreements for developing projects state a philosophy of equity regarding the division of the work to be executed by each side. The unclear definition of what "equal parts" means is the prime source of inbred interest-based conflicts, which also affect the culture of the project.

The Development of a Project Culture

Experience in managing binational projects indicates that, for cultural convergence to take place, managers of both sides need to understand the culture of the other side, analyzing the different patterns that make up that culture. This means learning the other country's history, geography, economy, religion, traditions, and politics. Both sides, therefore, need to become fully aware of basic differences involving educational level, professional experience, experience on this kind of project, knowledge of the language, and host country way of life.

Aside from this information, which can be readily obtained and assimilated, other perceptions must be taken into consideration, such as beliefs, feelings, informal actions and interactions, group norms, and values. These factors strongly affect behavior patterns. A simple way of tabulating the different factors that affect cultural behavior is shown in Exhibit 39-2. Although the judgment criteria are basically subjective, the chart pinpoints some of the basic differences in culture that tend to affect managerial behavior. In the binational situation used as a basis for this discussion, both sides filled out the charts and jointly evaluated the results.

Based on the analysis of the cultural differences, behavioral standards need to be developed. The objective is to define a desirable behavior or a "project culture" most suitable to the project objectives and the group's culture. In other words, cross-cultural team building must take place so that the individuals' inputs can be effectively channeled to meet the project goals. Forming a project culture is a project in itself; therefore, it must have an objective, a schedule, resources, and a development

Exhibit 39-2. Evaluation of cultural patterns of two countries involved in a joint venture.

Characteristic	Country 1 — Minimum 1	2	3	4	Maximum 5	Country 2 — Minimum 1	2	3	4	Maximum 5
Gregariousness			X					X		
Technically Oriented		X							X	
Formal Behavior		X					X			
Consensus-Oriented				X						X
Internal Project Experience	X					X				
Rational Behavior	X									X
Nonnationalistic Posture		X							X	
TOTAL	16					24				

Column headers span: "Country 1 — Values" and "Country 2 — Values", each with Minimum (1) and Maximum (5).

plan. Its execution becomes the responsibility of the management team. The objective of building a project culture is to attain a cooperative spirit, to supplant the our-side-versus-your-side feeling with a strong "our project" view. The project culture is developed around the commonalities of both groups, identified in the analysis shown in Exhibit 39-2. As other desirable traits are identified, they must be developed through a training program designed to stimulate those traits.

The Project Culture Over the Life Cycle of the Project

Culture on international projects begins to establish itself during the early stages of the project. The participative process in the development of the work breakdown structure and the project activities network can stimulate the "our project" spirit. It is also then that the first problems arise. Problems at this stage are relatively easy to solve, because enthusiasm on the part of the team members is generally high. The cultural model to be established at this stage is that of strong cooperation of all parties where and when necessary, in the spirit of "all for one, one for all."

If some individuals at this stage don't demonstrate efforts toward integration or show uncooperative attitudes, project managers should seriously consider taking them off the project, because if they create problems in blue-sky conditions, they may be impossible to work with when stormy weather appears. On the other hand, emerging team leaders need to be identified and motivated early on in the project.

During the maturing stages of international projects, when the organization is well defined and each unit or department is supposed to take care of its own tasks, the culture tends to become competitive as project groups try to show efficiency in relation to the other groups. Problems mainly arise at this stage because of unbalanced work loads. Some groups may claim to be overworked while others have little work to do. Strong coordination and regular follow-up meetings are required during these intermediate project stages.

The final stage of the project is particularly difficult in terms of cultural integration. There is less work to do, and people are leaving to go on to other new international projects, ofttimes earning more than on "this old and uninteresting project." At this point, project managers are hard-strapped to maintain the spirit of the remaining group. This is the moment for the managers to show their leadership capabilities to make sure that the final activities of the project are performed with the same efficiency as the previous ones.

Bibliography

Casse, Pierre. *Training for the Multicultural Manager.* Washington, D.C.: SIETAR, 1982.

Halpin, Daniel W. "The International Challenge in Design and Construction." *Construction Business Review Magazine* (January-February 1992).

Seaden, George. "The International Transfer of Building." *Construction Business Review Magazine* (January-February 1992).

Index

About the Editor

Paul C. Dinsmore is an international speaker and seminar leader on project management. He is the author of five books, including *Human Factors in Project Management* (second edition, AMACOM, 1990), and he has written more than sixty professional papers and articles. Mr. Dinsmore is president of Dinsmore Associates, a training and development group, and director of Management Consultants International, a consulting firm specializing in project management. Prior to establishing his consulting practice in 1985, he worked for twenty years as a project manager and executive in the construction and engineering industry for Daniel International, Morrison Knudsen International, and Engevix Engineering.

Mr. Dinsmore has performed consulting and training services for major companies including IBM, ENI-Italy, Petrobrás, General Electric, Mercedes Benz, Shell, Control Data, Morrison Knudsen, the World Trade Institute, Westinghouse, Ford, Caterpillar, and Alcoa. His consulting practice has included projects on company reorganization, project start-up, development and implementation of project management systems, and training programs, as well as special advisory functions for the presidents of several organizations. Project management applications include the areas of product development, concurrent engineering, software development, company reorganization, and engineering and construction.

Mr. Dinsmore is feature editor of the column "Up & Down the Organization," published in *PMNET,* the magazine of the Project Management Institute. He participates actively in such professional associations as INTERNET (the International Association of Project Management), NSA (the National Speakers Association), and PMI, which awarded him its Distinguished Contributions Award.

Mr. Dinsmore graduated from Texas Tech University and completed the Advanced Management Program at Harvard Business School.

About the Supporting Editor

Frank Galopin is currently the sole proprietor of FEG Services, a consulting firm providing hands-on expertise in the general field of project control and specifically in the areas of cost estimating, cost control, and project scheduling. Before that, he spent thirty years working (including teaching and writing) in these same areas in many countries of North America, South America, and Europe, being employed in supervisory and managerial positions by the Bechtel Organization (a Morrison Knudsen subsidiary), Ebasco Services, and Westinghouse Electric.

About the Contributors

John R. Adams is a professor of Project Management at Western Carolina University in Cullowhee, N.C., and director of its Master of Project Management Degree Program. He is president of DMI and has been active with the Institute's Board of Directors for more than fifteen years. A frequent contributor to the literature of project management, his book *Management by Project Management* has been translated into Japanese and used as a basis for courses and workshops in Australia, Canada, Japan, and throughout the United States. Dr. Adams's practical management experience includes over twenty years of applied research work with U.S. Air Force weapon systems development projects.

Russell D. Archibald of Integrated Project Systems in Los Angeles is an independent management consultant with broad international experience in program and project management. His consulting clients include major industrial, engineering, construction, consumer products, and services companies in twelve countries, plus federal and local government agencies and development banks. Mr. Archibald is the author of *Managing High Technology Programs and Projects* (which has been translated into Japanese and Italian) and, with R. L. Villoria, *Network-Based Management Information Systems (PERT/CPM)*. He has also written numerous articles and papers. Mr. Archibald is a certified management consultant and a certified project management professional.

George C. Belev became associated with General Electric Company in 1971 and was instrumental in the design, development, and manufacture of reactor plant components for the Navy Nuclear Propulsion Program. He is now manager of Technical Support Procurement at General Electric. Mr. Belev has served as speaker and facilitator in numerous contract management and procurement seminars. He is an ASQC-certified quality engineer, an ICA-certified cost analyst, and an SME-certified manufacturing engineer. He holds the professional designation in contract management from the U.S. Air Force and is a registered professional engineer.

Manuel M. Benitez Codas is a consultant in project management and strategic planning with M. M. Benitez Codas in Brazil. Prior to starting his own consulting company in 1990, he worked for more than twenty years in large Brazilian and Paraguayan engineering organizations, involved in such large undertakings as hydroelectric projects and mass transport projects. Mr. Codas also developed intensive training activities related to project management for several companies in Brazil. He has published articles in the *International Journal of Project Management* and *RAE—Business Administration Magazine*. Mr. Codas is the founder and former president of the São Paulo Project Management Association and a member of the Project Management Institute and the Association of Project Managers.

Jasjit S. Dhillon has over eight years of experience in business process reengineering, strategic planning, and has performed in and managed a variety of multi-disciplinary projects in the public sector, aerospace, electronic systems, telecommunications, and gas/electric utility industries for the past six years. His experience also includes strategic planning, decision analysis, technology planning, and project management engagements. Mr. Dhillon's specific areas of expertise are strategic planning, business reengineering, decision analysis in operations, economic analysis, risk analysis, project management, contingency analysis and management, variance mitigation, technology studies and evaluation, competitive analysis, information systems planning, and logistics management.

Ralph D. Ellis, Jr., is a professor of Construction Engineering and Engineering Management in the Department of Civil Engineering at the University of Florida. Dr. Ellis has had more than fifteen years of experience as a manager of his own company providing construction services on both domestic and overseas projects. Principal clients have included the U.S. Army Corps of Engineers, the U.S. Department of the Navy, and the Panama Canal Commission. Dr. Ellis is a registered professional engineer and a member of the American Society of Civil Engineers, the American Society of Cost Engineers, the American Society for Engineering Education, and the Project Management Institute. He is also a member of the Construction Industry Research Council and serves on several national professional committees.

Irving M. Fogel is founder and president of Fogel & Associates, a New York City-based consulting engineering and project management firm. Fogel & Associates has served as project management, scheduling, and claims consultant to builders, developers, contractors, engineers, architects, manufacturers, and government agencies. Mr. Fogel is a registered professional engineer in twenty-two states, the District of Columbia, and the state of Israel. He has worked on projects worldwide.

David Gordon has been affiliated with the University of Dallas since 1969 as a member of the resident faculty of the Graduate School of Management. He serves as director of MBA Programs in Engineering and Industrial Management. Prior to joining the university, Dr. Gordon held several senior industrial management positions. He has authored numerous scholarly articles in the field of operations management and is a recognized expert in the area of total quality management. He has delivered consulting services both nationally and internationally to organizations ranging from *Fortune* 100 companies to U.S. government agencies and military commands.

Robert J. Graham of R. J. Graham and Associates in Philadelphia is an independent management consultant in the areas of international project management and organizational change. He is also a senior associate with the Strategic Management Group in Philadelphia. Dr. Graham teaches in the project management program at Henley-The Management College in England and has been a visiting professor at the University of the German Armed Forces in Munich. Previously, he was a member of the senior staff at the Management and Behavioral Sciences Center at the Wharton School, University of Pennsylvania.

Jerry Haar is an international management consultant specializing in marketing, strategic planning, trade and investment analysis and promotion, and project evaluation. He presently is director of the Inter-American Business and Labor program as well as the Canada Program at the North-South Center, University of Miami. Additionally, he is a senior research associate at the center and teaches international business and international marketing in the university. Dr. Haar is also an adjunct scholar of the American Enterprise Institute in Washington, D.C. Prior to his current assignment, he was a business professor at Florida International University. From 1981 to 1984, Dr. Haar was director of Washington Programs for the Council of the Americas, a New York-based business association of over 200 corporations comprising a majority of U.S. private investment in Latin America. Prior to joining the council, Dr. Haar held several senior staff positions with the federal government in the areas of policy planning, management evaluation, and organizational development. He also served as special assistant to two cabinet secretaries. Dr. Haar is a graduate of Harvard University's Executive Program in Management and Health Finance. He has authored or co-authored four books and a number of articles and has served as consultant to public and private organizations in the United States and abroad.

Brian Hobbs has been a professor at the University of Quebec at Montreal since 1983, where he was director of the Master's Program in Project Management between 1985 and 1987. He has presented papers at PMI and INTERNET conferences in recent years and is coauthor of a reference book entitled *Project Management: The Mapping of the Field*. Dr. Hobbs has acted as a consultant with many project management firms.

William N. Hosley is the president of All-Tech Project Management Services, Inc. in Rochester, New York, a project management consulting group and producer of project management software packages. He was employed by the Eastman Kodak Company for thirty-five years until he retired in 1986. At Kodak, he was head of Management Services at the Kodak Research Laboratories, head of project planning support for new product programs, and coordinator of project management training in the Management Services Division. Mr. Hosley is the principal author of *Project Management Advantage*™, an artificial intelligence/expert system applied to the principal issues in project management, and the *All-Tech Project Simulator*™. He has taught project management courses at the Rochester Institute of Technology and is a certified project management professional.

Darrel G. Hubbard is vice-president of Management Systems for Management Analysis Company, Inc., in San Diego. His career of more than twenty-five years includes broad experience in management, consulting, and technical positions. Mr. Hubbard has over fifteen years of project-related experience in a wide variety of applications areas, having applied management systems to financial, administrative, and human resources processes and to research, development, fossil, geothermal, hydroelectric, nuclear, and waste management projects. He is a registered professional engineer in control systems and is a member of the Project Management Institute and the Instrument Society of America.

Lewis R. Ireland is president of L. R. Ireland & Associates in Reston, Va., a company specializing in project management consulting. He has more than sixteen years of experience in planning and implementing projects ranging in value from $6,500 to $178 million in both the public and private sectors. Dr. Ireland is a fellow of the

Project Management Institute and a recipient of PMI's Person of the Year and Distinguished Contribution awards.

Lee R. Lambert of Lee R. Lambert & Associates in Worthington, Ohio, is known throughout the world as an authority on the development and implementation of project management processes especially suited for high technology and fast-track projects in all technical disciplines in commercial and government environments. Mr. Lambert has developed management systems, procedures, and training for major corporations, including the Citicorp Executive Development Center, Niagara Mohawk Power, the Battelle Memorial Institute, and the Kuwait Institute for Scientific Research. He has held senior management positions in such corporations as the Lawrence Livermore Laboratory, General Electric, and the Battelle Memorial Institute. Mr. Lambert has published twenty articles and is the author of a book on cost/ schedule control system criteria. He is also a founding member of the Project Management Institute's Project Management Professional Certification Committee.

Harvey A. Levine is president of the Project Knowledge Group in Saratoga Springs, New York, a consulting firm specializing in project management training; project management software selection, evaluation, and implementation; and project management using microcomputers. With over thirty-one years of practice and service to the project management profession, Mr. Levine has taught for several universities and technical organizations. A prolific writer on project management, he has written several books and close to a hundred articles for leading technical publishers and periodicals. Mr. Levine is a consultant to a wide variety of businesses in both the private and government sectors. In addition to consulting for project management practitioners, Mr. Levine is the leading consultant to the project management software industry. Mr. Levine recently served on the board of directors of the Project Management Institute as president and chairman of the board. He received PMI's 1989 Distinguished Contribution to Project Management award.

J. Royce Lummus, Jr., is manager of New Aircraft Programs within the Advanced Programs Department of the General Dynamics Corporation's Fort Worth Division. As adjunct professor in the Graduate School of Management at the University of Dallas, he teaches Technical Project Management and also serves on the Industry Advisory Board for the graduate school. A registered professional engineer, Dr. Lummus has published numerous articles in technical journals on the subjects of aerodynamics and aircraft design and development.

Jacques Marcovitch is a professor at the University of São Paulo in Brazil. At the university, he served as director of Advanced Studies and as editor of the business magazine. He was also president of the Latin America Association of Technical Management. Dr. Marcovitch did postgraduate work at the International Management Institute in Geneva. He is the author of two books on the management of technology.

M. Dean Martin at the time of his death was a professor in the Department of Management and Marketing at the School of Business, Western Carolina University, in Cullowhee, N.C. He had extensive experience as a project manager, a procurement contracting officer, an administrative contracting officer, and a price and cost analyst within the federal government policy setting and operation areas. He managed a

Defense Contract Administration Services Office, served as chief of Management Engineering, and held major procurement and pricing responsibilities for several Department of Defense weapon systems acquisition programs. Dr. Martin was active in the Project Management Institute, holding several offices in both the Ohio Chapter and the national PMI. He served as an instructor in the weekend workshops held in conjunction with the PMI's annual International Symposium/Seminar, was a member of the PMI's Annual Student Award Committee, and was a frequent contributor of papers to both the *Project Management Journal* and the annual Symposium/Seminar.

Antonio C. A. Maximiano is an associate professor and coordinator of the Graduate Program of Management at the University of São Paulo in Brazil. He is also a lecturer in management development programs for such organizations as the university's Institute of Administration, Mercedes Benz of Brazil, and IBM of Brazil. Dr. Maximiano is the author of *Introduction to Management* and *Management of Teamwork*.

Pierre Ménard had an eight-year professional career as a project engineer and project manager in the telecommunications industry before joining the University of Quebec at Montreal in 1972. In 1976, he launched the Master's Program in Project Management to be established at any major university. This program also became the first to be officially accredited by the Project Management Institute at its 1988 Symposium in San Francisco. Dr. Ménard is currently the director of the program for the University of Quebec network.

Alan S. Mendelssohn is currently director of quality with Budget Rent a Car Corporation. For many years, he was with Florida Power & Light Company's Project Management Department, where he was extensively involved in all aspects of FPL's quality improvement process and played a lead role in its incorporation into that department. He is also serving as a quality management consultant with the U.S. Army Material Command. Mr. Mendelssohn is a registered professional engineer in Florida and has been designated by the American Association of Cost Engineers (AACE) as a Certified Cost Engineer. He is a member of the AACE, the Project Management Institute, and the American Society for Quality Control. Mr. Mendelssohn has also made numerous presentations on a variety of project-management-related subjects, including several papers on quality management.

Peter W. G. Morris is director of Special Projects with Bovis Ltd., in London. Among his particular responsibilities are Bovis business in Central and Eastern Europe and public sector and multilateral financing. He also heads Bovis's feasibility and concept studies practice. Dr. Morris is an associate fellow of Templeton College, Oxford, and is on the faculty of the University of Oxford. He is also a member of the board of the International Association of Macro Engineering Societies, is on the Council of the U.K. Association of Project Managers, and is on the Accreditation Committee of the Project Management Institute.

Rainer A. Otto is manager of computer applications with the Southern California Gas Company in Los Angeles. SoCalGas is the largest gas distributor in the United States serving approximately 13 million people throughout the southern half of Southern California. Prior to 1993, Mr. Rainer was in charge of support of financial and administrative systems for the company. He has also been responsible for development and support of the methods, techniques, policies, procedures, and tools used to develop, enhance, and support computer applications. This included the development of project management methods, roles, and responsibilities and the selection of project management software tools. Mr. Otto has also held positions in Pacific Enterprises, Southern California Gas Company's parent corporation, as a financial planning analyst, operations research manager, and was in charge of office systems and end-user computing support and computer technology evaluation.

Stephen D. Owens of the Department of Management and Marketing of Western Carolina University in Cullowhee, N.C., has over twenty years of university teaching experience. He has taught human resources management, organizational behavior, and labor relations both in and outside the United States. He has also led workshops and seminars to improve managerial skills for supervisory and midlevel managers in both the private and public sectors. Dr. Owens has lectured at North Texas State University, Louisiana State University, and Central Michigan University. His principal areas of research and consulting include a variety of topics related to the field of project management, industrial relations, and human resources management. He has presented papers at the Project Management Institute's national symposia, the annual meetings of the Industrial Relations Research Association, and meetings of the World Congress of Project Management, as well as other professional organizations. Dr. Owens has also served as editor of the *Project Management Journal*.

Alfred I. Paley is president of NRI Associates in Oceanport, N.J. A certified value specialist, he is also Value Engineering Program Manager and chief of the VE Office of the U.S. Army Communications Electronics Command (CECOM) in Ft. Monmouth, N.J. Mr. Paley has been recognized with numerous VE awards by the U.S. Army and was chosen by CECOM to accept the Department of Defense Command VE Achievement Award for 1989. He has served on the Certification Board of the Society of American Value Engineers (SAVE), is past president of the Metropolitan New York Chapter of SAVE, and was honored with the chapter's Value Engineer of the Year award for 1985–1986. Mr. Paley has lectured on VE for the American Management Association and developed a SAVE-certified course on VE that was taught at Hofstra University and Monmouth College.

David L. Pells is principal of Strategic Project Management International, a senior consultant assigned to the Superconducting Super Collider Laboratory in Dallas. He has broad experience in planning and developing project management systems. He has worked as a project manager of management information systems and as a consultant to the Department of Energy. Mr. Pells also directed the planning for the government validation of project tracking systems (C/SCSC) and has prepared project plans and project management plans for projects ranging from tens of thousands to billions of dollars. In the Project Management Institute, he has been president of two chapters (Idaho and Dallas). A certified project management professional, Mr. Pells has presented numerous technical papers on planning and tracking strategies at PMI and INTERNET symposia.

Joseph S. Reams is a partner in Brennan Construction, a general contractor specializing in commercial and industrial building. He is a registered professional engineer, a certified cost engineer, a certified constructor, and an appointed arbitrator to the American Arbitration Association. Mr. Reams has over fifteen years of experience in the management of construction and related projects. As a consultant with Administrative Controls Management, Inc., in Ann Arbor, Mich., he analyzed claims and provided expert witness support for both contractors and owners. Mr. Reams has presented construction claims seminars and was a professor of construction management and scheduling at Eastern Michigan University.

William H. Roetzheim is a senior associate with the technical consulting firm of Booz-Allen and Hamilton, Inc., in San Diego. He is a noted author and lecturer on software engineering and software project management. Books written by Mr. Roetzheim include *Structures Computer Project Management* and *Developing Software to Government Standards Management.*

Milton D. Rosenau, Jr., a certified management consultant, founded Rosenau Consulting Company in 1978. The company, twice named as one of the 100 leading management consulting firms in the United States, helps clients to move profitable new product ideas to market quickly, and also offers management training seminars. Mr. Rosenau has been Vice-President–Science and Technology for Avery International, vice-president and general manager of Optigon Research & Development Corporation, and has spent seventeen years in management, marketing, and engineering positions. His personal background includes successful new-product development for industrial and consumer markets as well as commercial diversification from technology developed on government contract programs. Mr. Rosenau has degrees in engineering physics from Cornell University and management programs at MIT, Cornell, and UCLA. He is the author of five books including *Faster New Product Development: Getting the Right Product to Market Quickly; Innovation: Managing the Development of Profitable New Products;* and *Successful Project Management.* Mr. Rosenau is vice-president of the Product Development & Management Association (PDMA), a member of the Steering Committee for PDMA-WEST, and vice-chairman of the Institute of Management Consultants.

Larry A. Smith is an associate professor in the College of Business at Florida International University. He is also president of Applied Management Associates in Plantation, Fla. Dr. Smith served on the editorial board of the *Project Management Journal* and has published over forty articles in such publications as the *Project Management Journal,* the *International Journal of Project Management, Management Science, Industrial Engineering, Data Management,* and *Managerial Planning.* His research is in all areas of project and production management.

Sri Sridharan has been a project manager developing new telecommunications products with the Network Transmission Systems division of Rockwell International (now Alcatel Network Systems) for over fifteen years. He is a certified manager and a project management professional. Mr. Sridharan has taught courses in project management topics at the University of Texas at Dallas and has served as vice-president of Education for the Project Management Institute's DFW chapter.

Alan M. Stretton is a visiting professor at the Faculty of Architecture and Building, University of Technology, in Sydney, Australia, where his primary interest has been the development and running of a Master of Project Management course. Mr. Stretton has relevant work experience in civil engineering and heavy construction, including seven years working on hydroelectric projects in Australia, three years in consulting engineering, and two years in heavy construction. He also spent eighteen years with a major Australian building project management organization in a variety of roles, including development of information and control systems, management of the planning department and of research and development, and development of internal education programs in construction planning and project management. Mr. Stretton has been affiliated with the Project Management Institute as chairman of the Standards (PMBOK) Committee. He has published thirty professional articles.

Hans J. Thamhain is an associate professor of management at Bentley College in Waltham, Mass. He received masters degrees in engineering and business administration and a doctorate in management from Syracuse University. Dr. Thamhain has held engineering and management positions with GTE, General Electric, and Westinghouse, and is well known for his research on engineering team building and project management. Dr. Thamhain is a frequent speaker at major conferences, has written over sixty research papers and four books on engineering/project management, and is consulted in all phases of technology management.

John Tuman, Jr., is senior vice-president with Management Technologies Group, Inc., a consulting firm in Morgantown, Pa., that provides consulting, training, and implementation services in organizational development, project management, change management, and information technology. Mr. Tuman's career spans thirty years of diverse engineering and project management experience. He was a project manager and a program manager on several major military and commercial aerospace programs for General Electric and the AVCO Corporation. He also held various management positions with Gilbert/Commonwealth, where he was responsible for developing computer-based management systems as well as providing consulting services and training. Mr. Tuman has given numerous presentations and seminars in the United States and abroad. He has written extensively on management methods, systems, and trends. He is a registered professional engineer.

Thomas P. Watkins has over eight years of experience in project management, operations research, organizational analysis, and process reengineering for both commercial and government industries. He has over three years of experience in regulatory analysis for telecommunications, utility, and transportation industries. Mr. Watkins has worked as senior manager for Decision Management Associates since 1989, managing various organizational and process analysis projects, including a one-year study at the Los Angeles County Transportation Commission. He has also worked for GTEL GTE as program manager, responsible for the development of operational and project management procedures for GTE's multi-city/state private network projects. As project engineer for Veda, Incorporated, Mr. Watkins was responsible for flight data analysis and parametric evaluation of flight test data for the F-14A as well as other Department of Navy weapon systems. He is the co-author of two abstracts published by PMI in 1989 and 1990.

Francis M. Webster, Jr., is a retired professor emeritus of management at the School of Business, Western Carolina University, in Cullowhee, N.C., where he specialized in teaching project management courses and concepts. He serves as editor-in-chief for the Project Management Institute, responsible for the editorial content and publication of the *Project Management Journal* and *PM NETwork*. Dr. Webster has had extensive experience in the design and application of project management software and in the management of project work. He was manager of Operations Research at Chrysler Corporation and served on the DOD/NASA PERT/COST Coordinating Council during the early days of the development of modern project management concepts and practices. He has published widely and contributed in a variety of ways to defining the profession of project management through his activities at PMI.

A. J. Werderitsch is executive vice-president of Administrative Controls Management, Inc., in Ann Arbor, Mich. He is a registered professional engineer and a certified cost engineer and has been elected a fellow of the American Association of Cost Engineers. He has over twenty-five years of experience in management and project controls, is a recognized expert on project controls and management, and has provided testimony in construction litigations. Mr. Werderitsch's professional responsibilities have entailed corporate, operations, and department management for project management, estimating, planning, scheduling, and cost analysis. He presents seminars on project management, planning, and construction delay claims and is an appointed arbitrator to the American Arbitration Association.

Richard E. Westney is widely known as a teacher, writer, and consultant in practical project management. Founder of Spectrum Consultants International, Inc., in 1978, he has assisted companies worldwide in the development and implementation of effective project management methods. Spectrum, based in Spring, Tex., specializes in computer-based methods and has done pioneering work in such areas as artificial intelligence, probabilistic analysis, integrated modeling, and computer-aided design. Mr. Westney has served as an instructor for the Construction Executive Programs at Texas A&M and Stanford Universities. He is the author of *Managing the Engineering and Construction of Small Projects* and is a contributor to *The Project & Cost Engineer's Handbook*. In addition to writing many papers and articles, from 1984 to 1989 he wrote the monthly computer column "Getting Personal" in *Cost Engineering* magazine. Mr. Westney is a licensed professional engineer in Texas and New Jersey. He is president of AACE International (formerly American Association of Cost Engineers).

Robert B. Youker of Management, Planning & Control Systems is an independent consultant and trainer in project implementation operating from Bethesda, Md. He is also an adjunct professor of Project Management in the Engineering Management School of George Washington University. In recent years, he has taught short courses at Harvard, the University of Wisconsin, the Asian Development Bank, Arthur D. Little, and the University of Bradford in England. Mr. Youker's consulting assignments include evaluating the training program of the Caribbean Development Bank, designing a Project Monitoring System for the island of St. Kitts for the Organization of American States, and evaluating the project implementation process for the African Development Bank. Mr. Youker took doctoral studies in Behavioral Science at George Washington University.

Lois Zells is an international author, lecturer, and business consultant in software engineering, specializing in software total quality management, software process maturity assessments, systems development methodologies and techniques, and project management. She has authored the best seller, *Managing Software Projects*, the popular, totally integrated, three-tier learning program on software engineering project management called *Successful Projects: The Common Sense Approach*, the introductory chapter for *Total Quality Management for Software*, (James McManus and Gordon Schulmyer, editors, New York: Van Nostrand Reinhold, 1992), and has published many articles in major periodicals of the industry. Ms. Zells is now also working on two books: *Applying Japanese Quality Management in U.S. Software Engineering* and *The Complete Guide to Quality Software Project Management*.